LOST ON DIVISION

Party Unity in the Canadian Parliament

Compared to other parliamentary democracies around the world, Canada's Parliament shows a high level of party unity when it comes to legislative voting. This was not always the case, however. One hundred years ago, this sort of party discipline was not as evident, leading scholars to wonder what explains the growing influence of political parties in the Canadian Parliament.

In *Lost on Division*, Jean-François Godbout analyses more than two million individual votes recorded in the House of Commons and the Senate since Confederation, demonstrating that the increase in partisanship is linked to changes in the content of the legislative agenda, itself a product of more restrictive parliamentary rules instituted after 1900. These rules reduced the independence of private members, polarized voting along partisan lines, and undermined Parliament's ability to represent distinct regional interests, resulting in – among other things – the rise of third parties.

Bridging the scholarship on party politics, legislatures, and elections, *Lost on Division* builds a powerful case for bringing institutions back into our understanding of how party systems change. It represents a significant contribution to legislative studies, political development, and the comparative study of parliaments.

(Political Development: Comparative Perspectives)

JEAN-FRANÇOIS GODBOUT is a professor in the Department of Political Science at the University of Montreal.

Political Development: Comparative Perspectives

Editors: JACK LUCAS (University of Calgary) and
ROBERT C. VIPOND (University of Toronto)

Political Development: Comparative Perspectives publishes books that explore political development with a comparative lens, with a particular focus on studies of Canadian, American, or British political development. Books in this series use historical data and narratives to explain long-term patterns of institutional change, public policy, social movement politics, elections and party systems, and other key aspects of political authority and state power. They employ cross-country comparison, within-country comparison, or single-case analysis to illuminate important debates in comparative political science and history.

Lost on Division

Party Unity in the Canadian Parliament

JEAN-FRANÇOIS GODBOUT

UNIVERSITY OF TORONTO PRESS
Toronto Buffalo London

Toronto Buffalo London
utorontopress.com

ISBN 978-1-4875-0703-9 (cloth)
ISBN 978-1-4875-2475-3 (paper)
ISBN 978-1-4875-3543-8 (EPUB)
ISBN 978-1-4875-3542-1 (PDF)

Library and Archives Canada Cataloguing in Publication

Title: Lost on division: Party unity in the Canadian parliament / Jean-François Godbout.
Names: Godbout, Jean-François, 1976– author.
Description: Series statement: Political development: comparative perspectives
Identifiers: Canadiana (print) 20200159399 | Canadiana (ebook) 20200159526 | ISBN 9781487507039 (hardcover) | ISBN 9781487524753 (softcover) | ISBN 9781487535438 (EPUB) | ISBN 9781487535421 (PDF)
Subjects: LCSH: Canada. Parliament – Voting – History. | LCSH: Canada. Parliament – Voting. | LCSH: Political parties – Canada – History. | LCSH: Political parties – Canada. | LCSH: Canada – Politics and government. | LCSH: Political participation – Canada.
Classification: LCC JL136.G63 2020 | DDC 328.71/0775 – dc23

This book has been published with the help of a grant from the Federation for the Humanities and Social Sciences, through the Awards to Scholarly Publications Program, using funds provided by the Social Sciences and Humanities Research Council of Canada.

University of Toronto Press acknowledges the financial assistance to its publishing program of the Canada Council for the Arts and the Ontario Arts Council, an agency of the Government of Ontario.

Canada Council for the Arts
Conseil des Arts du Canada

Funded by the Government of Canada
Financé par le gouvernement du Canada
Canada

Contents

Figures and Tables

Figures

Tables

SIR WILFRID LAURIER: The only difference in the deciding of questions in this House is, not that some are decided by a vote and some are decided otherwise, but that, while all are decided by a vote, in some cases the vote is recorded, and in other cases it is not recorded.

MR. MEIGHEN: I do not think that is the theory at all. A motion may be lost on division without a vote. The effect of that is to declare that large numbers do not vote. There is only one way by which a member can vote, and that is by recording his vote. Mr. Speaker comes to the conclusion according to the number cast for or against ...

SIR WILFRID LAURIER: The Speaker calls for an expression of opinion, and on the basis of that expression he says "I think the yeas have it; I think the nays have it." That is a vote, but it is not a recorded vote.

MR. MEIGHEN: As I understand it, that is not a vote. It is a motion decided on division, but it cannot be argued that a number voted "yea" and a number voted "nay." That is the difference between a vote and an unrecorded division. The point is important because, if it were decided by a vote, then the party division would be there which the hon. gentleman sought to establish, but there is no such record. It seemed to be the consensus of opinion of the House at the time that this was the course to pursue, and that is all about it.

– *House of Commons Debates*, 14 May 1917

Preface

It took me ten years to write this book. I began working on this project at the University of Oslo in 2008 with my very good friend and colleague Bjørn Høyland. Together, we set out on a journey to collect and analyse all of the recorded divisions in the Canadian Parliament. Along the way, we benefited from the support of several universities, research centres, and funding agencies, as well as from the advice and comments of numerous colleagues, students, and friends. But without Bjørn's contribution, I could never have written this book, and for that I owe him a great deal of gratitude and thanks.

Completing this book also would not have been possible without the diligent work of undergraduate and graduate students. I was fortunate enough to have at my disposal a very competent group of research assistants who, over the years, helped me collect and code more than two million votes in the Canadian House of Commons and Senate. I want to especially acknowledge the work of Eve Bourgeois, Juliette Charpentier, J.-F. Daoust, Geneviève Gosselin, Simon Guertin-Armstrong, Martin Leduc, Philippe Mongrain, Simon Poirier, Indraneel Sircar, Alexis St-Maurice, and Monika Smaz. I also want to thank Semra Sevi and Allison Smith for reading earlier drafts of different chapters in the book. Finally, I am very grateful for the invaluable assistance provided by Florence Vallée-Dubois, who put a lot of time and effort into getting this manuscript into shape and ready for publication. Florence deserves high praise for her work. She is an outstanding scholar, and I have learned a lot from her research skills. Florence was always patient, professional, and cheerful with my many requests – *alors, merci beaucoup*.

The main funding for this project came from a Social Sciences and Humanities Research Council grant (no. 410-2009-2907) that Bjørn and I received while I was working at Simon Fraser University. Living on the west coast of Canada provided me the perfect intellectual environment to begin researching dissension in Parliament. I want to especially thank Andy Heard, Dick Johnston, Campbell Sharman, and Steve Weldon for their help in the earlier stages of this project. But above all I am thankful for the advice and support of David

Laycock, who has always been a great champion of my work, as well as a mentor and a friend. His expertise on western populism has been invaluable to my understanding of Canadian politics. Although I left Vancouver for Montreal in 2010, David has continued to show great interest in this project by reading several different drafts of the manuscript. I am greatly indebted to him for his support and encouragements over the years.

I also received invaluable help from my colleagues on the east coast. The most important support came from Éric Montpetit and Christine Rothmayr, who were, successively, chairs of the Department of Political Science at the Université de Montréal. Christine Rothmayr was instrumental in clearing my teaching schedule so that I could have enough time to finish this book. I also want to thank several current and former colleagues from the Department of Political Science for their advice and support: Vincent Arel-Bundock, André Blais, Ruth Dassonneville, Martial Foucault, Lee Seymour, and our Librarian Mathieu Thomas. Finally, I want to thank the students who participated in all the seminars I taught on Canadian politics, Parliament, and research methods. In these classes, I was able to learn a lot about the topics covered in this book, and students have always been very supportive of my obsession with nineteenth-century Canadian political history. Also, many thanks to the students who read parts of my manuscript in class for all of their comments and suggestions, which greatly improved the overall framing of the arguments.

Three research centres were instrumental in helping me complete this book. The Political Institutions and Public Choice Program (PIPC) of Duke University was the first to provide me with a very stimulating environment in which to begin thinking about this project in 2007. There, I was fortunate to receive the generous assistance and mentorship of David Rohde and John Aldrich. Their influence in this book is apparent, and I want to thank them for sharing their insights on party development and legislative organization. The Center for the Study of Democratic Politics (CSDP) at Princeton University also played a crucial role in getting this project off the ground. As a visiting scholar of the CSDP in the 2013–14 academic year, I benefited from the generous assistance provided by the Woodrow Wilson School of Public and International Affairs and the incredible intellectual environment offered by Princeton and members of the Center. I want to thank all the students, staff, and colleagues at CSDP, but especially Chris Achen, Doug Arnold, David Bateman, Chuck Cameron, Brandice Canes-Wrone, Michele Epstein, Nolan McCarty, Markus Prior, and Miguel Rueda. Another centre, but this one the Centre for the Study of Democratic Citizenship (CSDC), provided me invaluable assistance to complete this project in Montreal. Several current and former CSDC members deserve high praise for their help and support: Marc Bodet, Elizabeth Gidengil, Sven-Oliver Proksch, and Dietlind Stolle.

This book also benefited from the feedback I received during several invited conferences and seminar presentations. In particular, I want to thank the following colleagues, research centres, and departments for inviting me to speak about the book, and for the excellent comments I received from members of these audiences: Elizabeth Goodyear-Grant and the participants of Queen's University's Department of Political Studies seminar; Arthur Spirling and the participants of the Westminster Model of Democracy in Crisis workshop at Harvard University; Bill Cross and the participants of the seminar of the Bell Chair in Parliamentary Democracy at Carleton University; Antoine Yoshinaka and the participants of the research seminar in the Department of Government at American University; Cristina Bucur, Bjørn-Erik Rasch and Elisabetta Cassina Wolff and the participants of the Historical Parliamentarism: Early Instances, Evolution, and Constitutional Design workshop at the University of Oslo; Mark Pickup and the participants of the speaker series of the Department of Political Science at Simon Fraser University; Chris Cochrane and the participants of the University of Toronto's Department of Political Science research seminar; and Campbell Sherman and the participants of the University of British Columbia's Department of Political Science research seminar.

Many other colleagues, students, and friends helped me along the way to finish this book. I have been fortunate enough to benefit from the collective wisdom of several people who read and commented parts of the manuscript, and I want to thank them for their help, especially Chris Cochrane, Simon Hug, Demetra Kasimis, Peter Loewen, Emmett Macfarlane, Jonathan Malloy, Alex Marland, Shane Martin, John McAndrews, and Graham White. Chris along with the Lipad folks deserve special thanks for sharing their parliamentary speech data used in chapter 3. In writing this book, I have drawn upon some material that was previously published in the *Canadian Journal of Political Science* ("The Emergence of Parties in the Canadian House of Commons (1867–1908)," co-authored with Bjørn Høyland), the *British Journal of Political Science* ("Unity in Diversity? The Development of Political Parties in the Parliament of Canada (1867–2011)," co-authored with Bjørn Høyland), and the *Australian Journal of Political Science* ("Party Development in the Early Decades of the Australian Parliament: A New Perspective," co-authored with Monika Smaz).

Additional funding for the research presented in this book was provided by the Norwegian Research Council (grant no. 222442) and the James R. Mallory Research Grant for the Study of Parliament. This last grant helped collect most of the data from the Senate. Research funds provided by the CSDP at Princeton, the CSDC in Quebec, and the Université de Montréal were also instrumental in helping me complete some of the data-collection tasks.

Many thanks to the University of Toronto Press, and especially my editor, Daniel Quinlan, for his help and patience in waiting for this book to be completed. Daniel read the first draft of the manuscript and gave me valuable suggestions to improve my writing and the framing of the book. Thanks also to freelancer Barry Norris, who edited the final draft of this manuscript for the Press. I am grateful as well for the excellent comments I received from three anonymous reviewers, which greatly improved the overall quality of my arguments. Lastly, I want to thank Rob Vipond and Jack Lucas for selecting this book to be the first to appear in the University of Toronto Press Political Development: Comparative Perspectives series. It is a great honour to contribute to this collection. Rob and Jack have done a lot to reinvigorate the field of historical political development in Canada, and this new series promises to be an invaluable resource for our growing research community.

I want to end this preface by thanking Alexandra Matus, who has always been my most ardent supporter. Alexandra has made many personal sacrifices to help my academic career. She followed me across Canada, the United States, and Europe, and has always been willing to leave me alone during the long hours I was reading or working on the computer. Alexandra also deserves high praises for having proofread the whole manuscript while she was pregnant with our daughter Angélique. Her suggestions greatly improved the quality of the text, and since she read the whole thing aloud, our daughter was born with an extensive knowledge of Canadian parliamentary procedures.

I was inspired by my family's history in writing this book. From an early age, I learned a lot about politics and the importance of patronage when I heard rumours that my grandfather got a job in the federal government after writing a letter to Senator Adélard Godbout. More recently, while doing research for this book, I also learned that my other grandfather, Antonio Reny, was good friends with Senator Chubby Power, who, as you will find out shortly, plays an important role in this book as well. For me, then, politics has always been a family affair. And so, for all of these reasons and for many more, I dedicate this book to my own family: Alexandra and Angélique.

LOST ON DIVISION

Party Unity in the Canadian Parliament

Chapter One

Introduction

Canada's Parliament is increasingly considered irrelevant. While many argue that this situation is linked to the development of party discipline and the growing influence of government in the legislative arena, very few studies have attempted to determine the origins of these changes. The empirical core of this book provides an answer to this puzzle. By analysing the outcome of every single recorded vote in the House of Commons and Senate since Confederation, I explain how partisanship increased over time and modified the structure of the Canadian party system more broadly. My argument is that the heightened levels of party discipline observed in the legislature today are primarily linked to changes in the content of the legislative agenda, which resulted from the adoption of more restrictive parliamentary rules around the turn of the previous century. These new rules reduced the independence of private members by limiting their ability to speak, amend, or introduce bills during debates. They also polarized voting along partisan lines, and undermined Parliament's ability to represent distinct regional interests. In the final part of the book, I demonstrate that these changes ultimately contributed to the rise of third parties in Canada.

Although members today almost always support their own party during legislative votes, this has not always been the case. Over the past 150 years, the country's national legislature has transformed from being governed by a loosely based coalition of independent members to one governed by strict party discipline. In his historical description of the first two national parties in Canada, Underhill (1935, 369) notes that party unity was much weaker in the years following Confederation. For instance, we know that the earliest Parliaments contained several Liberal or Conservative "loose fish" who were gradually replaced by more loyal party supporters, or what Prime Minister Pierre Elliott Trudeau referred to as "trained seals" (Reid [1932] 1963, 15; Debates 1976, 11238). Prior to 1900, it was not uncommon for legislators to influence the content of the legislative agenda, introduce bills, and hold members of the executive accountable for their actions. At some point during the twentieth century, however, this independence was lost as party leaders discovered ways of imposing their will on the assembly. Today, party discipline is so rigid that not a single member of the Conservative Party voted against the government's legislative program during the forty-first Parliament (2011–15).

This situation is by no means exceptional. More than a century ago, critics were already claiming that party discipline was an obstacle to effective democratic representation in Canada. For example, Henri Bourassa compared party members to "a flock of ignorant slaves" who blindly followed their leaders in the assembly, and were thus unable to represent the interests of their constituents (Dumont, Montminy, and Hamelin 1978, 264). But the most virulent opposition came from the Prairies, where supporters of the progressive movement believed that political parties were being corrupted by banks and great corporations that financed electoral machines and controlled governments. Representatives were thus powerless to resist their influence, and ultimately unwilling to oppose party leaders. Advocates of this movement pushed for a more radical transformation of legislatures, replacing ministerial responsibility, cabinet solidarity, and the vote of confidence with constituency conventions, direct legislation, and recall elections.

Although such extreme proposals were never fully implemented at the national level, several other reforms have since been adopted to reduce the apparent influence of parties in the legislative arena. Most notably, these proposals aimed to increase the amount of nongovernment or private members' business in the debates, to allow greater parliamentary committee scrutiny, or to relax the confidence convention during certain votes. Unfortunately, these attempts to change parliamentary procedures have done little to improve the overall independence of members, perhaps because party discipline is such an essential component of the Westminster system of government (Lemco 1988, 83; White 2005, 15). Indeed, without a leadership structure to organize the legislature, it would be difficult for members to coordinate their actions and support a stable governing coalition. It would also be harder for parties to enact their legislative program and for voters to hold parties accountable for their record of accomplishments in Parliament. From a collective perspective, then, party unity improves democratic accountability. However, it can also weaken the link between representatives and their constituents, especially if the party's interests do not coincide with those of people in the district. When this situation arises, legislators usually have three options: they can vote with their caucus, and risk being punished by the electorate; they can openly dissent, and risk being sanctioned by their leaders; or they can abstain from voting, and refrain from expressing an opinion. Given that parties are rarely openly challenged today, it seems that leaders now have at their disposal sufficient resources to control the fate of their candidates both inside and outside Parliament.

The example of Bill Casey, a Member of Parliament (MP) from Cumberland-Colchester-Musquodoboit Valley, is illustrative of this point. A Conservative for almost twenty years, Casey was expelled from his caucus when he voted against the government's budget in 2007. At the time, he believed that oil and gas revenues should not reduce equalization payments to Nova Scotia, a promise made under the Progressive Conservative (PC) government of Brian Mulroney (O'Neil 2007). After the vote, the chief Conservative whip told Casey that he was "done" and "no longer a member of the party." The fact that Casey had supported all other government bills during the session does not seem to have influenced the final decision to expel him from the caucus.

We can contrast Casey's experience with the career of former Liberal Charles "Chubby" Power, of Quebec-South, who served in Parliament from 1917 to 1968. Power spent the better part of his first eighteen years in the House of Commons as a government backbencher. During this time, he voted on several occasions against his party's own budget, most notably to reduce spending in the Department of National Defence or to remove certain staples from the tariff list. Power recognized that such open dissension would have been impossible towards the end of his career. As he explained, "the ordinary member [today] is made to feel that he is a voting machine and nothing else," since "unquestioned loyalty on divisions" is always expected "with little or no occasion to express personal views or to deviate from government policies" (Ward 1966, 263–9). This sentiment has led some members even to question the relevancy of Parliament. "We know what people are saying," declared John Evans, who represented Ottawa Centre from 1979 to 1984, "'You're a bunch of clowns' and they're right: we are a bunch of clowns" (*Gazette* [Montreal] 1982).

The experience of these MPs is by no means unique. Over the years, both scholars and legislators have criticized the increasing domination of parties in the legislative arena (see, for example, Docherty 1997; Franks 1987; Guay 2002, 5; Savoie 1999; Stewart 1977; Strahl 2001, 2; Venne 2003, 2). The most common approach to measuring this lack of responsiveness has been through the analysis of recorded votes, where party discipline – or what I refer to as legislative party voting unity – is usually estimated by calculating how frequently members vote together in the legislature. Figure 1.1 displays the results of such an analysis by reporting the evolution of parliamentary voting unity for Canada's two historically dominant parties, the Conservatives and the Liberals. The measure used to summarize party influence represents the median value of the distribution of individual loyalty scores in each of the forty-one Parliaments since Confederation (1867–2015). These loyalty scores are obtained by averaging the proportion of times individual members voted with the majority of their caucus in a legislative term. A median of .90 implies that at least half the caucus supported the party in 90 per cent of the votes (the bars indicate a plus or minus one absolute deviation from this value). The first plot of figure 1.1 highlights the medians for all of the votes recorded during a term, whereas the second plot displays the same measure but for government-sponsored motions only (that is, whipped divisions).

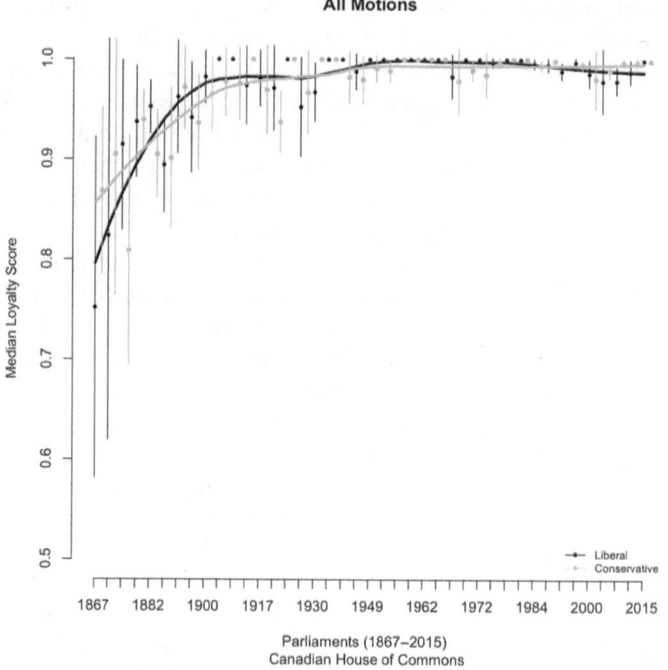

Figure 1.1 Party Loyalty in the House of Commons, 1867–2015

Both graphs confirm that the Conservatives and the Liberals experienced a marked increase in the level of individual party loyalty between 1867 and 1900. This was followed by a second, more gradual period of transformation that lasted until the end of the Second World War. After this point, deviations from the median converge towards zero, which implies that almost all members now support their party in the legislature. We find a similar trend if we look at voting on government business only (the second plot): party unity also seems to have peaked around 1900, but this time the Liberals became more unified earlier than did the Conservatives, who reached their apex after the end of the First World War. In the remaining period, there seems to have been much less variation around the median values for both parties, which suggests that there was almost no dissension on government-sponsored motions or bills.

From these two plots, one can confirm that strict party discipline has been the norm in the House of Commons for almost a century now – longer still if we consider only votes related to government business. Variations observed around the medians also confirm, however, that an important level of internal dissension remained within both the Conservative and Liberal caucuses

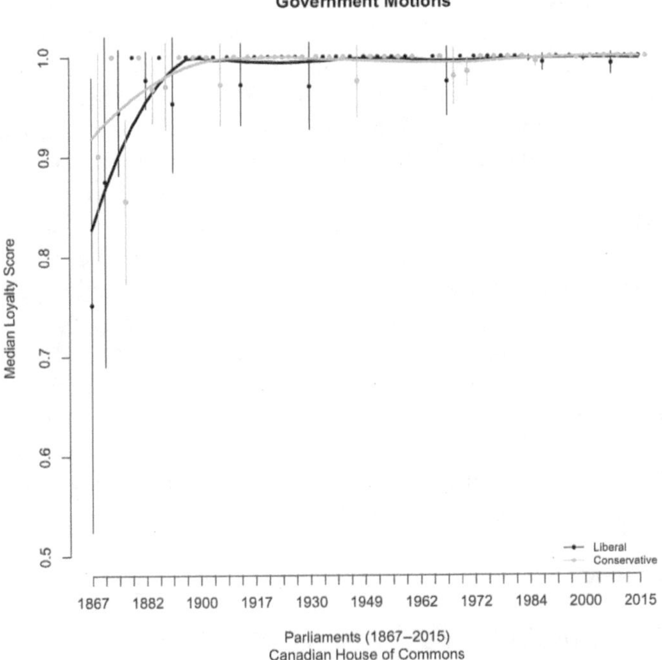

Figure 1.1 continued

for many years after Confederation. If anything, the two plots indicate that near-perfect party voting unity was not achieved until much later and that the influence of parties appears to have fluctuated over time.

This overall transformation raises several important questions about the influence of parties in the House of Commons. First, how can the sharp increase in the development of partisanship in the first few decades following Confederation be explained? Can the professionalization and replacement of members account for this change? Or, rather, is this increasing partisanship linked to the gradual expansion of the franchise or the changing political alignments of Canadians? Second, what explains the subsequent less dramatic increase in party voting unity observed during the twentieth century? Is this more gradual transformation a consequence of the changing content of the legislative agenda or of the emergence of the welfare state? Can this change be explained by the increasing dominance of government in the legislature or by the declining influence of backbench members in the legislative process? Finally, what has been the broader effect of these heightened levels of voting unity on the organization of political parties? Did the development of strict party discipline raise the incentives for some members to leave their party's caucus? Can these transformations be linked to the introduction of third parties in Parliament?

In this book, I provide answers to these questions by analysing the legislative behaviour of every single member of Parliament who served between 1867 and 2015. The research focuses on both the actions of members in the legislature and on the transformation of the rules and regulations governing the parliamentary process. Although I consider several different theories of legislative party development, I find that these conventional explanations are incapable of accounting for the Canadian case if they are not considered in sequence and within the country's historical context. The overarching goal of this book is thus to understand both the causes and consequences of this growth in partisanship observed in Parliament since Confederation. To this end, I examine how parties influence the behaviour of their members by looking at the outcomes of recorded votes and by analysing the content of legislative speeches and bills. I also consider how the modification of the rules of the House could have affected the representation of sectional interests in Parliament and promoted the development of new political parties within its walls.

The Argument

In Canada the rise of partisan voting in the federal Parliament occurred through three successive transformations connected to historical events that permanently modified the organization of the House of Commons. The first one began in the years immediately following Confederation, when Parliament was debating the most important aspects of Canada's nation-building projects. During this period, it was common for members to oppose their own party in order to represent the interests of their local constituency. Most of these local rivalries disappeared when the Conservative government of John A. Macdonald settled on a protectionist economic policy – the National Policy – in 1879 centred around national industries, agriculture, railway development, and the colonization of western territories. This state-building program remained silent, however, on the linguistic and religious rights of French and Roman Catholic Canadians who resided outside the province of Quebec. This omission proved to be the source of great difficulties for Macdonald, primarily because parties were divided internally on issues of ethnicity and religion, which weakened their overall levels of party unity in the legislature. These sectional divisions eventually led to the first transformation of the Canadian party system towards the end of the nineteenth century, when virtually all French Catholic MPs came to be associated with the Liberal Party, while most English Protestant members came to be associated with the Conservative Party.

After Parliament settled on the National Policy and parties became more ideologically cohesive on matters of religion and language, the rules of the House of Commons were modified to limit the rights of backbenchers and increase the ability of party leaders to control the legislative agenda. These rule changes affected the organization of the House and promoted partisanship within it. The modification of parliamentary procedures became necessary to manage the increasing amount of government business on the legislative agenda, but also to control the systematic obstruction of members from the opposition. This is the second transformation, which took place during the first two decades of the twentieth century.

The third transformation followed from the adoption of these new rules, and contributed to the breakup of Canada's two-party system. Although party discipline increased after backbenchers lost most of their influence in the legislative arena, this newfound rigidity added pressure on legislators to conform with the views of party leaders in the House. For several MPs, representing agricultural ridings in Western Canada or Quebec nationalists, it became increasingly difficult to support either of the two dominant parties, especially after the adoption of the Civil Service Reform Act of 1918, which abolished the distribution of patronage in ridings. The lack of opportunities to express grievances in the legislature, combined with a reduction of the "spoils of office," reduced the incentives for some members to remain loyal to their party. Ultimately, these changes contributed to the development of several new protest parties after the 1921 election, such as the Progressives and the United Farmers, whose roots can be traced back to frontier politics and radical western populism, but also – and perhaps more surprisingly – to changes in parliamentary procedures.

The removal of these factions from the two main parties raised levels of voting unity even more, and they remained very high until the rules of the House of Commons were once again modified during the 1980s to increase the influence of backbenchers in the legislative process. After the introduction of these reforms, there was a resurgence in the amount of private members' business in the legislature, which led to an increase in the number of dissenting party votes. This change proved to be temporary, however; rapidly, the time set aside to discuss private members' affairs was gradually taken over by party leaders to promote their own legislative program. As a consequence, the level of partisan conflicts observed in Parliament began to rise again, and eventually reached unprecedented heights under the Conservative governments of Stephen Harper (2006–15).

Ultimately, this book argues that the emergence of several distinct regional parties in the House of Commons can be linked to parliamentary rules and party discipline. For members who often found themselves at odds with the positions defended by the Liberal and Conservative caucuses, the incentives to create their own separate caucus grew significantly after losing most of their influence in the legislative process. Several of these new parties were tied to specific regional factions from Western Canada, but also from Quebec, which failed to find a place within the dominant two-party system. This interpretation stands in sharp contrast to existing theories of party system change in Canada. For authors such as Carty (1988) or Johnston (2017), the era of Liberal and Conservative dominance came to an end during the 1920s because of changing voter preferences. Central to this argument is the idea that the number of parties in a given political system reflects the principal ideological conflicts that divide the electorate (Carty, Cross, and Young 2000, 4). Thus, in a country like Canada, with a plurality voting system, an increase in the number of parties can be understood only in terms of electoral consequences: voters are pushed away from the existing parties when they fail to address important issues. This realignment thesis, popular in the American political science literature, ignores the role that legislative institutions could have played in this process as well. In the following pages, I show that this role is indeed an important factor in understanding why new parties are sometimes created within the confines of Parliament, mainly because parliamentary rules and party discipline can limit the ability of members to meet the demands of their constituents. It is often they, not the voters, who are first alienated by the party system.

Objectives and Contributions

This book has two main objectives. The first is empirical: it aims to analyse a new dataset of parliamentary votes in the House of Commons and the Senate from 1867 to 2015. The goal here is to explain why partisanship has increased over time and why it is so high in Parliament today. The second objective is to evaluate the consequences of this change on the organization of the legislature and on the structure of the Canadian party system more broadly. Note that the overall argument presented in this book builds on these two objectives in sequence. The first part introduces the voting data and the different theories of party development, and tests the effectiveness of these theories in explaining the growth of partisanship after Confederation. In the second part, I move beyond a simple analysis of the determinants of party voting unity to assess whether the changing preferences of members or the introduction of new parliamentary rules promoted the emergence of new parties in the legislative arena.

By pursuing these objectives, the book makes four important contributions to the study of Canadian political institutions and parties. For one, it is the first study of its kind to analyse systematically the legislative voting behaviour of all Members of Parliament from Confederation to the present day. Although some empirical researchers – such as Blidook (2012), Docherty (1997), Kam (2009), Kornberg (1967), and March (1974) – have looked at different aspects of parliamentary behaviour in one or more specific legislative terms, there has been no comprehensive analysis of legislative voting records covering all Parliaments since Confederation. Such an investigation is important because scholars still do not understand fully how party discipline and modern political parties have evolved over time in Canada (Atkinson and Thomas 1993, 442; Heard 1991, 80–1; Malloy 2003, 119–20; Thomas 1996, 257). There is a wide consensus in the political science literature that party unity was much weaker in the years following Confederation (Eggleston 1988; Forsey 1963; Ward 1966). We also know that partisanship increased dramatically in the first two decades of the twentieth century (March 1974; Wearing 1998), and that it has reached unprecedented heights since then (Kam 2009; Malloy 2003). To date, the most widely accepted explanation of this transformation comes from the historical analysis of party organization in Canada (Carty, Cross, and Young 2000; Johnston et al. 1992). This line of research usually divides the development of political parties into several distinctive periods or party systems.[1] What little information there is about the emergence of partisanship in the House of Commons can be found in the description of the first party system (1867–1917), a period when a large number of independent members were gradually replaced by more partisan supporters (Carty 1988, 15–19; Patten 2017, 5–7). Until now, these observations have been based mostly on anecdotal evidence or on the comparison of a handful of recorded votes over time, usually across one or two parliamentary terms.[2] Still, the absence of raw data on legislative voting has not prevented political scientists, pundits, or historians from developing different theories to account for the development of parties in the legislative arena. Below, I review the most common of these applied to the Canadian context.

Scholars have known for some time now that party unity is very high in Canada. "It is the universal testimony of foreign as well as Canadian observers that Canadian parties display a notable coherence and subservience to their leaders," noted Hugh Clokie more than seventy-five years ago (1944, 135). He and other prominent political scientists from this era believed that party leaders, particularly those who controlled the government, maintained discipline by either offering or withholding patronage in the district or by threatening to dissolve Parliament (Clokie 1944, 136; Corry 1946, 162–3). Parliamentary caucus meetings were also seen as mechanisms for encouraging solidarity and negotiating compromises among members (Dawson [1947] 1960, 244–7). Relatively few studies from this period, however, focused on explaining why party unity grew over time. Frank Underhill (1935) and Escott Reid ([1932] 1963) were the first to argue that Canada's antiquated electoral system contributed to weakening party discipline in Parliament after Confederation. During the 1867–78 period, elections were held at different dates, while voting was done in public by a show of hands. The first government of John A. Macdonald took advantage of this situation by holding earlier elections in the most partisan districts in order to secure an important number of seats and count on a bandwagon effect in the later, more competitive contests. Several candidates also benefited from this system by waiting to align themselves with either one of the two major parties until they could predict the most likely winner. Reid ([1932]

1963, 14–15) maintained that these men were usually elected by acclamation and that, once in office, they tended to support the government in exchange for patronage in their district. On record, they were affiliated with the majority party; in practice, they remained highly independent (see also Forsey 1964, 5). The introduction of the secret ballot and simultaneous elections in 1878 put an end to this practice and encouraged the election of more loyal candidates afterwards.

Another common explanation found in the literature to account for the development of partisanship in Parliament is related to the membership of the first political parties. Since national parties did not really exist in the first two decades after Confederation, authors such as Hougham (1963, 1–2) have argued that the first MPs remained highly independent of parties because they could rely on their own resources and reputation to get elected. During this period, the Liberal and Conservative caucuses were roughly composed of sectional factions controlled by strong regional leaders such as John A. Macdonald in Ontario, George-Étienne Cartier in Quebec, and Joseph Howe in Nova Scotia. As members of local elites, most candidates had enough influence to win an election without a party's help (March 1974, 2). Once in Parliament, these members remained highly independent from party caucuses, and were more likely to dissent and promote the interests of their constituents (Forsey 1963, 367). The change in partisanship observed over time thus could be explained by the gradual replacement of these older cohorts of members from the party ranks.

A third explanation for the emergence of party voting unity in Parliament is related to the expansion of the franchise and the development of mass political parties (March 1974, 47). Although the voting franchise was relatively inclusive at the time of Confederation, a large percentage of the electorate was still unable to vote because of gender, ethnic origin (for example, Indigenous and Asian peoples), or income and property requirements. Some of these restrictions were removed in 1898, when universal manhood suffrage was introduced in federal elections, and others in 1918, when women acquired the right to vote.[3] Scholars have argued that a main consequence of these changes was to weaken the independence of MPs (March 1974, 7–8). With the increasing size of the electorate, candidates could no longer rely strictly on their wealth and reputation to get elected; they now required help from a party to finance their own campaign and mobilize voters in the district. The first permanent mass political party organization in Canada was thus created in response to these demands. By relying increasingly on the party for their (re)election, candidates had to change their campaign strategy to make broader programmatic appeals to voters. This also reinforced the party's influence by tying the electoral fortune of incumbents to the party's success in the legislature. Thus, by becoming more dependent on party resources, members had an increased incentive to support their caucus during legislative votes.

Another set of explanations Canadian scholars have raised to account for the increase in partisanship is linked to the professionalization and the socialization of members. For instance, C.E.S. Franks (1987, 257–8) argues that party leaders have more influence in the House of Commons because legislative careers are short, and new and inexperienced cohorts of members regularly replace incumbents. Kornberg (1964, 49–52), Docherty (1997, 25–8), and later Kam (2009, 57–8) also highlight the important role that social norms and informal rules play in accounting for the high levels of party unity. Their survey analysis and interviews of MPs confirm that legislators go through an apprenticeship in their first term, after which they tend to remain loyal to the party for the remainder of their legislative career. More recently, Malloy (2003, 122) has argued that the ideological heterogeneity of Liberal and Conservative caucuses has put a premium on party discipline. According to this view, the high levels of voting unity observed in Parliament today are not explained by the common policy preferences of members; rather, they are a consequence of the pressure exerted by party leaders. For Carty, Cross and Young (2000, 36), the reason for this artificial cohesion is linked to the idea that Canadian political parties practise "brokerage politics," characterized by a "desire to maintain national unity" by promoting a balance between the interests of "different regional, linguistic, ethnic, and other groups" inside party caucuses (see also Malloy 2003, 122; Porter 1965, 373–4). These accommodations are negotiated in private, away from the public eye, so that a party can present a united front in the legislature (see also Thomas 1996, 259–60). The challenge then is not only to explain how regionally diverse parties have been able to maintain cohesion over time, but also how they managed to increase their dominance in the legislative arena during the twentieth century.

Faced with these diverse accounts, the first contribution of this book is thus to determine which of these factors, if any, explains the growth of partisanship in the Canadian Parliament over time. These explanations are drawn from the existing literature on party development in Canada, but also from related work in the United States, the United Kingdom, and other relevant comparative studies of legislative behaviour. So far, the most popular accounts have tended to focus on a limited number of factors to explain this change, whether they be the replacement of older cohorts of MPs by newer ones, the professionalization of parliamentary careers, electoral pressure, or the changing ideological composition of party caucuses. The lack of systematic data on legislative voting behaviour, however, has prevented researchers from assessing the relative effect of these factors on the development of party unity over time, so the patterns observed in Parliament remain unexplained to this day.

The second contribution of this book is to demonstrate how Parliament's rules and regulations can influence legislative behaviour. Although authors such as Epstein (1964), Lemco (1988), and Atkinson and Thomas (1993) long ago demonstrated the relevance of parliamentary organization and procedure to individual actions in the House of Commons, little progress has been made since then to understand how parliamentary rules affect party organization. Aside from the obvious differences that can be attributed to the parliamentary system and the confidence convention to explain party voting unity in Canada, Corry (1954) and MacGuigan (1978), for example, have noted that modifying the procedures of the House can alter the behaviour of legislators – most notably when they aim to strengthen the influence of party leaders. Stewart (1977) has shown that the most important of these changes occurred around the turn of the twentieth century, when the cabinet modified the rules of the House to limit debates by adopting closure and by permanently increasing the time allocated to government business on the legislative agenda. Although Stewart does not explicitly measure the effect of these new rules on the behaviour of members, he argues that they greatly reduced the independence of backbenchers in the legislative process and contributed to increasing party voting unity over time. His argument rests on his own experience as a Member of Parliament, but also on a detailed analysis of the evolution of the daily proceedings of the House, which looks at changes in the proportion of government business in legislative records since 1867.

To date, Stewart's study remains the most complete analysis of the influence of parliamentary rules and procedures on the organization of the House of Commons. The absence of data, however, also prevented Stewart – and other researchers – from fully understanding how parties increase their dominance over the legislative process through time. One main advantage of having information on all recorded votes between 1867 and 2015 is that we can see how modifying certain rules or the content of the legislative agenda can influence the behaviour of members, thus imposing limits on speculation about what explains the growth of partisanship in Parliament.

The third contribution of this book is to understand the evolution of the Canadian party system from the perspective of Parliament as an institution. Unlike work that focuses on election results to describe the historical development of Canadian parties (for example, Cairns 1968; Carty, Cross, and Young 2000; Johnston 2017; Johnston et al. 1992), this study attempts to determine if institutional rules affect legislative behaviour, and how the modification of these rules could have influenced the structure of the Canadian party system in turn. To date, studies of the Canadian Parliament have had limited interest in political parties outside the legislative arena; while studies focused more on the transformation of the party system have often ignored how parties behave in Parliament. In this book, I combine these two largely separate literatures to develop an endogenous theory of party system change, where the introduction of restrictive parliamentary rules increases the incentives not only for members to support the party line, but also to create new parties in the legislative arena.

The final contribution of this book is to provide a reference tool for researchers and students of Canadian politics to analyse both historical and current aspects of the development of party organization. The study relies on an extensive and completely original dataset of recorded votes collected in each of the forty-one Parliaments elected since Confederation. Overall, these data contain information on 12,119 recorded divisions (or roll call votes) in the House of Commons and 1,453 recorded divisions in the Senate. The data files also include the voting records and biographical information of 4,216 unique members of the House of Commons and 925 senators.

By using a dataset that combines information on the background and behaviour of legislators, the content and topic of each recorded division, and the rules and procedures of the legislature, this book presents a comprehensive account to explain the historical development of party discipline and voting unity in the Canadian Parliament. The study also addresses the more general question of the development of legislative party organization in Westminster-style parliamentary systems. Since legislatures often deal with the most important issues of the day, the historical analysis of parliamentary voting can give researchers a unique tool with which to learn effectively about the evolution of political conflicts. Identifying the nature of these potential divisions is important because contemporary parties tend to reflect the political divisions present at the time of their creation (Lijphart 1977, 3–4; Lipset and Rokkan 1967, 2–3). This analysis should thus increase our current understanding of the role of Members of Parliament in the Canadian political system.

In exploring the historical development of party unity in Canada, the study employs both narrative accounts of political conflicts and systematic quantitative data analyses. Because of the sheer volume of the information collected, it would be difficult to present a detailed description of the evolution of Parliament over the past 150 years. Consequently, the study focuses on several distinct periods when a series of crises had an important influence on the actions of MPs and contributed to strengthen or weaken party influence in the legislative arena.

I present my own interpretation of these events, and it is by no means the only one. Nevertheless, I have done my best to provide historical evidence, either from the records of Parliaments, the personal archives of members, or newspaper accounts of that period, to explain how Canadian parties responded to these challenges. The core empirical findings of the book also include numerous analyses of parliamentary speeches, recorded divisions, and election results to measure how parties and parliamentary rules influence the behaviour of members in the legislature. Since it is extremely difficult to identify the causal mechanisms behind large-scale social changes, in the analysis presented in the following chapters I adopt a historical and institutional perspective.[4] I ask the reader to bear this in mind until I return to these considerations in the conclusion of the book. Those who want to learn more about the historical context of the development of Parliament are encouraged to consult the excellent books of Azoulay (1999); Beck (1968); Bourinot (1916); Carty, Cross, and Young (2000); Dawson (1962); March (1974); English (1977); and Ward (1963). I also warn the reader that this book is not a historiography of the development of political parties in Canada. Much more talented scholars have written on this subject as well; I invite the interested reader to consult Brown and Cook (1974); English (1977); Lemieux (2008); Lower (1961); Morton (1950); Neatby (1973); and Wade (1955).

Plan of the Book

The remainder of the book is divided into nine chapters. I begin in chapter 2 by presenting a historical survey of the development of party voting unity in Parliament. The main focus of this chapter is to describe in greater detail the events that led to the transformation of the party system over time. Here I show how certain historical facts influenced the political alignments of MPs and, in turn, contributed to increasing partisanship in the legislative arena. In chapter 3, I introduce my own theory of legislative voting behaviour, and review the different factors identified in both the Canadian and comparative political science literature to explain the historical development of political parties inside and outside the legislative arena. The focus here is primarily on the British and American cases, but I also show how these factors could be related to the Canadian context. Chapter 4 takes a more in-depth look at the parliamentary records collected from the Canadian Parliament. Here I describe in greater detail the legislative voting data used in the analysis, and take a closer look at different measures of party voting unity over time. The next two chapters test the validity of the different factors identified in chapter 3 to explain legislative party development: first by looking at the individual-level determinants of party loyalty (chapter 5); and then by considering how parliamentary rules and the legislative agenda influence party unity (chapter 6). From these empirical analyses, I conclude that the conventional factors identified in the literature to explain the development of party voting unity, such as the professionalization of the legislature, electoral pressure, or career and socialization effects, have little influence on the behaviour of members in Canada. Instead, I find that both the content of the legislative agenda and parliamentary rules have a much more important effect on the development of partisanship in the legislature. Still, the lack of historical context in the empirical analyses prevents me from fully understanding how the content of the legislative agenda might have changed over time, or why certain rules might have been modified during the past 150 years to promote party unity. This is the focus of the second part of the book.

Each of the next two chapters presents a distinct case study to explain how the combination of historical events and institutional rule changes might have contributed to increasing partisanship in Canada. The aim here is to identify and categorize the issues that have been known to split parties internally, and to determine whether parliamentary rule and procedural changes have strengthened or weakened party influence during two distinct periods. The first case study, presented in chapter 7, focuses on the 1867–1900 period to explain the religious realignment of Roman Catholic and Protestant MPs within the Conservative and Liberal parties. This chapter provides evidence to show that the issues dividing parties internally were first linked to nation-building projects, and later to religious questions, and that each of these conflicts successively increased the ideological cohesion of the two major parties. The second case study, in chapter 8, covers the next three decades (1900–30), and analyses the effect of rule changes on the organization of the House of Commons. In this chapter, I demonstrate that the introduction of restrictive parliamentary procedures between 1906 and 1913 to control the legislative agenda reduced the influence of backbenchers and created incentives for some members to defect from their parties. I also look at how the modification of these rules influenced the content of legislative debates and ultimately contributed to change the structure of the party system between 1918 and 1930. Here, I focus on western alienation and Quebec nationalism to show the limits of representing heterogeneous interests in Westminster-style parliamentary systems.

In the last empirical chapter (chapter 9), I use a different approach to analyse the development of parties in the legislative arena by considering the Canadian Senate. This chapter stands apart from the rest of the book in that it provides a contrasting case to the House of Commons for evaluating how institutional rules affect legislative behaviour. Indeed, the upper chamber offers an interesting perspective on the study of party influence in Parliament for three reasons. First, the Senate historically has been less affected by party discipline, primarily because the confidence convention applies only to the lower house, but also because senators are appointed to their seats and thus are isolated from electoral pressure. Second, the Senate recently has undergone important institutional changes: all former Liberal senators now sit as independent in this chamber. This transformation presents us with a rare opportunity to measure the influence of party leaders on legislative behaviour by comparing the voting records of senators before and after they were removed from the Liberal caucus. Here I find that the unity of the Liberal caucus was barely affected by this change, and show that reducing party discipline did not increase the independence of senators much, even in the most recent Parliament (2015–19), when all new senator appointments were based on the recommendations of a nonpartisan commission.

In the conclusion, chapter 10, I summarize the main findings presented in the book, emphasize the limits of my argument, and offer several avenues for future comparative research by outlining a broader theory of party system change. I also discuss some of the more recent proposals for reforms to increase the influence of private members in Parliament. I explain that the changes made to the parliamentary order of business following the recommendations of the 1985 report of the Special Committee on the Reform of the House of Commons (Canada 1985) – referred to as the McGrath Report – increased the effective legislative function of backbenchers in the House of Commons and temporarily weakened the hold of party leaders on their members. I also argue, however, that increasing the independence of Members of Parliament, which is often viewed as a panacea for improving democratic representation, might not necessarily lead to a more responsive system of parliamentary government.

Chapter Two

The Emergence of Parties in Parliament

When the first Canadian Parliament assembled in November 1867, John A. Macdonald had an enormous challenge. He needed to find a way to maintain a unified caucus and garner enough support to enact the country's first national legislative program. This was not an easy task. Macdonald's governing coalition was composed of parliamentarians with distinct sectional interests who for the most part had served in the former colonial assemblies of British North America. Worse still, Macdonald had to rely on an unstable majority made up of "several independent members, or loose fish" who tended to support the government whenever it served their own personal interests (Macdonald letter, 2 September 1872, cited in Pope 1921, 175).

Prior to Confederation, it was not uncommon for individual lawmakers to break party lines and hold members of the executive accountable for their actions, even if they were elected under the same party banner. Macdonald knew the importance of caucus unity. Because of a lack of discipline, the United Province of Canada had been governed by twelve different ministries since 1848, which lasted on average eighteen months (Lower 1961, 303). The "irreconcilable differences of opinion" between members of what are now the provinces of Ontario and Quebec over questions of religion, language, education, and democratic representation were such that the union was in "danger of impending anarchy" (Debates 1865, 26). "We had election after election" and "ministry after ministry," declared Macdonald in his opening speech in the Confederation Debates, all with the same results: "a succession of weak governments – weak in numerical support, weak in force, and weak in the power of doing good." In fact, "parties were so equally balanced," he continued, "that the vote of one member might decide the fate of the Administration for a year or a series of years" (26).

The struggle to build a stable governing coalition had been a constant problem in United Canada ever since Lafontaine and Baldwin formed the first responsible government in 1848. "What to do I do not know," wrote Macdonald to one of his allies in a letter discussing the voting situation in his party after the 1858 election (Macdonald letter, 12 January 1858, cited in Johnson 1930, 6–7). Even as leader of the government, Macdonald did not know how many members would support him before Parliament convened for its first session. "Cook of Dundas, you put down for us – doubtful," he stated in the same letter. "Dorland you put down for us. Is this so? McLeod and Hogan (and I think Burwell) will vote for us. Holmes is nearly certain. Wallbridge will not I think go in the opposition *mais nous verrons*" (6–7).

In the end, the solution to this chronic ministerial instability proved to be constitutional, and was resolved with the federal union of British North American colonies. By assigning the most controversial issues, such as education and local expenditures, to the provincial legislatures, the Fathers of Confederation were able to remove most of the sectional difficulties that threatened to make government on the federal stage impossible. "We have formed a scheme of government which unites the advantages of a legislative union and the sectional freedom of a federal union, with protection to local interests," Macdonald explained in the Confederation debates, where "all the great questions which affect the general interests of the Confederacy as a whole, are confined to the Federal Parliament, while the local interests and local laws of each section are preserved intact, and entrusted to the care of the local bodies." Only under these conditions could the legislature attempt to break "the dead-lock," the "anarchy," and the "evils" that "threatened the future of Canada" and promote the formation of a "strong government" (Debates 1865, 25–44).

History has shown that Macdonald was right. The federal union of the Canadian provinces did indeed remove most of these "sectional difficulties" from the national Parliament, while the remaining obstacles were dealt with through a combination of patronage and ministerial appointments. Ultimately, Macdonald was able to secure the loyalty of enough members to build a stable governing coalition throughout his tenure as prime minister. And this has been the case for all other ministries since then. Not one government in Ottawa has ever fallen due to a lack of party unity in Parliament.[1] In fact, over the past 150 years, legislative parties have become so cohesive in Canada that they are now considered among the most disciplined in the world. How did this country move from a Parliament dominated by a disorganized rump of independent members to one controlled by parties, where dissension is rarely expressed in public?

The following chapter begins to answer this question by providing a historical account of the emergence of the first political parties in Canada. The objective here is to offer background from secondary sources to the original empirical analysis that follows. The story is centred on two main events that occurred before the end of the First World War, one related to ethnic and religious diversity and the rise of French-Canadian nationalism, the other linked to western colonization and the emergence of agrarian populism. Both changes had a profound influence on the country's first major political conflicts, which led to the rapid consolidation of party unity in the legislature and ultimately to the demise of the two-party system in Parliament.

My argument can be summarized as follows. For a time, Confederation did indeed appear to reduce the number of regional, ethnic, and religious conflicts in Parliament. The new constitution transferred jurisdiction over these controversial matters to the provincial assemblies, but also added safeguards to protect the rights of the French and English minorities across the country. The acquisition of Rupert's Land in 1869, however, which led to the establishment of the province of Manitoba and the Northwest Territories in 1870, created two new problems for the national legislature. First, government needed to deal with the Métis, French, and Roman Catholic population in this area; second, it had to reconcile Canada's industrial policy with the economic needs of the new frontier. As I argue below – and later demonstrate empirically – each of these events reduced the unity of the Liberal and Conservative caucuses in Parliament. Both parties first began to divide internally over questions related to religion and language, and later broke down on the debates surrounding Canada's role in the British Empire and the economic subordination of the western provinces.

Ultimately, these issues led to the creation of two distinct party factions within the Liberal and Conservative caucuses: French-Canadian nationalists and western agrarian populists. For a time, members of these groups remained loyal to the existing two-party system. However, many saw their influence waning as party leaders increased their domination over the legislative process in the first two decades of the twentieth century. Since the imposition of strict party discipline left little room for dissension, supporters of the nationalist and agrarian movements eventually left the old parties to sit on their own in the legislature. It was in part because of the development of party discipline that several regional parties, such as the Progressive Party (1920–42) and the Bloc Populaire (1942–7), were created in Parliament after members defected from the Liberal and Conservative caucuses. Paradoxically, the removal of these factions further increased cohesion within the two old parties and ultimately contributed to reducing the influence of private members in the legislative process even more. From now on, backbenchers had to compete with the leaders of three or more parties to gain access to the floor.

In what follows, I describe in greater detail the events that led to these transformations by focusing primarily on the period between 1867 and 1935, when the party system was in flux. I begin by explaining the origins of the first political parties in Canada. In the next section, I describe how party discipline and caucus unity has changed over five different periods: one dominated by sectional, religious, and language conflicts (1867–96); one characterized by the emergence of a nationalist party faction (1896–1917); one defined by the western agrarian movement (1917–21); one that saw the introduction of the first regional parties in Parliament (1921–35); and finally, one in which parties consolidated into highly cohesive voting blocs (1935–2015). This periodization highlights how members' preferences might have interacted with parliamentary rules to affect the structure of the party system. It also emphasizes how the Liberal and Conservative parties became more unified over time, and how this newfound rigidity contributed to the creation of the first regional parties in Parliament.

The Origin of the First Canadian Parties

Until the end of the First World War, the Conservative and Liberal parties almost exclusively dominated the Parliament of Canada. Both originated from the former legislative assemblies of Ontario, Quebec, New Brunswick, and Nova Scotia, where the main political conflict was between supporters of the colonial administration and democratic reformers. In the years immediately following Confederation, the Conservative and Liberal parties were not clearly defined as parliamentary groups. There was a Liberal-Conservative alliance led by John A. Macdonald, who campaigned in favour of the union. This coalition was loosely based on four regional factions found in the former United Province of Canada: moderate reformists, with followers of the Tory "Family Compact," in Ontario; and Conservative French Canadians (the "Bleus"), with English mercantile interests, in Quebec (Hougham 1963, 1–2). In addition, at times several independent MPs could have joined the governing coalition on certain votes. Others, such as Joseph Howe from Nova Scotia, became government supporters only after they entered the cabinet.

A similar regional organization was found within the Liberal Party, which was roughly composed of former anti-Catholic radical "Clear Grits" reformers, led by George Brown in Ontario, and anti-clerical radicals (Rouges), who favoured closer ties with the United States, led by Antoine-Aimé Dorion in Quebec. These factions remained relatively independent until a Liberal Party leader was elected towards the end of the first Parliament. Finally, the two Maritime colonies, New Brunswick and Nova Scotia, had their own separate party systems independent of the ones found in Ontario and Quebec. One group campaigned in favour of the union, whereas the other was opposed to the project. This latter group, composed of Liberal (New Brunswick) and Anti-Confederate (Nova Scotia) legislators, won the most seats in the first federal election.

The first five decades after Confederation saw the consolidation of the two-party system in the legislative arena. Party unity increased and partisan conflict intensified as the House of Commons alternated between successive Conservative and Liberal governments (see table 2.1). During this period, Canada experienced unprecedented economic growth, with the expansion of

Table 2.1 Party Standings in the House of Commons, 1867–1935

		Party (number of seats)			
Parliament	Term	Conservatives	Liberals	Others	Independents
1st	1867–72	100	61	18[a]	–
2nd	1873–4	95	98	–	6
3rd	1874–8	64	130	–	11
4th	1879–82	136	61	1[b]	8
5th	1883–7	133	71	1[b]	6
6th	1887–91	121	78	3[c]	11
7th	1891–6	115	90	2[d]	7
8th	1896–1900	86	116	3[e]	6
9th	1901–4	79	127	–	6
10th	1905–8	74	135	–	2
11th	1909–11	84	131	1[f]	2
12th	1911–17	131	84	1[f]	3
13th	1918–21	151	81	–	–
14th	1922–5	49	119	63[g]	4
15th	1926	115	100	26[h]	4
16th	1926–30	89	117	34[i]	3
17th	1930–5	136	89	17[j]	3

Note: Numbers are taken from the party standing following the first vote taken in the first session of the Parliament. The other party categories are distributed as follows:
(a) Anti-Confederate Party of Nova Scotia (18);
(b) Nationalist Party of Quebec (1);
(c) Nationalist Party of Quebec (3);
(d) Nationalist Party of Quebec (2);
(e) Patron of Industry (2), McCarthyite (1);
(f) Labour (1);
(g) Progressives (57), Labour (3), United Farmers (3);
(h) Progressives (22), Labour (2), United Farmers (2);
(i) United Farmers (12), Progressives (10), Liberal Progressives (8), Labour (4);
(j) United Farmers (9), Progressives (3), Liberal Progressives (3), Labour (2).
Sources: Godbout and Høyland (2017), parliamentary data files; Parlinfo, Information Service of the Parliament of Canada.

railroads, first to the east and then to the west, in an effort to colonize western territories and develop new markets. Originally comprised of four provinces in 1867 (Ontario, Quebec, New Brunswick, and Nova Scotia), the federation grew in size with the addition of Manitoba and the Northwest Territories (1870), British Columbia (1871), Prince Edward Island (1873), Yukon (1901), and Alberta and Saskatchewan (1905). Attachment to provincial identity remained high. Local governments had a much greater effect on the daily lives of the average Canadian than did the federal bureaucracy, whose chief function was primarily limited to strengthening the economy through different nation-building projects.

The presence of distinct sectional interests in the first Canadian Parliament presupposes some level of regional conflict that transcended party lines, at least in the first years following Confederation. Because Canada is the product of a federal union among four formerly independent colonies, it is quite possible that, during certain legislative votes, members from the same province were more likely to band together and break party lines. These splits would have been more likely to occur over localized interests when certain legislation affected specific parts of the country. For example, the creation of a uniform currency and banking system in 1871 generated a great deal of controversy because each former colony had to integrate its own monetary system into that of the new union (Easterbrook and Aitken 1988, 462–3). Furthermore, the fact that MPs had dual representation – for example, they could occupy seats in both provincial and federal legislatures until 1874 – probably served to strengthen ties between both levels of government. Finally, the presence of an anti-Confederate party in Nova Scotia and the reluctance of Maritime leaders to align with either one of the major parties during the first Parliament also guaranteed that regionalism would play an important role in shaping political debates. Still, we should expect the importance of these regional conflicts to have declined over time, especially since many of the most divisive issues, such as banking, insolvency law, or major railway developments, were more or less settled by the end of the third Parliament (1874–8). It was after this term that the Conservative Party introduced the National Policy. This project proposed a comprehensive approach to promoting the development and industrialization of the Canadian economy through higher tariffs, western expansion, and an increase in trade and economic integration among the different provinces. The National Policy also clearly polarized both parties along economic lines, with the Conservatives favouring protectionism and the Liberals promoting free trade. In return, this new political alignment consolidated the positions of each party in the minds of voters, who could now more easily distinguish between them.

Ethnic and Religious Conflicts, 1867–1896

Although the Conservative Party of John A. Macdonald was very successful on the economic front, several political events seriously weakened its popular support in the years following Confederation. Most of these problems were related to the role of the Roman Catholic Church and language rights outside of the predominantly French-speaking province of Quebec (Morton 1950, 9). Although today language debates are frequently associated with Quebec, this issue was not entirely regional at the time, mainly because there was an important proportion of Roman Catholics and French speakers outside that province: according to the

1871 census, for example, 86 per cent of the population of Quebec was Catholic, while the proportion reached 21 per cent in the rest of Canada.

As we saw earlier, one of the primary goals of Confederation was to restrict the powers of the central government by transferring jurisdiction over local and private matters to provincial assemblies. This was done in order to break the deadlock created under the Act of Union of 1840, which had united Upper and Lower Canada into a single colony (Wade 1955, 321). The objective of this union had been to assimilate the French-speaking population to the English-speaking majority: each section of Canada was represented by an equal number of legislators sitting in a single assembly, where the use of French was prohibited. This situation created so much tension that chronic ministerial instability became the norm in the legislature between 1848 and 1864. These conflicts were fuelled primarily by ethnic and religious cleavages, but also by weak party unity, which often failed to give the government a working majority. Confederation was thus seen as a solution to these problems because it would prevent the central government from interfering in local affairs. French speakers would now become a majority in the provincial assembly of Quebec, and free to adopt their own laws in the spheres of education, religion, and private property. They would also form a minority, however, inside the new federal Parliament, where legislators would be asked to consider matters of common interest to the whole dominion. Provisions to protect the rights of Protestants in Quebec and Roman Catholics outside that province were added to the new Constitution as well. Thus, the Fathers of Confederation believed that the separation-of-powers scheme proposed in the British North America Act would remove most of the important sources of ethnic and religious tension from the national legislature, and promote stability within it.

Unfortunately, this legislative harmony never came to pass, primarily because the new federal Parliament proved incapable of protecting the rights of Roman Catholics and French speakers outside Quebec. The problems for the Conservative Party began shortly after Confederation, when New Brunswick abolished confessional education in 1871.[2] This decision rapidly transformed into a national crisis when John Costigan, a Catholic member of Macdonald's Conservatives, introduced a motion in the House of Commons requesting that the federal government disallow the New Brunswick act by using the remedial provision outlined in section 93 of the Constitution.[3] Although this motion was ultimately defeated, several other conflicts over language and religion emerged elsewhere in the country as well. As a result, the division between French and English, Catholic and Protestant, gradually increased over time (Wade 1955, 460–1).

This fundamental conflict surrounding language and religion defined the colonial history of Canada, and remained salient in the minds of the electorate well into the twentieth century (Blais 2005, 830).[4] Perhaps the best example of this struggle relates to the Manitoba (1869) and Northwest Territories (1885) rebellions of Catholic Métis against the influx of anglophone Protestant settlers, and a federal court decision to execute their leader, Louis Riel, a former Member of Parliament. The culmination of this crisis occurred in 1890, when Manitoba passed a law to abolish French as an official language and removed public funding for Catholic schools in the province – rights that were protected under Manitoba's constitution. Following the Conservative government's inaction on this matter, Catholic voters across Canada began to realign their votes towards the Liberal Party, now led by a French-Catholic representative from Quebec, Wilfrid Laurier. The primary consequence of this partisan realignment was that the French-speaking population of Quebec basically rejected the Conservative Party for several decades to come, while Roman Catholic voters across Canada began to support the Liberal Party disproportionately after the 1896 election.

It is important not to underestimate the salience of religion in Canadian political life during the nineteenth century. Both the Conservative and the Liberal parties originally emerged from religious alliances: Catholic ultramontanes with the established Protestant churches for the Conservative Party; Catholic Gallicans with other Protestant reformed churches for the Liberals. These fragile coalitions, however, were seriously put to the test after Confederation (Azoulay 1999, 55–6; Stewart 1986, 62–3). Partisan loyalty was often trumped by religious identity. Divisions on issues such as divorce, marriage, temperance, education, and language generally split the Conservative and Liberal parties internally. It was also common for clergymen to preach politics from the pulpit or to attempt to influence the behaviour of voters and elected officials directly. For example, the Catholic Church told voters that they had "the right and the duty to speak not only to the electors and to the candidates, but also to the constituted authorities," and that their votes should conform "with the wishes and instructions set forth by the bishops in their pastoral" (Siegfried [1906] 1966, 43). Religious interference was not limited to Catholic clergymen. Members of the Methodist Church were also known to voice their opposition to French domination and popery, while several different political organizations existed to defend the rights of Protestants – for example, the Orange Lodge, the Equal Rights Association, the Imperial Federation League, and the Protestant Protective Association (Fay 2002, 144).

The fact that both the Liberal and Conservative caucuses were a mix of Roman Catholic and Protestant MPs constantly threatened the unity of each party. Whenever an issue related to language or religion was raised during a debate, such as over the North-West Rebellion (1869–70), the incorporation of the Orange Association of British America (1883), or the hanging of Louis Riel (1885), both parties were at risk of dividing internally along confessional lines. It was only after Wilfrid Laurier became prime minister in 1896 that intra-party splits over these issues slowly began to decline in Parliament. After this point, most Catholic members in the House of Commons were elected under the Liberal

Party banner, while religious and linguistic conflicts became closely associated with the partisan division opposing the two main parties.

To summarize, the first Canadian political parties were characterized by weak levels of party unity for two reasons. First, members tended to be more independent of their party, and a great number of controversial issues – mostly related to state-building projects and the national economy – had to be settled rapidly in the new federal Parliament. Debates over the tariff rate, the development of railways, and the establishment of the first banking system created many controversies inside the legislature, with opposing members of the same party representing different sections of the country. Second, although party unity increased somewhat after the adoption of the National Policy in 1879, conflicts over language and religion remained an important source of intra-party division. Under the new federal Constitution, these debates should have been settled in provincial legislatures, but several different events, such as the creation of the Northwest Territories and the province of Manitoba, pushed the question of Catholic and French-speaking minority rights onto the national stage. The debates surrounding theses crises eventually led to the realignment of Catholic voters with the Liberals and the end of the Liberal-Conservative coalition of John A. Macdonald in Parliament.

Quebec Nationalists, 1896–1917

Although the realignment of Catholic voters appeared to have settled most of the controversial debates related to language and religion in Parliament, the Liberal Party's positions on several other related questions, such as Imperial relations and, later, conscription, were often perceived by many members of the French-Canadian elite to be insufficient compromises for protecting their rights in the federation. As a consequence, Quebec voters often elected nationalist representatives to Parliament, such as during the 1911 election, when conflicts over culture and language became salient again. These candidates usually ran under the Conservative Party banner. Once in Parliament, however, they regularly failed to support their caucus during important legislative votes.

Henri Bourassa is perhaps the best representative of this movement. The grandson of Louis-Joseph Papineau, Bourassa was first elected to Parliament as a Liberal in 1896. Extremely weary of party discipline, he refused to submit to the directives of party leaders, which he compared to a modern form of slavery: "Our parties are nothing more than flocks of ignorant and venal slaves who blindly follow their leaders. The stultifying discipline of parties and, more importantly, election resources, make most candidates and Members of Parliament docile instruments of their masters who have bought, fed and watered them, while promising opulent pasture for their old days" (Dumont, Montminy, and Hamelin 1978, 264).[5] This fierce independent spirit led him to resign from the Liberal caucus in 1899 to protest Canada's involvement in the South African War. Bourassa was, however, immediately re-elected by acclamation to the House of Commons, and continued to serve as a member of the Liberal Party until he resigned once again in 1907, this time to run as a Conservative candidate in the Quebec provincial election.

While in Parliament, Bourassa adopted a nationalist and anti-imperialist ideology that was never fully embraced by either of the two major party caucuses. On the one hand, Bourassa was critical of Laurier's ambiguous position of compromise over questions of religion, language, and Imperial relations, which were to become the hallmarks of his tenure as prime minister. On the other hand, he was even more critical of the views defended by the English-speaking members of the Conservative Party, who favoured closer ties with the British Empire and the assimilation of the French-Canadian minority outside Quebec (Wade 1955, 495–6). Bourassa's ambivalence towards Laurier's conciliatory positions eventually forced him to switch sides and to support an alliance with the Conservative Party during the 1911 federal election.

This election was fought primarily on the issues of reciprocity and the free trade agreement with the United States. In Quebec, however, the campaign was dominated by the question of Imperial relations and by Laurier's decision to create a Canadian naval force. For Quebec nationalists, this proposal was viewed as a step closer to war and conscription, whereas for the remaining members of the Conservative Party, Laurier's "tin-pot navy" was perceived as an inadequate compromise to defend the Empire against German aggression. With help from *La Ligue nationaliste canadienne* – an organization founded in 1903 to promote the interests of French Canadians and the autonomy of Canada within the Empire – Bourassa encouraged nationalists to run as Conservatives during the 1911 campaign. The anti-imperialist sentiment weakened support for the Liberals in Quebec, and Laurier lost enough seats in the province to give a majority to the Conservatives.

Although united in their struggle against the Liberal Party, the Conservatives ended up dividing shortly after the election. Most nationalists left the caucus as soon as they understood that there would be no concession on the question of Imperial relations in a party dominated by "vociferous Orangemen" with a "strong attachment to the British connection" and a "Protestant, Anglo-Saxon Weltanschauung" (English 1977, 84). For instance, Prime Minister Robert Borden caused quite a stir among the remaining nationalists of his caucus when he refused to consider remedial actions against Regulation 17 in Ontario, which virtually banned French education in schools. "As the matter was entirely of provincial concern," he explained in his memoirs, "I felt strongly that discussion in the House of Commons would be not only futile but exasperating and even dangerous" (Borden 1938, 573). The opposition between English- and French-speaking MPs became even more virulent later in this term when Laurier took a stand against conscription and refused to join the wartime coalition government of Robert Borden in 1917.[6] Parliament was dissolved the same year, and Laurier – along with every single French-speaking MP from Quebec – won re-election under an anti-conscription banner against a Conservative-Liberal Unionist government composed almost exclusively of Protestant English Canadians. This represents the only instance in Canada's political history when the party system was completely divided along ethnic lines. The imposition of conscription ended up alienating the Conservative Party in Quebec for decades to come (Cairns 1968, 62; English 1977, 190).

A relatively strong level of partisan conflict in Parliament characterized the period between the 1896 and 1917 elections. However, the presence of nationalist members from Quebec – such as Henri Bourassa, Armand Lavergne, and Joseph Israël Tarte – who, for a time, supported the Liberals, then later switched sides to the Conservatives, prevented both parties from achieving complete unity. A second group of rebellious MPs also emerged towards the end of this period, as the debates surrounding wartime industrial production led to the growth of the farmers' movement in Western Canada (Brown and Cook 1974, 315). It is the presence of this last faction that contributed the most to the demise of the two-party system in the federal Parliament.

Agrarian Revolt, 1917–1921

Nationalist Members of Parliament were not the only faction that shifted party allegiance during the first two decades of the twentieth century. Like Bourassa's supporters in Quebec, western farmers were at odds with the position of the two dominant parties on several important issues. On the one hand, they were more likely to favour lower tariffs and free trade, a position championed by the Liberals but opposed by the Conservatives. On the other hand, they were also more likely to be socially conservative on issues such as prohibition and temperance, and to oppose the Liberals on questions of French-language rights and confessional education outside Quebec (Brown and Cook 1974, 317).

In the first decades following Confederation, western MPs from Manitoba, British Columbia, and the Northwest Territories frequently ran as independent candidates by pledging to support whichever party won the most seats in Parliament. This was done in order to secure patronage in the districts and acquire funds for the transcontinental railway (Macpherson 1953, 22). Most of these "moderate" government supporters, however, eventually gravitated towards the Liberals, who were opposed to the Conservatives' National Policy of higher tariffs and import restrictions. Adopted in the fourth Parliament, this economic platform aimed to protect eastern industries at the expense of Prairie farmers, who were forced to pay inflated prices for manufactured goods and higher railway freight rates (7). The unequal effect of the National Policy across the country confirmed the quasi-colonial status of the western provinces (10). Major regional grievances arose over the control of banks, railways, and the grain trade, which were primarily administered from Central Canada (Morton 1950, 7). Some of these injustices were partially resolved following the adoption of the Crow's Nest Pass Agreement between the Canadian Pacific Railway and the Laurier government in 1897. As a result of this agreement, freight rates temporarily fell for western farmers until the First World War. The fact that the federal government owned the natural resources of the Prairies well into the 1930s also fostered strong sectional feelings in this region.

As the population of the Prairies increased through immigration and land settlement policies – from 7 per cent of Canada's total population in 1901 to 23 per cent in 1921 (Friesen 1984, 248) – the influence of the western provinces grew in the legislature as well. After 1900, the majority of candidates from this region were elected under the Liberal Party banner to represent agricultural ridings in Ottawa. Most were supported by different provincial farmers' associations, such as the Manitoba and Saskatchewan Grain Growers' Associations and the United Farmers of Alberta, all affiliated with the Canadian Council of Agriculture (Morton 1950, 63–4). Like French-Canadian nationalists, these candidates remained highly independent from parties and often failed to support their caucus during legislative votes. Still, the "demands for independent political action" from the Prairies grew steadily over time, especially after Laurier lost the 1911 election by proposing a free trade agreement with the United States (Macpherson 1953, 25). As I argue later in the book, these demands were also fuelled by changes to parliamentary rules that aimed to limit the influence of backbenchers in the legislative process (Smith 1981, 39–40). Now unable to represent the interests of farmers effectively within the existing party system, several members from the Prairies opted to create their own independent Progressive caucus in the legislature right before the 1921 election.

Like Henri Bourassa and his nationalist supporters in Quebec, the career of Thomas Crerar, a prominent leader of the Manitoba Grain Growers' Association, illustrates how the farmers' movement remained highly independent of the parties in Parliament. Although a Liberal, Crerar was first elected to the House of Commons as a Unionist member of Robert Borden's wartime government (1917–21). He was immediately promoted to the cabinet as minister of agriculture despite his strong opposition to tariff protection, a central component of the Conservative Party's National Policy. This irreconcilable difference of interest led him to resign from the party after he voted in favour of an amendment to reduce tariff rates in the first post-war budget (Morton 1950, 69). Along with seven other rebel western members from the government side, Crerar went on to found the Progressive caucus (Beck 1968, 151; Morton 1950, 96).

The emergence of this new party in Parliament can be linked to the waning influence of private members in the legislative process. Until Crerar's decision to cross the floor and sit as an independent, western farmers believed they could transform the old parties from within – as long as they could win enough seats to have their voices heard in government (Brown and Cook 1974, 317). We can see this strategy clearly in the 1916 program of the Canadian Council of Agriculture. Candidates from all parties were invited to join the movement, but they had to pledge their support for the council's platform and agree to challenge the National Policy and the tariff once in Parliament (Morton 1950, 63–4). The problem with this approach was that several representatives of the farmers' movement had already been elected under the Liberal or Conservative Party banner, and no major agrarian reform had been adopted since then. In fact, it was very difficult for western MPs to have their voices heard within the existing party structures, let alone inside the cabinet. The parliamentary system imposed too many restraints on regional groups, which could not be effectively managed within the two major parties (Smith 1963, 130–1). As Brown and Cook (1974) explain, "for men like Henry Wise Wood of Alberta, and J.J. Morrison of Ontario" who were important leaders in the cooperative and farmers' movements, "the political system itself had to be changed," "the iron chains of party discipline had to be broken," and the "parties abolished" (317). The most radical agrarian reformers believed that only under these conditions could elected officials truly represent the interests not only of farmers, but also those of other major societal groups, such as industrial workers and business owners, in a new kind of corporate assembly where members would deal with issues based on their merit, not partisan or political considerations (Macpherson 1953, 26).

The farmers' distrust of the existing party system was nothing new. It had existed since the time of the North-West uprising and had become a permanent feature of western agrarian radicalism – more so with the emergence of the Nonpartisan League in Alberta during the First World War (Macpherson 1953, 25). Farmers assumed that elected representatives were corrupted by moneyed interests and patronage networks, two hallmarks of the traditional party system (Laycock 1990, 50). Mistrust of "partyism," however, made it difficult for supporters of the movement to justify joining the Liberal Party once they had left the Unionist government in 1920. Not only were the Liberals corrupted by party discipline; they were also mostly Catholic, French-speaking, and "anti-prohibition elements that held little appeal for the righteous farmer" (Brown and Cook 1974, 317). The only option left for farmers' representatives was to sit on their own and form an independent caucus in the House of Commons.

As Smith (1963, 130) explains, supporters of the farmers' movement left the traditional parties "because they saw that it was a loose federation of provincial groups, dominated by the members from the populous, industrious provinces." Thus, a new, farmer-controlled party appeared to be the most promising avenue for the agrarian political movement. Such a party might hold the balance of power in Parliament by winning enough seats to deny the government a majority; just as the Irish Home Rule party had done in Britain in the last two decades of the nineteenth century (Morton 1950, 18). It was these considerations that led the Canadian Council of Agriculture to recognize the members of the Progressive caucus as their official representatives in Parliament, to acknowledge Crerar as its national leader, and to endorse Progressive candidates in the 1921 election (106). This strategy proved successful, since the Progressive Party did indeed hold the balance of power in three successive Liberal minority governments between 1921 and 1930.

A Multiparty System, 1921–1935

The arrival of the Progressive Party had a profound effect on the organization of Parliament. For the first time, the legislature had to accommodate members from three different political parties, and the rules of the House had to be modified to recognize more than one opposition leader. These changes further centralized into the hands of party leaders the time set aside to discuss government business in the debates. As a consequence, the limited opportunities for backbenchers to influence the legislative process were reduced even more, while the concentration of power in Parliament increased significantly (Dawson 1962, 25; Morton 1950, 153).

Although the Progressives won the second-highest number of seats in the 1921 election, they never fully "achieved internal harmony" in Parliament (Morton 1950, 106). At its core, the party was loosely based on an alliance of provincial and local farmers' organizations controlled by two distinct factions. One was led by Crerar, and composed of other former members of the Unionist government from Manitoba. This faction favoured an alliance with the Liberals and a governing coalition in Parliament. The other faction, however – consisting of Henry Wise Wood and other more radical elements of the caucus from Alberta, and elected to promote a radical new form of government based on the representation of occupational groups – rapidly rejected this idea because they suspected that such a deal would require strong party leaders and party discipline (Morton 1950, 147, 166). Under their proposed system, the convention of responsible party government would be abolished, there would no longer be a need for party discipline, and Parliament would cease to be divided along partisan lines (Macpherson 1953, 45; Morton 1950, 229). Wood and his supporters believed these reforms would prevent members from being corrupted by the party system, since cabinet dominance would be replaced by direct legislation, referendums, and recall elections (Macpherson 1953, 71; Morton 1950, 15–16).

In the end, neither faction managed to impose its will on the other, and these internal conflicts led to the gradual destruction of the Progressive Party over the next three federal elections. When it became apparent that a formal alliance with the Liberal Party was impossible, Crerar was offered the position of leader of the opposition in Parliament. He refused to accept this role, however, and it was taken over by the Conservatives' new leader, Arthur Meighen, whose party finished third in the 1921 election. Nonetheless, internal divisions between the Alberta and Manitoba factions of the Progressive Party did not end there: other conflicts emerged over time between the more practical wing of the caucus, which wanted to work within the existing party system to reduce the tariff, and the more radical elements, who wanted to implement constituency autonomy and a new form of political representation (Morton 1950, 167).

Crerar eventually resigned as party leader in 1922, and joined the Liberals in 1930 as a cabinet minister in the government of William L. Mackenzie King. By 1925, ten other members from Manitoba had also left the party to sit as Liberals in Parliament. The remaining more radical elements – the so-called Ginger Group – abandoned the Progressive Party as well, mostly to run as candidates of the United Farmers Party of Alberta in the 1925, 1926, and 1930 federal elections. It is revealing to note that this split was not caused by difference of opinion or policy, as Morton claims, but rather, by "parliamentary organization and procedure," since the Ginger Group carried "the principle of constituency autonomy to the point of the complete independence of the individual member" (1950, 221).

The disintegration of the Progressive caucus was by no means the end of third-party representation in Parliament. The farmers' movement, which had first organized at the local level under the United Farmers banner, was much more successful in provincial elections, forming a government in Ontario (1919–23), Alberta (1921–35), and Manitoba (1922–32). At the federal level, the farmers' vote remained highly divided regionally, with Manitoba, Saskatchewan, and Ontario continuing to support the Progressive Party for most of the 1920s and Alberta moving towards the United Farmers. Candidates from the distinct provincial Labour parties also won a handful of seats in more urban ridings during this period.[7] And so, after the 1930 election, it became apparent to the supporters of these different agrarian and labour organizations that co-operation was necessary to "undertake the fundamental economic and social reconstruction" that would put an end to the National Policy and its agents, the traditional political parties (Morton 1950, 283). Such a broader alliance was needed because, as stand-alone groups, their numbers were insufficient to control the government (281). As table 2.1 shows, third parties represented only 11 per cent, 14 per cent, and 7 per cent of the elected members in the fifteenth (1926), sixteenth (1926–30), and seventeenth (1930–5) Parliaments. Collaboration among these different political parties was seen as necessary if farmers and workers wanted to preserve and exercise their rights in the economic and political spheres (Young 1969, 18). Thus, an alliance was formed between labour and farming organizations to constitute the Co-operative Commonwealth

Federation (CCF) in 1932. This new party adopted a platform in Regina a year later to support, among other things, "the security of tenure for farmers," "the replacement of the capitalist system" (CCF 1933), and the "full extension of democratic rights and practices within the parliamentary system" (Laycock 1990, 20).

Punctuated Regionalism, 1935–2015

The arrival of the CCF, which became the New Democratic Party in 1962, represents the final stage in the transformation of the Canadian party system. Although several other regional parties have emerged in Parliament since then, none could claim to have developed a comparable national basis of support.[8] After 1935, three common features can be identified as defining most federal elections. First, this date marks the beginning of almost fifty years of uninterrupted Liberal governments: by relying on a strong basis of support in Quebec, the Liberal Party managed to form the government after eleven of the fifteen elections between 1935 and 1980.[9] Second, the period illustrates what is referred to as Canada's two-and-a-half party system (Blondel 1968, 185), where electoral competition at the national level occurs primarily between three major parties: the Conservatives, the Liberals, and the New Democrats. Figure 2.1 illustrates this point by reporting the mean of the effective number of candidates in each riding for all elections held between 1867 and 2015.[10] This measure ranges from 1 to 6.29 in the data, where 1 represents an election in which there was only one candidate, who won 100 per cent of the votes – that is, the candidate won by acclamation – and 2 represents an election where two candidates shared 50 per cent of the vote. Any value greater than 1 implies that competition increased in a district election, with an index of 2.67 corresponding, for example, to a 50-25-25 split among three candidates, and so on.

Here we see that the local level of competition in federal elections increased significantly in 1935, reaching an average value of around 2.5 for most of the subsequent elections. It is important to note, however, that there are deviations in the level of competition during certain elections – for example, 1945, 1957, and 1993 – when the index value approaches three candidates. These elections were characterized by periods of punctuated regionalism, when minor party candidates managed to win several seats in local contests, mostly in Alberta and Quebec. This represents the third feature of the national party system after 1935.

Although the Canadian political science literature generally identifies at least three other distinct party systems following the arrival of the CCF (later, the New Democratic Party, NDP) on the national stage (Carty, Cross, and Young 2000; Johnston et al. 1992), these shifts had only minor consequences for the organization of parties in Parliament. At different times, regional parties emerged to represent the political interests of groups that did not quite fit within the

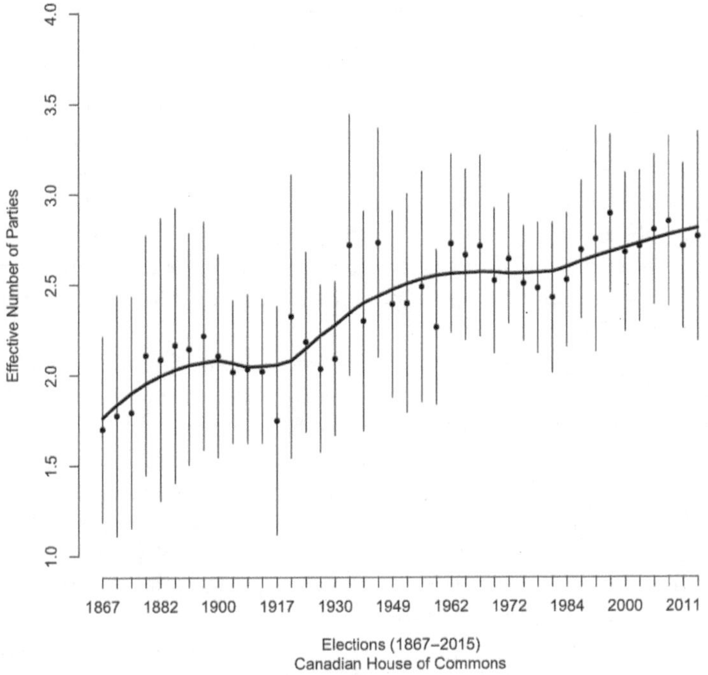

Figure 2.1 Effective Number of Parties in Federal Elections, 1867–2015

framework of the NDP, Liberal, or Conservative parties. For example, two regional parties, Social Credit (1935–80) and Reform (1987–2000), elected members to Parliament in order to defend the interests of the western provinces. Likewise, three parties from Quebec, the Bloc Populaire (1942–7), the Ralliement Créditiste (1963–71), and the Bloc Québécois (1991–) were founded in part to defend nationalist ideology in Ottawa (Pinard 1971, 22, 83). Not all of these parties were created by defecting MPs. Only the Bloc Populaire and the Bloc Québécois were founded by Liberal and Conservative Party members, first over the question of conscription in the 1940s and later over the failure of the Meech Lake Accord in the 1990s. Perhaps Maxime Bernier's new People's Party of Canada falls into this category as well. In Alberta, the Social Credit Party was created by supporters of the agrarian movement who represented the right wing of the United Farmers and Progressive parties (Morton 1950, 287).

To a certain extent, these new parties attempted to fill a void left by Liberals and Conservatives who were incapable of brokering the interests of an increasingly complex Canadian electorate that now divided along ethnic, regional, and class lines. Certain parties, such as the Progressives – but also the United

Farmers, Social Credit, and later Reform – were founded in part to combat party discipline and to increase the responsiveness of elected representatives in Parliament (Malloy 2003, 124). The old parties were viewed as biased towards the interests of Central Canada, corrupted by money, and "made up of party-picked lawyers and professional politicians under obligation to the suppliers of party funds" (Morton 1950, 120). The most radical elements of the Progressive Party proposed to respond to these problems by adopting a new form of parliamentary government, one without votes of confidence but with recall elections and direct legislation, where representatives would be free of party ties and mandated to support their local constituency in Parliament (Macpherson 1953, 71).

In Quebec, the emergence of the Bloc Populaire during the Second World War is also in part explained by the corrupted practices of the old parties, especially the Liberals, who were accused of being agents of big business: "For too long electoral corruption has allowed the predators of finance to slyly lead the old parties" (Bloc Populaire 1943, 12).[11] For Quebec nationalists who had been supporting the Liberal Party since the conscription crisis of 1917, a return to the Conservative fold was inconceivable, but so was supporting Mackenzie King, whose government imposed conscription following the results of the 1942 plebiscite on this question. As a consequence, Liberal MP Maxime Raymond from Quebec left the party in 1943 to establish the Bloc Populaire canadien in the federal Parliament. Although the Bloc Populaire counted only two elected members after the 1945 election, the party promoted a traditional French-Canadian nationalist ideology, which previously had been defended by Henri Bourassa and other French-speaking Conservatives from Quebec in the first two decades of the twentieth century (Behiels 1982, 488).

In 1990 the situation was reversed. It was now Lucien Bouchard, a nationalist member of the Conservative Party, who left his caucus to create the Bloc Québécois after the failure of the Meech Lake Accord. Crossing the floor to the Liberals was not an option, since the party was opposed to recognizing Quebec as a distinct society. The Bloc went on to win fifty-four of the seventy-five seats in the province during the 1993 election and form the official opposition in Ottawa during the thirty-fifth Parliament. The ideology defended by Bouchard and his supporters was different from the more traditional French-Canadian nationalism of Bourassa: it was more progressive, and promoted the independence of Quebec from the rest of Canada.

Although fifty years separate the creation of the Bloc Populaire and the Bloc Québécois, in each of these cases, members left the two old parties because their views could not be represented adequately. The emergence of the Progressive Party was also linked to a similar process, with Crerar and other western MPs leaving Borden's Unionist government, but refusing to join the ranks of the Liberal Party, which they viewed as corrupted. From the standpoint of party unity, the removal of these factions led to an increase in party cohesion in Parliament for two reasons. First, the new regional parties contributed to a reduction in the number of dissenting votes within the Conservative and Liberal caucuses by allowing the representation of different views – such as agrarian populism or Quebec nationalism – in the national legislature. Second, these new parties not only reduced the size of the Conservative and Liberal caucuses in Parliament, they also increased ideological cohesion within the assembly. Rebellious farmer MPs from Western Canada or nationalist ones from Quebec no longer sat with the old parties, but now had an independent caucus and were free to act on their own. Those who remained loyal to the two old parties could be trusted to behave like "trained donkeys," to "file in when the division bell rang" (Trudeau 1958, 308). Paradoxically, the presence of third parties also weakened the influence of backbenchers, mostly because House rules had to be modified to recognize more than one opposition leader, further reducing the opportunities for private members to intervene during debates.

Conclusion

This brief historical overview of the transformation of the Canadian party system offers some evidence to support the idea that the lower levels of party unity first observed in Parliament were linked to religious, language, and regional grievances. Each of these issues related to a cross-cutting political cleavage that divided Canada's two major parties internally. In return, these conflicts weakened party unity in the legislative arena. For example, the Liberals and Conservatives divided over questions of religion, with Catholics sometimes banding together to vote against Protestants regardless of their party affiliation. Later, the conflict moved on to Imperial relations, and mostly weakened the unity of the Conservative Party, which split between nationalist and pro-British factions. On this issue, it was two extreme positions against the more moderate middle represented by the Liberal Party. Finally, the emergence of the farmers' movement created tensions within the two major parties on the question of tariffs. Although farmers initially supported the Liberals' position on trade, the onset of the First World War and the conscription crisis led many to join Borden's Unionist government. In this case, the post-war budget split both ends of the Conservative Party against the middle: farmers supported free trade, while the rest favoured protectionism and the National Policy. The Liberals occupied a more moderate position in the centre by supporting lower tariffs without fully embracing free trade.

In this chapter, we saw how these internal divisions affected the political careers of Thomas Crerar and Henri Bourassa. Both were weary of party discipline and patronage-oriented party organizations, and each had the support of powerful regional interest groups: agrarian reformers in Western Canada and nationalists from Quebec. At first, Bourassa and Crerar attempted to find a place within the existing two-party system. Bourassa began his career as a Liberal, but later joined the Conservative Party as a nationalist to oppose Laurier's support of the Empire. Crerar, on the other hand, was a Liberal who joined the Unionist government of Robert Borden, a Conservative. This put him in a difficult position over the tariff question, and he subsequently resigned from the cabinet to become leader of the Progressive caucus in Parliament. The Canadian Council of Agriculture then quickly recognized this group of MPs as its official representatives in Ottawa (Morton 1950, 106), and this party won the second-highest number of seats in the 1921 election. Crerar, however, remained a member of the Progressive Party only for one term, and eventually returned to Parliament as a Liberal in 1930.

The analysis clearly shows that these members and their factions did not really fit within the existing two-party system that dominated Parliament after Confederation. Bourassa chose to switch allegiance for a brief period, but ultimately returned to the Liberal fold after the conscription crisis unravelled. On the other hand, Crerar and his supporters chose to leave the two-party system altogether, at least for a time, in order to create their own caucus in the legislative arena. Although Crerar, too, eventually became a Liberal again, Parliament never fully returned to the two-party equilibrium after the 1921 election. Three reasons explain this outcome.

First, until the beginning of the First World War, the farmers' movement had supported the Liberal Party. In a sense, the decision to join Borden's Unionist government already represented a change of allegiance for this group. Either they could decide to return to the Liberal Party (like Crerar and several other members did after the 1925 election) or continue to support their own farmers' caucus (Progressives, United Farmers) in the legislature.

Second, unlike the religious realignment of Conservative Catholics towards the Liberal Party around the end of the nineteenth century, debates over questions of tariffs and Imperial relations implied the formation of a coalition of two factions with opposing views. In the first case, nationalist and pro-British members created an alliance against the more centrist position of the Liberal Party. In the second case, free traders and protectionists banded together in the Unionist government to oppose the Liberals. Under these conditions, it was much more difficult to maintain a coalition of "two ends against the middle" in Parliament (Johnston 2008, 829), especially if members were expected to follow the party line.

The final explanation of the presence of third parties in Canada relates to party discipline. It is important not to underestimate the role legislative voting played in the decision to establish the Progressive Party. Indeed, the party was created in part to break away from the discipline imposed by the two old parties. Moreover, the changing rules and regulations of the House of Commons between 1906 and 1913 put additional pressure on members to conform with the views of party leaders and limited their influence in the legislative arena. At its core, the more radical members of the Progressive caucus wanted more freedom to represent the interests of their constituents – to vote for whatever legislation they felt best served the interests of their constituents, even if it meant a fundamental transformation of the parliamentary system. This critical view of Parliament is still present today in Western Canada, where voters "tend to be put off by rigid party discipline, block voting, and the polarization of all issues between government and opposition" (Flanagan 2001, 627–8).

In the remainder of this book, I will demonstrate how the introduction of new procedures in the House of Commons profoundly transformed the Canadian party system around the turn of the last century. Before these rules were modified, it was much easier for factions and members to break away from their parties to represent the interests of their constituents. Hence, brokerage between these different groups was done primarily on the floor of the House. The Assembly of the United Canadas provides a good example of how regional factions of MPs could switch their allegiance from one party to the next, depending on the issue considered in the debates. For a time, this might have been possible in the House of Commons. However, once the rules were modified to limit the influence of individual members in the legislative process, representatives had to adapt, while the incentives for some to organize as a separate caucus grew significantly.

Before getting into the empirical evidence to support this claim, it is important to present a theoretical account to explain why members join parties in the legislative arena and why party systems change. This theory should help us understand why party unity has increased over time in Canada.

Chapter Three

Theories of Party Development

The emergence of permanently organized and disciplined political parties represents one of the most important developments in the history of modern parliaments.[1] Although there exists a vast literature on the influence of parties in the legislative arena, we still lack a clear understanding of how parties transformed over time. Scholars generally agree that, as the influence of representative assemblies increased during the nineteenth century, a number of countries began experiencing major political changes that prompted lawmakers to modify their behaviour in the legislature. As a result, parties became increasingly unified in response to the extension of suffrage and the modernization of parliamentary procedures.

Previous research suggests a direct relationship between parliamentary organization and electoral politics, but we find a wide range of competing theories to explain the emergence of partisanship in the legislative arena. Thus far, scholars have claimed that factors such as the centralization of the leadership structure or the changing ideological preferences of members (either through their replacement or socialization) contributed to increasing partisan votes in the UK Parliament and US Congress during the nineteenth century. And while this trend has been observed in many other established democracies since then, empirical studies of these older cases are scarce, and offer an incomplete picture of the development of party unity because they focus only on a relatively short period of time. The lack of comparable historical data makes it difficult for researchers to determine whether a common set of factors in fact might explain the emergence of organized political parties outside the Anglo-American context.

This is unfortunate, especially if we consider that disciplined and cohesive political parties now represent a central feature of virtually all parliamentary democracies today. Nowhere has this development been more apparent than in Canada. As we saw in chapter 1, party voting unity increased dramatically in the years following Confederation, and there has been very little dissension since the 1920s. Given that parties have remained relatively cohesive for a century now, can we find some theoretical explanation to account for this trend? Is the Canadian experience unique? Or does it follow the same pattern of development found in other, older democracies, such as those of the United Kingdom and the United States?

I begin to answer these questions in this chapter by reviewing the most commonly identified factors that have been proposed to explain the increase in party voting unity over time. Although the focus of this book is on the Canadian Parliament, there are good reasons to expect that the development of party voting unity in this country closely follows the US and UK experiences. Canada has one of the oldest continuous parliamentary systems in the world: its first colonial legislative institutions were established during the late eighteenth century, and the Westminster model of government was fully transplanted by the time of Confederation in 1867. Canada also shares many of the characteristics of its nineteenth-century American neighbour, such as federalism, the absence of a feudal class system, a homestead frontier economy, and a relatively broad electoral franchise (Epstein 1964, 47–8). But perhaps more important, the United States, the United Kingdom, and Canada have maintained a set of common political institutions over the years, such as geographically based representation and plurality elections, which cultivate a strong direct link between legislators and their constituents. Taken together, these institutional features suggest that Canada represents an ideal case for explaining the emergence of parties in Anglo-American democracies precisely because it provides a bridge between these two types of political system.

In this chapter, I also consider what factors influence the structure of party systems. Unlike the literature on the emergence of political parties in the legislative arena, there is a strong tradition of research on party-system change in Canada. Most of this work attempts to explain why the number of parties represented in Parliament fluctuates over time by looking at election results, party membership, candidate recruitment, or political financing. I argue, however, that the structure of the party system can be influenced by parliamentary rules and party discipline as well. Although I focus here mostly on the factors that influence the development of party voting unity over time, it makes sense to assume that the number of parties in Parliament could also affect party cohesion and party-line voting. There thus could be a reciprocal relationship between the structure of the party system and party voting unity. I explore the nature of this relationship more fully in the second part of the book.

I begin by introducing a simple theoretical framework to explain why members support their party in the legislative arena during parliamentary votes. I then review some of the most important studies that focus on explaining the development of party voting unity in the US and British cases, and relate them to the Canadian context. In the final section, I discuss the different theories of party system change in Canada.

The first objective here is thus to identify a set of common factors that could explain the growth of partisanship in the legislative arena over time. The second objective is to show how this change could affect the structure of the party system in turn. Later in the book, I conduct different empirical analyses to validate the relevance of these hypotheses in the Canadian context: first, by testing how they influence the loyalty of individual members (chapter 5); second, by looking at how they could affect the unity of parties during legislative votes (chapter 6); and third, by evaluating how the ideology of members (chapter 7) and changes in parliamentary rules (chapter 8) transformed parties around the turn of the previous century.

A Theory of Legislative Party Support

Here, I present a theory of legislative voting, and show how this framework could be used to account for variations in the aggregate level of party unity observed over time. The foundations of this theory rest on two widely accepted assumptions in the study of parliamentary behaviour (Godbout and Smaz 2016, 482). The first assumption is that elected members have three specific career objectives: they care about being re-elected, their advancement in the legislature, and implementing good public policies (see, for example, Müller and Strøm 1999, 5–9). The second assumption is that the decision to support the party leader during a recorded vote is affected by each of these goals (Kam 2009, 33–5).

Although certain members will gladly toe the party line most of the time, others might be tempted to rebel occasionally and oppose their leader in the legislature. This could be for electoral reasons or because they disagree with the party on a specific issue. It could also be because they feel that their chances of being promoted to the cabinet are limited, or that their influence in the legislature is waning. For whatever reason, a member's decision to dissent will be weighed against any potential sanctions imposed for breaking the party line and the rewards offered in exchange for support.

It follows that members will always vote with their caucus if they believe that the party's objectives do not conflict with their own. In other words, members who approve of the government's policy agenda will remain loyal to the party during legislative votes, especially if they think this will improve their odds of being re-elected. If, on the other hand, the party's objectives do not completely match a member's career ambitions, the incentive to dissent will increase. This situation might occur, for example, if the party supports a policy that is unpopular in a representative's district or, alternatively, if a member prefers a different policy than the one put forward by the leadership. In either of these scenarios, voting with the party clearly would be in conflict with the legislator's policy and re-election goals.

It is important to understand that a mismatch between the interests of legislator and party does not necessarily lead to open dissension. Indeed, the decision to vote against the party should be weighed against the member's own career objectives (see Dawson [1947] 1960, 247; Kam 2009, 32; Thomas 1996, 257). For instance, members who oppose their party on important votes risk compromising their chances of advancement in Parliament. They might also lose the support of their party during an election campaign. This could have major consequences for an incumbent, primarily because candidates who represent a major political party have an enormous electoral advantage over those who run as independents. Indeed, party candidates can expect to benefit from the party's brand, its electoral resources, and the national campaign. They can also expect to ride the coattails of a popular party leader. Once in office, members benefit from their party affiliation as well. In the Canadian Parliament, any group of twelve or more members is recognized as an official party in the House of Commons. This status brings certain privileges, such as additional allowances for the leadership, financial support for research, and special consideration during debates. In addition, since the party that controls the largest number of seats in Parliament usually forms the government, its supporters expect to benefit from the spoils of office and have a greater influence on the orientation of public policies. Ultimately, members who break the party line to a marked degree risk being expelled from their caucus. Although party expulsions are rare, they do occur from time to time, with about twenty-nine members expelled from their caucus between 1990 and 2015 – 3 per cent of all elected members during this period. In earlier Parliaments, expulsions from the party also occurred frequently. Armand Lavergne, who represented the Quebec riding of Montmagny during the tenth Parliament, was removed from the Liberal caucus in 1907 for opposing the government on the North-West Schools Question. Laurier even personally "took away the exercise of patronage" in his riding as a punishment for his disloyalty (*Le Nationaliste* 1907).

To summarize, the three career objectives of MPs – re-election, influence in the legislature, and the adoption of good public policies – are easier to achieve through a political party, and so we should expect members to support their party most of the time. Still, we know from voting records that there have been periods when members were much more likely to challenge party leaders – most notably, in the first few decades following Confederation. The theory I outlined above suggests that this could have been possible only if members relied less on political parties to achieve their career objectives in the legislature (Boily 1982, 47). For example, one way members could maintain their career ambitions was by cultivating a more direct link with the electorate. Another way was by having greater individual influence in the legislative process. A third way was through opportunities for promotion outside the usual party channels. One thing is certain: at some point this independence was lost, as members increasingly began to rely on parties to get elected.

The Development of the First Political Parties: The US and British Cases

Modern political parties are essential for the re-election goals of members. This was not always the case. The principal incentive for the development of the first political parties came not from electoral pressure, but from collective action and social choice problems faced by members who sat in the democratically elected assemblies that emerged during the second half of the eighteenth century (Aldrich 1995, 28–9; Squire 2012, 6). These problems included unstable or cyclical voting majority decisions in assemblies, and the classic "prisoner's dilemma," where Pareto-inferior outcomes (or detrimental laws) are adopted by the whole legislature (Saalfeld and Strøm 2014, 382). Although at the time representatives were distrustful of factions and parties, especially in the United States, it became apparent that a permanent and stable coalition of members could more easily control political power and the spoils of office. In the British case, the incentives to organize parties arose primarily after the principle of responsible government was fully recognized in Parliament. Members then were not focused so much on re-election – since the limited franchise meant it was relatively easy to get elected without the support of national party machinery (Ostrogorski 1902, 135) – but rather on controlling government policy and distributing patronage in their district.

The first political parties thus were highly unstable, with different factions often changing sides during legislative votes. A series of democratic reforms, however, provided enough incentives for members gradually to change their behaviour, first in the United States and later in Britain, when the number of voters dramatically increased following the introduction of universal male suffrage (Cox 1987, 128–9; Gerring 1998, 45–6; Rae 2007, 171–2). Indeed, Cox (1987, 56–7) has confirmed that, during the early nineteenth century in the British House of Commons, elected officials represented relatively few voters, who could easily be swayed by patronage opportunities or by a member's personal fortune. This all changed between 1832 and 1884 after the adoption of a series of reforms aimed at reducing corrupt election practices and increasing the franchise. In return, the influx of newly qualified voters forced members to rely more on vote brokers and party workers to win election. As the size of the electorate grew, vote buying – or the provision of money or other rewards in exchange for support – became harder to organize at the constituency level, especially after the secret ballot was introduced in 1888 (Engstrom 2012, 374).

The development of responsible party government also increased the influence of local party organizations in Britain. The "efficient secret" – the fusion of the executive and the legislative branches – put a premium on caucus unity in the legislative arena, which now allowed the most organized group of members to control the government and implement their own political program (Cox 1987, 5–6). In exchange for their help during election campaigns, local partisan organizations began to require that candidates pledge to support the party platform in Parliament (70). The efficient secret also centralized patronage opportunities in the hands of party leaders, further weakening the influence of incumbents in their district (56–7).

The combination of these reforms suggests that, towards the end of the nineteenth century, parties in Britain controlled most of the tools necessary to help candidates in their re-election goals. Indeed, party members developed a collective incentive to protect the party's reputation in Parliament: first, by promoting a common set of public policies; and second, by supporting their leaders in the legislature. In the same vein, the emergence of a more partisan electorate also provided additional incentives for supporting the caucus, mostly because voters expected their representatives to follow the party line once in Parliament. Given the increasing value of the party brand among the electorate, the incentives to dissent in the legislature declined because voters now based their choices on party platforms, rather than on the personal voting records of their representative (Cox 1987, 146). Two mechanisms were thus simultaneously at work to increase party unity: first, members had more incentives to support their party's program in the legislative arena; and second, party leaders could demand loyalty in exchange for support at election time.

Of course, the expansion of the franchise represents one potential explanation for the growth of partisanship. Although the shift from a vote-buying or clientelistic relationship between voters and their elected representatives to a system dominated by party-centred programmatic appeals has been observed elsewhere, other factors have been proposed to explain the rising influence of parties in the legislative arena. Not all of these are relevant to the Canadian context, though. For example, we know that party voting unity is higher in a parliamentary system or when there is a proportional electoral system (Carey 2007, 94). Neither of these institutional features on its own, however, can explain why party discipline is so high in Canada, because this country has always followed the Westminster model of government, with a plurality electoral system. Likewise, the introduction of responsible party government and the organization of the first political parties both predate the inaugural meeting of the federal Parliament in 1867. Since we are interested in understanding the growth of partisanship in Canada over time, the analysis presented in the following pages focuses primarily on the elements that can explain the development of party voting unity in more than one legislative term.

The Factors That Explain Party Development

The most common approach to studying the development of partisanship in the legislature has been through the analysis of roll call votes or recorded divisions, where party unity is usually measured by calculating how frequently members vote together in the legislature. Starting with the work of Lowell (1908) and Rice (1925), studies have shown that parties tend to become more cohesive over time, not only in more established democracies such as the United Kingdom, but also in newer ones such as those found in eastern Europe or in the European Parliament.[2] Several different theories have been proposed to explain these transformations (see, for example, Depauw and Martin 2009). From those, I identify six groups of factors that have been shown to influence members' behaviour in the legislative arena: (1) electoral pressure, (2) promotions and patronage, (3) career and candidate selection, (4) parliamentary rules and procedures, (5) ideology and partisan preferences, and (6) the party system.[3]

Electoral Pressure

The first group of factors identified in the literature to explain the growth of partisanship in the legislative arena is linked to extra-parliamentary party organization and electoral incentives. As we saw earlier, the most important of these is the expansion of the franchise. In his historical study of the evolution of legislative voting in the British House of Commons, Cox (1987) noticed a surge in voting unity after the enlargement of the electorate around the time of the Reform Act of 1884. In the first half of the nineteenth century, in contrast, MPs generally enjoyed a great deal of liberty, and private members' business played an important role in shaping the legislative agenda. The rapid growth of the British economy, however, created new problems for the government, and put pressure on the cabinet to control debates and increase legislative productivity. Cox argues that, since independent members faced a much more diverse electorate after the franchise was expanded, party leaders were able to trade some of their campaign resources in exchange for loyalty in the Commons.

In the Canadian context, we have reason to suspect that the increasing number of voters and industrialization will have had a much smaller effect on the growth in partisanship, at least in the years following Confederation. During this period, Canada was still largely a rural country, and the voting franchise remained comparatively larger than in Britain – in fact, closer to what was found in the United States at that time (Garner 1969, 3–4). Prior to 1900, the average winning candidate received around 1,400 votes in Canadian federal elections; some, such as in the new, sparsely colonized provinces of British Columbia and Manitoba, even won with the support of fewer than a hundred voters. Still, there was a significant increase in the number of voters after 1898, when universal male suffrage was introduced throughout the Dominion, and again in 1918, when most women were allowed to vote for the first time. After this, just as in the British case, we must consider the possibility that candidates faced not just a larger but also more diverse electorate.

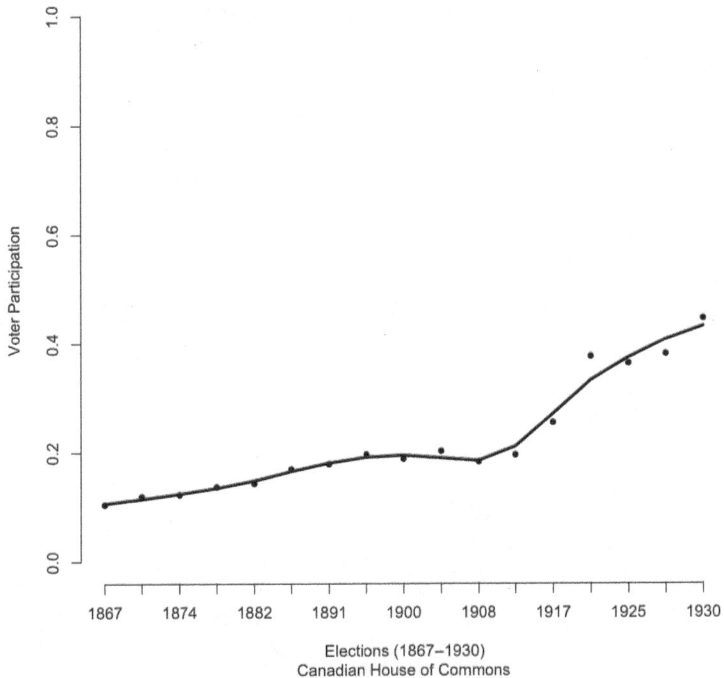

Figure 3.1 Average Number of Voters Relative to Total Riding Population, Federal Elections, 1867–1930

Figure 3.1 reports this change by showing the average number of voters in each election as a percentage of the total population in the riding between the 1867 and 1930 elections. As we can see, there was a slight increase in the overall number of voters over time, more so after the 1885 election, when the Electoral Franchise Act was adopted. The most important change, however, came in the 1917 election, when the right to vote was extended to spouses and families of men who served in the Canadian forces, and in 1921, after universal suffrage was introduced.[4]

Even with a limited franchise, those who were eligible to vote could still influence the behaviour of elected representatives by monitoring their voting records in the House of Commons. Indeed, as we saw earlier in the UK case, it was not uncommon during the nineteenth century for local partisan organizations to demand pledges from their candidates to commit to particular policy positions in Parliament; in a subsequent election, voters could then punish incumbents who failed to do so (Cox 1987, 70). Furthermore, the decline in the number of uncontested seats and the increase in electoral competition

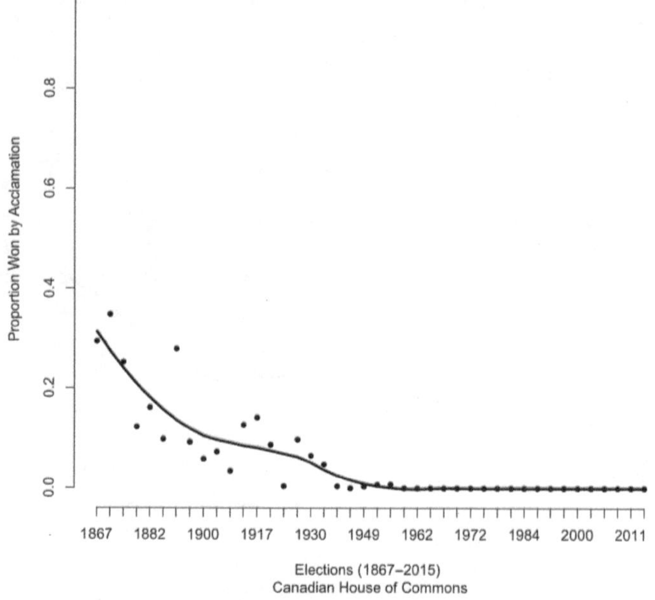

Figure 3.2 Proportion of Elections Won by Acclamation / Median Proportion of Support for Winning Candidate, 1867–2015

created additional pressure for members to conform to the party's directives in exchange for its support (Franks 1987, 110; Hamelin 1974, 129–30; Thomas 1996, 255).

In the Canadian context, the number of uncontested elections declined dramatically in the years following Confederation, while the level of electoral competition gradually increased over time, especially after the First World War, when third parties began to elect more candidates. Figure 3.2 details this change by showing two different measures of party competition: first, the proportion of seats won by acclamation in each election after Confederation (above); and second, the median proportion of votes received by each winning candidate for every election during the same period (next page).

As we can see, there was a decline in the number of uncontested elections between 1867 and 1940. Almost one-quarter of seats were won by acclamation in the first three elections following Confederation, but that proportion fell below 20 per cent in later years. The reason for such a high number of uncontested elections during this period is related to the fact that any sitting member of the

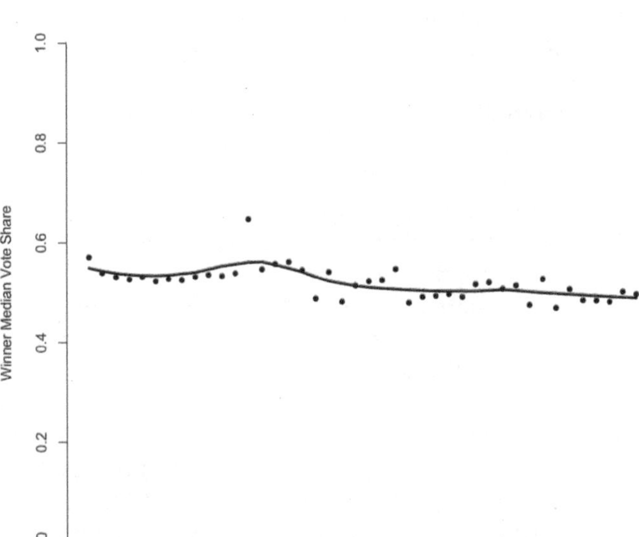

Figure 3.2 continued

House of Commons who was appointed to the cabinet (after the first meeting of a new Parliament) was required to stand for re-election. Until 1931, when the practice was abolished, the opposition parties generally did not contest these elections.

The second plot, reporting the median proportion of total votes received by the winning candidate, shows there was a gradual increase in the level of competition in riding elections over time. Two trends are notable here. First, until 1935, most candidates won with more than 50 per cent of the vote (median of 54.4 per cent); after that, competition increased somewhat, with the winning candidate's median share decreasing to 49.9 per cent. Of course, the addition of the Progressive Party following the 1921 election and the arrival of the CCF in 1935 explain some of this change. Perhaps more surprising is the absence of more electoral competition over the whole period. A majority of candidates won their seat with more than half of the popular vote in twenty-eight of the forty-one elections since Confederation. Still, both panels of figure 3.2 suggest there was an increase in the level of party competition after the First World War, which could imply sharper ideological divisions between the parties at election time. The link between electoral competition and more partisan behaviour in the legislature remains tentative at best, especially given that most of the increase in party voting unity occurred before that time.

Nevertheless, we must consider the possibility of a connection between a member's voting record and voters in the riding in the years following Confederation, especially given that major newspapers often published detailed records of debates and parliamentary votes during this period.[5] Thus, we can assume that some qualified electors might have held incumbents accountable for their voting decisions in Parliament. Knowing this, MPs could have been influenced by electoral pressure, especially in competitive elections when they dared not risk alienating their supporters (Corry 1946, 241). On the other hand, it is also possible that members elected with wider margins could be pressured to support their party more in the legislature, especially if voters expected them to follow the party line. There is also the distinct possibility that some MPs were rewarded for their independence, since, in the years following Confederation, electoral rules favoured candidates who remained independent of parties, but aligned themselves with the government once they took their seat in Parliament.

Indeed, in the first three Parliaments, elections were conducted over several weeks, and voting was done in public by a show of hands. The practice at the time was for the governing party to hold earlier elections in the most partisan districts in order to secure an important number of seats, and to count on a bandwagon effect in the later, more competitive races. Several candidates took advantage of such a situation by waiting to align themselves with the most likely winner of the election. Underhill (1935, 369) explains that, once in Parliament, these "shaky fellows" tended to vote with the cabinet to secure the patronage offered by the government. On the record, these men were affiliated with the majority party; in practice, they remained highly independent. In this context, voters would have rewarded such members even if they broke the party line from time to time. We should expect, however, that, over time, the introduction of the secret ballot and the same-day election (in the third Parliament) will have reduced the number of these independent-minded MPs and contributed to the consolidation of party unity after this term.

Promotions and Patronage

Another important factor that could help explain why members might have become more inclined to support parties in the legislative arena is related to different types of promotions controlled by the leadership (Cox 1987, 75). Presumably, the biggest prize is to be named to the cabinet, followed by other promotions, such as becoming a committee chairman or a parliamentary secretary (Docherty 1997, 220–1; Malloy 2003, 119; Thomas 1996, 257). Loyal members in the earlier Parliaments would also have been awarded civil service jobs, judgeships, provincial governorships, or senatorial seats (Dawson [1947] 1960, 247, 376; Lemieux 2008, 29). For instance, Ward (1963, 145) found that 22 per cent of members who left the House between 1867 and 1896 were nominated as senators, judges, or provincial governors; the proportion declined to 19 per cent between 1911 and 1935. Since the availability of these patronage opportunities remained relatively limited, however, they are unlikely to explain on their own the growth of partisanship in the legislature over time.

Another important incentive to remain loyal to parties could also have been removed when the Civil Service Act was adopted in 1918. Prior to this, it was relatively easy for parties to sustain loyalty through the distribution of federal patronage in a representative's riding (Dawson 1947 [1960], 246), and parties came to view patronage as an electoral resource to reward supporters and punish opponents. Unquestionably, the patronage networks of post-Confederation Canada were highly sophisticated and organized. Local patronage opportunities were controlled by party organizations in the ridings, and the custom was to offer work to loyal party supporters. Any such appointments were then approved by the responsible minister or even, in some cases, by the prime minister (Stewart 1986, 77–8). Both Macdonald and Laurier were personally involved in the distribution of federal patronage opportunities in the different ministries (Carty 1988, 16). For example, they would approve the appointment of particular individuals to civil service jobs – such as postmasters or inspectors of weights and measures; others could find work as firemen or brakemen for the Intercolonial Railway, which was owned by the federal government (Cruikshank 1986, 82–3). And all of these positions were always given to loyal party supporters. According to Stewart (1986, 93), patronage was the cement that unified the first political parties in the Canadian federation. Party leaders used these rewards to influence voters in the district, and to promote party loyalty among Members of Parliament (68).

Conservative and Liberal candidates thus could benefit from this system if their party was in power, especially since they could participate in the establishment of the list of potential candidates for government jobs (Stewart 1980, 6). Federal employees also had a strong incentive to work hard for their representative: they could lose their job if the other party won the next election. This system reinforced the link between the local party organization, MPs, and voters. In order to benefit from patronage and the party's electoral machine, a member had to side with the government in the House of Commons. Note, however, that it was the local party organization, not the member, that ultimately controlled the patronage list in the riding (Simpson 1988, 77). Thus, Nova Scotia's Joseph Howe, who had opposed Confederation, could be lured into the cabinet with the promise of patronage (Stevenson 1997, 39). Those who remained independent or who sided with the opposition would be left in the lurch. Since parties controlled patronage, it could be withdrawn as a penalty for disloyalty (Corry 1946, 163).

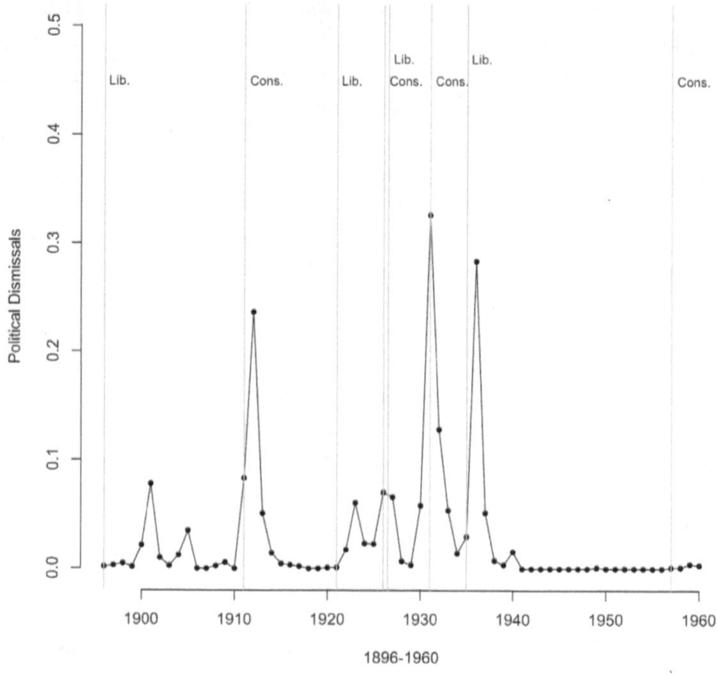

Figure 3.3 Patronage Dismissals of Postmasters as a Proportion of All Vacancies, 1896–1960

Figure 3.3 provides an example of the relationship between partisanship and patronage in the federal bureaucracy by reporting the number of postmasters who were dismissed for political reasons between 1867 and 1960. Each point in the plot corresponds to the number of political dismissals of postmasters as a proportion of all combined vacancies in a given year. This information comes from the Post Offices and Postmasters database of Library and Archives Canada, which contains more than 170,605 records of individual postmasters who served from 1851 to 1981. These data also indicate why postmasters left their position (death, retirement, resignation, and so on), as well as the reason behind any dismissal – such as abscondence, deportation, or political partisanship.

From figure 3.3, we can see that the peaks in the numbers of postmasters removed for political reasons roughly correspond to a change in the majority in the House, such as after the 1896, 1911, and 1921 elections. In 1912, for example, 589 of the 2,492 dismissals were because of partisanship, meaning that these postmasters were fired because they were Liberals. In 1923, this number was 72 out of 1,185 dismissals, but this time it was Conservatives who were removed from office. The fact that postmasters continued to lose their jobs for political reasons after the adoption of the Civil Service Act in 1918 shows the limits of this reform. The new rules required that all hires be based on merit and be granted by an independent federal commission, but only for the more senior civil servant positions. Political appointments were still used for about half of all the positions controlled by the federal government, and postmasters clearly fall into this category (Dawson 1936, 288–9). Figure 3.3 shows that, between the 1930 and 1935 federal elections, a significantly large number of postmasters were removed for political reasons, but the number appears to have declined after the Second World War.

After this point, it seems, the process of appointing postmasters was taken over fully by the federal bureaucracy, and parliamentarians lost an important resource for providing their constituents direct employment (Lemieux 2008, 28). This was especially important in rural ridings, where government jobs were usually scarce. Of course, postmasters represented just one example of federal patronage in the riding – many other employment opportunities existed, and even more were created as the size of the federal government increased. Nonetheless, over time, the availability of these positions declined as the various civil service reforms transformed the federal bureaucracy (Gordon 1999, 29). As a consequence, it is possible that some members, especially those who depended on patronage to improve their chances of re-election, lost a strong incentive to support their party in the legislature.

Career and Candidate Selection

The third group of factors that could have influenced the development of party voting unity is linked to the socialization of members (Rush and Giddings 2011, 174). Scholars have noted that members tend to become more loyal as they progress in their legislative career. This socialization process also might have played differently over time, so that members elected earlier could have adopted a different kind of behaviour than those elected in later terms. In this context, party unity could result from internalized norms of caucus solidarity, which can then be reinforced over the course of a legislative career (Docherty 1997, 136–7; Franks 1987, 108; Kam 2009, 13–14; Thomas 1996, 258).

It is also possible that the development of party unity was linked to the gradual replacement of independent members elected in earlier terms, when party leaders might have been less influential (Eggers and Spirling 2016, 568). If so, the surge in partisanship observed in Canada could be explained by the professionalization of the legislature and the subsequent election of more career-oriented cohorts of loyal members. Two mechanisms thus could have been at play here simultaneously: first, members might have become more loyal as their careers progressed in the legislature; second, new cohorts of more loyal

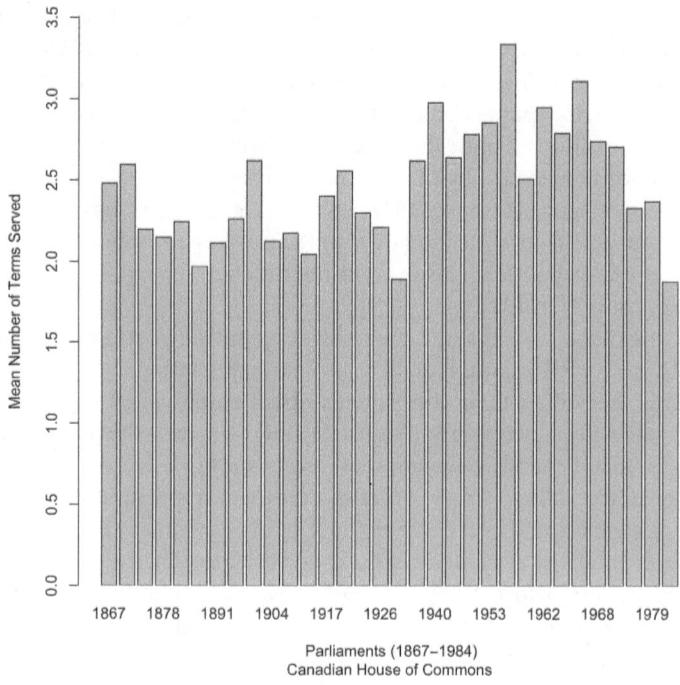

Figure 3.4 Average Career Length by Cohorts of Elected Members, 1867–1984

members gradually could have replaced those elected earlier who might have been more inclined to remain independent of their party.

Figure 3.4 reports the average length of legislative careers for different cohorts of members elected between 1867 and 1980 – note that the 1980 cohort represents the most recent group of members that no longer has any sitting in the House. The figure demonstrates that there was a marked increase in the number of terms served by members of the cohorts elected after 1935. The average for the whole period is 2.5 terms served, with 2.3 before 1935 and 2.7 after. This represents evidence of the professionalization of the career of parliamentarian, especially given that the incumbency re-election rate remained relatively low in Canada during most of this period (Kerby and Blidook 2011, 625–6).

Another example of the importance of legislative careers in the development of party voting unity is linked to the selection of candidates. Parties that do not fully control the nomination process run the risk of having more independent members in their ranks (Corry 1946, 166). However, if party leaders have the power to remove undesirable nominees from the ballot, we should expect an increase in loyalty among elected representatives (Franks 1987, 111; Malloy

2003, 119; Morgenstern 2004, 86; Thomas 1996, 255). Today, Canadian party leaders appear to have full control over the selection of candidates, since they can always refuse to sign the nomination papers of anyone selected by a riding association. This has only been possible since 1970, when the Canada Elections Act was modified to allow party names to be shown on the ballot. Prior to this change, only the names and professions of candidates were recorded on the ballot, not their party affiliations.

In addition, the process of selecting candidates remained highly decentralized for most of the twentieth century. Candidates were usually elected by local riding associations that operated more or less like open conventions in which anyone in the riding could vote, just like in primary elections in the United States (Dawson [1960] 1947, 517–18; Epstein 1967, 230; Meisel 1962, 121; 1964, 54). Because legislative party organizations had very little control over the nomination process before the 1970s, we should expect this factor to have had a limited effect on the development of partisan behaviour, especially since voting unity was already relatively high by then.

Parliamentary Rules and Procedures

The fourth group of factors that could influence the development of partisanship in the legislature relates to the internal organization of Parliament. The fact that the House of Commons operates under a Westminster parliamentary system likely explains why party discipline is so high in the first place, since caucus solidarity is necessary for a government to remain in office (Franks 1987, 100; Heard 1991, 91; Thomas 1996, 256). In this type of government, members have an incentive to support their leader, even when in opposition, because cohesive parties are more likely to be rewarded by voters (Cox 1987, 128–9). Figure 3.5 reports the difference in party unity in both government and opposition parties in each term since 1867. As the graph shows, unity is almost always higher for the governing party than for the opposition. There are a few exceptions, such as in Borden's Conservative and Unionist governments (1911–17) and Paul Martin's Liberal government (2004–6). These are outliers, however: in 90 per cent of the electoral terms, loyalty has been higher on the government side than in all other parties in opposition.

It is important to note, though, that the confidence convention of responsible government cannot, on its own, explain the development of party unity in Canada. Indeed, as I pointed out earlier, this custom was already in place at the time of Confederation, when partisanship was much lower. The same can be said about using the threat of dissolution of Parliament to promote loyalty among government supporters (Dawson [1960] 1947, 246): it is fair to assume that most members do not want an early election if they can avoid it, and that this was the case even in the years following Confederation.

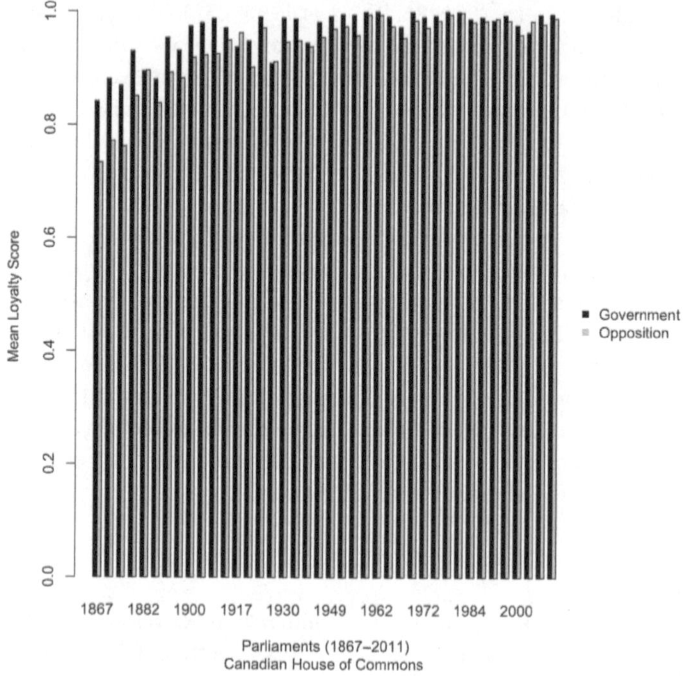

Figure 3.5 Average Party Loyalty, Government and Opposition Members, 1867–2011

Moreover, there is the important power of the party whip, who can use sanctions to impose discipline within the caucus. Whips have been a fixture in Parliament since Confederation. They usually promote unity by making sure that enough members are present for debates and votes; they also direct members how to vote on certain bills and motions. Whips have many resources at their disposal to impose party discipline. For example, they control the allocation of office space, committee assignments, and official international travel opportunities. They also decide the duty roster of MPs, or who will be allowed to speak during debates (Westmacott 1983, 17–18). As such, whips have a direct influence on the life of a representative, and members who are loyal to the party can expect to be rewarded for their services (Franks 1987, 105; Heard 1991, 81; Malloy 2003, 118–19).

Another important aspect of legislative organization that can influence party unity relates to agenda-setting powers (Berrington 1968, 338). Cox and McCubbins (2005, 9–10) explain that a majority party can use either strict discipline or the legislative agenda to maintain loyalty among its members. Since imposing discipline can be costly, leaders might prefer to keep some of the most divisive issues off the agenda, thus avoiding votes that could create disunity within their caucus. This is most likely to be true when the leadership controls the debates. This concept of negative agenda control has been used mostly to analyse party voting in the US Congress, although we find traces of this strategy in other legislatures as well (Eggers and Spirling 2018, 346; Jones and Hwang 2005, 268).

In the Canadian context, there is clear evidence pointing towards an increase in agenda control by the government over time. Indeed, after Confederation, a number of important modifications to the legislative rules took place to increase the influence of party leaders. These changes were related primarily to the daily proceedings of the House and the schedule of debates. In the first Parliament, most of the business conducted in the legislature was evenly split between private members' business and government affairs.[6] It soon became apparent, however, that the time allocated for government activities was insufficient, and special rules to modify the calendar were adopted on an ad hoc basis to increase the number of days when government business would be discussed (Bourinot 1884, 258). In subsequent years, these special sittings increased with such frequency that, between 1906 and 1913, the legislative calendar was permanently changed to increase the number of government business days (Beauchesne 1922, 80–1; Stewart 1977, 197). Once the government won the right to control most of the debates in the House, it became easier for party leaders to prevent private members from discussing controversial issues such as regional concerns or language or religious rights. It also increased the incentives for members to support their party, since the confidence convention of the Westminster system could be applied to most government bills – as opposed to bills sponsored by private members. Finally, since the issues raised in Parliament were increasingly related to government business, the content of political debates took a more adversarial tone, with supporters of the two main parties vying for control of the agenda (March 1974, 202).

Figure 3.6 illustrates these changes by showing the proportion of private and public bills adopted by Parliament over time. Note that public bills have a much broader effect on society since they relate to matters of national interest, while private bills affect only individuals or corporations by granting them extraordinary powers or exempting them from "the general application of the law" – for example, a divorce or the incorporation of a railway company (O'Brien and Bosc 2009, 1177). Nevertheless, it is important not to underestimate the significance of private bills in the years following Confederation. Indeed, the "House dealt with a large volume of private legislation to establish companies to build and operate railways and to incorporate interprovincial companies since no other legal authority allowed such corporations to be formed" (1179). Only noncabinet members can introduce private bills in the House of Commons; however,

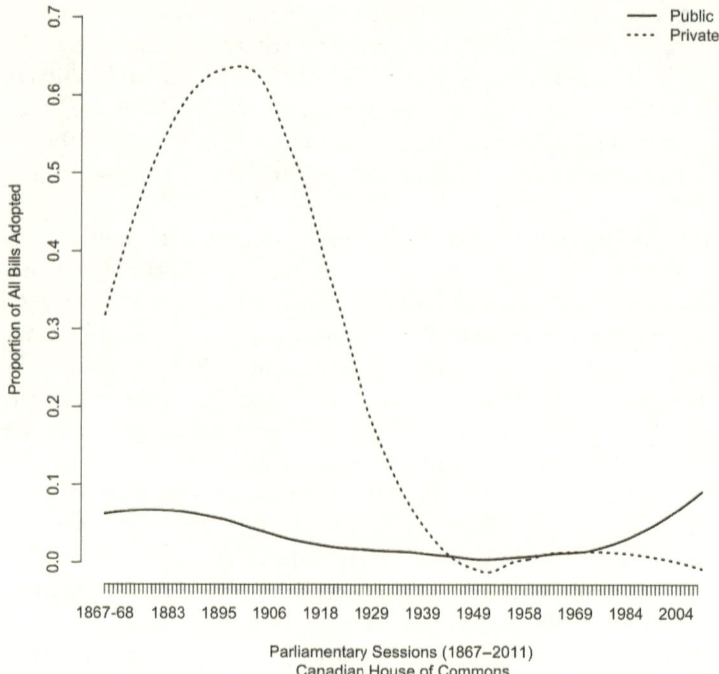

Figure 3.6 Proportions of Public Acts and Private Acts by Private Members Adopted, 1867–2011

both ministers and private members can introduce public bills, while only the government is allowed to provide for the expenditure of treasury funds (718).

The figure reports two different trends. The first, shown by the solid line, indicates how many private members' public bills passed as a proportion of all public bills adopted by Parliament in each session between 1867 and 2011.[7] The second trend, represented by the dotted line, indicates the proportion of private bills adopted as a fraction of the total number of bills passed (public and private) by Parliament during the same period.

From the figure, we note the continuous decline in the proportion of private members' bills, starting from around 1885 until the 1950s, when it reaches zero. In fact, between 1906 and 1955, the government took over most of the remaining private members' business time on the agenda for its own purposes (O'Brien and Bosc 2009, 1103). Consequently, it became extremely difficult for private members' motions or private members' public bills to be debated and voted on in Parliament – a clear indication of the diminishing influence of backbenchers in the House of Commons. The subsequent surge observed in the post-war period is explained by the introduction of a series of new rules that gradually increased the time allotted for private members' business in the proceedings of the House: first, in 1955, when a minimal number of fixed days were set on the calendar to discuss private members' business; and second, in 1962, when one hour every day was set aside to discuss such business. Other minor modifications have been made since then, all of which have had the effect of increasing somewhat the number of bills or motions by private members debated and passed in Parliament (see Blidook 2012, 31–6).

Nevertheless, the declining influence of backbenchers is more noticeable when we look at the number of private bills adopted in Parliament over time. Recall that noncabinet members are the only ones allowed to introduce these types of bills in the legislature, and that this must be done during the time set aside for private members' business. Although they are infrequent today, private bills once represented a majority of legislation passed by Parliament. Part of this decline is explained by the fact that private bills tend to be introduced first in the Senate, where the fees for processing these measures have been lower than in the House of Commons since 1934 (O'Brien and Bosc 2009, 1178n4). Nevertheless, as we can see in figure 3.6, a relatively important amount of private legislation was introduced and passed in the House until the early 1900s, when it represented more than 60 per cent of all legislation adopted by Parliament. Aside from the difference of fees between the House and Senate, other factors also contributed to the decline in the number of private bills introduced in the lower chamber, such as the adoption of the first federal divorce law in 1968 and the Canada Corporations Act in 1970, which created permanent rules to regulate what once required acts of Parliament (1179).

Overall, then, both trends demonstrate a clear decline in the influence of private members in the legislature, which began around the turn of the previous century and culminated in the 1950s. Interestingly, the rise in the level of partisanship observed in the House of Commons seems to have gone in the opposite direction during the same period. In other words, there could be a link between the reduction in the legislative influence of private members and the subsequent increase in party voting unity in Parliament. One must be careful in making such a connection, however, since the number of successful bills introduced by private members represents only a small fraction of all of their activities in the legislature. Backbenchers can also influence the legislative process by other means, such as by introducing motions or amendments, or by speaking during debates.

In fact, for almost one hundred years after Confederation, members had numerous opportunities to determine the topics of debates in the House of Commons, even during the time set aside to consider government business exclusively (see Stewart 1977, 208–18). For instance, backbenchers could introduce a motion to adjourn at any moment during debates, thereby taking precedence over any other motion being considered (including government measures). In this context, a member could propose to adjourn the House to discuss an important matter, and this motion was debatable until the rules were changed in 1906 (Bourinot 1916, 349–50).

Another method members could use to air their grievances in the House was through the process of going either into the committee of the whole, ways and means, or supply, where all government bills and budget resolutions had to be debated. During these debates, any member could propose an amendment to the motion of moving to such a committee, and nongermane amendments were often permitted. Just as for adjournment debates, these motions could be related to any topic – such as the hanging of Louis Riel or the salary of the governor general. Once in these grand committees, the House operated under an open rule that permitted any number of amendments to be proposed after a government bill reached the floor (Bourinot 1916, 521–6). Although the number of opportunities to amend motions to consider budget resolutions was eventually restricted in 1913, this legislative process remained basically unchanged until 1968, when the procedures of the House were modified to allow reference of all government bills – except supply and ways and means motions – to standing committees (O'Brien and Bosc 2009, 917–19).

The final major opportunity for backbenchers to influence debates relates to the Speech from the Throne. After hearing the speech, all members had the chance to discuss the government's legislative program or any other topic of their choosing (O'Brien and Bosc 2009, 678). Prior to 1955, there were no limits on the duration of these debates, which could last anywhere between one and twenty-eight days (681). Other minor changes were adopted over the years to limit the influence of private members in the legislative process, such as in 1910, when irrelevant or repetitive speeches were no longer permitted in the House, or in 1913, when closure was introduced, and then later in 1927, when time limits were imposed on individual speeches (Stewart 1977, 211, 317n25).

One consequence of the ability of private members to engage in debates was that the government often did not have enough time to consider all of its business during a legislative session; this became a real problem as the size of the federal public administration grew during the twentieth century. This explains why several new rules were introduced after 1900 – such as a time limit on speeches and closure – to reduce the number of these opportunities, so that the government could get its business done in Parliament within a reasonable amount of time (Stewart 1977, 197).

Figure 3.7, by using the transcripts of parliamentary debates provided by the online Linked Parliamentary Data Project (Beelen et al. 2017), shows that this is precisely what occurred between 1900 and 1974. In order to understand how changing the rules in the House of Commons increased the dominance of the executive in the legislative process, the figure reports the proportion

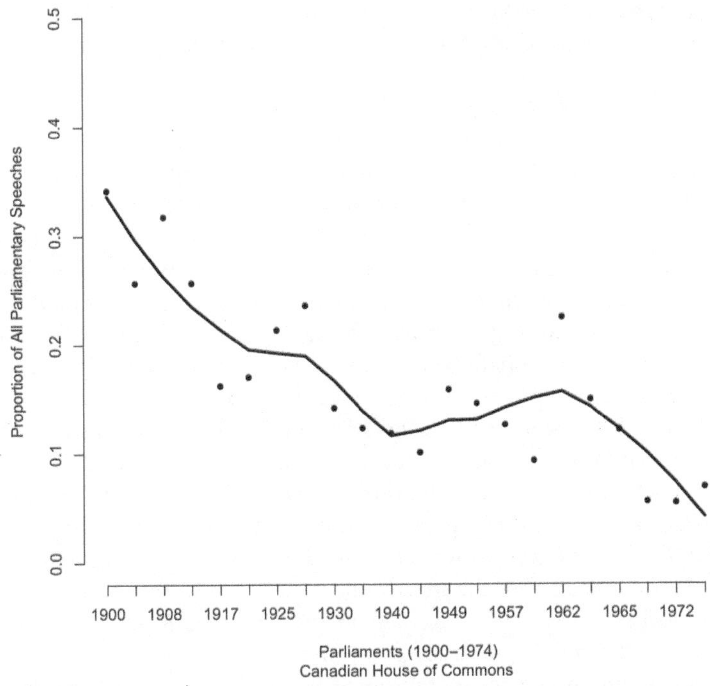

Figure 3.7 Proportion of Debates Controlled by Backbenchers, 1900–1974

of adjournment, throne speech, and supply debates controlled by noncabinet members. Each of these categories represented opportunities when private members could encroach on the time set aside to consider government business. Here, I measure the control of debates by counting the number of words spoken by backbenchers as a proportion of all the words spoken during these three types of debates. As we can see, there was a marked increase in the proportion of words spoken by cabinet members, especially in the twelfth Parliament, when the Standing Orders were modified to introduce closure and to restrict the number of amendments that would go to the committee of supply. The figure also confirms that the proportion of words spoken by backbenchers further declined during this period, especially after 1968, when the supply procedure was partially transferred to standing committees.

To summarize, the increase in party voting unity observed in the Canadian House of Commons could be linked to the declining influence of backbenchers in the legislative process. To support this claim, we first saw that the number of private member bills adopted by Parliament declined over time. We also saw that the proportion of debates controlled by backbenchers in the House was reduced during the past century. Both trends were linked to procedural changes, which enhanced the government's ability to control the legislative agenda.

Ideology and Partisan Preferences

The fifth factor linked to the development of party voting unity is related to the ideology of members and partisan sorting. As Özbudun (1970, 330–1) and later Krehbiel (2000, 213–14) explain, party members who have similar preferences might vote together consistently in a legislature, not because they are forced to do so, but because they share common beliefs on a wide range of public policy issues. In this context, a growth in partisanship could simply reflect a better match between party affiliation and the ideological views of legislators. In Canada, this was less likely to be the case in the years following Confederation. Indeed, during this period, the Conservative and Liberal parties were not clearly defined as parliamentary groups; rather, both parties were loosely based on regional coalitions of interests. Powerful provincial leaders led these factions, and it was not uncommon for parties to divide internally when voting occurred over sectional issues. As we saw in chapter 2, the early history of Parliament is filled with such examples, the most important of which relate to the rights of French speakers and Catholics outside the province of Quebec, the relationship with the British Empire, and trade policy in the West.

One of the main arguments presented in this book is that the increase in party voting unity observed in Parliament is partially explained by the position taken by the parties over these issues. Solving sectional conflicts in the legislature polarized both Liberal and Conservative members over time, first on tariff rates (the National Policy), then along religious lines and over Imperial relations. Once the parties began to polarize on these questions, it became easier for voters to distinguish between the positions of their candidates at election time – for example, a Liberal would defend provincial autonomy, minority rights, and free trade; a Conservative would promote closer ties with the Empire, support the established churches, and favour protectionism. It is important to understand that neither party always had a clear position on these issues in the years following Confederation. The ranks of both parties were made up of a relatively important proportion of French-speaking or Catholic members, and members from the different regions of Canada. A consequence of this diversity was that party unity was often weakened when voting occurred over questions of religion or sectional divisions – for example, western or Catholic members would band together to support the same position, regardless of their party affiliation.

Even though members often broke party lines to represent the views of their riding, voters eventually began to associate the positions of the parties with these different issues and to support them accordingly, regardless of the voting records of their representatives in Parliament. As a result, the electorate became more partisan while the preferences of the newly elected candidates from the same party became increasingly similar.

Unfortunately, it is difficult to disentangle the influence of party discipline and ideological cohesion when analysing the sources of party loyalty. Members might vote with the majority of their party because they agree with the position defended by the leadership. In other cases, members could disagree with their leader but be forced by the whip to support the party anyway. In both cases, we should observe the same outcome, even if the decision to vote for the party was motivated by different reasons. To make matters worse, we might observe that some members systematically oppose government proposals for strategic reasons, regardless of their ideological preferences (Dewan and Spirling 2011, 338). Under these conditions, it would be impossible to identify the influence of ideology or even party discipline on legislative behaviour, since members would support the same position whether in the government or in the opposition (Lee 2016, 162–4). High levels of party unity thus could be explained simply by bipartisanship or unanimous voting (Brady, Cooper, and Hurley 1979, 382).

In the empirical analyses that follow, I circumvent these problems by using extraparliamentary measures of members' and riding preferences to identify regional factions within the two major parties, and to assess their influence on caucus cohesiveness over time.[8] These indicators for members are linked to religion, language, and geography, while the information on riding characteristics is linked to historical census data and election results. With this approach, I can infer both the preferences of members on a certain number of issues, such as language, education, and trade, as well as those of voters, by looking at the proportion of Roman Catholics or farmers in a riding over time. Thus, it becomes possible to measure the influence of a member's ideology during specific votes or to look at how Catholic voters across Canada might have realigned their votes towards the Liberal Party near the end of the nineteenth century.

The Party System

The sixth and final group of factors that can influence the development of party unity over time is linked to the structure of the party system. In what follows, I use the definition of party systems by Carty, Cross, and Young (2000, 4), which is characterized by the "number of parties" represented in Parliament and the "nature of the issues that divide them." As I argued earlier, the party system can affect partisanship and voting unity through two distinctive mechanisms. The first is related to Sartori's claim that the ideological distance between parties is more extreme when the number of parties in competition is high (Sartori 1976, 126). If only two major parties compete, as in the United Kingdom or the United States, one should expect a more moderate political system, characterized by a small ideological distance between the parties. In terms of party unity, this would imply some level of cross-party voting, especially if the legislature represents a diverse set of interests. This is what we observe in the earlier decades of the Canadian Parliament and even in the US Congress, when party competition was much lower and the Democrats almost always won a majority in the House between 1933 and 1981 (Lee 2016, 3). In cases where the number of parties is high, such as in the Weimar Republic of Germany or in post-war Italy, one should expect a more polarized system, where the ideological distance between the parties will be greater. This polarized pluralism will translate into higher levels of party voting unity, most notably because the multiplication of parties in the legislative arena is more likely to reflect disagreements on a wider range of issues (Sartori 1976, 137). We thus should find that the ideological distance between parties in Canada – along with their levels of ideological cohesion – grew when party competition increased from two, to three, to four, to even five parties during the 1990s (for a similar argument, see Johnston 2008). Put another way, the removal of dissenting members from the Conservative and Liberal parties, the creation of the CCF (later, the NDP), and the cyclical appearance of smaller regional parties in Alberta or Quebec should all have contributed to increase party voting unity in the legislative arena, precisely because those parties created smaller and more ideologically cohesive caucuses in the legislature (Malloy 2003, 122–3).

The second mechanism by which the number of parties represented in Parliament could affect party voting unity is linked to parliamentary procedures. As I indicated earlier, the arrival of third parties could have increased caucus unity by reducing the influence of backbenchers in the legislative process. Since Parliament has only a limited amount of time to consider its business during a session, competition for access to the floor is usually very high. The cabinet controls most of this time, but opposition party leaders also have special rights: they can respond to ministerial statements, propose motions on opposition days, or participate in the leadership of standing committees (O'Brien and Bosc 2009, 38–9). Before third parties were officially recognized in the Standing Orders, these privileges were given only to the leader of the official opposition. Backbenchers thus had many more opportunities to intervene during debates, since they were competing with fewer party leaders for access to the floor. When the rules were modified, however, to recognize more than one opposition party, the time available for private members to make speeches or introduce motions, amendments, and bills was significantly reduced. This is because the speaker usually gives opposition party leaders special rights to speak during debates, a privilege that extends to opposition critics or spokespersons (O'Brien and Bosc 2009, 595). Therefore, when the number of opposition parties increases, the opportunities for backbenchers to participate in debates is reduced. One consequence of this is that the legislative agenda becomes increasingly dominated by partisan affairs, with a greater emphasis on "government-versus-opposition" voting, which should translate in higher levels of party unity (Dewan and Spirling 2011, 337).

Factors That Explain Party System Change

In the previous section, I considered six different factors that could influence the level of party voting unity in Parliament. The last of these, linked to the structure of the party system, is set apart from the rest because it is both an independent and a dependent variable in the empirical analysis that follows. The number of parties in the legislature can be used to explain variations in the levels of party voting unity over time, but it can also be influenced in turn by party discipline. Recall from the Introduction that one of my arguments is that the structure of the party system can change when parliamentary rules reduce the influence of backbenchers in the legislative process. Later in the book, I argue that some of these rules can provide enough incentives for members to leave their own party to form a new caucus in the legislature. This endogenous account of party system change is not new. As we saw earlier in this chapter, the development of the first "elite" or "cadre" parties in Britain and the United States during the eighteenth century were formed inside the legislature to solve coordination problems among members (Saalfeld and Strøm 2014, 378). Later transformations of the party system, on the other hand, can often be explained by exogenous factors, such as the extension of the franchise, which led to a broader and more diverse electorate, or the adoption of proportional representation, which tended to lower the threshold of representation and increase the number of parties in the legislature (Boix 2007, 518).

In Canada, the literature on party system change usually considers the emergence of new parties to be a reflection of exogenous electoral forces. Blake (1979) was the first to use the American concept of "critical elections" and "electoral volatility" to describe how the Canadian party system has transformed over time. According to this view, both the fluctuations in electoral results and changes across the distribution of party support can lead to a partisan realignment or even, in some cases, to the creation of a new party. Although Smith (1985), Carty (1988), Johnston et al. (1992), and Carty, Cross, and Young (2000) have since added nuances and historical context to characterize the transformation of the Canadian party system, the explanation of how new parties emerge remains for the most part the same: new parties are created when existing ones are incapable of responding to the demands of a changing electorate. These new arrivals usually take the form of temporary, regionally based "insurgent parties" such as the Progressives and Social Credit (Johnston 2017), or a more permanent national alliance such as that between labour and farmers as represented by the CCF and later the NDP (Brodie and Jenson 1988). In each of these examples, the emergence of a new party followed from an abrupt change in the electoral market. There is, of course, more to party system change than this simple voter realignment thesis. As Carty, Cross, and Young (2000, 7–9) explain, this transition can also occur when new internal party practices are adopted, such as for selecting leaders and candidates, financing the party, or determining policy orientation. This textbook account of Canadian political parties, however, does not consider the role Parliament could play in this process as well. This is somewhat surprising, as it is frequently the case that new parties emerge first in Parliament (Boily 1982, 37–40). These new parties, such as the Progressives or the Bloc Québécois, were created by dissatisfied MPs who later chose to compete under a new party banner in the general election. Authors such as Epstein (1964), Lemco (1988), Lipset (1954), and Smith (1963) have suggested that the development of parties inside Parliament can be linked to party discipline, but there is no empirical evidence to support this notion in the literature. In the second part of the book, I address this shortcoming by developing and empirically testing a theory of endogenous party system change in the Canadian context.

Conclusion

I began this chapter by outlining a theory to explain why legislators support their party in Parliament, and argued that this decision is guided by three career objectives: being re-elected, having influence in the legislature, and adopting good public policy. I claimed that, over time, each of these goals has become easier to achieve with the help of political parties. For example, it is now extremely difficult for a candidate to get elected without the resources provided by the party machinery. In earlier Canadian elections, however, the context was different. Some candidates could rely on their own reputation (and money) to run a campaign and win a seat in the House of Commons. Others had to compete in ridings with only a few hundred eligible voters. These candidates knew their constituents by name, and they could promise and deliver patronage opportunities at election time. Once in Parliament, these members tended to remain independent. And since the legislative agenda was divided equally between government and private members' business, most backbenchers had ample opportunities to influence the orientation of public policy debates by introducing their own motions or bills on the floor of the House. All of this could be done without the direct help of political parties, so members did not have very strong incentives to remain loyal during legislative votes.

I also argued that several changes occurred later and directly affected the career objectives of MPs. These transformations increased incentives for members to support their party. I organized these changes into six specific factors to explain the development of legislative party organization in the decades following Confederation.

The first factor relates to electoral pressure and the growing partisanship of voters. After the expansion of the franchise in federal elections at the end of the nineteenth century, it is possible that certain MPs had to rely more on their party's brand to get elected, especially if voters cared more about the overall program of the parties than they did about the individual accomplishments of members in the House.

The second factor is linked to legislative ambition and patronage. Here again, we can determine that certain members learned that promotions or patronage opportunities were more likely to be awarded to loyal party supporters, even at the riding level. A member's re-election bid would also depend more on the party, especially if patronage appointments were an essential tool for the re-election of incumbents.

The third factor relates to legislative careers and candidate selection. Perhaps over the course of their tenure in office, members were socialized into supporting their caucus to the point that their own career objectives began to match closely those of the party. Likewise, the party could also have become more adept at recruiting suitable candidates. In both scenarios, two aspects of the member's career objectives – either the desire to have influence in the legislature or to adopt good public policy – increasingly would match the broader goals of the party.

The fourth factor is linked to parliamentary rules and procedures. I argued that the decline in private members' business forced backbenchers to rely increasingly on parties to influence the legislative process. Without doubt, once the rules of the House were permanently modified to make more room for the government's program, it became much more difficult for ordinary members to influence debates by introducing motions or bills. Increasingly, party leaders – both government and opposition – controlled the agenda, and individual members lost their ability to air grievances in the House. This increase in government business also promoted a more adversarial and partisan tone during debates and more votes on questions related to potential issues of confidence.

The fifth factor identified to explain the growth in partisanship relates to the changing preferences and ideology of members. As we saw, the nationalization of political debates on religion, language, trade, and Imperial relations polarized supporters of the Liberal and Conservative parties in Parliament. These conflicts also fuelled a succession of partisan realignments around the turn of the twentieth century – first with Catholic voters and later with western farmers – that eventually led to the breakup of the two-party system. As a consequence, parties became increasingly ideologically cohesive, while the interests of members and their leaders were more likely to match in Parliament.

The sixth and final factor identified to explain the growth of partisanship follows from the latter, and is linked to the number of parties in the legislative arena. When only two parties competed in Parliament, members were much more likely to have heterogeneous preferences over the main ideological dimensions of political conflict, but also to have more access to the floor. Once third parties entered the House, however, caucus unity increased along with partisan divisions, while opportunities for private members to initiate legislation, introduce amendments, or to intervene during debates declined significantly.

One could conclude, then, that the previous theory of legislative behaviour and party support is capable of accounting for the increase in partisanship observed in the Canadian Parliament. To date, however, none of the previous factors has been evaluated simultaneously in an empirical setting to determine if it is, in fact, related to the development of party voting unity in Canada. So far, in the British case, the focus generally has been on measuring the effects of electoral incentives on party loyalty and on determining whether cohort or replacement effects account for the increase in partisanship observed during the Victorian era (see, for example, Cox 1987, 75–9; Eggers and Spirling 2016, 568). In the United States, much more attention has focused on the effects of parliamentary rules and legislative organization to explain the growth of partisan polarization in the past few decades (see, for example, Lee 2009, 18–21; Rohde 1991, 1–16; Sinclair 2016, 259).

In the remainder of this book, I propose a unique empirical strategy to estimate the independent effects of each of these factors on the development of partisanship in the Canadian Parliament. The analysis is divided into two parts. The first part focuses on individual voting behaviour, and attempts to determine if electoral pressure, the socialization and replacement of members, or career incentives has influenced the development of party loyalty over time. The results of this analysis are reported in chapter 5. The empirical investigation then moves on to parties by considering what influence the legislative agenda and parliamentary rules could have had on caucus unity during recorded votes. The results of this analysis are reported in chapter 6.

I find that none of the six factors, taken on its own, can account for the development of partisanship in the Canadian Parliament. Although this increase in partisan behaviour appears to have followed the Anglo-American example during the second half of the nineteenth century, I demonstrate that different mechanisms were involved. Canada was still very much a rural country with a relatively small electorate until the end of the First World War. The rules and procedures of the House of Commons were also simple – the government's struggle to control the agenda was largely over by 1913, and the next wave of important reforms did not occur until 1968 (March 1974, 51–4). In the end, a bicultural and regionally diverse population, combined with a single-member-plurality electoral system, produced unusual tensions in Parliament. This ultimately resulted in the multiplication of regional parties and in more frequent minority governments after the First World War, in sharp contrast to the British and US experiences, where electoral and legislative reforms were introduced earlier and preceded the consolidation of parties in the legislature (see Brady and Althoff 1974, 754; and Cox 1987, 56–9).

This argument is the focus of the second part of the book, where I demonstrate in chapters 7 and 8 how partisan sorting and the preferences of members help to explain the growth of partisanship over time. For instance, the analysis evaluates whether the gradual economic integration of the provinces and the increasingly divergent views adopted by both parties on language and religion explain the consolidation of the party system after Confederation. Since the data employ historical voting records, the sequencing of these events can help one to estimate their independent effects on the development of parties as cohesive voting groups. In this part of the book, I also consider how the growth in the number of parties increased partisanship in the House of Commons and how the modification of parliamentary rules – which reduced the influence of private members in the legislative process – can explain the creation of new parties in the legislature. Before turning to these empirical analyses, in the next chapter I present the different datasets of legislative voting behaviour and elections used throughout the rest of this book.

Chapter Four

Legislative Records and Parliamentary Voting

In the late 1970s, William O. Ayedelotte urged scholars to use available computer techniques to analyse the parliamentary historical records of different democracies (Ayedelotte 1977, 3–9). According to him, these records provided a rare opportunity to study the opinions of elected officials. He believed that, because legislatures tend to deal with the most important issues of the day, an analysis of parliamentary voting could unveil the evolution of political conflicts over time. Indeed, this type of analysis is analogous to measuring public opinion when there are no available surveys. By looking at the particular voting records of members, it is possible to know how supporters of the Liberal or the Conservative parties or, say, Roman Catholics voters in Ontario felt about a particular issue. This is especially useful for understanding what issues influenced the organization of the Canadian party system before the Second World War and the advent of modern public opinion studies.

This type of historical work on legislative voting so far has focused primarily on the United States, perhaps because Poole and Rosenthal (2007, 1997) have analysed, and widely distributed, the complete set of roll call votes recorded in Congress since 1789. Still, several scholars have attempted to analyse historical voting records outside the US context over the years – most notably to explain the development of different characteristics of modern legislatures, such as the rise of partisanship in Victorian Britain (Eggers and Spirling 2016), the influence of emerging party groups on legislative behaviour in France (Godbout and Foucault 2013), or the development of parties in the Irish Seanad (Sircar and Høyland 2010).

In Canada, several scholars – such as Carty (1988), Kornberg and Mishler (1976), Reid ([1932] 1963), and Underhill (1935) – noted that party unity was much lower in the first few decades after Confederation than was later the case. These studies, however, were mostly based on anecdotal evidence or on a very limited sample of legislative votes collected from the House of Commons. In fact, aside from the work of Massicotte (2009), covering all the voting records of the Quebec legislature from 1867 to 1986, no comparable study exists of legislative voting in the federal Parliament.

This lack of raw empirical data has rendered a significant number of studies on Parliament "highly judgmental," "normative," and "impressionistic" (Atkinson and Thomas 1993, 432). In his review of work on parliamentary voting in Canada, Malloy (2003, 128n3) notes that, "even leading works such as C.E.S. Franks's *The Parliament of Canada* (1987) contain no systematic data on voting trends." Later, he adds that "the absence of more systematic data prevents us from exploring these patterns further in search of clarification and findings to compare with other jurisdictions." Elsewhere, he comments that "there is little sense of an ongoing and robust agenda of positive, empirical research on Canadian legislatures" (Malloy 2002, 1). This absence of empirical information on legislative behaviour further complicates the puzzle surrounding the origins of party discipline in Canada and its effect on democratic representation and parliamentary government more broadly.

The objective of this chapter is thus to present a detailed description of the legislative voting data used in the analysis presented in the remainder of this book. The first part describes the different datasets, and explains how the voting records were collected from the parliamentary archives. The second part takes a closer look at how many votes were recorded over time in the House of Commons and the Senate, and considers the link between legislative voting and parliamentary obstruction (note that the data related to the Senate are analysed in chapter 9). The third part discusses the different methods used to measure party unity throughout the remainder of this book, and highlights some of the limits of these techniques to analyse the concept of party discipline.

How the Votes Were Collected

The voting data used in the analysis were collected by Bjørn Høyland and me from the Journals of the House of Commons and the Senate from 1867 to 2015 – that is, from the first Parliament to the forty-first Parliament.[1] The coding of the outcome of each vote followed a similar procedure for each chamber. For the House, a team of research assistants identified visually from the Journals all of the recorded divisions in the first thirty-four Parliaments (1867–1993), and transcribed them directly into separate datasets (one for each parliamentary term). For the subsequent three Parliaments (1993–2004), an automated coding scheme was used to locate and download votes from the online published records available on the parliamentary website. Finally, for the last five Parliaments (2004–15), votes were taken from files provided by the parliamentary website (under the section "votes in the Chamber Business"). Since there are fewer legislative votes in the Senate, research assistants collected data from the Journals and transcribed them into different data files.

Voting procedures in the House and the Senate follow different degrees of complexity depending on the formality of the vote under consideration. In the House, the most common method of voting is by voice, whereby the speaker tries to ascertain whether the yeas or the nays have the majority. The official recording of a division in Hansard – the official record of debates – follows from this decision: if five or more members rise to demand a recorded vote, the members will be called in to vote on the motion by ringing the division bell in Parliament.[2] This bell is supposed to warn other members who are scattered about on Parliament Hill that a recorded division is about to occur. The bell usually rings for fifteen or thirty minutes, depending on the importance of the vote, and stops when all the party whips have taken their seats. The speaker then officially puts the question to the House again. Members in favour of the motion rise, and the clerk notes their names in the record. The same procedure is used to identify members who are opposed to the motion. Once voting is done, the clerk reports the outcome to the speaker, who declares "the motion carried or lost on division" (O'Brien and Bosc 2009, 567). The speaker is allowed to vote only if the vote is tied.

This process has remained basically unchanged for the whole period under investigation.[3] A sitting member can either vote yea, nay, or be paired – which occurs when two members, one from the government and one from the opposition, are matched and agree to abstain from participation in a particular vote. This is usually done to allow both members to be absent from the House. Paired members were not reported in the Journals before 1991, although the practice was commonly used in the House before this change, and sometimes reported in the more extensive Hansard debates. Abstentions are not recorded either, therefore it is impossible to distinguish between members who abstained from voting voluntarily or involuntarily – although, in the first few decades after Confederation, a strict attendance rule was maintained in the House (Dawson 1962, 89).[4]

In the Senate, a vote is recorded when at least two senators make a request. The voting process is much the same as in the House of Commons: senators can either vote yea or nay, but there is no official recording of voting pairs. Also, since 1982, senators have been able to abstain from voting on a division, a decision that is recorded officially in the Journal of the Debates. Before this change, senators had to obtain the permission of the whole chamber to abstain on a particular vote.[5] Finally, the speaker of the Senate is always allowed to vote, and in the case of a tie, the motion is negatived.

Because divisions are recorded only by surname in the Journals (and sometimes with the riding name when more than one MP has the same surname), the recorded vote data were matched with a biographical file built directly from the historical listing of members of the House of Commons and the Senate available on the parliamentary website. These data were supplemented by the online records of Elections Canada's Historical Results in Federal Electoral Ridings.[6] The general topic of the motion under consideration was also identified for each recorded division, as well as the sponsors of the motion and, in the case of amendments, the original sponsor(s) of the motion being amended.

How Frequently Members Vote

From these various records, Høyland and I collected the biographical information of 4,216 MPs and 925 senators who served between 1867 and 2015. This number ranges from the 215 sitting members of the House in the second Parliament to the 323 in the forty-first Parliament (a mean of 270 for the period), and 86 sitting senators in the second Parliament to 138 in the thirty-fourth Parliament (a mean of 111 for the period). The reasons for these fluctuations are twofold. First, some MPs were replaced in by-elections because they left the chamber (following retirement, death, expulsion, and so on). Note that senators could also be replaced if they retired or died in office. Second, the number of seats also increased in the House of Commons with population growth and the redistribution of federal electoral ridings following the decennial census, and in the Senate with the addition of new provinces and territories.

Høyland and I also collected the voting records of every member who participated in one or more of the recorded divisions in the House of Commons or the Senate. This gave us a total of 12,119 votes in the House, or 2,346,490 individual voting decisions. In the Senate, the total number of votes was 1,453, with 83,695 individual voting decisions. In terms of frequency of voting, there was an average of 296 recorded votes per term in the House between 1867 and 2015 (a standard deviation of 394).[7] In the Senate, the average was just 35 votes per parliamentary term (a standard deviation of 34).[8]

A more detailed description of the frequency with which members participated in recorded divisions is reported in figure 4.1. Each point represents the average turnout rate by term for both Conservative and Liberal members of the House of Commons and the Senate. Note that the bars correspond to a one standard deviation increase or decline from this value. The analysis confirms that the participation rate in the House of Commons was higher than in the Senate, although the difference is not very large. In each chamber, the trend appears to follow a convex pattern, with a decline in the level of participation culminating in the middle of the twentieth century and a subsequent increase

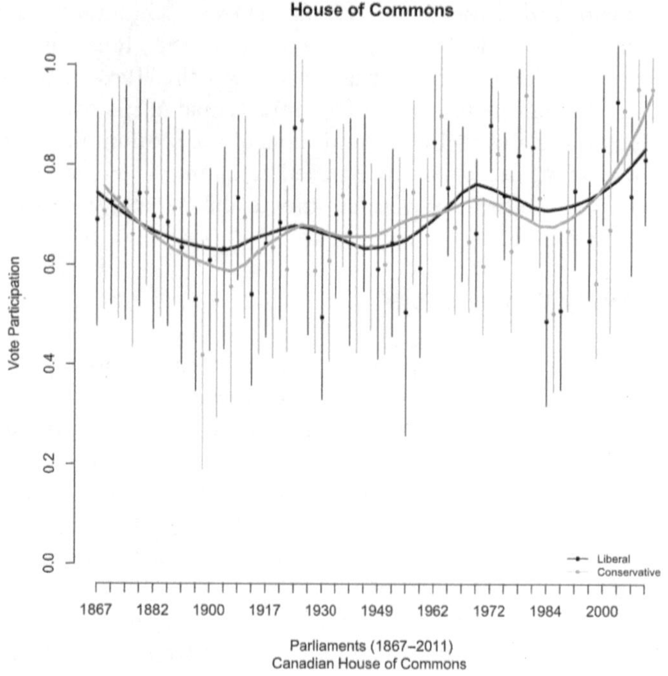

Figure 4.1 Average Participation Rate in Recorded Divisions, House of Commons and Senate, 1867–2011

in more recent years. The variation in turnout around the mean is also higher in the Senate – in other words, there were several senators who systematically abstained from voting, while others participated in almost all legislative votes. In the House, this type of behaviour appears to have been less frequent, as members were more likely to be closer to the House average in each term. Of course, these values are highly influenced by the number of divisions recorded during a session. If, for example, there were only a handful of votes in a parliamentary term, turnout was much more likely to be affected by the absence of one or two members, as opposed to a term where several hundred votes were recorded.

Figure 4.2 demonstrates that this was indeed a possibility by reporting the actual number of divisions in each legislative term in both the House and the Senate. The figure confirms that the number of votes recorded by term varied considerably. There were slightly more votes in the House during the nineteenth century, but this number was relatively low compared with the dramatic increase observed in the period after the Second World War. In

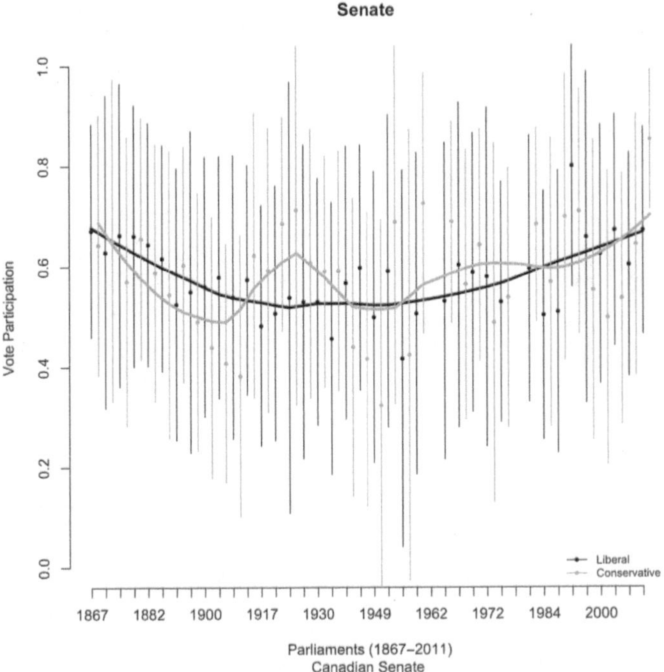

Figure 4.1 continued

fact, more than 62 per cent of all the divisions in the House occurred between the thirty-third and forty-first Parliaments (1993–2015). Another way to look at the data is to consider the number of votes recorded on average per sitting day. According to this measure, we find that the mean number of votes was almost one per day (0.72) in the House between 1867 and 2015, with an average of 388 sitting days per Parliament. The highest number of votes recorded in the House during a single day occurred on 7 December 1999, when the Reform Party attempted to filibuster the adoption of the Nisga'a First Nation land claim treaty by recording 472 votes. The Senate appears to have experienced a similar shift in the number of recorded divisions over time, with more than 45 per cent of the voting data recorded after 1993. In terms of daily average, the number of votes in the Senate was much lower, with less than one vote per day (0.14) and an average of 238 sitting days per Parliament.

This increase in the number of votes recorded in the House and the Senate is explained by several factors. It could be, for example, related to the additional workload in the legislature over time, or even to the increase in the partisanship

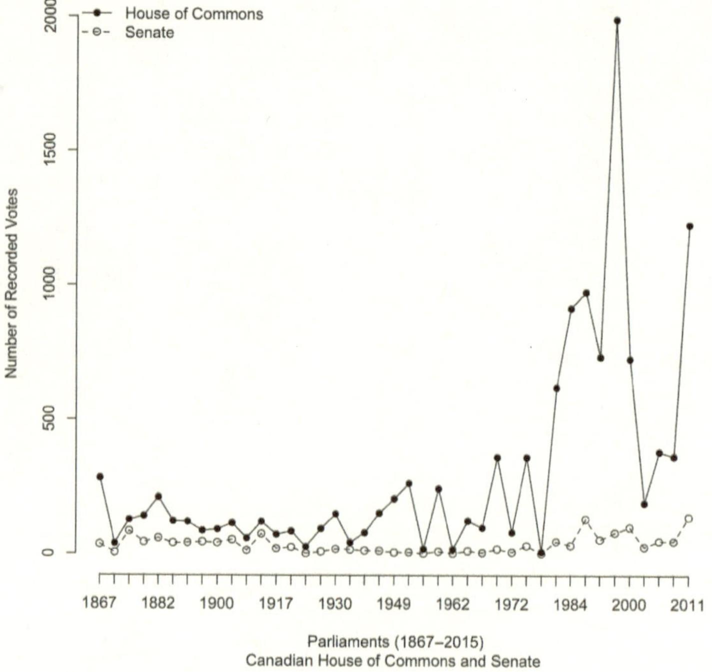

Figure 4.2 Total Recorded Votes, House of Commons and Senate, 1867–2015

of MPs. The most likely explanation for this change, however, is linked to the adoption of new tactics by the opposition to obstruct legislative proceedings. Since parliamentarians over the years have used several different tools to slow down or delay the adoption of legislation in the House, the government has had to change the rules to limit their participation in the legislative process. When Parliament first met after Confederation, the time set aside to discuss private members' and government business was about equally divided during a session. It quickly became apparent, however, that more days were needed to consider government legislation, especially as the size and scope of the federal bureaucracy increased. Several temporary measures were adopted to add time on the agenda for government business, until only a few hours of the week were reserved for private members (O'Brien and Bosc 2009, 475–6). This scheduling eventually became permanent in the Standing Orders at the beginning of the twentieth century and, as a consequence, backbenchers lost a great deal of influence in the legislative process.

Since private members' activities now encroached on government time, backbenchers and opposition party leaders had to seek other ways to be heard in Parliament. For many, obstruction began to be seen as a tactic to obtain concessions from the government side. For example, before the adoption of the closure rule in 1913, members could discuss issues almost indefinitely on the floor of the House to prevent the adjournment of debates. In the most extreme cases, these debates could last for several days, or even lead to the dissolution of Parliament, as in 1896, when Parliament was dissolved over the Manitoba Schools Question, or in 1911, when the Conservative Party filibustered the adoption of a reciprocity trade agreement with the United States. Although the adoption of closure put an end to this practice, members found other means to slow down the proceedings, either by introducing amendments or by raising points of order, which often had to be dealt with by a recorded division. Each time the opposition discovered a new dilatory tactic to obstruct the debate, the Standing Orders of the House of Commons were subsequently modified by the government to place time limits on these activities.

It follows that part of the increase in the number of recorded divisions observed in the last three decades of the twentieth century is a direct consequence of the opposition's continuing attempts to obstruct government business. For instance, members used the division bell to prevent the adoption of controversial bills on several occasions (Stewart 1977, 47). Since the presence of the chief government and opposition whips is necessary before a recorded vote can begin, each whip has the power to bring the House to a standstill by refusing to appear in the chamber during a vote. However, after an episode in 1982 in which the bell rang nonstop for more than fourteen days, the Standing Orders were changed to set time limits on the calling of members (Francis 1984, 26; O'Brien and Bosc 2009, 570n285).

Because the process of recording divisions also takes time, opposition parties have used them to slow down the proceedings by requesting, for example, individual votes on hundreds of their own amendments introduced in the reporting stage of a bill. Once again, the rules had to be modified to accommodate the increasing number of votes called by the opposition. A good example is related to the implementation of deferring votes, whereby the House agrees to carry all of its legislative votes successively at a particular time during the week, either on Tuesdays or Wednesdays, usually before the daily adjournment (O'Brien and Bosc 2009, 574). Another practice is to apply the results of one vote to a series of successive votes. Here, the government and the opposition whips agree on a common position for their parties, which is announced to the speaker. Members who want to cast a vote at odds with the party's position must declare their position to the speaker (this is done automatically for independent members). In recent years, this practice has been increasingly used in concert with deferred divisions in the House. Both have saved a lot of time during debates (O'Brien and Bosc 2009, 578–9). In fact, 74 per cent of the 1,294 divisions recorded during the thirty-fifth Parliament (1994–7) were "applied votes" (Marleau and Montpetit 2000, 488n280). Of course, it remains possible for a group of determined members to use recorded divisions to slow the proceedings. We saw that the Reform Party requested the highest number of votes in one day during the adoption of the Nisga'a treaty in 1999. The Progressive Conservative Party used a similar obstruction tactic in 1984, when voting over the amendments of a particularly controversial bill took almost a full sitting day of the House (578n333).

Although still significant, the increase in the number of votes in the Senate has not been as dramatic as in the House of Commons. Because the rules of the Senate have more or less remained the same since Confederation (O'Brien 1981, 28), this change must be explained by something else. Senator Lynch-Staunton (2000, 11) has suggested that the increasing number of divisions in the Senate can be explained by the more frequent partisan conflicts observed between this chamber and the House of Commons over the past three decades. This era of intra-parliamentary division began with the election of the PC government of Brian Mulroney in 1984. Because the PCs had been in the opposition for all but one of the previous thirty years, the Senate at the time was dominated by a large majority of Liberals, who began to oppose the PC government by frequently blocking or delaying legislation in the upper house. The successive alternation between four Liberal (1993–2006) and three Conservative (2006–15) governments prolonged this situation for many years, until new senators could be named to change the party standings in the Senate. As a consequence, the average number of recorded divisions was higher in the Senate during these terms. But this cannot be the whole story, since we still find a relatively large number of votes recorded when the Liberals and Conservatives controlled a majority in both chambers.

An additional explanation for the Senate's increasing legislative activity relates to the fact that bills originating from the House of Commons now require more scrutiny because they are frequently poorly drafted (Lynch-Staunton 2000, 11). This is a direct consequence of the government's renewed attempts to control the legislative agenda. Indeed, the speaker now has the power to determine the number of amendments that can be proposed to a bill, therefore limiting the opportunities for members to modify and improve proposed legislation (O'Brien and Bosc 2009, 777). The government can also use time allocation motions to reduce the length of debate on a specific piece of legislation introduced in the House (Pelletier 2000, 20). These new rules, adopted in 1969, have been used not only to silence the opposition, but also to push controversial bills through the legislature more quickly (25). Once in the Senate, these bills require extensive modification, which has led to the adoption of more amendments and, ultimately, to an increase in the number of recorded divisions in that chamber. A cursory look at the number of bills introduced in the House and amended in the Senate also reveals an increase in the number of successful amendments adopted in the upper chamber after 1984, although this number is much higher when Parliament is divided (see chapter 9). This suggests that the Senate indeed might have improved on some of the legislation sent up by the House, but that this is much more likely to occur when different parties control the majority of the House and Senate.

To summarize, this first look at the voting data of the Canadian Parliament shows that there was a marked increase in the number of recorded divisions over time. In the House of Commons, this surge can be explained by the modification of the rules, mainly those that resulted in more time being allocated to the consideration of government business in the legislative agenda. This was done first through the adoption in 1906 of a new weekly order of business to increase permanently the number of government business days, then by the introduction in 1913 of the closure rule, and later, in the 1960s, by the placing of limits on the length of debates and on the possibilities for introducing amendments. The adoption of these new rules led opposition members to find new ways to obstruct government business, such as by using the time-consuming process of recording divisions.

Although changes in the Senate were not as expansive, that chamber also has seen an increase in the number of divisions in recent Parliaments. Because the Standing Orders in the Senate have remained almost unchanged since Confederation, this surge in the number of divisions in the upper chamber might be explained either by the rise in the number of divided Parliaments or by the increase in the number of amendments. Although both explanations are validated somewhat by empirical data, the evidence is tentative at best, as there are simply too few recorded divisions in the Senate. I return to this puzzle in chapter 9, where I consider the development of partisanship in this chamber more directly.

How Party Unity Is Measured

Before proceeding further, it is important to provide a more complete definition of the concept of party voting unity, which represents the dependent variable in most of the empirical analysis in the next chapters, and its relationship to party discipline. The legislative voting dataset used in this book consists of the outcome of individual voting decisions (that is, of votes cast). It does not tell us what motivates these votes. The presence or absence of party discipline has to be inferred using additional considerations. Several factors could influence the decision to support or oppose a party during a legislative vote. It should not be controversial to say that, when party members vote the same way as their leadership, it is not necessarily because they are pressured to do so. Some might vote with the party because they share the same view as their leader on the issue being debated. And it also should not be controversial to say that sometimes members vote with their party because they feel pressured to do so and want to avoid paying the cost of disobedience. As we saw earlier, this cost can take several forms, such as being stripped of certain duties in the legislature or, in extreme cases, being expelled from the caucus.

So it can be assumed that members sometimes end up supporting their party in the legislature even though they would rather have voted differently on some particular issues. It is true that, during especially difficult votes, party whips may allow members to abstain from voting, instead of forcing them to cast a vote that could have negative electoral consequences in their riding. Allowing members to abstain when there is a disagreement is a practice confirmed during several informal interviews I conducted with the whips of three of the major parties in the House of Commons. In other special circumstances, the leadership may also permit a free vote. Free votes are extremely rare, however, and occur only over particularly controversial issues. In those circumstances, no direction is given by the whips, and the members are free to "vote their consciences." A recent example of this in the House concerned the 2005 same-sex marriage bill when Liberal, Bloc Québécois, and Conservative backbenchers were allowed a free vote. On this vote, however, the NDP imposed the party line. NDP member Bev Desjarlais nevertheless voted against the bill, and as a consequence she was removed from her two official critic positions in the House by the party leadership (*CBC News* 2005).

So party discipline is not absolute in Parliament: there have been numerous instances when party unity broke down during legislative votes, but this has become less frequent over time. Should we thus assume that this is because the parties have found a more efficient method to discipline their members? Or is it because the ideological preferences of party members have become increasingly similar? In order to bracket these questions, it is common to speak of party voting unity, rather than party discipline or party cohesion. The more frequently members vote together in the legislature, the greater the party unity. When party members support or oppose the same motions because they share a common ideology, they are said to be cohesive. If members support or oppose the same motions because they are pressured to vote with their party, they are said to be disciplined (Kam 2014, 402). "Party voting unity" thus can be the result of party discipline, ideological cohesion, or both – and there are other possible factors as well, such as strategic voting.

To understand the development of partisanship in the Canadian legislature, I use two different measures of party unity. The first is based on individual party members, and measures party unity by means of an index of "loyalty."

The index reports the proportion of votes (ranging from 0 to 1) on which a member voted with a majority of their caucus on all the recorded divisions in a given parliamentary term. Thus, if a member sits in more than one Parliament, we have multiple records of loyalty for this MP. The more a member votes with his/her party, the higher the member's loyalty index should be. So far, the analysis of party voting unity presented in this book has been based on this measure.

The second measure of party voting unity is based on legislative votes, and is aggregated at the party level. It is obtained, first, by subtracting the number of votes cast in a division by the majority position of a party (either yeas or nays) from the number of votes cast by the minority position of the same party (either yeas or nays). This difference is then divided by the total number of votes recorded by the party (minority + majority positions). This is known as the Rice index, which ranges from 0 (perfect split) to 1 (perfect unity).

I use both of these measures throughout the book but the loyalty scores are found primarily in the analysis of the individual determinants of legislative voting, presented in chapter 5, while the Rice index measures are associated with the analysis of the aggregate determinants of voting unity at the party level, presented in chapter 6. Although each measure has clear substantive interpretations and has been widely used in the literature, they both also have important methodological and conceptual limitations. Neither exactly captures what I am ultimately trying to estimate. For example, these scores could inflate the level of party unity for smaller parties, mainly because there will be more variance in the outcome of recorded votes when few MPs participate in a division (Desposato 2005, 735). The Liberals and Conservatives have elected a significant number of MPs in almost every parliamentary term, however, so this should not represent a problem, especially when we look at the development of partisanship in the first few decades following Confederation, when there were only two parties in the House of Commons. An additional problem is related to the number of votes recorded in each Parliament, which, as with party size, could affect the value of party unity. This is more likely to be true if the issues that come up for a vote are not randomly selected (Hug 2010, 226). As we will see in later chapters, one primary factor explaining the rise in party voting unity in the House is related precisely to the gradual modification of the legislative agenda and the increase in the number of government-related divisions in Parliament.

Thus, problems related to the measurement of party voting unity remain a valid concern in the Canadian case. First, we saw that, in certain parliamentary terms, such as the minority government of the thirty-first Parliament (1979–80), there were only a handful of recorded divisions in the House of Commons. In the Senate, this problem is even more serious, since the average number of recorded divisions is consistently lower than in the House. Second, the caucus

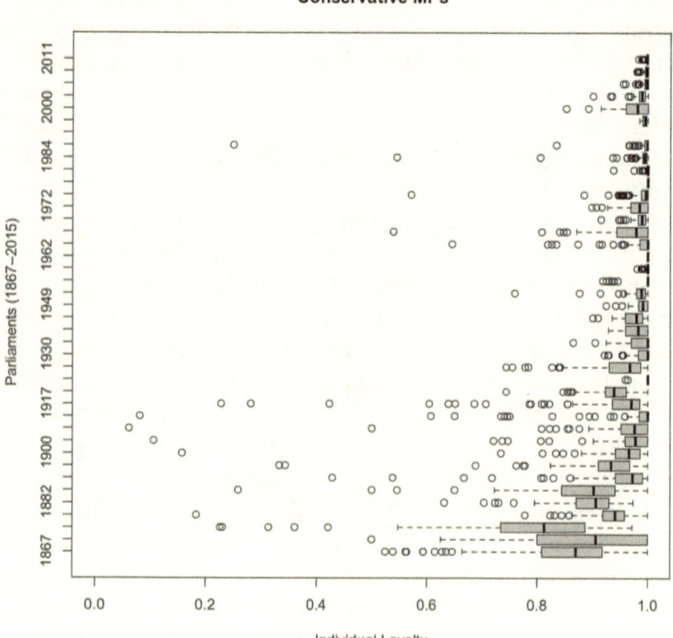

Figure 4.3 Distribution of Loyalty Scores, by Party, 1867–2015

size of each party could also be problematic, especially if we consider several of the third parties that have elected only a limited number of representatives over the years, or the Progressive Conservative Party in the thirty-fifth Parliament (1993–7), with only two MPs.

To get a sense of how caucus size could influence the measurement of party voting unity, figure 4.3 shows the box plots of the distribution of individual loyalty scores for each major party that elected more than five members to the House of Commons between 1867 and 2015. Because the Conservatives and the Liberals are the only parties to have members in every parliamentary term since Confederation, the plots combine two or more minor parties in the same graph whenever their representation in the House does not overlap. If we exclude the CCF/NDP, which has had more than five members in every Parliament since 1935, third parties have been present in the House for only short periods. These parties are: the Progressive Party (fourteenth to sixteenth Parliaments), the different United Farmer Parties (sixteenth and seventeenth), the Social Credit Party (eighteenth to thirty-first), the Ralliement Créditiste

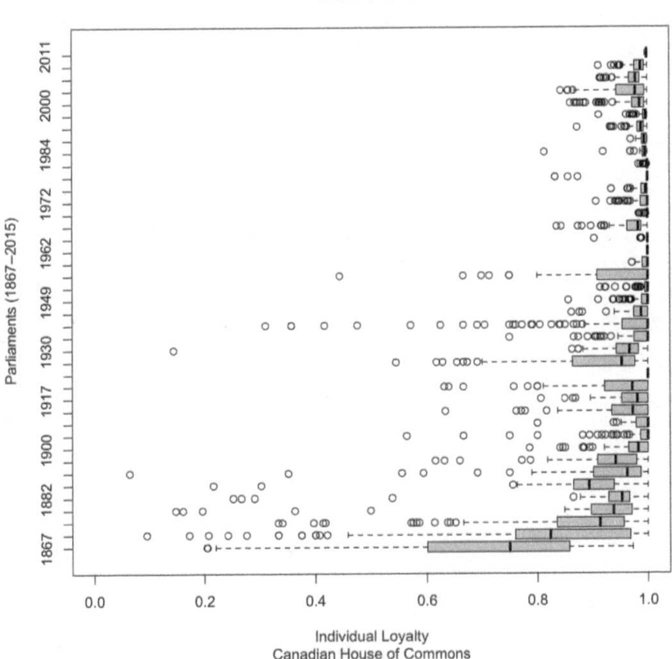

Figure 4.3 continued

(twenty-sixth to twenty-eighth), the Reform Party/Canadian Alliance (thirty-fifth to thirty-eighth), and the Bloc Québécois (thirty-fifth to fortieth).

The box plots show that the median loyalty score (the bold bars in each box) is more or less always in the range of 75 to 100 per cent for the Conservatives and Liberals. It is lowest during the first term, and reaches almost 100 per cent by the tenth Parliament (1904). After this point, the median loyalty level never falls below 95 per cent. This last result does not imply that all members were systematically loyal to their respective parties. In fact, we find only three terms when every elected member followed the party line perfectly: the Liberals in the fifteenth and twenty-fifth Parliaments, and the Conservatives in the twenty-fifth and the thirty-first Parliaments (all shorter minority Parliaments with a handful of votes). We can also see that the variation in loyalty scores decreases over time: the standard deviation is never above ten points for the two major parties after the twentieth Parliament.[9]

Not surprisingly, the box plots also show that the average level of individual party loyalty is much lower for the Progressive Party, the first major

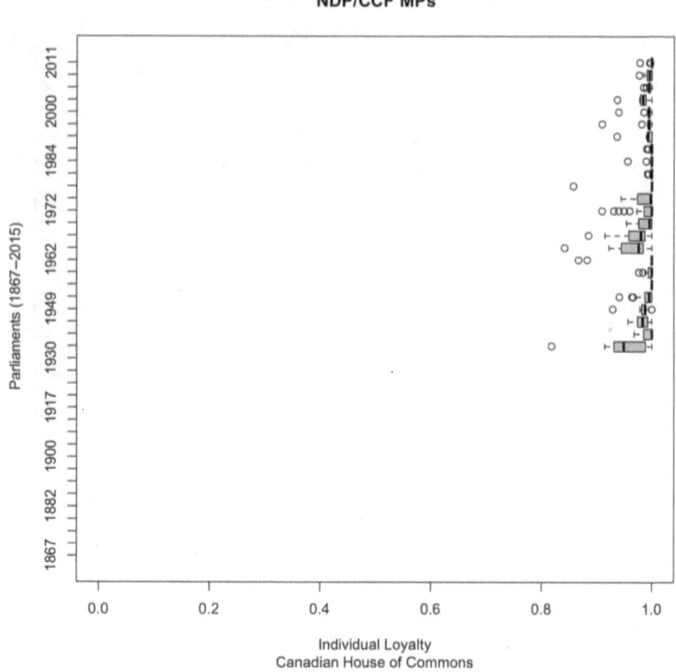

Figure 4.3 Distribution of Loyalty Scores, by Party, 1867–2015 (continued)

third party, which elected members to Parliament in 1921. The high level of variance observed among the Progressive caucus is most likely explained by the leaders' refusal to impose discipline on their ranks. It is perhaps more interesting to look at the levels of party unity for the CCF/NDP, which are always high, as is the case for most other major third parties, such as the Bloc Québécois and Reform/Canadian Alliance. In this last case, it is surprising to find such a high level of party unity for Reformists, especially given that one of their objectives was to weaken party discipline in the House (Laycock 2002, 102). The explanation could be the strong leadership of Preston Manning, or perhaps most of the caucus simply agreed on the issues debated in the House.

We can infer from the individual party loyalty scores presented in figure 4.3 that party unity is also high for most of the third parties in the House of Commons – the only exception being the Progressive Party. We also cannot discount the fact that the unity scores of some third parties, such as the United Farmers group or the Ralliement Créditiste, could be inflated by the smaller size of their membership. The results also demonstrate, however, that

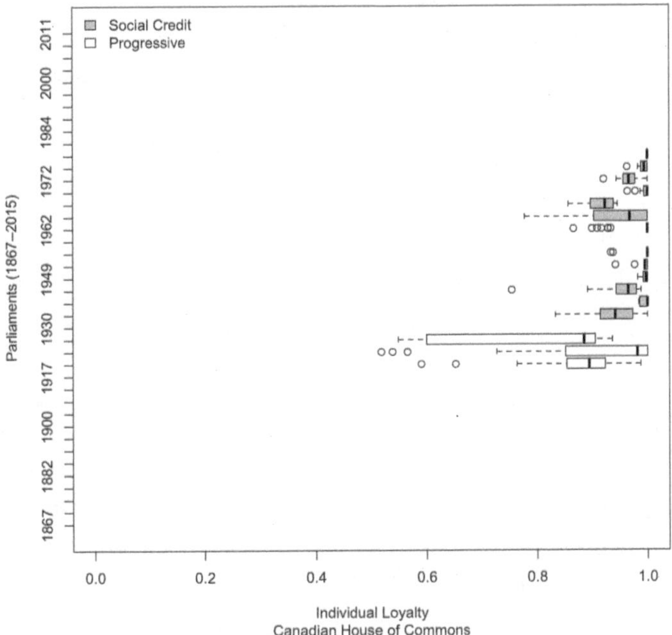

Figure 4.3 continued

party unity is very high for parties with a strong contingent of representatives in the House, such as the NDP, Reform/Canadian Alliance, and the Bloc Québécois.

Because the level of party voting unity is already high when most third parties elect members for the first time – notable exceptions being the Progressive Party and perhaps Social Credit – and because this measure tends to increase over time, it is more important to understand why partisanship developed during the first few decades following Confederation. And since the Liberals and Conservatives are the only two parties present in the legislature throughout the period under study, the analysis in the rest of this book focuses primarily on those two, which have controlled every Canadian federal government. Indeed, because the size of their caucuses has almost always been large, we can be confident that the measure of voting unity used in this study will not be artificially inflated. Still, given that third parties played an important role in consolidating party unity during the 1920s, I consider their influence on the development of partisanship in the legislature in chapter 8 and the conclusion.

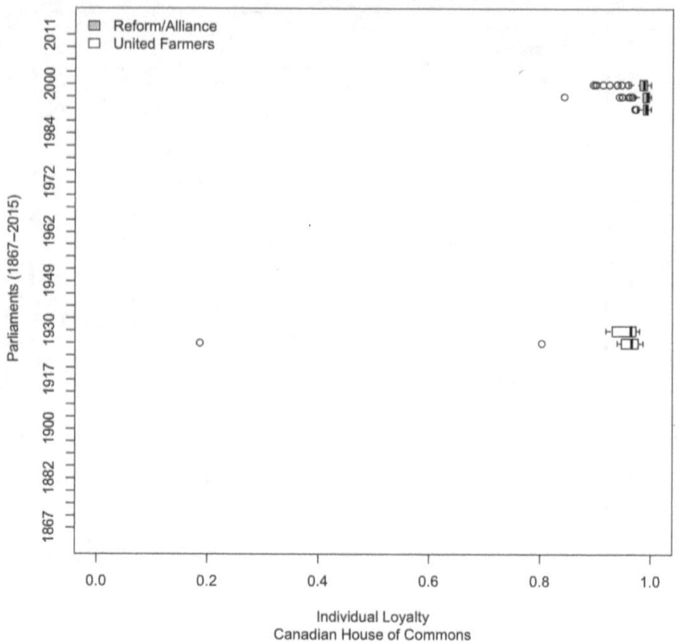

Figure 4.3 Distribution of Loyalty Scores, by Party, 1867–2015 (continued)

I explained earlier that the type of motion or bill under consideration could also influence the level of party unity observed during legislative votes. For example, if all recorded divisions in Parliament were free votes, involving no party discipline, we would probably observe much lower levels of party unity. Likewise, if most votes were related to bills introduced by private members, party unity would probably be weaker, since this type of legislative activity does not constitute a question of confidence in the government. The effect of the origins of a motion on partisanship can be seen in figure 4.4, which compares the Rice index, my second measure of party voting unity, on motions sponsored by the government with motions sponsored by private members. Note that I do not include a similar analysis for the Senate because of the absence of the confidence convention and because there have been only a limited number of divisions in that chamber in each term.

The motions included in this analysis are from all the legislative votes recorded between 1867 and 2011. They could be related to several different types of legislative activity, such as voting on a bill, an amendment to a bill,

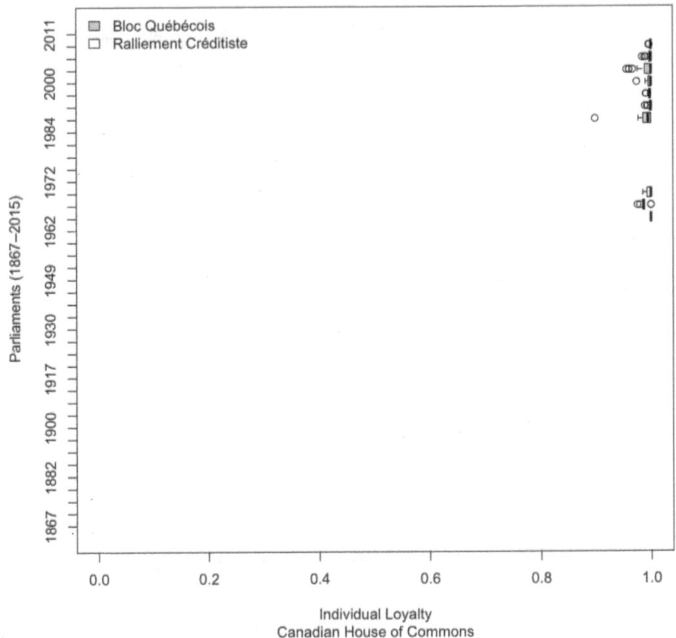

Figure 4.3 continued

or a procedural motion (such as an adjournment motion). They could also be linked to a budget vote (ways and means or supply resolutions), a concordance in committee report, or a motion to amend the throne speech. The analysis presented in the figure separates motions introduced by members of the government from those introduced by other members. Thus, an amendment to the budget is categorized as government business, even if an opposition leader or backbencher introduced it. On the other hand, a bill or motion introduced by a backbencher is considered private members' business, even if a member of the cabinet amended it.

Figure 4.4 reports the average unity scores for voting over these two types of motions (originating from the cabinet or from private members). The first plot shows the mean Rice index for these votes for the party controlling the government (either the Liberals or the Conservatives, depending on the term). The second plot shows the same measure for the official opposition (once again, either Liberal or Conservative, depending on the term). The results demonstrate that voting unity is much higher on average when voting occurs on a

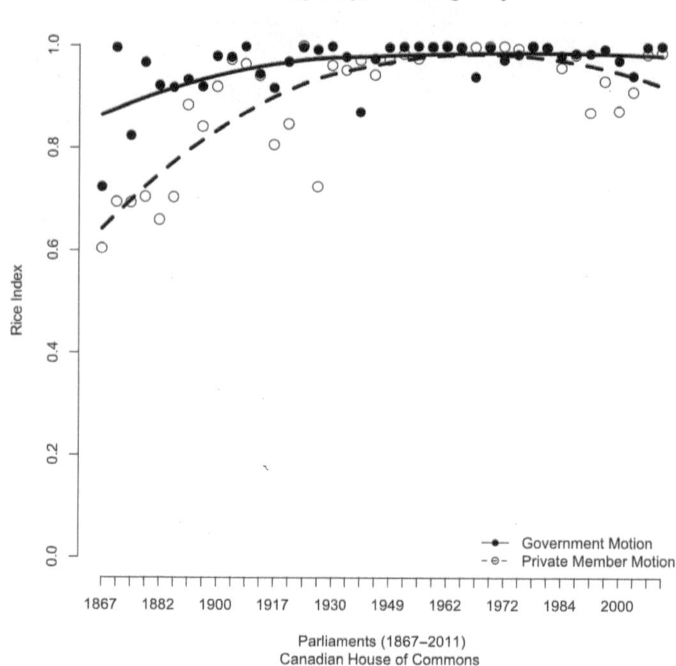

Figure 4.4 Voting Unity, Governing and Opposition Parties, 1867–2011

motion related to government business, and this is true for both the Liberal and Conservative parties when they are in government. This trend converges much earlier towards the maximum value of the Rice index (100 per cent, or 1 on the index), which implies that there is no observable dissension within the governing party. On the other hand, the Rice index for private members' business remains much lower throughout the whole period, although we see a small decline in the unity of the governing party towards the end. This last drop corresponds to the return of private members' business in the House of Commons after rules were modified in the 1980s and 1990s so as to increase the influence of backbenchers in the legislative process.

Since partisan voting appears to be a function of the type of issue being debated, it is important to take this into consideration when trying to explain the development of party unity in the empirical analysis that follows. Indeed, it is possible that a large proportion of the consolidation of partisanship is explained by the increase in government business and by the reduction of the influence of backbenchers in the legislative process. Still, figure 4.4 shows that party unity,

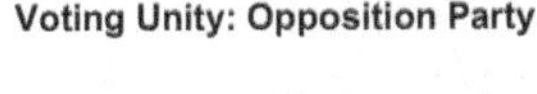

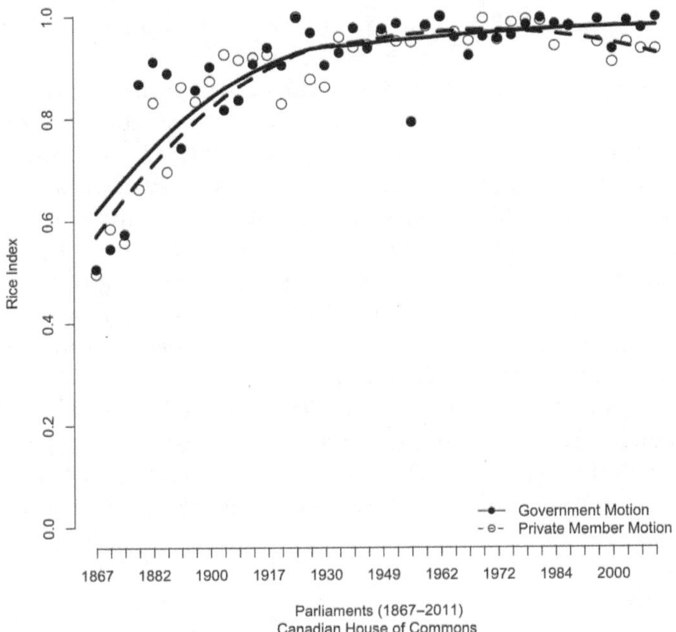

Figure 4.4 continued

even for government-related business, was much lower in the years following Confederation, so something other than the increase in government business must explain this earlier change. One possibility is that, over time, members became more ideologically cohesive and thus more likely to vote together in the legislature. It is also possible that the introduction of the secret ballot and the increasing size of the voting population could have led members to become more partisan in the legislature. Still another possibility is that governments found more efficient ways to impose discipline in the House of Commons – for example, by rewarding loyal supporters with patronage or by promoting them to the cabinet. In the next two chapters, I consider each of these possibilities, and several more, to explain the development of party unity in the Canadian Parliament.

A final concern with the distribution of these indices is that a standard statistical model could fail to capture historical changes in the relationship between the variables in the analysis. To address this problem, I estimated (and compared) different change-point models (one for each Parliament) to locate potential structural breaks in the data. I identified these breaks by comparing the deviance of different statistical models with a limited number of variables. The models include the number of the Parliament (linear and squared).[10] I then interacted both of these variables with a binary measure identifying the change points; I thus coded all parliamentary terms 1 after a model-specific change point was located – for a similar approach, see Western and Kleykamp (2004). From this analysis, I identified two distinct breaks: one around the sixteenth Parliament (1926) for the loyalty scores, and one around the seventeenth Parliament (1926–30) for the unity scores. Both of these changes are relevant, as they occurred in the middle of the transition period towards a multiparty system in Canada, when the growth in voting unity appears to have levelled off. Therefore, in order to control for the potential effects of these change points, the analysis presented in chapters 5 and 6 considers all of the Parliaments in a cumulative model (1867–2011), but also separately by dividing the data into two distinct periods (before and after the change points). These two periods are: the first through fifteenth Parliaments and sixteenth through fortieth Parliaments for the loyalty scores; and the first through sixteenth Parliaments and seventeenth through fortieth Parliaments for the unity scores.

Conclusion

I began this chapter by looking more closely at the data on legislative voting in the Canadian Parliament. We saw that there was an increase in the yearly average of the number of recorded divisions in the House of Commons. The same pattern was observed in the Senate, but to a lesser extent. I argued that this increase could be attributed to renewed attempts by the opposition to obstruct government legislative activities in the House. The struggle between the government and the opposition led to several modifications of the rules of this chamber, most notably to increase the government's ability to control the legislative agenda. Because the request to record a division can be made by as few as five members, this procedure gradually became a way to obstruct the proceedings of the House, as the adoption of new rules progressively reduced the influence of ordinary members in the legislative process.

I then defined the concept of party voting unity, and explained how party discipline, members' preferences, and the legislative agenda could all influence a member's decision to support the party during a legislative vote. As we saw, the type of motion under consideration is likely to have an effect on the outcome of a division. In addition, the size of the party caucus and the number of legislative votes could influence both of these measures of partisanship in the legislature. For these reasons, I decided to focus most of the empirical analysis in the remainder of the book on the two major parties, the Liberals and

Conservatives, which have also been present in the House in every Parliament since Confederation. Considering that voting in the Senate is less frequent, and since the development of party unity in that chamber occurred later than in the House, I analyse the development of partisanship in that chamber subsequently, in chapter 9. My goal in the previous pages was to reveal the sharp increase in party voting unity in Parliament by looking at all the recorded votes in the House of Commons. The objective of the next four chapters is to identify what factors best explain this increase over time.

Chapter Five

How Members Vote

I begin my empirical investigation of how MPs vote by looking at the determinants of legislative voting in Parliament. The focus of this chapter is related to the main objective of this book, which is to determine what factors explain the growth of partisanship in Parliament over time. I conduct this analysis at the level of individual members to verify whether or not existing theories of party support are relevant in the Canadian context. These theories, outlined in chapter 3, are linked to the following three sets of factors: (1) electoral pressure; (2) promotions and patronage opportunities; and (3) the socialization of members and candidate selection. The goal here is to confirm if these factors are associated with higher levels of party loyalty, but also to determine if they can account for the development of partisanship in the House of Commons over time. If I find, for example, that members who represent populous ridings are more likely to support their party during legislative votes, I can infer that the size of the electorate is associated with higher levels of party loyalty in the House. Still, this does not tell us much about the development of party loyalty over time or when exactly electoral pressure began to influence legislative behaviour. If, on the other hand, I can show that the relationship between the size of the electorate and partisan voting became considerably stronger after the franchise expanded in 1898, I will have much stronger evidence to support the claim that this is one cause of the increase in party voting unity observed around the turn of the previous century.

The mere mention of causality in the context of an observational study is bound to be highly controversial. After all, the dataset I use in this analysis comes from the historical voting records of actual Members of Parliament. In this context, causal inference is problematic, because one cannot be certain that the relationship observed between party loyalty and electoral pressure is not explained by something else. If, for example, one takes the size of the voting population, it would be questionable to claim that increasing the number of voters in the riding causes members to support their party more in the legislative arena, even if there is a high correlation between these two variables. Other unobservable factors could influence this relationship. For instance, it is possible that loyal party supporters are more likely to be assigned to more populous ridings, or that maverick members seek out smaller ridings to represent. In this context, the assignment to the treatment (representing a large or a small riding) would be correlated with an unobserved variable (the member's ideology), so any attempt to estimate the causal effect of population size on party loyalty would be biased. Unless one can directly observe and compare the legislative behaviour of a member who simultaneously represents a large and a small riding at the same time (or assign all candidates randomly across different types of districts), it is impossible to estimate directly the counterfactual causal effect that the size of the electorate has on individual legislative behaviour – or any other co-factors listed above, for that matter.[1]

Fortunately, researchers have at their disposal several different methodological tools to approximate the influence of independent variables in the context of observational studies. These approaches are primarily associated with natural (or quasi) experiments, regression discontinuity, and matching methods (Sekhon 2008, 272). In this chapter and the next, I use a much simpler approach by taking advantage of the longitudinal structure of the voting data to identify specific events that might have influenced the development of partisan behaviour in the legislative arena. As mentioned before, I can compare the loyalty of MPs before and after the franchise was expanded in 1898, when most adult men were allowed to vote for the first time. If the analysis shows that party voting unity increased significantly after this point, I can infer that this change played an important role in the development of party-line voting in the legislature. The expansion of the franchise in 1898 then would represent a form of exogenous treatment applied uniformly to all MPs in what could be conceived as a quasi-experiment design (Carson and Sievert 2015, 89).

Since I use historical voting data in the analysis, several other events like these, such as the introduction of same-day elections in 1874 and the adoption of the Civil Service Act in 1918, could be used as points of comparison to estimate their independent effects on the development of party voting unity. Thus, the structure of the data allows me to determine whether most factors identified in the literature to explain the growth of partisanship could indeed be responsible for the changes observed in Parliament. Nevertheless, not all of the variables of interest fall into this category. Certain factors, such as the socialization of members and their legislative experience, did not suddenly change from one Parliament to the next. Although the number of claims one can make about the causal effect of these variables is limited, I find that three of the most common explanations for the rise in partisanship are related to specific institutional rule changes: the introduction of same-day elections in 1874; the expansion of the franchise in 1898, 1917, and 1921; and finally, civil service reforms in 1918 that abolished most patronage appointments. The analysis I present below takes advantage of these events to estimate their influence on legislative voting.

I begin by discussing some of the limits of using loyalty scores as a dependent variable in the analysis and propose ways to address this issue. I then look at the relationship between electoral pressure and party loyalty over time. Here, I attempt to determine whether same-day elections, the size of the franchise, or electoral competitiveness in the riding explain why members would support their party more. Moving away from party loyalty as a dependent variable, I then assess how patronage opportunities influence legislative behaviour, in order to determine if members who were promoted to either the cabinet or the Senate were more likely previously to have been strong party supporters in the House of Commons. I also verify if members were rewarded for their loyalty by receiving more patronage appointments in their ridings. I then look at how the socialization of members influences party support. More precisely, I consider whether two sets of factors – career length and cohort replacement effects – are related to higher individual loyalty scores. The goal here is to determine if members who served for longer periods, or who were elected in more recent terms, had higher loyalty scores on average. Finally, I present the results of a cumulative analysis that integrates both the electoral and socialization variables into a single model to estimate their effects on individual loyalty scores. The objective here is to adjudicate between these two different explanations of party support.

Modelling Individual Party Loyalty Scores

I should note at the outset that several MPs, especially towards the latter part of the twentieth century, have perfect or near-perfect individual party loyalty scores – as confirmed in the previous chapter, where I presented a more detailed analysis of their distribution over time (the same is true for the aggregated measure of party unity used in chapter 6). The values of these indices imply that a standard linear model can be problematic, because it assumes that the dependent variable is free from upper or lower bounds. In my case, the dependent variable – the individual loyalty score – cannot be above 1 or below 0, where 1 represents perfect loyalty towards the party, and 0 represents a member who always opposed the party during a legislative term. Although failure to take this into consideration might bias the results, the empirical analysis I present below uses standard linear regression models, which allows for a much more straightforward interpretation of the coefficients. Nevertheless, to minimize these concerns, in all the models presented below, I adjusted the standard errors to control for autocorrelation and heteroscedasticity.[2]

Another potential pitfall associated with my measure of party loyalty is linked to the type of vote recorded in the House of Commons. Recall that I calculate party loyalty for each individual MP, and report the proportion of times a member sided with a majority of his or her caucus during all the votes in a legislative term. This measure is likely to be influenced by the type of division being recorded. Of course, party unity will be much higher when voting occurs over government-related business. When these votes are recorded in the debates, parties are expected to pressure their members to support (or oppose) the government. Failure to do so could lead to a loss of confidence in the cabinet and new elections. Since recorded divisions on government and private members' business are not randomly determined in the course of a legislative session, it is important to distinguish between these two types of votes in the analysis. As we saw in chapter 4, an important proportion of the variation observed in the voting data can be explained by private members' business. Since voting on this type of motion is less likely to be whipped by party leaders, but also less likely to bring the government down (unless it is a motion of no-confidence), then party unity should be much lower in these votes than in motions sponsored by the front bench of government.

It is important, therefore, to distinguish between private members' and government business in the House. In the Westminster parliamentary system tradition, the government and opposition parties usually assign their whips as tellers to verify the count during important legislative votes. This is done to make sure that the rank and file support the official party position. If, on the other hand, voting occurs over a private members' bill or any other motion that does not require party intervention, the tellers are selected from the backbenchers of the House. Scholars traditionally have used these separate whipped and unwhipped divisions in their analyses of voting in the United Kingdom: simply put, a vote is classified as whipped whenever the government party whip is identified in the records as the teller for a division (see, for example, Eggers and Spirling 2016, 572). Unfortunately, in the Canadian context, there are no party tellers to speak of, so one cannot use their names to identify whipped divisions (voting is done by calling the names of MPs, not by walking through the division lobbies). Nevertheless, since party pressure is much more likely to be applied when voting occurs on a government motion, I used a different strategy to determine whether or not the party whipped a vote. This coding method determined if voting occurred on motions introduced by members of the cabinet (which should be closest to whipped divisions) or by a private member. I employ this distinction in the last analysis of this chapter, where one model uses the individual loyalty score for all votes and another only government-related votes (these last results are presented in the online appendix to this chapter). In the latter model, I identified these divisions by locating the original sponsor of the motion in Hansard: whenever a division occurred over a motion or bill introduced by a member of the cabinet, I coded it as a government vote. I also considered amendments to these motions or bills to be government-related.

Electoral Pressure

I begin by looking at the influence of electoral pressure on party loyalty using three different types of analysis: the relationship between election timing and party loyalty; the influence of the size of the electorate on party support; and the relationship between electoral competition and legislative votes. I conducted these empirical analyses to validate three of the most common hypotheses found in the literature about the development of partisanship in the Canadian Parliament – namely, that (1) the timing of elections favoured the selection of more independent candidates; (2) the increase in the franchise and the growth of the voting population promoted greater party unity; and (3) electoral competition at the riding level led to a surge in partisan activities in the legislative arena.

Election Timing, 1867–1878

Recall that the first three federal elections were conducted by a show of hands in public and held over the course of several weeks.[3] Most political scientists consider the introduction of same-day elections and the secret ballot to explain why party unity surged after the third Parliament (see, for example, Patten 2017, 3). This transformation can be explained by the governing party's holding earlier elections in the most partisan ridings first, and elections in the more competitive ridings later. Candidates took advantage of this situation by waiting to align themselves with the party most likely to win the general election. Once in Parliament, these "loose fish" tended to side with the cabinet during legislative votes to secure patronage in their riding. These "ministerialists," however, also remained highly independent, and thus contributed to reducing the overall unity of the governing party.

If this account is correct, we should expect that candidates elected in the later stages of an election to have, on average, lower levels of party loyalty. Table 5.1 shows the results of a linear regression analysis where the dependent variable measures how frequently each member voted with the cabinet in the first three Parliaments. Note that this model uses a slightly different measure of party loyalty than the one described above. Since party lines were often blurred in the first few parliamentary terms, it is much easier to measure how often an individual MP voted with the majority position of the cabinet, while controlling for party affiliation in the analysis.[4] Because I am primarily interested in establishing whether MPs elected later were more likely to be independent from the party in government, the main variable of interest in this model is the day of the election, which ranges from 0 (the first day of polling) to 83 (the last possible day of polling). Election polling day is also interacted with a dummy variable indicating whether an MP is identified as a member of the governing party – Liberal or Conservative, depending on the term.[5] Finally, the model adds three

Table 5.1 Election Timing, 1867–1874

Variable	
Intercept	0.43 (0.05)***
Ministry	0.10 (0.02)***
Government	0.45 (0.04)***
Colonial	−0.01 (0.02)
Maritimes	0.14 (0.02)***
Quebec	−0.09 (0.02)***
Parliament 2	−0.00 (0.02)
Parliament 3	−0.04 (0.03)
Days	−0.00 (0.00)˙
Government × Days	0.00 (0.00)
Adj. R^2	0.68
N	575

***$p < 0.001$; **$p < 0.01$; *$p < 0.05$; ˙$p < 0.1$.

Note: Ordinary least squares regression. Standard errors were corrected to control for autocorrelation and heteroscedasticity. The dependent variable is an index ranging from 0 to 1, indicating how often a member supported the governing party during legislative votes.

additional control variables: the region of the member's riding, whether or not the member was in the cabinet, and whether or not the member previously had served in a colonial assembly.[6] Since the model pools data from three different parliamentary terms, it also contains two dummy variables to control for specific time effects in the estimations (the baseline is the first Parliament).[7]

The results in table 5.1 confirm that members elected at later polling dates are more likely to have lower levels of party loyalty when compared to members elected at the beginning of the election. However, there are no differences between members of the opposition and supporters of the governing party (either Liberal or Conservative, depending on the term). Had government patronage played a more important role, we would have expected lower levels of loyalty in this latter group.[8] The most important finding, however, is that members of the governing party were more likely to be loyal to the cabinet. The same is true for ministers. On average, if we compare members who were classified as government supporters and those who were in the opposition, we find a forty-five-point difference in their loyalty score in the first three Parliaments.[9] Since Westminster-style parliamentary systems provide the most incentives for members to be loyal when they are in government, it is not surprising that unity is much higher when the party controls the executive. The results also indicate that members who held a seat in a colonial assembly were also more likely to remain independent from the parties, which suggests that these members might have relied more on their local standings to get elected in earlier terms.

Population Size, 1867–1935

The second analysis of the influence of electoral pressure on party loyalty considers the effect of the size of the population in a riding and the extent of the electoral franchise. One of the most popular explanations of why party unity increased over time is linked to the expansion of the franchise and the growing number of voters, especially after 1898. This account follows from the British experience, where researchers have argued that the franchise reforms of the nineteenth century increased incentives for members to support their party in the legislative arena. Two processes explain this change. First, with the growing number of voters, members no longer could rely exclusively on their own resources to get elected. Most candidates now had to work with vote brokers and party associations to mobilize a large number of supporters in their district, and ultimately to win a seat in Parliament. In turn, this new approach forced members to collaborate more with party leaders, both in the legislature and back at home. Second, because parties increasingly had to mobilize a growing number of voters, they also began to make more programmatic appeals during election campaigns. A consequence of this new strategy was that voters now expected their representatives to deliver on these promises. Thus, incentives to support the party rose even more because voters now could be mobilized not only on the basis of the party's electoral promises, but also on its record of achievement in the legislature.

This was the British experience. As we saw in chapter 3, however, the relationship between the increasing size of the electorate and party unity is not as straightforward in the Canadian case. First, although it excluded poorer voters, the franchise in Canada was always relatively larger than in Britain. Second, the population of Canadian ridings remained comparatively small during most of the nineteenth and early twentieth centuries, even after the franchise was expanded in 1898 to remove most of the property and income qualifications for voting.[10] Nevertheless, since the franchise narrative is such a powerful account of party development, in the analysis presented below I attempt to validate this hypothesis by looking at the relationship between the size of the electorate in the riding and the loyalty of members towards their party.

I begin by considering the statistical association between population size and party loyalty. Figure 5.1 summarizes the results of a series of linear regression models run separately by parliamentary term. In these analyses, the dependent variable is the loyalty score index for either the Conservatives or Liberals, depending on the party affiliation of the member. Note that I removed independents and third party candidates from the data. I limited the analysis to the period between 1867 and 1935 because those years saw the most growth in partisanship in the House of Commons. I obtained the population in each riding

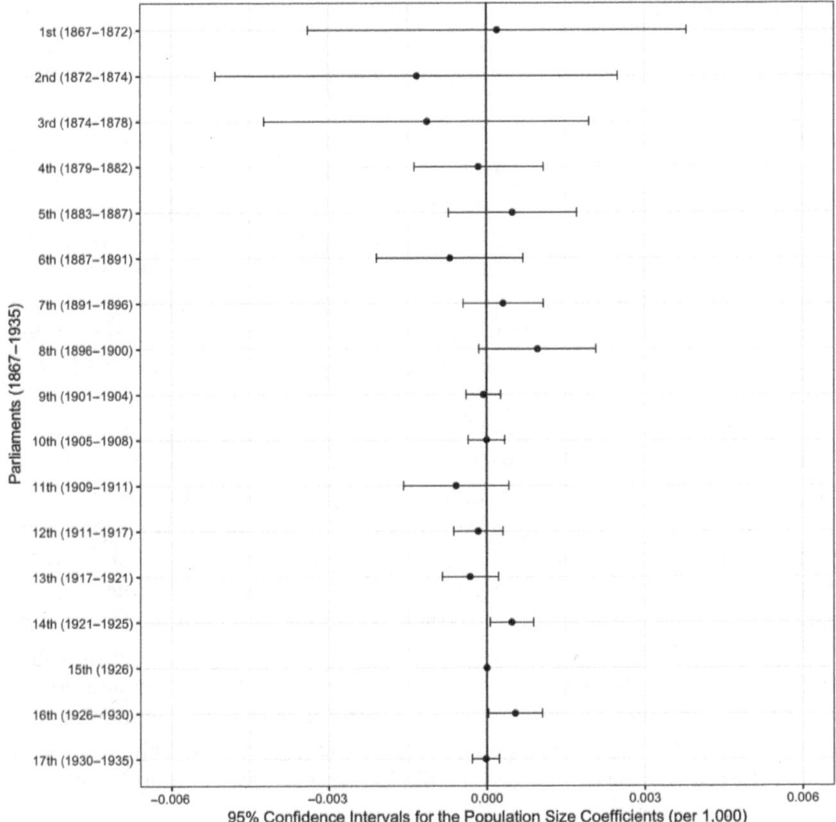

Figure 5.1 Influence of the Franchise on Party Loyalty, 1867–1935

from the decennial censuses.[11] The other variables included in the regression are the same as those found in table 5.1.[12] Note also that I did not pool the datasets into a single model because the goal here was to see whether the growth in the number of voters is associated with higher loyalty scores over time.[13]

In figure 5.1, each dot represents the unique effect that riding population size (per 1,000 residents) has on loyalty scores during a specific term. I obtained these estimates from the regression coefficients, holding other variables (region, cabinet member, and governing party member) constant. The bars on the left- and right-hand sides of each point estimate show the 95 per cent confidence intervals; whenever confidence intervals overlap with zero on the *x* axis, one cannot conclude that population size had a significant effect on loyalty scores in that term.

The figure shows that this lack of significant effect was indeed the case in fifteen out of seventeen Parliaments between 1867 and 1935. In other words, population size does not seem to have had a major influence on the growth of partisanship over time, especially during the first seven parliamentary terms, or even after 1898, when the franchise was expanded to include most men over age twenty-one. We do see a positive relationship between riding population size and party loyalty in 1921, after most women were allowed to vote for the first time, but by then party unity was already high in the legislative arena. Note also that the relationship between population size and party loyalty was negative (but not significant) in the previous term, which also witnessed an increase in the size of the voting population when the franchise was partially expanded to include women in the Canadian armed forces and any female relatives of soldiers.

To summarize, there is not much evidence that riding population size is associated with higher levels of party loyalty for either Conservative or Liberal MPs before 1935. In other words, comparing members who sat in the same Parliament, those who represented larger ridings were not, on average, more likely to have higher loyalty scores than those from less populous ridings. Furthermore, the relationship between these two variables does not become stronger over time. Canada's population experienced unprecedented growth between 1867 and 1935, and the franchise was expanded in 1898 and again in 1917 and 1921, yet except for the Parliaments of 1921–5 and 1926–30, the models do not confirm the existence of a positive relationship between riding population size and party loyalty. These findings suggest that the growth of the eligible voting population cannot be on its own a valid explanation for the development of legislative party voting unity in Canada.

Electoral Competition, 1867–1974

If the size of the voting population cannot account for the growth of party voting unity over time, perhaps electoral competition is a more relevant and revealing factor. The relationship between these two variables can be explained by two distinct processes. First, it is possible that members who were elected with smaller margins were more likely to remain independent of their party than those elected with larger margins. Second, it is also possible that, during the late nineteenth and early twentieth centuries, the relationship between these two variables became stronger as the number of parties competing in each riding increased and elections became more competitive.

Since incumbents who represent safe ridings receive very little electoral advantage from dissent (Kam 2009, 158), we should find that a high (low) margin of victory in the previous election is associated with a higher (lower) level of party loyalty in the subsequent Parliament. There is also the possibility that members who were elected with wider margins might have represented less partisan ridings on average, and that these members were rewarded for their independence. I return to these considerations below.

To determine whether electoral competition is related to higher levels of party loyalty, figure 5.2 presents the results of a series of linear regressions for each Parliament between 1867 and 1974. The period ends in 1974 because a change to the ballot structure in 1970 placed the party affiliation below the candidate's name for the first time. The figure also includes two different measures of electoral competition. On the first plot, the variable of interest is the effective number of parties (Laakso and Taagepera's index presented in figure 2.1 in chapter 2).[14] On the next plot is the winning candidate's margin of victory, obtained by subtracting the percentage of the vote received by the second-place candidate from the winner's percentage.

As in the previous analysis, each plot in figure 5.2 reports the estimated unique effects that the effective number of parties (or the margin of victory) had on a member's loyalty score during a specific parliamentary term. I obtained these results from the same models used in figure 5.1, but I substituted population size for the measures of electoral competitiveness.[15]

The regression analysis fails to confirm that electoral pressure systematically influenced legislative voting. This holds true for all but a total of five Parliaments in the two models. There are no clear patterns in the relationship between electoral competition and party loyalty. In some Parliaments, the effect is positive, meaning that members elected with larger margins (or with a lower effective number of parties) were more likely to have higher loyalty scores, while in others, the opposite is true.

These results are in sharp contrast with those of Cox (1987, 150), who found that the increasing competition in British elections explains the development of party unity during the nineteenth century. Although Cox's expectation is that MPs elected in more partisan districts would be pressured to support their party more, we must also consider the possibility that electoral security provided some incumbents with a greater level of independence from their caucus, and that this behaviour could even have been rewarded by voters in certain constituencies. Unfortunately, it is not possible to test this two-effect hypothesis directly because the dataset does not have an independent measure of riding partisanship – the proxy for such partisanship is election result, which is determined by other factors as well. However, the fact that I find no significant influence of electoral competition on party loyalty in the first Parliament (by either electoral margin or the effective number of parties) suggests, at least for this term, that electoral safety did not influence legislative behaviour. Since all the MPs in this Parliament were elected for the first time, their nonexistent voting records in the House of Commons could not have influenced the results of the first election.

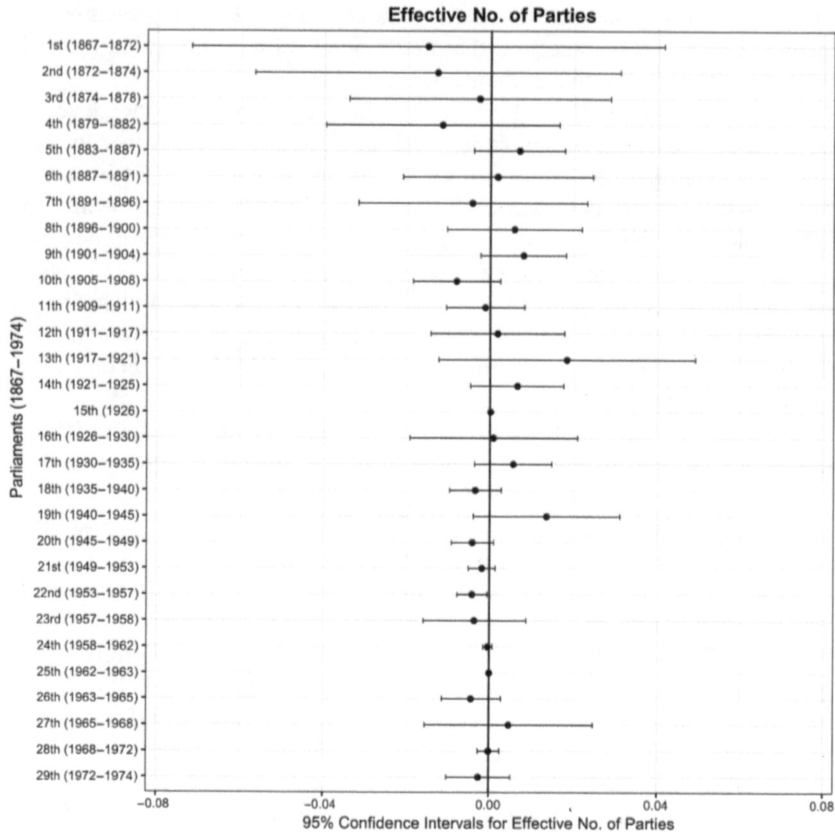

Figure 5.2 Influence of Competition on Party Loyalty, 1867–1974

Promotions and Patronage

Could the lure of promotions and patronage opportunities provide incentives for members to support their party in the legislative arena? Both Cox (1987, 75) and Eggers and Spirling (2016, 583) argue that, in the British case, MPs might have been induced into voting with their party because of the promise of rewards offered by the government. Ministerial ambition thus could offer an incentive to toe the party line, especially if leaders tend to promote party faithfuls to the cabinet. In Canada, there are reasons to suspect that a similar set of incentives existed in Parliament, because the principle of responsible government was already in place at the time of Confederation. Between 1867 and 2015, more than 750 appointments were made to the cabinet, representing around

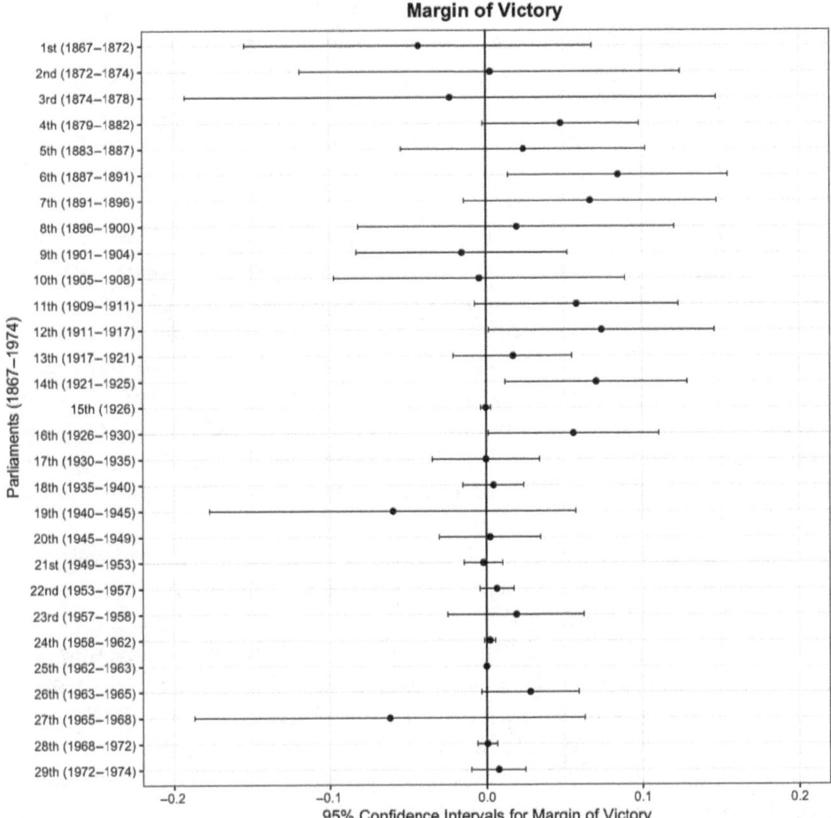

Figure 5.2 continued

17 per cent of all members elected to the House of Commons. On the other hand, there is also the possibility that promotions to the cabinet might not always have been awarded to the most loyal party supporters in the House, especially considering Canada's particular constitutional conventions. In fact, aside from making sure that each region is represented in the cabinet, prime ministers have long had also to appoint at least one English-speaking Catholic member, as well as one Protestant member from Quebec (Kam 2006, 562). These special requirements could have greatly limited the number of qualified candidates for ministerial appointments, especially if a party was unpopular in a region or among a group of voters.

Another promotion that could have been used to reward loyalty was Senate appointments. Prior to 1952, there was no pension plan to speak of for MPs

(O'Brien and Bosc 2009, 235). Instead, they mostly relied on their own personal fortunes to finance their retirement once they left Parliament. For many, an appointment to the Senate represented a guaranteed source of income into their old age, especially since senators had life-long tenure prior to 1965. Chubby Power was one who benefited from this tradition: after serving for thirty-eight years in the House of Commons, in 1955 he was appointed to the Senate, where he served until his death in 1968.

Being appointed to the Senate was not the only sinecure available to faithful party supporters. Some were appointed to the Bench, others served as lieutenant-governor or ended up in the public service. These types of patronage opportunities, however, became less frequent over time; only appointments to the Senate remained a constant post-parliamentary career source for those who left the House of Commons throughout the twentieth century (Ward 1963, 145). This explains why I consider this type of promotion as a reward for loyalty in the analysis presented below. These represent a total of 310 Senate appointments between 1867 and 2015, or around 7 per cent of all post-parliamentary careers (including deaths and retirements).

Finally, another type of reward granted in exchange for party loyalty was linked to patronage opportunities in the district. Recall that, following Confederation, Macdonald centralized the process of appointments to the bureaucracy in the hands of the executive. This assured that all these federal jobs now were controlled by the party leaders, either in Ottawa or back home in the ridings. Laurier and later Borden also perpetuated this practice, until the Civil Service Reform Act was adopted in 1918. Thus, the explanation for the rise in party loyalty could stem from the provision of patronage opportunities: members would support their party in the legislature if they received their fair share of jobs in the riding. These appointments could take several forms – inspector of weights and measures, sheriff, collector of customs, and so on – but these jobs were relatively limited and more frequently available in larger cities such as Montreal, Toronto, or Halifax.

A more readily available source of patronage, however, is found across almost all federal ridings at the time of Confederation: local postmasters. Postmasters were appointed by the federal government. They managed the local post offices in Canadian towns throughout the nineteenth and most of the twentieth centuries. In 1871 there were around four thousand rural post offices in Canada; this number peaked at thirteen thousand in 1911 and remained steady at twelve thousand until the 1950s (Amyot and Willis 2003, 38). As we saw in chapter 3, there is strong historical evidence that postmasters were appointed to office as a reward for their political service to the party. As Amyot and Willis explain: "Politics and politicians were quintessential players of the Canadian rural postal system ... and the available data largely confirms this preconception" (2003, 89). Postmasters were usually replaced (or fired) when there was a change of government in Ottawa. A former postmaster from Quebec summarized this practice by stating: "When the government changes, the post office changes."[16]

Since the position of postmaster was considered a political reward by MPs who supported the government, and since they expected to have the final say in the nomination of postmasters in their riding, we should expect to find a relationship between these appointments and party loyalty. Although MPs could recommend a specific candidate for the position of postmaster when a vacancy occurred in their riding, party leaders did not always follow these suggestions. They could be overridden by the minister of the post office or other cabinet ministers (Amyot and Willis 2003, 88). In this context, we can assume that these demands were much more likely to be heard when they originated from loyal party supporters on the government side (Gordon 1999, 10). Hence, we should find that MPs received on average more postmaster appointments in their ridings (or new post offices) as a reward for their service to the party.

In summary, I have identified three different sources of patronage opportunities that could have influenced legislative behaviour. The first two are linked to the rewards bestowed upon members for their support of the party in the legislature: appointments to the cabinet and the Senate. The third is only indirectly related to members and considers patronage in the riding. Here, the assumption is that members who were loyal to the government should have received more postmaster appointments than did less loyal members (or members of the opposition). I have no way of verifying if members actually fully controlled the appointment process for these positions. But the evidence provided above and in chapter 3 suggests that this is likely to have been the case, even after the adoption of the Civil Service Act reform in 1918, and possibly even until Canada Post became a Crown corporation in 1981.

To validate this inducement account of party development, I report in table 5.2 the results of three different analyses of the influence of party loyalty on (1) the probability of being named to the cabinet; (2) the probability of being named to the Senate; and (3) the number of postmaster appointments in an MP's riding. In all three models, the loyalty scores of members are lagged and averaged throughout their legislative career. In other words, unlike in the analyses presented above, which considered party loyalty in each term as the dependent variable, the model presented below includes a unique measure of party loyalty calculated across a member's career, until the parliamentary term when the MP was appointed to the cabinet or the Senate.[17] For postmaster appointments, the model uses a similar strategy by calculating the total number of new appointments in a member's riding throughout his or her career. I also use the same career loyalty average for this model as well.

Table 5.2 Promotion and Patronage Appointments, 1867–2011

Variable	Cabinet, 1867–2011	Senate, 1867–1984	Postal, 1867–1945
Intercept	−7.42 (1.50)***	−3.34 (0.59)***	−0.30 (6.08)
Career loyalty	6.64 (1.53)***	0.17 (0.57)	−1.39 (6.17)
Career length	0.08 (0.05)˙	0.12 (0.05)**	6.51 (1.01)***
Government side	−0.68 (0.07)***	0.21 (0.07)**	4.91 (1.84)**
Term served in cabinet		−0.08 (0.07)	
Quebec	0.31 (0.13)*	0.16 (0.18)	−9.58 (2.40)***
Maritimes	−0.08 (0.15)	0.87 (0.17)***	0.79 (3.83)
West	−0.24 (0.13)˙	0.40 (0.19)*	10.51 (4.52)*
Adj. R^2			0.24
N	3,146	2,864	1,356

***$p < 0.001$; **$p < 0.01$; *$p < 0.05$; ˙$p < 0.1$.

Note: The results in the first two columns are logistic regressions; the results in the third column are from an ordinary least squares regression. Standard errors were corrected to control for autocorrelation and heteroscedasticity. The dependent variable in the first (second) model indicates whether or not a member was promoted to the cabinet (Senate); the dependent variable in the third model is the number of postmasters appointed throughout a member's career.

The records of postmaster appointments come from the Post Offices and Postmasters database at Library and Archives Canada. This dataset indicates the name of the riding in which each postmaster was appointed between 1851 and 1981. I used an automated algorithm to match these riding names with the records from Elections Canada. Unfortunately, I could not match all of the records, so caution in the interpretation of the results is warranted.[18]

The second column of table 5.2 reports the results of the cabinet appointment analysis between 1867 and 2011. Since the dependent variable is a binary outcome, the model uses a logistic regression to determine the probability of being promoted to the front bench.[19] Aside from average career loyalty scores, the model also controls for the length of a member's tenure in the legislature (how many terms the MP served before retiring or being appointed to the cabinet), how many terms a member served on the government's side (when the MPs' party was in power), and regional dummy variables. The results confirm that previous loyalty mattered when it came to cabinet promotions. The coefficient for this variable is positive and significant. For instance, the likelihood of being appointed to the cabinet increased by 9 per cent for members with a perfect voting record over members who supported the party 90 per cent of the time during their legislative career. As well, the probability of being appointed to the cabinet declined with the time spent as a government backbencher: about 12 per cent after three terms. In short, this first analysis offers strong evidence to support the claim that party leaders rewarded party loyalty: MPs who supported their party more were also more likely to be promoted to the front benches of the House.

The third column of table 5.2 looks at the influence of loyalty on the probability of being appointed to the Senate. The model controls for the same variables as before, but this time the dependent variable is coded 1 if a member ended his or her career in the Senate, 0 otherwise. The period for this analysis ranges from 1867 to 2011, and excludes members who were elected after 1984, since some of these members have not yet retired or left the House of Commons. In other words, the analysis considers only members who completed their legislative career and left the House of Commons, voluntarily or involuntarily, between 1867 and 1984.

Unlike cabinet promotions, the model confirms that career loyalty did not increase the probability of being appointed to the Senate. Beside regional controls, the only two variables significant in this model are length of service and time spent on the government bench. Members such as Chubby Power who had longer legislative careers tended to be rewarded more. For each additional term served, the probability of being appointed to the Senate increased by about 1 per cent. The same was true for members who sat on the government side of the House: each additional term served increased the probability of being appointed to the Senate by about 1.7 per cent.

Finally, the fourth column of table 5.2 considers the relationship between party loyalty and postmaster appointments in the riding between 1867 and 1945, a period selected to maximize the chances of detecting a relationship between these two variables. Although MPs could still influence the appointment of postmasters after the Second World War, this practice was already becoming highly unpopular in the 1930s and appointments increasingly favoured veterans and more qualified candidates (see, for example, Debates 1932, 4955; Debates 1942, 4514).

The results presented in table 5.2 are from a linear regression, since the dependent variable is the total number of postmasters appointed in a member's riding throughout his or her career (this variable ranges from 1 to 286, with a mean of 18). The results demonstrate that party loyalty had no significant influence on the number of appointments in the riding. As expected, members who served longer careers, or who spent more time on the government side, did appoint more postmasters on average: since the dependent variable measures the total number of appointments in the riding during the MP's whole career, the longer the member served, the more appointments they should have received. Nevertheless, it is reassuring to confirm that members who sat on the government side for longer periods received more postmaster appointments on average than did members of the opposition party. Were MPs more likely to be rewarded for their loyalty only when they sat on the government side? One can verify this hypothesis by adding an interactive term to measure the relationship between career loyalty and the total number of terms served on the government

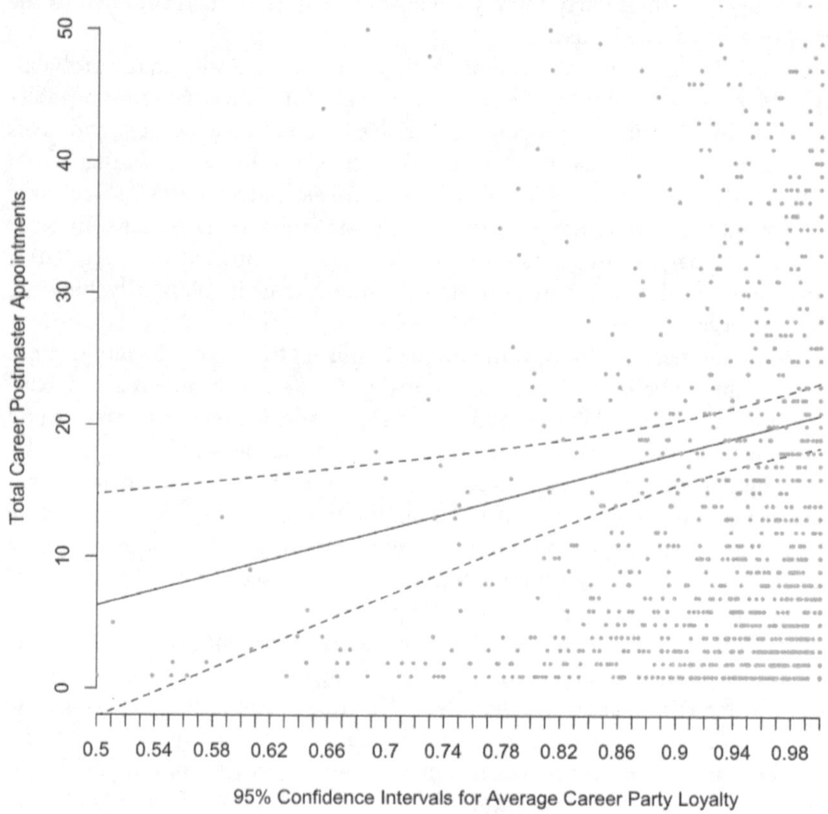

Figure 5.3 Influence of Party Loyalty on Patronage, 1867–1945

side (career loyalty × total government terms). This new variable changes the results somewhat. We now find that party loyalty had a positive and significant influence on the number of postmaster appointments in the riding. Figure 5.3 summarizes this finding by showing the relationship between party loyalty and the total number of postmaster appointments in a member's riding between 1867 and 1945.[20] Essentially, this is the same model as in table 5.2 (fourth column), with an added interaction variable between the total number of terms served in the government and career loyalty.

The figure shows the positive relationship between the two variables. I obtained these predictions from the regression equation by setting the values of the model at their mean (for a hypothetical government member from Ontario). Each point in the figure represents the intersection between the average career loyalty score of a member and the total number of postmasters appointed in the member's riding. The solid line represents the predicted values calculated from the model (with the 95 per cent confidence intervals represented by the dotted lines). We can see that supporting the party when a member sat on the government side was rewarded more: those who were loyal throughout their career tended to receive additional postmaster appointments. If we assume that the parties rewarded loyal members with additional patronage positions in their riding, and that these kinds of appointments increased a member's chance of re-election, then we are given a powerful inducement mechanism to explain why government supporters were more likely to be loyal.

To summarize, MPs could expect to be rewarded for their loyalty by being appointed to the cabinet or by receiving more patronage positions in their riding. This does not hold, however, for Senate appointments; perhaps nominations to this chamber were not frequent enough to be statistically significant. It might be interesting to consider other post-career opportunities, such as judgeships, lieutenant-governorships, or additional public service positions, to see if members were also granted these promotions in exchange for their record of service to the party. Although the inducement account provides the first potential explanation for the rise of partisanship observed in the House of Commons over time, this cannot be the whole story. Indeed, cabinet positions were always available to MPs at the time of Confederation, yet party unity gradually increased after the meeting of the first Parliament. So unless members "learned" about the potential rewards of being promoted to the cabinet, this finding cannot on its own explain the development of party-line voting in the House. Patronage appointments perhaps better account for this development: any new member could have quickly realized that federal jobs in the riding were more likely to be awarded to loyal government supporters. Still, even though the analysis looked at only one set of appointments and the data were only partially matched, it is striking even to find a relationship between these two variables: this is the first systematic empirical evidence showing a direct link between legislative behaviour and patronage appointments in Canadian political science research.

Career and Replacement Effects

It remains to be seen whether the socialization of members can explain the development of legislative party voting unity over time. Recall that this account presupposes that members learn to collaborate together throughout their legislative careers. Thus, the process of socialization implies that lawmakers rapidly learn the importance of loyalty and solidarity when they first enter Parliament

(Kam 2009, 13). These norms are also expected to become stronger over time, since new MPs are "less likely to have been socialized into acceptable patterns of parliamentary behaviour," and thus "are more likely to dissent than their more experienced colleagues" (58).

The second mechanism by which socialization could have affected the development of party loyalty relates to the period in which MPs began their legislative career – that is, an increase in party unity might be observed because of the changing norms and values of members. We know that MPs who were elected in the decades following Confederation were likely to be less disciplined than those elected in later terms, especially after 1900. In this context, party unity could have increased with the gradual replacement of these less loyal party supporters (Eggers and Spirling 2016, 578–9). It is also possible that members who entered Parliament at different times (such as when their party was in the opposition, or right after the election of a new popular party leader) collectively could have experienced a different environment, which might have influenced their willingness to support the party throughout their career. The case of Jean Chrétien's first years as prime minister serves as a good example here. Kam (2006, 570–3) shows that Liberal Party members who had previously supported his rivals in the leadership campaign (John Nunziata, for example) were less likely to be promoted to the cabinet and more likely to dissent in subsequent terms.

In short, the socialization account of party support potentially operates at two distinct levels: one through legislative careers, the other relating to the period in which members first entered Parliament. In the analysis below, I conceptualize legislative careers by counting the number of terms each member served.[21] This variable ranges from 1 to 13, depending on the member. I measure the moment when members entered the House of Commons by grouping them into different cohorts, ranging from 1 to 40. Note that the cohort number remains constant throughout a member's legislative career.[22]

The goal of this analysis is thus to determine if legislative career length and election cohorts are associated with higher levels of party loyalty. Much like the analysis of the influence of electoral competition above, I include in figure 5.4 the results of a series of linear regressions for each Parliament between 1872 and 2011. The figure reports the estimated unique effects of the number of terms served (first plot) and of election cohorts (second plot) on the individual loyalty score of a member during each legislative term. The models also control for whether an MP was a member of the governing party (Liberal or Conservative, depending on the term), the region the member represented, or whether the member had a position in the cabinet.[23]

The findings reported in figure 5.4 do not provide enough evidence to support the claim that the socialization of members influenced legislative behaviour.

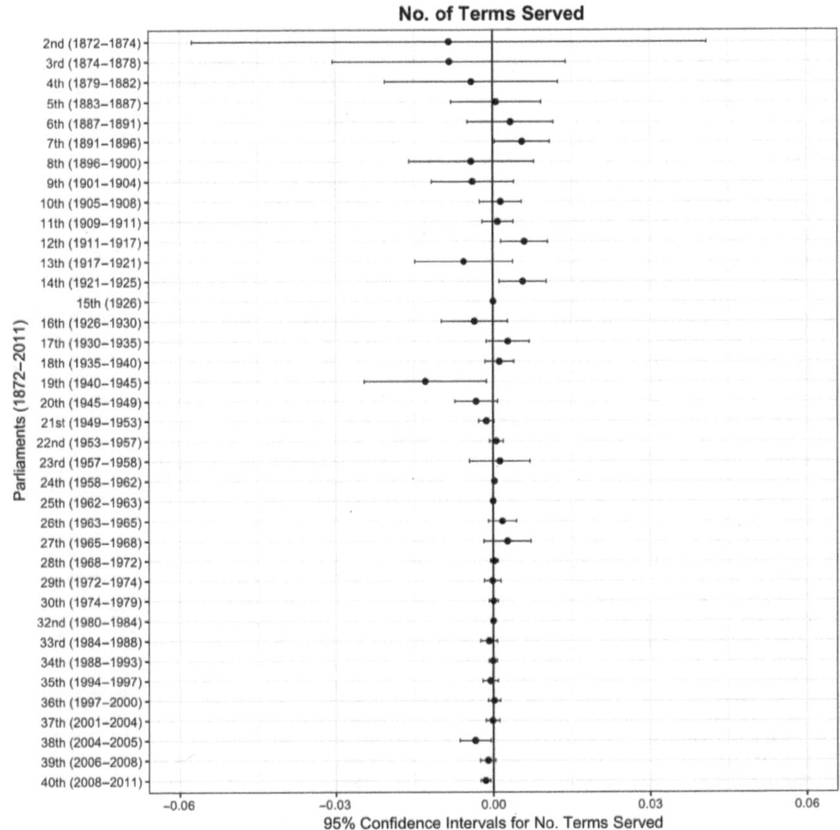

Figure 5.4 Influence of Careers and Cohorts on Party Loyalty, 1872–2011

Both the number of terms served and the election cohorts of a member are not systematically related to loyalty scores. With regards to the number of terms served, the influence of this variable does seem to increase over the first seven Parliaments, but the effect becomes positive only in the fifth term (1883–7) and statistically significant only in the seventh (1891–6). After Wilfrid Laurier became prime minister in 1896 (the eighth Parliament), the influence of legislative career length again turns negative, and remains more or less close to zero for the remainder of the study period.

Likewise, the effect of cohorts also appears to be weakly related to individual party loyalty scores. For instance, members elected in later terms seem to have been more loyal on average during the nineteenth century, but this relationship is not statistically significant. Furthermore, it appears that members elected in

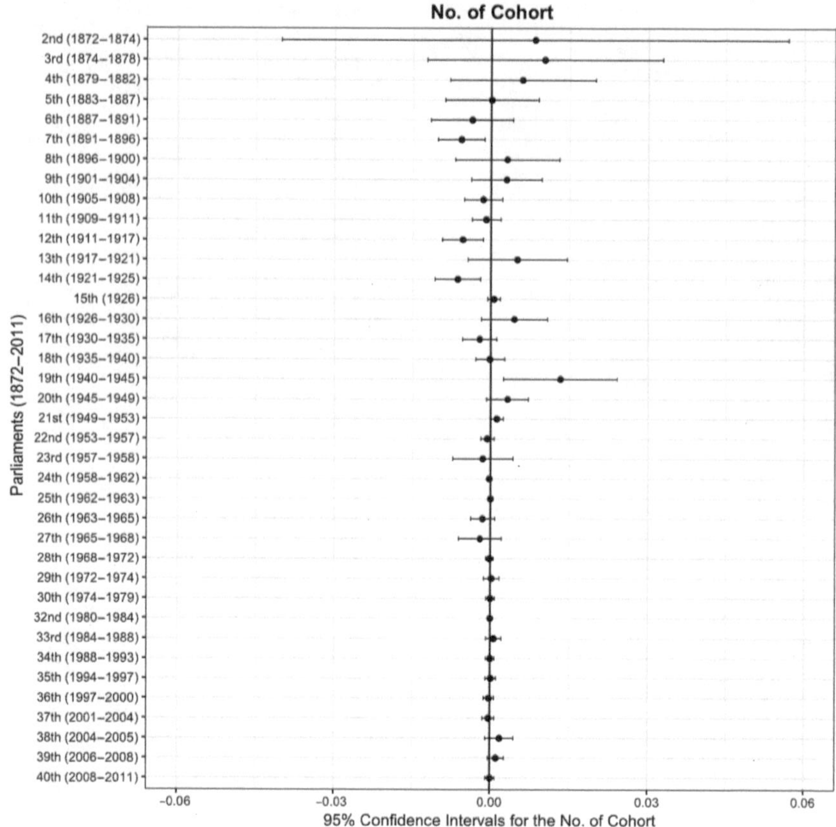

Figure 5.4 continued

later cohorts actually could have been less loyal, such as in the seventh Parliament. In this term, the average marginal effect of this variable is around 0.75 per cent, meaning that, if we compare members who were first elected in the sixth Parliament with members elected in the seventh Parliament (while holding all the other variables in the model constant), the second group of MPs has a loyalty score 1.5 percentage points lower than the first. Similar to career length, as we move towards the end of the period under study, the average marginal effect of cohorts on loyalty scores becomes smaller, mainly because there is increasingly less variation in the dependent variable, which is now closer to 1 (perfect loyalty) for most members of the House.

Overall, then, neither of the last two analyses offers much evidence to confirm that the length of legislative careers and election cohorts are systematically related to higher levels of party loyalty – especially during the first few parliamentary terms, when the growth in partisanship was strongest. These findings cast doubt on the sociological explanation of party development in the Canadian Parliament. If we assume that career length represents an adequate representation of the socialization process that members experienced within their party while in office, then we must conclude that this cannot on its own explain the development of party loyalty in the House of Commons. The same could be said about the election cohorts of members: those elected in later terms do not appear to have been more loyal on average.

Cumulative Analysis

It is now possible to take a more comprehensive look at the different factors that could influence legislative behaviour, and try to verify if electoral pressure and cohort or career incentive variables explain the rise in partisanship observed over time in Canada.[24] Aside from loyalty scores, which represent the dependent variable in the regressions described below, the models also add several new control variables to capture the effects of other determinants of legislative behaviour. First, the analysis controls for the voting participation of members, which I calculated by how often a member voted in a given term.[25] Second, the model controls for electoral competition in a riding by using the effective number of candidates in an election (Laakso and Taagepera's index). Third, the model includes a measure of the size of the electorate by adding a variable that reports the total number of voters in the riding in an election.[26] These last two measures evaluate the effects of electoral pressure on partisan loyalty.

The models contain several parliamentary status variables as well, such as cabinet membership, whether an MP was a member of the governing party, whether the MP was elected as part of a minority government, and the number of terms the MP served in Parliament.[27] I added these variables to measure career incentives and the effects of being in the governing party. As before, the model includes regional dummy variables (Quebec, Ontario, the Maritimes, and the western provinces), and identifies the forty different election cohorts for every sitting MP.[28] The analysis also adds a parliamentary term component to the models that represents the number of the Parliament. I also squared these last two variables, and added them to control for variations over time and for the replacement of members.[29]

Table 5.3 presents the results of the analysis separately for Liberal and Conservative MPs; this was necessary because the election data were pooled into one cumulative data file.[30] The table includes three different specifications: the second and fifth columns report the results of a linear regression for the whole period, while columns 3–4 and 6–7 divide the data according to the structural break points previously identified in chapter 4 (before/after the sixteenth Parliament).[31]

One of the most important results from this table relates to the influence of the government variable: government backbenchers were systematically more likely to toe the party line. The electoral pressure variable in the cumulative models for the whole period appear to have the expected effect on the dependent variable for both the Liberal and Conservative parties. In both cases, the total number of voters in the riding is related to higher levels of party loyalty. This effect is not robust, however, across model specifications (or in the negative binomial analysis included in the online appendix to this chapter). On the other hand, we find mixed results for the socialization variables (cohort and number of terms served). For the cohort variable (cohort number + cohort number squared), the signs imply a convex relationship, meaning that this effect was negative in the first few parliamentary terms, then stabilized in the later terms; however, these variables are not significant across specifications. Similarly, the number of terms served had a negative influence on the loyalty scores of Conservative Party members, a result that is contrary to the socialization hypothesis. Finally, we find some evidence that electoral incentives matter. For both Liberal and Conservative MPs, the impact of the effective number of candidates fails to influence loyalty in the House significantly in three of the six models (the results in the online appendix that focus on government divisions show this as well). In the cumulative models, an increase in competitiveness is associated with higher levels of party loyalty for the Conservatives – although this result is not robust across specifications – but not for the Liberals.

The analysis also confirms that party loyalty increased over time but at a decreasing rate for both parties. This finding is illustrated in figure 5.5, which reports the mean-centred, term-specific effects of this variable, as measured by the cumulative models (the predicted level of loyalty of Conservative and Liberal members). Clearly, the plots show that the parliamentary term matters in explaining the growth of partisanship: the effect becomes increasingly important as we approach the 1940s, but stabilizes thereafter.

Furthermore, the analysis confirms that the influence of certain variables was not constant across the two periods identified by the change point models. Most of these differences were minor, but there are a few exceptions. For example, cabinet membership was not always significant for both parties, depending on the period under study. Even more surprising are the differences between the governing party variable before and after the sixteenth Parliament for the Liberals, a result that can be explained by the presence of minority governments. Indeed, this variable does not differentiate between opposition and

Table 5.3 Determinants of Individual Party Loyalty, by Party, Cumulative Analysis, 1867–2011

	Conservative Party			Liberal Party		
	Parliament					
Variable	1st–40th	1st–15th	16th–40th	1st–40th	1st–15th	16th–40th
Intercept	0.81 (0.01)***	0.76 (0.02)***	0.90 (0.01)***	0.79 (0.01)***	0.68 (0.03)***	0.73 (0.02)***
Government	0.02 (0.00)***	0.02 (0.01)**	0.01 (0.00)***	0.01 (0.00)***	0.03 (0.01)***	–0.01 (0.00)***
Cabinet	0.01 (0.00)***	0.03 (0.01)***	0.00 (0.00)	0.00 (0.00)	0.01 (0.01)	0.01 (0.00)***
Minority	–0.01 (0.00)***	0.04 (0.02)**	–0.01 (0.00)***	–0.02 (0.00)***	–0.02 (0.01)˙	–0.02 (0.00)***
Number of terms	–0.01 (0.00)***	–0.01 (0.00)*	0.00 (0.00)	0.00 (0.00)	0.00 (0.01)	0.00 (0.00)
Participation	0.04 (0.01)***	0.05 (0.02)***	0.04 (0.01)***	0.04 (0.01)***	0.09 (0.02)***	0.03 (0.01)***
Effective number of parties	0.01 (0.00)**	0.01 (0.00)*	0.00 (0.00)	0.00 (0.00)	–0.01 (0.01)	0.01 (0.00)***
Total number of voters	0.00 (0.00)***	0.00 (0.00)	0.00 (0.00)	0.00 (0.00)***	0.00 (0.00)	0.00 (0.00)
Maritimes	–0.01 (0.00)˙	–0.01 (0.01)	0.00 (0.00)	–0.02 (0.01)***	–0.07 (0.01)***	0.00 (0.00)*
Quebec	–0.03 (0.01)***	–0.04 (0.01)***	–0.01 (0.00)***	–0.01 (0.00)***	–0.05 (0.01)***	0.00 (0.00)
West	–0.01 (0.00)***	–0.01 (0.01)	0.00 (0.00)	–0.04 (0.01)***	–0.11 (0.02)***	–0.02 (0.00)***
Parliament	0.02 (0.00)***	0.03 (0.00)***	0.01 (0.00)***	0.02 (0.00)***	0.05 (0.01)***	0.01 (0.00)**
Parliament^2	0.00 (0.00)***	0.00 (0.00)**	0.00 (0.00)**	0.00 (0.00)***	0.00 (0.00)***	0.01 (0.00)***
Cohort	–0.01 (0.00)***	0.00 (0.00)	0.00 (0.00)	–0.01 (0.00)	0.00 (0.01)	0.01 (0.00)
Cohort^2	0.00 (0.00)	0.00 (0.00)	0.00 (0.00)	0.00 (0.00)***	0.00 (0.00)	0.00 (0.00)
Adj. R^2	0.30	0.19	0.11	0.27	0.35	0.14
N	3,975	1,629	2,346	4,643	1,580	3,063

***$p < 0.001$; **$p < 0.01$; *$p < 0.05$; ˙$p < 0.1$

Note: Ordinary least squares regressions. Standard errors were corrected to control for autocorrelation and heteroscedasticity. The dependent variable is the individual loyalty score by parliamentary term for each member of the Conservative Party (columns 2–4) and the Liberal Party (columns 5–7).

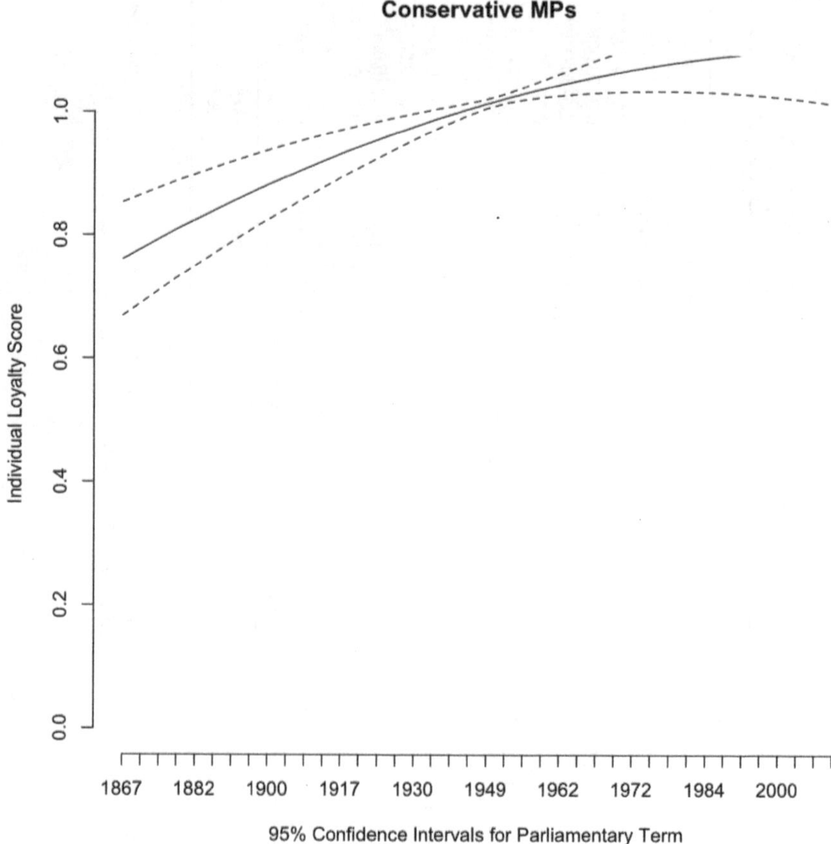

Figure 5.5 Influence of Time on Party Loyalty, 1867–2011

government status (that is, government × minority government). When this interaction term is included in the analysis, the conditional effect of being in the government becomes positive and significant for the Liberals in the second period. Another important determinant of individual party loyalty relates to participation in House of Commons votes: the results confirm that MPs who were regularly absent from the House were less likely to support their caucuses as well, a finding that suggests that abstentions represented an alternative to open dissension in Parliament.

Overall, the cumulative analysis confirms that being a member of the governing party is associated with higher levels of loyalty. There was also an important increase, however, in the average level of partisanship in the legislature over time, and this is true in all the models. Neither of these findings is particularly

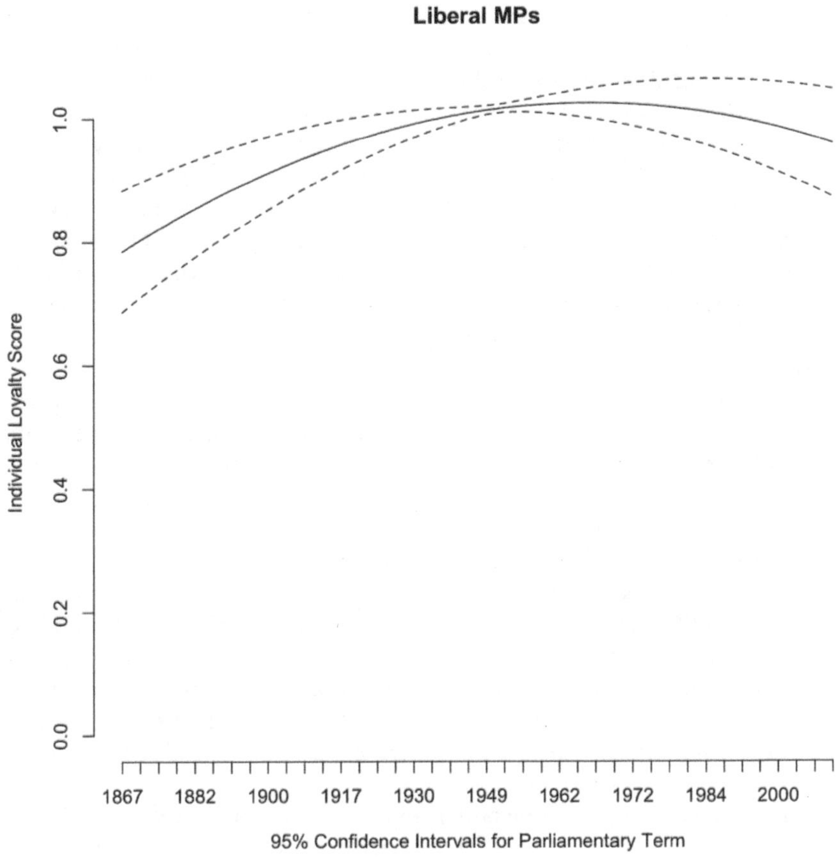

Figure 5.5 continued

surprising. What is perhaps more interesting is the confirmation that cohort- or career-specific effects are weakly related to this trend. The same is true for electoral incentives, which do not appear to be systematically associated with higher levels of party loyalty. There is strong evidence, therefore, that two of the most commonly identified mechanisms in the comparative literature to explain the development of party unity fail to be relevant in the Canadian context.

Conclusion

In this chapter, I set out to validate some of the most common theories found in the literature to explain the development of political parties in the Canadian House of Commons. The focus was on individual-level determinants of party voting loyalty, and I conducted different empirical tests to verify if electoral pressure, patronage opportunities, or the socialization of members could explain the rising levels in partisanship observed in the legislature over time.

The analysis found that electoral pressure – whether the day of the election, the number of voters in the riding, or electoral competition – is not systematically correlated with higher levels of party loyalty. Similarly, with respect to the socialization of Members of Parliament, those who served for longer periods or who were elected in later terms were not necessarily more likely to have been more loyal to their party than were other members. These results were confirmed not only in specific legislative terms, but also in a series of pooled regression analyses that combined all Conservative and Liberal members across parliamentary terms.

The only evidence found to explain why members supported their party more is linked to the inducement-based explanation of partisanship. Averaging individual members' loyalty scores across their whole career reveals that those who voted with their party frequently were also more likely to be promoted to the cabinet. The same is true for patronage in the riding: loyal party supporters were more likely to receive new postmaster appointments the longer they served on the government benches. This last result, however, comes with a caveat: since the data on postmaster appointments are only partially matched to electoral ridings, and since the analysis failed to confirm that Senate appointments were more likely to be attributed to loyal party supporters, one must be careful in interpreting this finding. More work is required before one can conclude that patronage opportunities were at one point offered as a reward for party loyalty in the Canadian House of Commons.

The analysis did confirm that both members of the cabinet and those who sat on the government's backbenches supported their party more in the legislative arena, especially in the first few decades after Confederation, but these findings on their own cannot explain the growth of partisanship. The same logic applies to the inducement account: the convention of responsible government already existed at the time of Confederation, so ministers knew about the potential rewards of supporting party leaders when Parliament first met in 1867. We might ask, then, why was party unity not higher? Similarly, the growth of party-line voting observed over time cannot be a reflection of an abrupt change in the career objectives of House members. The results lend support to this interpretation by confirming that those elected in later terms were not more likely to be loyal, and that those who had longer legislative careers were not necessarily socialized into supporting their party more.

There is, in summary, no "smoking gun" to suggest that any of the individual-level factors identified in the literature can explain the development of legislative party voting unity in the Canadian context. The results of the cumulative analysis I have presented here do confirm that time – as measured by the parliament and parliament squared variables in the model – is strongly correlated with higher levels of party loyalty. In other words, across parliamentary terms, members became much more likely to have higher loyalty scores – controlling for the other factors in the model, such as electoral pressure, the number of terms served, the legislative cohort, and the location of a member's riding. But what does time represent exactly in these models? Although I looked at whether specific events – such as the introduction of same-day elections, the secret ballot, and the expansion of the franchise – could explain the development of party unity after 1867, none of these changes seems to matter much for the growth in partisanship in the House of Commons. Perhaps this transformation more closely followed the changing content of the legislative agenda, to which I turn in the next chapter.

Chapter Six

How Parties Unite

In this chapter, I focus on the outcome of parliamentary votes to determine if particular bills or motions promoted or hindered party unity. This type of analysis was not possible in the previous chapter, because I measured party loyalty at the individual level and averaged it throughout each legislative term. Here I take a different approach by looking at the aggregate outcome of recorded divisions separately. The study thus moves away from individual members and instead examines whether the legislative agenda could have influenced party unity. The objective remains the same – to identify what factors best explain the growth of partisanship in the Canadian Parliament over time – but the level of analysis now changes.

In order to measure partisan divisions during legislative votes, the analysis presented below uses a common measure of party unity: the Rice index. As we saw in chapter 4, this measure is obtained by taking the absolute value of the difference between the numbers of votes cast by the majority position (either yeas or nays) minus the number of votes cast by the minority position (either yeas or nays) of a party in a recorded division. This difference is then divided by the total number of votes cast by the party (minority + majority votes in the caucus). Note that this index ranges from 0 (perfect split) to 1 (perfect unity). The analysis below covers more than 10,893 measures of this index for both the Liberal and Conservative parties: one for each individual recorded division between 1867 and 2011, when the data are available.

This level of analysis offers several advantages in estimating how parties were influenced by the legislative agenda. Indeed, we can look at the context in which each vote was recorded during the debates. For example, we can see if motions introduced by cabinet members (as opposed to private members) or by members of the same party (as opposed to members of the opposing party) influenced party unity. The same can be achieved by looking at certain types of bills (public or private), by considering budget votes (motions or resolutions from the committees of supply and ways and means), and by studying the specific stages of the legislative process (first, second, or third reading of a bill). In addition, we can use this information to determine if specific issues (religious questions, tariffs, civil service, railways, canals, and so on) were more likely to generate intra-party divisions. And finally, the Rice index allows us to consider different party-level variables when the data are pooled across parliamentary terms. For instance, we can determine if parties in government were on average more unified than those in the opposition. Similarly, we can see if smaller party caucuses (or minority governments) were less likely to experience dissension than larger ones.

Recall that the theory I outlined in chapter 3 made several predictions about the role of the legislative agenda in explaining the growth of partisanship in the Canadian Parliament over time. I argued that motions introduced by private members would be more likely to generate intra-party dissension than motions sponsored by cabinet members. The logic here is that, without party constraints, members would be more likely to introduce controversial bills, amendments, and motions. It follows that, in order to promote caucus unity, party leaders had a strong incentive to limit access to the floor during debates.

In the decades following Confederation, the Standing Orders of the House of Commons offered several opportunities for members to intervene in the legislative process. They could, for example, propose amendments to government bills, alter the budget, or introduce public and private bills in most of the sittings of the House. Several of these motions were debatable, which meant that they could be amended, and a recorded division could be taken on the amendment. In 1913, Conservative Prime Minister Robert Borden calculated that between fifty and seventy motions could be debated when a single financial bill was introduced in the House (Stewart 1977, 212). Most of these opportunities offered members the chance to introduce controversial amendments, and the government was virtually powerless to prevent them from reaching the floor. I identified several of these contentious issues in chapter 2, and noted that the country's party system was transformed after conflicts emerged over specific regional questions such as religion, language, foreign policy, and custom tariffs. Since members had the opportunity to discuss almost anything at will in the earlier days of Confederation, it should not be surprising to find that party unity was much weaker when voting occurred on these controversial issues – that is, until a general revision of the rules was carried out between 1906 and 1913. The new rules had a profound effect on the organization of the House of Commons: they formally centralized control of the legislative agenda in the hands of party leaders, and limited the number of opportunities for private members to intervene during debates.

Similar to my approach in the previous chapter, the analysis I present below looks at the topics of debates and the rule changes to determine if they help to explain the increase in party voting unity observed over time. For instance, we can see if the hanging of Louis Riel or the Manitoba Schools question reduced party unity, since several debates and recorded divisions on these topics took place. Likewise, we can estimate if the modification of the proceedings of the House or the reduction in the amount of private members' business on the legislative agenda promoted greater partisanship in the chamber. I consider some of these issues in this chapter; others, such as religion and the transformation of the rules of the House, are covered in greater detail in chapters 7 and 8.

I begin by discussing some of the limits of the Rice index as a measure of partisanship in the legislative arena. I then introduce a baseline model to measure the influence of private members' motions on party unity for both the Liberal and Conservative parties between 1867 and 2011, and use it to test the agenda-control hypothesis, which implies that noncabinet motions and bills are associated with lower levels of party unity. Then I look at the relationship between party unity and the topic of divisions between 1867 and 1930 to determine if certain issues – such as religion or the tariffs – were more likely to lead to intra-party divisions. This is followed by a closer look at the vote type by considering the origin of the motion (cabinet versus noncabinet member) and the vote category (second or third reading of a bill, supply or routine motion, and so on) between 1867 and 2011. The goal here is to see if specific types of votes had a different influence on party unity, depending on the sponsor of the motion. Finally, I present the results of a cumulative analysis that integrates both party- and agenda-level variables into a single model to estimate their effects on voting unity. Here, the goal is to determine whether minority/majority governments or the number of seats a party held during a term influenced party unity, while controlling for the origin and type of motions under consideration. As in the previous chapter, the objective is to adjudicate between the different explanations of party support in the Canadian Parliament.

Modelling Party Voting Unity

Before proceeding too far with the analysis, it is important to outline three notable limits to the use of the Rice index as a dependent variable in the analysis. First, recall that this measure ranges from 0 to 1, with most of the values being either very close to 1 (little dissension) or at 1 (perfect unity). This is especially true for votes recorded later in the period under study, although some variations in party unity occurred from the 1980s through the 2000s. Normally, it would be preferable to estimate a model accounting for these variations to correct for any potential biases in the results. However, just as in the previous chapter, the empirical analysis here uses standard linear regression models with robust standard errors.[1]

The second limit of the Rice index relates to abstentions during legislative votes. In the previous chapter, we saw that there was a negative correlation between lower loyalty scores and participation in recorded divisions. This result suggests that abstaining from voting could represent an alternative approach for dissenting from the party during legislative votes. Although a strict attendance rule was maintained in Parliament until 1877, it is possible that party unity was higher when certain divisions were recorded, but only because participation was low.[2] Unfortunately, it is impossible to distinguish between voluntary and involuntary abstentions – the division records indicate only whether a member voted yea or nay or if the member was paired with another member. Therefore, we cannot know for sure if someone was absent for a valid reason or abstained from voting to avoid antagonizing the party. To consider abstentions as a vote choice, the online appendix to this chapter includes an additional analysis in which the dependent variable is a weighted Rice index (see Hix, Noury, and Roland 2005, 216).

The third limitation of the Rice index relates to the number of votes found in each Parliament. As we saw in chapter 4, the total number of recorded divisions varied greatly by term. Some Parliaments, such as the twenty-fifth (1962–3) and the thirty-first (1979), had fewer than twenty votes; others, such as the thirty-sixth (1988–93), had close to 2,000. This disparity implies that conducting individual parliamentary analysis is not feasible in each term, since the total number of votes by Parliament can be lower than fifty (this is true for six of the forty Parliaments under study). Aside from the fact that this reduces the statistical power of the analysis, a small sample size also increases the likelihood that the estimates will be incorrect, especially if the votes recorded were whipped, as would have been the case for, among others, confidence motions, supply motions, and the Speech from the Throne. To minimize this potential problem, the models pool the data across several parliamentary terms, and although I report the results of the analysis of individual parliamentary terms where possible, the models consider only those in which at least thirty votes were recorded.[3]

Cabinet and Noncabinet Motions, 1867–2011

Can the origin of a motion influence party unity in the legislative arena? The theory of agenda control stipulates that party leaders can use parliamentary rules and procedures to select which motion may be introduced in the debates, and ultimately subjected to a vote on the floor of the House. In the analysis presented below, I hypothesize that motions introduced by cabinet members – as opposed to motions sponsored by private members – are associated with a higher degree of party unity. This is explained by two factors. First, in the Canadian Parliament, motions introduced by the government are widely assumed to follow the confidence convention, and thus are more likely to be monitored by party leaders. Although incorrect, this assumption stems from the idea that a government that loses a vote in the House must either resign or call for an election, so members feel intense pressure to support their own party during recorded divisions (Canada 1985, 6; Forsey 1963, 364; O'Brien and Bosc 2009, 50–2). Second, following the logic of agenda control, members of the executive also can avoid introducing motions that could split their own party. This logic might play differently for private members, who might want to insert their own controversial motions during debates, either to defend the interests of their constituents or to embarrass the government, even if this means challenging their own party leader. Chubby Power provides an example of this behaviour, explaining that he was "once fighting almost single-handedly against one of Mackenzie King's pieces of legislation, providing for the prohibition of the export of liquor from Canada to the then 'dry' United States." "We lost the vote," he recalled years later, "only eleven of us voting wet, but we won the argument" (Power 1968, 6). It is worth noting that, at the time, Power was sitting on the government's backbench. Other examples of this nature abound, but they have become less frequent in recent years as both government and opposition party leaders increased their control over the legislative agenda.

Below I look more closely at the influence of private members' business on party unity over time. Private members' business is defined as all the motions/bills introduced by members who were not in the cabinet when a vote was recorded. In other words, this variable lumps together all the motions made by opposition party leaders and backbenchers from both the government and opposition sides. It is important to note that not all private members' motions are related to private bills (such as divorce or railway bills); they can also be linked to public bills or other types of motions, such as motions of censure or motions to adjourn debates. The dataset contains 3,329 private members' motions recorded on division. Government business makes up the bulk, however, with 7,561 recorded votes.

To see if private members' business weakened party voting unity, figure 6.1 reports the results of a series of linear regressions for each Parliament between 1867 and 2011. Here the dependent variable is the Rice index for both the Conservatives and the Liberals (the first and second graphs of the figure). Both plots display only the estimated effects of private members' business, but these values are obtained from a model that also considers the origin of the motion under consideration. In other words, the model controls for whether or not the vote recorded occurred on a motion or bill introduced by a member of the same party.[4] Note that I did not pool the datasets into a single model because the goal here is to see whether private members' business reduced party unity in each specific term.

The results in figure 6.1 should be familiar by now. Each dot represents the unique effect that a vote on a private members' motion had on party unity. These estimates are obtained from the regression coefficients, holding other variables constant in the analysis (that is, the origin of the motion). The bars

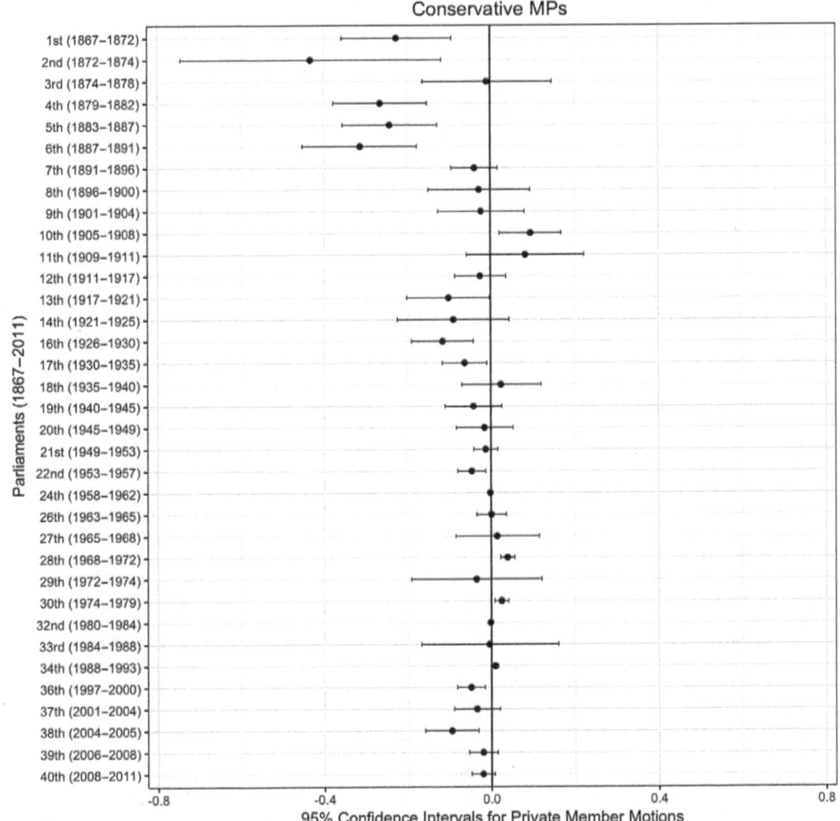

Figure 6.1 Influence of Private Members' Motions on Party Unity, 1867–2011

on the left- and right-hand sides of each point show the 95 per cent confidence intervals.

From the figure, we can see that party unity was lower when voting occurred on private members' motions, a result confirmed in nine out of thirty-six Parliaments for the Liberals, and eleven out of thirty-five for the Conservatives.[5] It is striking to see how strong this effect is on the Rice index, especially before 1930. It is also striking to see how much it reduced party unity after the 1980s, when the recommendations of the McGrath Report (Canada 1985) were put in place to increase the amount of private members' business on the agenda. Note that private members' motions also had a positive influence on party unity in certain parliamentary terms for several reasons. First, such motions did not distinguish between items introduced by opposition party leaders from those introduced by backbenchers of both major parties. Thus, it is possible that

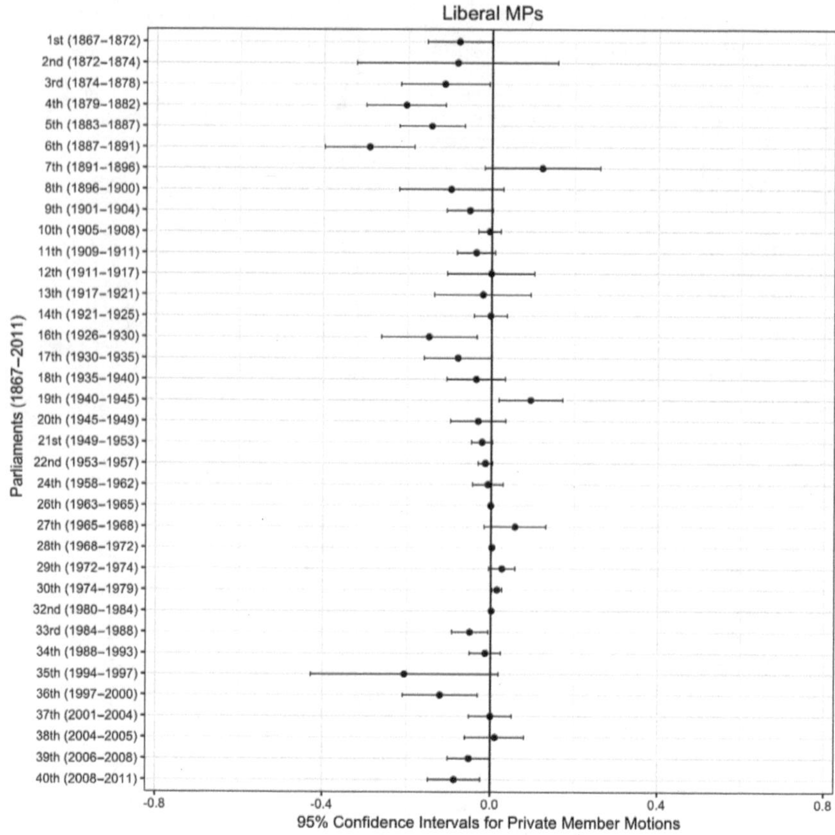

Figure 6.1 continued

some of these items were sponsored by opposition parties (instead of by a private member), such as for a motion of confidence or for questions of procedure. In addition, it is also possible that, in certain cases, party unity was abnormally low during government votes. This occurred in the thirtieth Parliament (1974–9), when there was a series of free votes to abolish the death penalty, a motion sponsored by the government. In this Parliament, average party unity was very high for both parties, but almost all of the votes that saw the greatest amount of dissension were related to this proposal. In other cases, such as in the nineteenth Parliament (1940–5), the number of votes recorded during the term was very low (a total of seventy-nine), which could also have affected the results.

Overall, then, this first analysis confirms that the type of motions sponsored by private members – such as private members' bills, motions to adjourn, or any other type of order or resolution – is associated on average with lower levels of party unity in the House of Commons. This was not true, however, in all Parliaments. The negative effect of this variable is mostly observed until the 1930s, but also after the increase of private members' business in the 1980s. In addition, the results are likely affected by the coding of the origin of the motion under consideration, since the analysis does not distinguish between motions sponsored by backbenchers and those introduced by leaders of the opposition. Separating these categories, one might find an even greater reduction in party unity for private members' business, since motions introduced by party leaders were more likely to be whipped. Another potential problem relates to the topic of the votes under consideration. Did the content of private members' motions make them more prone to create internal party divisions? Were they more likely to be associated with controversial issues, such as tariffs or religion? Or were they simply more divisive because they fell outside the confidence convention (unless, of course, a motion of no confidence was explicitly introduced by a member of the opposition party)?

Topics of the Votes, 1867–1930

We saw in chapter 2 that certain topics were more likely to create intra-party dissension in the Canadian Parliament.[6] For instance, votes related to banking and insurance, the adoption of tariffs, the establishment of the judiciary system, the development of railways and canals, and religious and language rights always had the potential to divide parties internally in the first years after Confederation. These issues were controversial because they often opposed the interests of members from the same party: Montrealers versus Haligonians, farmers versus city dwellers, Protestants versus Catholics. Most of these conflicts were eventually resolved by the 1880s, when the first federal financial system was firmly established and the National Policy was adopted by Parliament. Other questions, however, such as the issue of French and Catholic rights outside the province of Quebec and, later, tariffs and freight rates and Canada's involvement in Imperial wars, continued to divide parties internally for several decades to come.

To measure the influence of these different questions on party unity, I coded each recorded division into thirty-one issues from the first Parliament (1867–72) to the fifteenth (1926–30), a total of 1,785 recorded votes. I further reduced these issues to nine general categories of topics that I use in the analysis presented below. Table 6.1 reports their frequency within the voting data (column two) and the topics used in the analysis (column 3).

The model presented here reports the results of a simple linear regression to determine the relationship between the topic of recorded divisions and party unity, as measured by the Rice index. Since not all of the vote categories were

Table 6.1 Number of Votes, by Issue and Vote Category, 1867–1930

Issue	Number of Divisions	Category
Agriculture	38	Region
Banking/insurance	67	Budget
Bankruptcy	35	Budget
Budget	99	Budget
Canals	11	Region
Civil service	55	Budget
Commerce	35	Commerce
Communication	16	Commerce
Constitution/federalism	39	Region
Corruption	25	Democracy
Defence	48	Foreign
Democratic reform	122	Democracy
Divorce/marriage	96	Religion
Education	1	Budget
Election	110	Democracy
First Nations	5	Region
Foreign policy	35	Foreign
Hospital/health	4	Budget
Immigration/colonization	21	Immigration
Justice	55	Justice
Language/religion/prohibition	141	Religion
Member censure	9	Democracy
Natural resources	9	Region
Procedure	93	Procedure
Provinces/territories	98	Region
Public administration	2	Budget
Railway	269	Region
Social security/welfare	9	Budget
Tariff/taxation	168	Budget
Trade	42	Budget
Transportation	28	Region

found in each Parliament, I pooled the data across all sixteen Parliaments covering the 1867–1930 period. The results of this analysis are presented in table 6.2, for both the Liberal and Conservative parties separately. Each of the nine topics is represented by a dummy variable, with the baseline category of procedural votes. To avoid comparing only these voting categories to the reference level, the model uses a contrast coding approach (or deviation coding), where each vote category is compared to the average effect of all the others values of this variable in the model, instead of the baseline, as is common with the more traditional method for analysing dummy variables. This analytical approach should provide a more accurate estimate of how vote topics influence the Rice index. Note also that the model includes a dummy variable for each

Table 6.2 Issues as Determinants of Party Unity, by Party, 1867–1930

	Party	
Variable	Conservative	Liberal
Intercept	0.63 (0.02)***	0.48 (0.02)***
Budget	0.06 (0.01)***	0.04 (0.01)**
Commerce	−0.08 (0.04)·	−0.02 (0.03)
Democracy	0.12 (0.01)***	0.09 (0.01)***
Foreign	0.04 (0.02)·	0.02 (0.03)
Immigration	0.14 (0.01)***	0.07 (0.01)***
Justice	−0.14 (0.04)***	0.01 (0.03)
Region	0.08 (0.01)***	0.02 (0.01)
Religion	-0.25 (0.02)***	-0.22 (0.02)***
Parliamentary dummies (2–16)	✓	✓
Adj. R^2	0.32	0.41
N	1,794	1,794

***p < 0.001; **p < 0.01; *p < 0.05; ·p < 0.1.

Note : Ordinary least squares regressions. Standard errors were corrected to control for autocorrelation and heteroscedasticity. The dependent variable is the Rice index for the Conservative and Liberal parties.

parliamentary term (the baseline here is the first Parliament). Since this is simply to control for specific temporal effects, I used the standard coding scheme, and do not report the results in the table.

Table 6.2 shows the results of the analysis for both the Conservatives (second column) and Liberals (third column) separately. We find that several different voting categories had a positive influence on party voting unity. For instance, votes on the budget, democratic reforms, and immigration are all associated with higher values of the Rice index, and this is true for both parties. On the other hand, votes related to religious questions had a negative influence on party unity for both parties. A great number of controversial issues fall into this category, including Catholic and Protestant rights, language and education questions, temperance and prohibition, and divorce. These topics naturally weakened cohesion, as they were more likely to be opposed by Protestant and Catholic members of the same party.

Turning now to differences between the parties, there is slightly more variation in the results for the Conservatives. Here, certain issues, such as justice and commerce, are associated with lower levels of party unity, while others, such as foreign policy and regional questions, had a more positive effect. What can explain these differences? The model provides only a limited amount of information, but one can suppose that this variation is related to the Conservative Party's being in power during most of the nineteenth century, a time when party unity was more likely to fluctuate across different voting categories on the government side – that is, the overall mean of the Rice index is higher for the Conservatives, but there was more variation in party unity across voting categories. Although the data are pooled across several different parliamentary terms, we can still take a closer look at the issues that divided the Conservatives internally to understand the results of the analysis. First, on the issue of commerce, votes were related to patents, private companies, copyrights, the telegraph, telephones, mailing, and shipping. Since about half of these motions were linked to private members' bills establishing corporations or granting patents to particular individuals – not to be confused with a public bill, which can be introduced by either government or private members – it is not surprising that they generated more intra-party dissension. But then why did this voting category not reduce party unity for the Liberals as well? First, although not significant, the negative sign of this variable is in the right direction for the Liberals. Second, and perhaps more important, almost three-quarters of commerce motions introduced by members of the cabinet occurred when the Liberals were in power, which could explain why party unity was stronger in their case.

Nonetheless, to get a better sense of how specific issues might have influenced party unity over time, figure 6.2 presents a more detailed analysis of the effect of two different voting categories on the Rice index across each parliamentary term. In this plot, each dot represents the unique influence that budgetary and religious questions had on party voting unity between 1867 and 1930. These estimates are from the regression coefficients obtained in each parliamentary term, where a simple dummy variable is used to indicate whether or not a vote was related to the topic. Note that the figure superimposes these voting categories for both the Conservatives (first plot) and the Liberals (second plot).

The results in figure 6.2 confirm that, in all but three parliamentary terms, votes related to religious questions reduced party unity for both parties. Moreover, the effect is quite large: in some cases, it reaches almost fifty points, meaning that about one-quarter of the caucus could have voted against the party in these votes (for example, 75 per cent yeas – 25 per cent nays = 50 Rice index). Also note that the relationship between this variable and party unity remains more or less constant over time: it did not decline for the Liberal Party after Wilfrid Laurier became prime minister in 1896, and it continued to be an important factor throughout the period under study for the Conservatives, even after most Catholics left that party in 1917 (although this variable is not significant in this term). We saw earlier that the content of these votes was mostly associated with controversial issues such as marriage and divorce, schooling, language rights, prohibition, and the North-West Rebellion. In the years following Confederation, divorce bills were considered free votes (or votes of conscience), and all Catholic members were usually opposed to this practice. Other

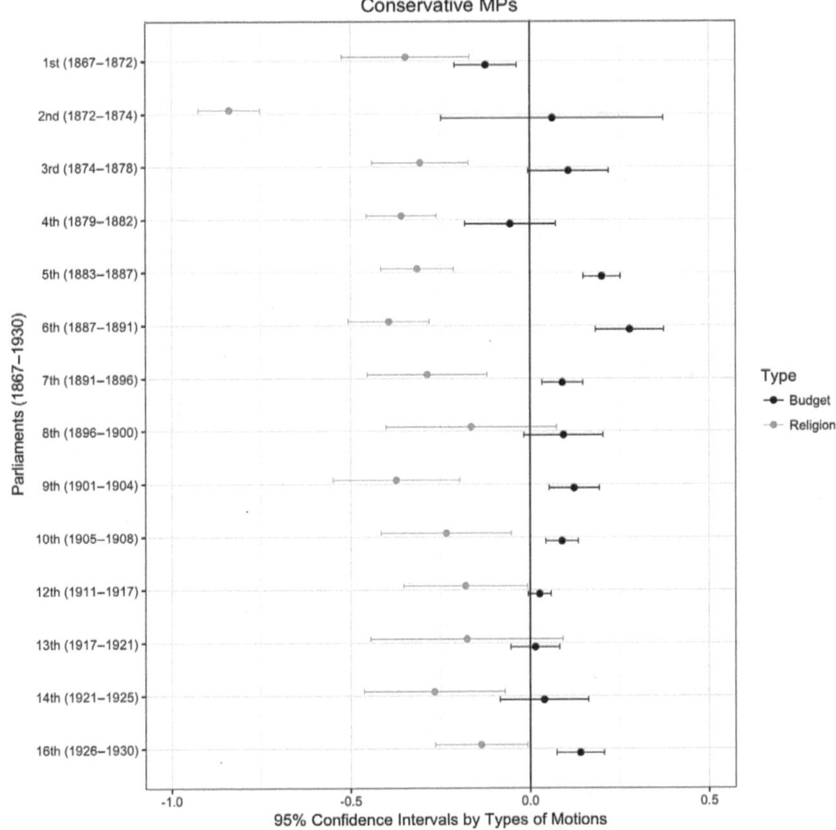

Figure 6.2 Influence of Motions Concerning the Budget and Religious Issues on Party Unity, 1867–1930

issues, such as the incorporation of the Orange Association of British America, a bill to allow a widower to marry his deceased wife's sister, or the expulsion of Louis Riel from Parliament, caused a similar uproar among Catholic MPs from both parties. Not surprisingly, the prohibition of Catholic and French-language education in several provinces outside Quebec represents another category of very divisive conflicts. For these votes, the Catholic MPs of both parties banded together to support their Church.

The effect of budgetary items on party unity was somewhat different. On average, voting on this type of motion tends to be associated with higher values of the Rice index; this is true in about half the terms for the Liberals and six for the Conservatives. As well, unlike with religious questions, the effect

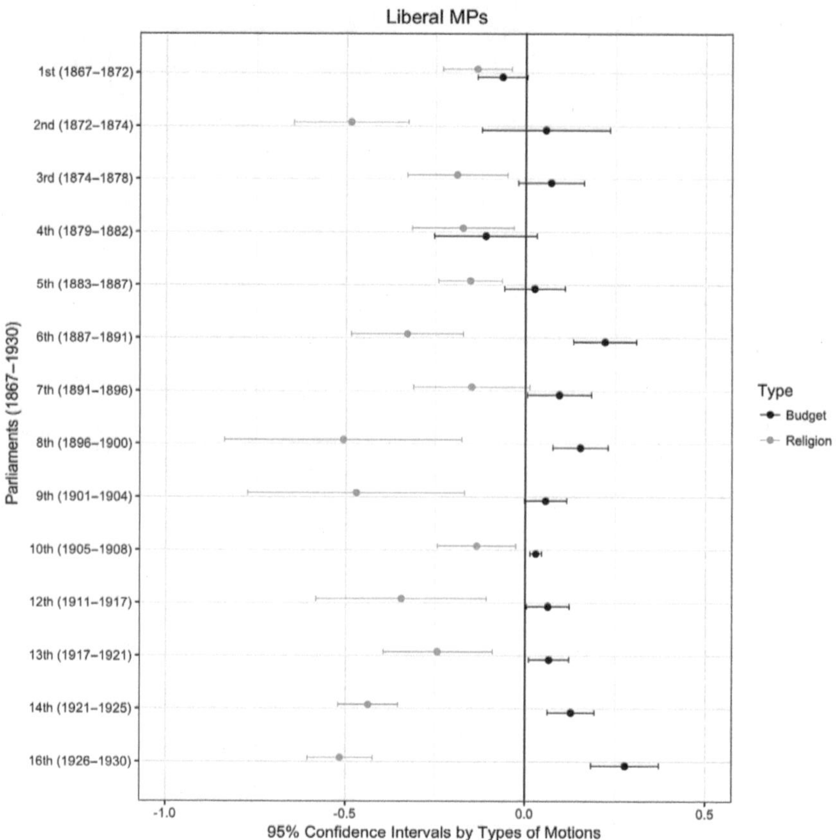

Figure 6.2 continued

of this variable is not very large. When significant, voting unity increased on average by fourteen and fifteen points for the Conservative and Liberal parties, respectively – representing a shift from, say, an 85–15 split to a 92–8 split during a division. The analysis also confirms that the positive influence of budgetary motions increased over time for the Liberals, meaning that the Rice index tends to be higher in later terms, when voting occurred on tariffs, the budget, and other aspects of government administration. This was not the case for the Conservatives, for whom the influence of this variable was more important in earlier terms, when that party was frequently in power. Another interesting finding is that voting on budgetary items actually reduced party unity in the first Parliament – a result significant only for the Conservative Party. This is not surprising: as indicated earlier, one of the first tasks of the new federal government was to adopt a common tariff and customs system, and most of the votes on these issues occurred immediately following Confederation. For example, whenever the government supported more aggressive tariffs on staples such as corn or tobacco, or the transfer of payments to certain provinces such as Nova Scotia or British Columbia, the economic interests of different sections of the country represented by the same party could be in direct conflict. Banking and bankruptcy is another voting category that frequently divided both parties internally, mainly because it transcended party lines by opposing the financial sectors of Montreal, Toronto, and Halifax. Not all of these issues, however, were resolved in the first few Parliaments. Others, such as the tariff question, lingered on for decades and contributed to reducing party unity until the 1920s.

To sum up, certain questions related to religion, commerce, and, to a lesser extent, tariffs and trade, are associated with lower levels of party unity in the House of Commons. We saw that other topics, such as the budget, can have a positive effect on the Rice index, especially for the party in government. Clearly, then, by controlling the content of the legislative agenda, party leaders effectively could keep some of the most controversial issues from reaching the floor of the House. As we saw earlier, an easy way to do this was to limit the amount of private members' business on the agenda. But what types of motions or bills are we talking about here? Is there a difference between the reading of a bill and a simple procedural motion? Are all motions/bills introduced by private members equally likely to reduce party unity? Or are all government votes always associated with strict party discipline?

Types of Votes, 1867–2011

It is possible to look more closely at the relationship between the origin of a motion (government versus private member) and the type of vote recorded. In the Canadian Parliament, voting can occur on several different types of questions. For instance, voting can be on the second or third reading of a bill ("shall the bill be read a third time?"). It can also occur on a routine motion, such as to adjourn a debate or to move for the previous question ("shall this question be now put?"). Since we know from the analysis presented earlier that private members' motions are usually associated with lower levels of party unity, should we expect this to be true for most types of votes recorded? Perhaps during certain debates – such as the address in reply to the Speech from the Throne or an amendment to the budget – a motion made by a private member will generate less dissension because these are considered to be matters of confidence in the government. But the same cannot be said about private bills, which remain outside of the realm of government business.

To distinguish between the potential effects of these different types of votes, the analysis presented below classifies each recorded division into eight

Table 6.3 Types of Votes, by Sponsor, 1867–2011

	Sponsor		
Type of Vote	Cabinet Member	Private Member	Total
Address	40	70	110
Reading of bills	2,057	670	2,727
Budget	856	600	1,456
Committee	3,856	271	4,127
Motion	110	868	978
Order	129	190	319
Throne speech	24	210	234
Procedure	492	447	939

Note: The values in the table represent the number of votes in each category.

categories: addresses to the Crown, readings of bills (first, second, and third readings), budget motions, concurrence in committee reports, general motions, orders, reply to the Speech from the Throne, and a residual baseline category of procedural votes. Table 6.3 reports the number of recorded divisions in each of these categories for motions sponsored by both noncabinet (that is, private members) and cabinet members between 1867 and 2011. I describe these categories in more detail below.

Addresses to the Crown. These motions generally contain a formal message to the monarch or governor general to "express a wish or an opinion of the House" or to make a specific demand (O'Brien and Bosc 2009, 942n191). When sponsored by a cabinet member, addresses are used, for example, to demand the modification of the Constitution. When sponsored by a private member, addresses can request that specific actions be taken – such as the disallowance of the New Brunswick School Act in 1872 – but also to ask for copies of government documents (1121).[7]

Concurrence in committee reports. This category refers to any vote taken to adopt a committee report – including amendments to bills in certain cases, especially after 1968, when bills began to be sent automatically to different standing committees after second reading (O'Brien and Bosc 2009, 777). Committee report votes are usually taken on government bills, although in earlier Parliaments the House mandated several different committees to consider specific questions (954). These earlier committees were chaired by noncabinet members and frequently reported to the House the results of their inquiries on such matters as printing, divorces, or banking and commerce (954n23).

Readings of bills. Votes related to the readings of bills correspond to the first, second, and third stages of the adoption of a piece of legislation in Parliament. All bills are required to be read three times in the House of Commons and the Senate before they are adopted, and votes are usually taken before the second and third reading stages. Two types of bills are considered here: public and private bills. Public bills can be introduced by either cabinet members or other members of the House, and deal with matters that concern society as a whole. Private bills are almost always introduced by noncabinet members, and grant "special powers or benefits" to private individuals, associations, or corporations (O'Brien and Bosc 2009, 719).

Budget motions. These votes relate to the adoption of the government's program for public expenditures (supply) and revenues (ways and means). Several different types of recorded divisions fall into this category, such as the adoption of the budget bill (second or third reading) and votes taken on specific resolutions adopted in the committees of supplies and ways and means. These resolutions can either increase or reduce expenditures. Note, however, that only cabinet members are allowed to grant the supplies needed to operate government, but other members of the House can propose to reduce specific expenditures or taxes in the budget (O'Brien and Bosc 2009, 833). Budget votes also relate to the discussion surrounding the debate "that the Speaker do now leave the Chair" before going into the committee of supplies and ways and means to consider the government's expenditures and revenues, a practice that was frequently used until 1968 when the financial procedures were changed. These motions are always made by noncabinet members to obtain concessions from the executive or to discuss issues of national importance (840–1). Although debated right before the budget, these motions may be related to almost any topic – historical examples include a resolution on restitution for the murder of Thomas Scott in Manitoba during the first Riel Rebellion (Debates 1871, 374), Home Rule in Ireland (Debates 1882, 1030), and Canada's participation in the South African War (Debates 1900, 82). As such, they usually generated numerous controversies during the debates, especially before a limit was placed in 1913 on the number of these motions. Today, the practice of going into the committees of supply and ways and means is automatic. In 1968, the House adopted a new set of rules to replace debates surrounding the adoption of the budget by a fixed number of supply or allotted days. After this point, opposition members were allowed to introduce only a certain number of debatable motions, the topic of which they could choose (O'Brien and Bosc 2009, 843–9).

General motions. Votes on general motions relate to directives or resolutions requiring the House to take a particular action or to consider a specific question or debate. Private members frequently use this type of motion to introduce a wide range of topics during debates. Their usage has become more frequent over time, especially after the rules were modified in 1913 to limit the number of amendments members could introduce. Today, private members' motions are debated during the time set aside for private members' business, and are selected by a lottery at the beginning of each session (the same method is used for selecting private members' bills).[8] Government motions are a little more difficult to define. I have placed in this category all the declarations of general principles made by cabinet members that required a vote. Falling into this category, for example, is the motion made by Prime Minister Alexander Mackenzie in the third Parliament that Louis Riel and Ambroise-Dydime Lépine be granted amnesty following a five-year banishment. Other examples are Jean Chrétien's 1995 motion that the House recognize Quebec as a distinct society and Stephen Harper's 2006 motion that the *Québécois* be recognized as a nation in a united Canada.

Orders. These votes are related to statements made by the House to organize its business or to give instructions to its members or committees (O'Brien and Bosc 2009, 493, 993). Both cabinet and private members can make them.

Reply to the Speech from the Throne. Votes related to the throne speech are either linked to amendments made by private members during its consideration by the House or to motions introduced by the cabinet formally to adopt the government's legislative program in the upcoming term. Note that motions moved to amend the Address in Reply motion can be linked to almost any topic, and are often considered to be matters of confidence in the government (O'Brien and Bosc 2009, 683).

Procedural motions. These votes apply primarily to superseding motions, which usually aim to proceed with the order of the day or to adjourn debates of the House of Commons (O'Brien and Bosc 2009, 529–30). Procedural votes can also be linked to points of order or to appeals to a ruling made by the speaker. Points of order were used more frequently in the House after the rules were modified between 1906 and 1913. These new rules limited backbenchers' opportunities to participate in debates, so members began to challenge the speaker's rulings in order to be heard (312). Because procedural matters usually involve routine House questions or special rules, these motions should be associated with higher levels of party unity. Indeed, Cox and McCubbins (2005, 29) argue that, in the US Congress, procedural votes generate less intra-party dissension, since leaders expect loyalty from their members when voting occurs on routine proceedings. In the analysis presented below, I use procedural votes as a reference category, although, as before, I also use a contrast coding scheme to compare the mean effect of each type of vote on the Rice index.

In order to distinguish the influence of these various government activities from one another, the analysis presented in table 6.4 separates motions originating from the cabinet from those sponsored by private members. Each model also covers every parliamentary term between 1867 and 2011, and considers the Conservative and Liberal parties separately. Aside from the vote types identified above, the model also includes a control variable indicating whether or not the motion was introduced by a member of the same party (either Liberal or Conservative), as well as a series of dummy variables for each parliamentary term (the baseline category is the first Parliament). Note that the table does not

Table 6.4 Determinants of Party Unity, Government versus Private Members' Business, by Party, 1867–2011

	Party			
	Conservative		Liberal	
Variable	Government Member	Private Member	Government Member	Private Member
Intercept	0.94 (0.02)***	0.80 (0.04)***	0.52 (0.03)***	0.78 (0.03)***
Own party	−0.19 (0.04)***	−0.02 (0.01)	0.44 (0.03)***	0.03 (0.01)**
Address	−0.01 (0.01)	−0.01 (0.03)	−0.07 (0.03)*	−0.00 (0.03)
Reading of bills	−0.00 (0.00)	−0.12 (0.01)***	0.01 (0.01)*	−0.14 (0.01)***
Budget	0.02 (0.01)**	0.08 (0.01)***	0.02 (0.01)**	0.06 (0.01)***
Committee report	−0.01 (0.01)	−0.01 (0.01)	0.01 (0.01)˙	−0.05 (0.02)*
Motion	−0.05 (0.01)˙	0.02 (0.01)˙	−0.05 (0.02)*	0.02 (0.01)˙
Order	0.01 (0.01)	−0.01 (0.02)	0.01 (0.01)	0.03 (0.01)**
Throne speech	0.02 (0.01)**	0.04 (0.01)***	0.03 (0.01)***	0.04 (0.01)***
Parliamentary dummies (2–40)	✓	✓	✓	✓
Adj. R^2	0.24	0.31	0.45	0.27
N	6,930	3,202	7,550	3,310

*** $p < 0.001$; ** $p < 0.01$; * $p < 0.05$; ˙$p < 0.1$.
Note: Ordinary least squares regressions. Standard errors were corrected to control for autocorrelation and heteroscedasticity. The dependent variable is the Rice index for the Conservative and Liberal parties, calculated separately for government- and private-member-related votes.

report the results for the parliamentary term dummies. Once again, I obtained the coefficients in this analysis from standard linear regression models, and the dependent variable is the Rice index.

The second and fourth columns of table 6.4 limit the sample to motions introduced by members of the cabinet from the Liberal or Conservative parties, while the third and fifth columns look at private members' motions only. Beginning with the cabinet, the results confirm that motions sponsored by members of the same party are associated with higher levels of party voting unity only for the Liberals. This is not really surprising, since we should expect members of the same caucus to support one another. For the Conservatives, however, cabinet motions actually reduced voting unity, since that party was in government for the longest time during the nineteenth century, when both parties were more likely to experience internal divisions. If we limit the sample to the twentieth century, this result becomes positive and significant. In terms of voting categories, only motions related to the budget and the throne speech are systematically associated with higher values of the Rice index for both parties. Once again, this is not surprising, since the confidence convention usually applies to these types of vote. What is perhaps more unusual here is that the general motion category had a negative effect on voting unity for the Liberals (and for the Conservatives, but not significant in their case). Recall that these motions were mostly related to statements of general principle made by members of the cabinet, often to discuss controversial topics such as the restriction of abortion rights, the promotion of the French Language Act, or the abolition of the death penalty. The analysis also reveals that the Liberals were slightly more unified during votes taken on the reading of bills or committee reports, while addresses to the Crown seem to have reduced unity in that party – by as much as seven points on the Rice index scale. Just as in the general motion category, motions of this type often occurred over highly controversial issues, such as the House's adoption of the Meech Lake Accord in 1987 (eleven Liberals voted against, thirty-three in favour).

Turning now to private members' motions, the results confirm that bills sponsored outside the cabinet are usually associated with lower levels of party unity. This is to be expected, as both public and private bills introduced by regular members do not constitute questions of confidence in the government. On the other hand, motions related to the budget (supply or ways and means motions) are associated with higher values of the Rice index. These motions are not strictly linked to financial matters. As we saw earlier, they can be related to almost any topic within the jurisdiction of Parliament. As such, they give noncabinet members a broad range of opportunities to air their grievances in the House, especially during supply debates. There was even a period in the history of Parliament when backbenchers from both parties could intervene directly in this type of debate by moving their own amendments. These opportunities declined significantly over time, however, especially after the rules were modified in 1913 to limit the number of supply or ways and means amendments to the budget. Since then, opposition party leaders have controlled almost all of the remaining opposition motions available to MPs. The third type of motions that has a positive effect on party unity relates to the general motions category. These private members' motions can also touch on a wide variety of topics but, unlike budget motions, their content is not supposed to be influenced by opposition party leaders (Blidook 2012). As such, we should have expected much lower levels of party unity in the first place. Perhaps the fact that around 75 per cent of these divisions were recorded after 1968, when partisanship was already very high in Parliament, explains part of this result. Recall that this analysis looks at the effect of these motions in relation to the average influence of all other types of votable items sponsored by private members in the data (the contrast coding scheme) – in this case, both public and private bills – which have a much stronger negative effect on party unity. Finally, votes taken during the address in reply to the Speech from the Throne also appear to have a positive influence on party unity. This is normal, since a successful amendment made to the throne speech normally would imply a loss of confidence in the government.

We can see, then, that certain legislative activities have influenced party unity more than others, depending on the type and origin of the motion. Not surprisingly, most of the votes tied to the confidence convention (the budget, government bills, the throne speech) are linked to higher values of the Rice index, while legislative initiatives sponsored by private members are much more likely to generate intra-party dissension. We find, however, several exceptions to this rule, such as the broader general motions category, which has a negative effect on party unity for government votes but a positive one for the private members category. Of course, these findings apply only to their respective sponsor, either in relationship to other cabinet motions or to noncabinet ones. Therefore, it is important to look at a cumulative model that combines all of the motions into one dataset to determine if certain types of votes were more likely than others to influence party unity.

Cumulative Analysis

This last analysis aims to determine if both the origin and the type of motions explain the rise in partisanship observed in the House of Commons over time. Aside from the Rice index, which represents the dependent variable in the regression models described below, the analysis includes several additional control variables to capture the effects of other determinants of party voting unity across parliamentary terms. Table 6.5 reports these results separately for the Conservatives (column 2) and Liberals (column 5). The dataset is further divided according to the periods identified previously by the change point models in chapter 4: either before or after the seventeenth Parliament (columns 3 and 4 for the Conservatives; 6 and 7 for the Liberals). As before, I conducted the analysis at the party level, and computed the aggregate unity scores for each of the 10,893 recorded divisions in the data between 1867 and 2011.

Since the goal here is to understand the outcome of legislative votes, the model includes several new variables to control for the types of divisions. To begin, I created a variable that combines both the origin and the nature of the motion under consideration. This variable has five categories: government bills, private members' public bills, private bills, government motions, and private members' motions.[9] The model also uses a contrast coding scheme, with government bills as the baseline category. Note that each type of motion or bill can be introduced either by a cabinet (government) member or noncabinet

Table 6.5 Determinants of Party Unity, by Party, Cumulative Analysis, 1867–2011

	Conservatives			Liberals		
	Parliament					
Variable	1st–40th	1st–16th	17th–40th	1st–40th	1st–16th	17th–40th
Intercept	0.65 (0.02)***	0.33 (0.07)***	0.93 (0.06)***	0.57 (0.03)***	0.56 (0.06)***	0.67 (0.08)***
Cabinet motion	0.06 (0.01)***	0.09 (0.02)***	0.03 (0.01)***	0.06 (0.01)***	0.08 (0.02)***	0.03 (0.01)***
Private members' motion	0.06 (0.01)***	0.11 (0.01)***	0.02 (0.01)***	0.07 (0.01)***	0.09 (0.01)***	0.04 (0.01)***
Private members' bill (private)	−0.15 (0.02)***	−0.20 (0.02)***	−0.05 (0.02)*	−0.12 (0.02)***	−0.20 (0.03)***	−0.01 (0.02)
Private members' bill (public)	−0.04 (0.01)***	−0.13 (0.03)***	−0.03 (0.01)**	−0.07 (0.02)***	−0.07 (0.03)**	−0.10 (0.02)***
Own party	0.00 (0.01)	0.00 (0.02)	0.00 (0.00)	0.04 (0.01)***	0.07 (0.02)***	0.02 (0.01)***
Minority government	0.02 (0.01)**	0.01 (0.03)	0.01 (0.01)	0.02 (0.01)*	−0.04 (0.03)	0.01 (0.01)
Governing party	0.06 (0.01)***	-0.05 (0.04)	0.01 (0.01)˙	−0.03 (0.01)**	0.13 (0.04)***	−0.03 (0.01)*
Percentage of seats	−0.08 (0.02)***	0.47 (0.15)***	0.00 (0.02)	0.04 (0.03)	−0.51 (0.17)***	0.04 (0.03)
Parliament	0.02 (0.00)***	0.04 (0.01)***	0.00 (0.00)	0.03 (0.00)***	0.09 (0.01)***	0.02 (0.00)***
Parliament^2	0.00 (0.00)***	0.00 (0.00)***	0.00 (0.00)	0.00 (0.00)***	0.00 (0.00)***	0.00 (0.00)***
Adj. R^2	0.26	0.26	0.02	0.34	0.40	0.11
N	10,132	1,794	8,338	10,860	1,794	9,066

***$p < 0.001$; **$p < 0.01$; *$p < 0.05$; ˙$p < 0.1$.

Note: Ordinary least squares regressions. Standard errors were corrected to control for autocorrelation and heteroscedasticity. The dependent variable is the Rice index by parliamentary term for the Conservatives (columns 2–4) and Liberals (columns 5–7).

(private) member. The model adds other control variables as well to indicate if the original sponsor of the motion was supported by a member of the same party, if it occurred when the party was in government, and if it occurred during a minority Parliament. Finally, the analysis controls for the size of the party in the House as a proportion of the seats controlled by the party at the time of the vote, and adds a parliamentary term component to represent the Parliament number (ranging from 1 to 40). This last variable is squared in the analysis to control for non-linear variations over time.

The results in table 6.5 confirm that several of the previous variables had an important influence on party voting unity. The most significant finding relates to the relationship between the Rice index and the type of vote recorded. For each party, unity was always lower when voting occurred over a bill introduced by a private member (either public or private). On the other hand, motions introduced by cabinet and noncabinet members usually had a positive influence on party unity, which means that the value of the Rice index is always higher when this type of recorded division is considered. In terms of the other controls, we can see that motions sponsored by a member of the same party, or votes recorded during minority governments, had a positive influence on party unity. The governing party variable had a positive effect on party unity, but the break point separation in the seventeenth Parliament shows that this was true only during the earlier period for the Liberals and in the later one for the Conservatives. The percentage of seats held by a party during a vote appears to have had a different effect on the dependent variable as well: either positive (for the Conservatives) or negative (for the Liberals), depending on the period. Finally, the influence of the parliamentary term seems to have been significant across time, with a positive increase in party unity in earlier terms, which later stabilized and thereafter declined.[10]

From this last set of results we can conclude that an important determinant of party unity is associated with the origin of the motion under consideration. Bills sponsored by noncabinet members are always associated with lower values of the Rice index, and this is true for both parties. Figure 6.3 illustrates this trend by showing the difference in party unity between government and private members' bills over time for both the Conservatives (the first plot) and Liberals (the second plot). These predictions were obtained from the regression equation of the cumulative models for the two parties in table 6.5, by setting the values of the variables to represent a vote taken on a motion introduced by a government member whose party controls 51 per cent of the seats in the House. The solid (black) line represents the intersection between: (1) the parliamentary term when a cabinet (noncabinet) vote was taken on a government (private members') bill; and (2) the predicted value of the Rice index calculated from the model (with the 95 per cent confidence intervals represented by the dotted lines). Clearly, both plots confirm that the parliamentary

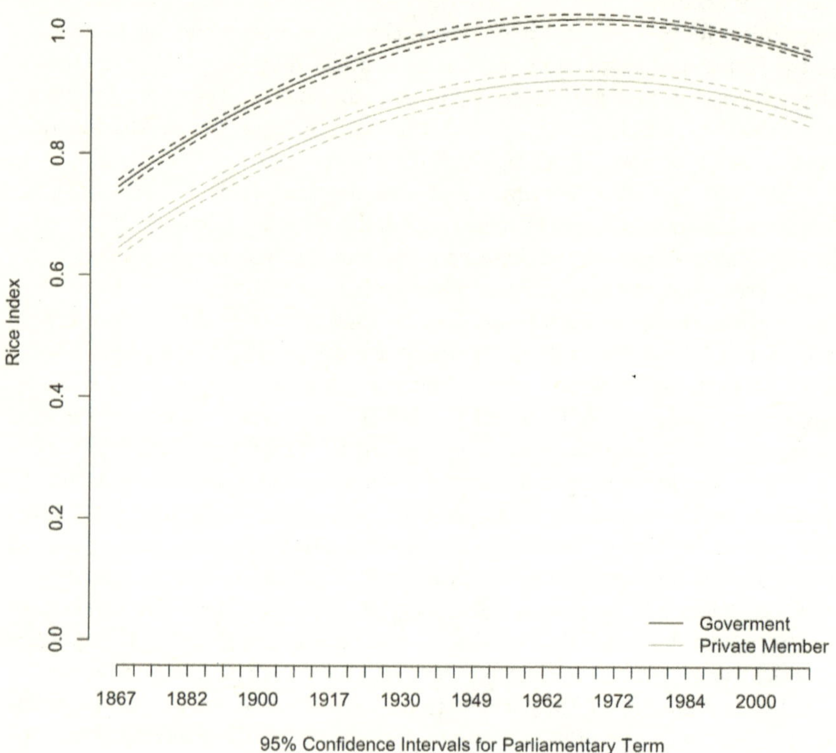

Figure 6.3 Public Bills and Party Unity, by Party, 1867–2011

term matters in explaining the growth of partisanship. The effects of government and private members' bills became increasingly important as the 1950s approached, but stabilized thereafter. The plots also show a striking difference between the two types of bills, with the latter having a very strong negative effect on party unity. Finally, note that party unity appears to decline near the end of the period under study for both government and private members' bills. This finding confirms a return to intra-party dissension in the House of Commons, partly because of the modification of the rules to increase the amount of private members' business on the agenda in the 1980s, but also because of infighting among both the Liberals (Kam 2006, 562–3) and the Conservatives (Malloy 2003, 120–3).

This last set of analyses suggests that government might have increased party unity during the twentieth century by reducing the amount of private

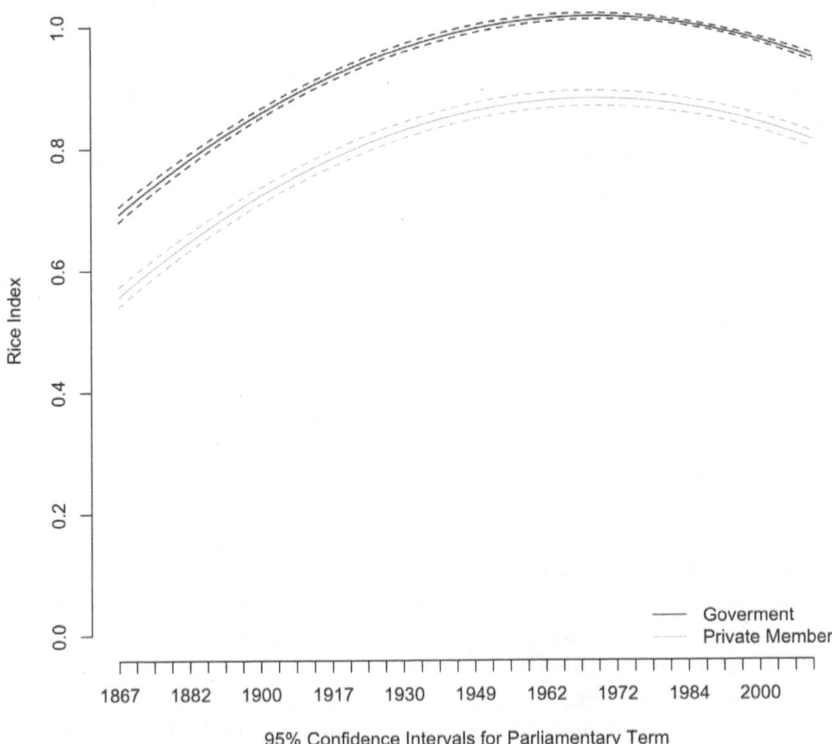

Figure 6.3 continued

members' business on the agenda. This is certainly true for the number of bills introduced by private members, which significantly declined after 1920 (see figure 3.6 in chapter 3). But private members' motions, in contrast, are actually linked to higher levels of party unity in almost all the models presented in table 6.3. The theory of agenda control predicts that this type of motion, where government party leaders do not determine the content, is more likely to generate intra-party dissension. Why was this not the case in the Canadian Parliament? Is the theory wrong? I return to this finding in chapter 8, when I look at the effect of rule changes on the organization of the House of Commons, but a few things are worth pointing out before proceeding further. First, private members' motions encompass a large number of votable items that do not necessarily allow members to introduce any topic of discussion during debates. Such opportunities are strictly limited to these types of motions: the address in reply to the throne speech; adjournment debates (after 1906, only for emergency debates); motions to go into the committee of the whole (prior to 1913), supply or ways and means (prior to 1968); and opposition or supply days (after 1968). Other motions frequently found in this category, such as concurrence in committee reports or points of order, are usually limited to the topic at hand. Second, although theoretically most of these motions can be sponsored by backbenchers from both sides of the House, party leaders of the official opposition have increasingly intervened in this type of debate. This trend accelerated even more after 1927, when third parties were officially recognized in the Standing Orders of the House of Commons (Stewart 1977, 113).

Conclusion

In this chapter, I set out to identify what factors have influenced party voting unity by analysing the outcome of legislative votes. The previous analysis was done at the party level to determine if the government's increasing control of the agenda could explain the growth of partisanship over time. Recall that the main hypothesis of the agenda-control theory is that motions introduced by government leaders would be associated, on average, with higher levels of party unity. In the first case, the Westminster system links the outcome of numerous legislative votes to the confidence convention (the budget, government bills, motions of no confidence), and failure to support the governing party can lead to a snap election. Thus, for government backbenchers, incentives to vote with their party are very high when a cabinet member introduces a motion, especially if they want to avoid going to the polls or being punished by their leader. The same logic would apply for members of the opposition, but for a different reason: they would want to be unified in their critique of the government.

Another way the legislative agenda could affect party unity is related to the content of motions during debates. Cabinet members can use the confidence convention to promote the adoption of controversial bills, but leaders of the government can also use their agenda-setting power to prevent the consideration of contentious questions in the House of Commons. This concept of negative agenda control thus could account for the growth in partisanship observed over time, especially because cabinet members now have almost absolute control over the daily proceedings of the House. O'Brien and Bosc (2009, 475) note that, over the years, "there have been many changes to the rules of the House in order to increase the time available to the government and to reduce the proportion of House time devoted to private bills or to matters brought forward by private members." The influence of backbenchers has been further reduced because remaining opportunities to influence debates increasingly are controlled by leaders of the opposition, who also have an incentive to promote party unity within their ranks.

This is the theory. What does the analysis of the outcome of all the votes recorded between 1867 and 2011 tell us about the influence of the legislative agenda on party unity? First, not surprisingly, the results confirm that private members' business is usually associated with lower levels of party unity. When we look at the type of votes in greater detail, however, we find that not all motions introduced by private members weakened party unity. In certain cases, such as public or private bills, the hypothesis was confirmed; in others, such as general motions or an address in reply to the Speech from the Throne, it was not. In fact, anything that could be linked to the confidence convention appeared to increase, not reduce, party unity. On the other hand, when we look at motions sponsored by cabinet members, we find that certain types of votes could be associated either with higher (government bills) or lower (general motions) levels of party unity. I proposed, without evaluating, several explanations to account for this difference – especially the one related to rule changes. Here, additional work is required, and this is the focus of chapter 8.

Finally, as we saw in the individual-level analysis presented in the previous chapter, the results reported here highlight the importance of time as an explanatory factor for the development of partisanship. Party unity increased after each term, and this effect remains strongly correlated with the Rice index across different periods, even after controlling for the type of vote, its sponsor, and the size of the governing party. This time-component variable, as measured by the Parliament number, cannot tell us much beyond what are included in the model as control variables. That is to say, the increase in party unity observed over time might be due to factors other than those included in the model specified above, and the parliamentary term component thus would act as a proxy for these unmeasured variables. An example of this could be linked to the issue of the vote. We did find earlier in this chapter that, between 1867 and 1930, the topic of certain motions tended to be associated with lower levels of party unity. The best example of this is religion, but other issues related to nation-building projects, such as banking and commerce, or foreign policy, could also have had the same kind of effect. Clearly, more work needs to be done before we can fully understand how the topic of certain motions influenced the development of partisanship in the House of Commons over time. This is the focus of the next two chapters.

Chapter Seven

Louis Riel and the Catholic Sort

One of the most enduring puzzles in Canadian politics today relates to the relationship between Catholics and the Liberal Party. Ever since the first Canadian Election Study survey was conducted in 1965, we have known that Roman Catholic voters are more likely to favour Liberal candidates; this connection has been confirmed in almost every other election since then (Johnston 2017, 123–6). In his 2005 Presidential Address to the Canadian Political Science Association, André Blais argued that the Catholic vote could explain why the Liberal Party was so adept at winning elections throughout most of the twentieth century; what remains unclear, however, is the origin of this religious cleavage, and how it has come to favour one party over the other (Blais 2005, 821–5).

Blais was quick to dismiss the importance of historical events as a potential source for the permanent relationship between religion and politics in Canada. For him, the Liberal-Catholic connection cannot be "construed as a residue of the past transmitted through family socialization," since the religious cleavage was as strong in 2005 as it was in 1965 (Blais 2005, 830). Other factors, such as differences in values, party identification, or the religion of candidates, do not seem to matter either. Thus, in the field of behavioural political science, explaining why Catholics historically have been more prone to support the Liberal Party remains somewhat of a mystery.

For scholars who take a more historical approach, such as Smith (1963, 128–9; but see also Power 1968, 14) and Johnston (2017, 102), accounting for the Liberals' success has more to do with the party's critical stance towards the British Empire than with Catholic support, which naturally flowed from the former. According to this view, it was the Liberals' own brand of nationalism that appealed to Catholics after Wilfrid Laurier became prime minister in 1896. By strongly opposing Imperial interference in domestic affairs, Laurier quickly won over members of this group, but also the support of newer immigrants who settled in the Prairies during the first two decades of the twentieth century.

The advantage of the Liberal Party among Catholic voters was not primarily related to religious dogma, but rather to an "ethnic conception of the Canadian nationality, as distinct from the ethnicity of its individual members" (Johnston 2017, 102).

The explanation of the Liberal dominance of Canadian politics I present in this chapter is, however, antecedent to this argument. Below, I demonstrate that certain historical events led Catholic voters away from the Conservatives in the decades following Confederation. I also show that this Catholic realignment was mostly elite driven, rather than popular. The consequence of this partisan realignment was that, after the First World War, there was a massive decline in the number of Catholic and French-speaking MPs in the Conservative Party, and this situation remained more or less unchanged until the election of Brian Mulroney in 1984.

To support this line of argument, I consider several different sources of data to demonstrate the link between religion, voters, and parliamentary behaviour. First, I show that the relationship between the proportion of Catholics and support for the Liberal Party increased in each electoral district between 1867 and 1974. Second, I take a closer look at the distribution of Catholic and French-speaking MPs within each party to confirm that there was a partisan movement (or sorting) away from the Conservative Party towards the end of the nineteenth century. I explain this shift by several factors, such as the execution of Louis Riel in 1885 and the premiership of Wilfrid Laurier in 1896. Lastly, I use the voting records of Members of Parliament to demonstrate that religious issues were more likely to divide parties internally in the House of Commons, mostly because they created coalitions of Protestant and Catholic members who voted along ethno-religious lines. However, I find that these conflicts basically disappeared from the agenda after the arrival of the Progressives in 1921.

My argument is not that the Conservative Party deliberately chose to alienate Catholic voters: John A. Macdonald knew the importance of the Catholic vote, not only in Quebec, but especially in Ontario, where their support often made the difference between winning and losing an election (Miller 1974, 34–5). As I explained in chapter 2, the Conservatives had the misfortune of being in power when a series of difficult decisions had to be made regarding the rights of Catholics and French speakers outside the province of Quebec during the nineteenth century. Events such as the hanging of Louis Riel by a federal court in 1885 and the Manitoba Schools Question in 1890 divided both parties internally, and Catholics across Canada largely blamed the Conservatives for their handling of these matters. The selection of Wilfrid Laurier as Liberal leader in 1887 convinced many Catholics to shift allegiance towards that party, despite the warnings of the clergy, who traditionally had supported the Conservatives. Unlike other issues linked to less controversial nation-building projects, such as the development of railways or the banking system, the question of language and religious rights outside Quebec could not be settled rapidly in the years following Confederation. Instead, ethno-religious divisions became even more important after the westward expansion of the Dominion, and remained a central feature of the ideological underpinnings of MPs for several decades to come.

Recall that, in chapter 3, I identified ideological sorting as a possible factor in the growth of partisanship in Parliament over time. The logic was that members who increasingly shared a common set of preferences on a wide range of issues would vote together more in the legislature, even in the absence of party discipline. I ignored this explanation in the empirical analysis presented earlier, however, mainly because it is extremely difficult to measure a member's ideology. Different approaches exist to counter this problem, such as conducting a survey of legislators (Docherty 1997; Kornberg 1966) or estimating the ideological ideal points of legislators from their voting records (Poole and Rosenthal 1997). Surveys of Canadian MPs, unfortunately, are few and far between, and the scaling of roll call votes in a parliamentary system can be misleading when party discipline is high (Spirling and McLean 2007, 92–3).

Below, I use the religion of Members of Parliament to determine whether Catholics and Protestants were more likely to sort towards the Conservatives or Liberals over time. I show that the division between the two denominations started in the legislative arena and later moved to the electorate. The observed realignment of Catholic and Protestant voters is thus a story of elite-driven polarization. Ultimately, I argue that, for a long time, these ethno-religious conflicts represented the main obstacle to the development of party unity in the House of Commons.

I begin this chapter by offering a brief historical account of the importance of religion as a political factor in the years following Confederation. This review is by no means exhaustive. Rather, I outline a series of religious conflicts in chronological order that began with the Act of Union in 1840 and culminated with the premiership of Wilfrid Laurier in 1896. I then consider the relationship between religion and voting between 1867 and 1965 by using census-level data to correlate aggregate election results with the religious composition of electoral districts. This is followed by an examination of changes in the distribution of French and Catholic MPs in the two major parties over time. Finally, I take a closer look at the relationship between parliamentary behaviour and ethno-religious conflicts in the House of Commons by reporting the results of a series of spatial analyses of legislative votes. These models allow us to identify the types of issues that were most likely to divide parties internally between 1867 and 1925, and to confirm that religion was indeed the most contentious issue of the time.

Historical Context: Religious Conflicts

Anti-Catholicism was an important movement in Canada during the Victorian era. Although a British colony since the Treaty of Paris in 1763, domestic affairs in Quebec were still largely dominated by the descendants of the first permanent European settlers, who were both of French origin and Roman Catholics. For many English speakers, this situation was simply unacceptable. Confederation had sought to reduce the influence of French Canadians in the political process. The failures of the United Province of Canada were a constant reminder, however, that sectional strife could be exploited by party leaders and lead to open ethnic and religious divisions in the party system. At its most extreme, the anti-Catholic nativism movement believed in a papal conspiracy to take over the state (Watt 1967, 45). "This is a Protestant country. Ours is a Protestant Queen," claimed a Nova Scotia newspaper in 1895 (*News of the Week*, 18 March 1895, quoted in Miller 1985, 478). Foreign elements, such as Roman Catholics or French Canadians, were perceived as a threat to the unity of British North America, which was based on a common language and culture – what Lord Durham referred to as the Anglo-Saxon race (Watt 1967, 47). For the nativists, the solution to this problem was simple: Catholics had to be assimilated (Durham 1839, 24–8) or at most be allowed only "limited political rights" (Miller 1985, 478).

The problem was only exacerbated during the nineteenth century by the high birthrate of French Canadians and the arrival of Catholic immigrants, mainly from Ireland and Scotland. Despite their increase in number, however, their proportion of the Canadian population remained relatively stable at around 40 per cent because of the massive influx of immigrants from the British Isles and other Protestant countries. The same pattern held for Canadians of French origin, who remained roughly 30 per cent of the total population in the first few decades following Confederation (Brown and Cook 1974, 127). Even more troubling for many English speakers was the decline in the proportion of Canadians of British origin, from 61 per cent of the total population in 1871 to 57 per cent in 1901, and finally to 52 per cent by 1931.[1]

These demographic shifts were accompanied by a significant change in attitudes towards Catholics among the Protestant majority, who created several political groups to protect their interests, such as the Equal Rights Association, the Protestant Protective Association, and the Orange Lodge (Breton 2005, 92; McLauchlin 1986, 38). These groups were primarily active in Ontario to prevent the encroachment of Roman Catholics and to condemn the interference of the Catholic Church in Canadian politics. According to Miller, in "the 1840s and 1850s there was anxiety about Catholic immigration, particularly the famine Irish, but from the 1870s onward the preoccupation was more with the Catholic Church in Quebec and its role in preserving, and, it was feared, extending the French-Canadian presence within Confederation" (Miller 1985, 477). This opposition was primarily directed against ultramontanism, a doctrine that emphasized papal supremacy and the domination of the Catholic Church over civilian government (476). Ultramontanism also promoted nationalism, "since it taught that the French-Canadian nation was divinely created with a special God-given purpose, and that French Canadians had a religious duty to maintain their nationality within Lower Canada" (Silver 1999, 49–50).

After the failed rebellion of 1837–8, ultramontanism became the dominant political ideology in Quebec (Balthazar 2013, 80–1). With the support of the clergy, moderate French-Canadian reformists such as Louis-Hippolyte Lafontaine forged an alliance with the nationalist and ultramontane wing of the Conservative Party to promote the interests of the Church in the Legislative Assembly of the United Province of Canada (Monet 1966, 49–50). In fact, throughout most of the latter half of the nineteenth century, the Conservative Party in Quebec (the "Bleus") could count systematically on the support of the Catholic Church in both federal and provincial elections (Hamelin 1974, 135, 221, 233).

The increasing political success of ultramontanism and nationalism added to the general Protestant anxiety in post-Confederation Canada (Miller 1985, 476). The adoption of several controversial bills to support the clergy in Quebec, such as to abolish the Ministry of Public Instruction in 1875 or to restore the Jesuit Estates in 1888, contributed to increasing anti-Catholic sentiment across most of the country (Fay 2002, 127). Several provinces reacted by adopting their own educational law to promote the assimilation of French speakers and Catholics. Although Confederation granted control over local affairs to provincial legislatures, the British North America Act remained unclear about what language and religious rights French speakers and Catholics would enjoy outside Quebec and Ontario. The most important of these related to education, which represented a central dimension of the social organization of Canadians at the time. Protestants and Catholics had fundamentally divergent views about the involvement of their churches in the school system (Neatby 1973, 52). Roman Catholics favoured separate schools, where each religious group would control the curriculum and teach in conformity with its beliefs. Protestants supported common schools, where the provincial government would dictate the content of the curriculum. Separate schools facilitated the survival of French and Catholic minorities outside Quebec, while common schools promoted homogeneity, and free and compulsory education for all (Neatby 1973, 52–3).

The conflict over the preservation of separate school systems across Canada was the first event that led to the realignment of French and Catholic voters towards the Liberal Party. Following Confederation, a series of restrictive laws was adopted to limit both the funding of Catholic schools and the right to

Table 7.1 Restrictions on the Rights of French Speakers and Catholics outside Quebec, 1864–1930

Year	Province	Restriction
1864	Nova Scotia	French-speaking Catholic Acadians forbidden to have French schools.
1871	New Brunswick	Catholic schools outlawed; teaching of French prohibited.
1877	Prince Edward Island	Catholic schools outlawed; teaching of French prohibited.
1890	Manitoba	Separate (Catholic) schools outlawed; teaching of French forbidden in high schools. French no longer an official language in the Legislative Assembly, civil service, government publications, or provincial courts.
1892	Northwest Territories	Catholic schools outlawed; teaching of French prohibited.
1905	Alberta and Saskatchewan	Catholic schools outlawed; teaching of French prohibited.
1915	Ontario	Regulation 17: French outlawed in schools.
1916	Manitoba	Teaching of French prohibited at all levels.
1930	Saskatchewan	Teaching of French prohibited outside school hours.

Source: Bernard (1978, 27).

educate children in French outside Quebec. In some cases, such as New Brunswick (1871) and Prince Edward Island (1877), teaching in French was simply prohibited; in others, such as Manitoba (1890), public funding of separate schools was abolished. Table 7.1 lists all these restrictive decisions between 1864 and 1930. During this period, most Canadian provinces adopted regulations to limit teaching in French or abolished separate school systems – in Ontario and Manitoba, this was done despite the guarantees provided by the Constitution.[2]

The case of Manitoba provides the most striking example of how religion and education could affect partisan conflicts in Parliament. The creation of Manitoba in 1870, which followed the Red River Rebellion of the Métis in 1869, explicitly guaranteed a system of denominational schools for educating the Catholic and French-speaking Indigenous population of the province. However, the arrival of Protestant settlers in the years following Confederation increased pressure to create a tax-based system of common schools, especially after English speakers became the majority. The Manitoba government went much further than that. In 1890, the provincial Legislative Assembly abolished French as an official language, even though this was a constitutionally protected right. It also abolished the separate school system, which had been in place since 1871, and replaced it with publicly funded nondenominational schools, where teaching in French was prohibited.

The struggle surrounding what became known as the Manitoba Schools Question extended far beyond the borders of the new province. Ever since the Red River Rebellion, the French-speaking population of Quebec had supported the Catholic Métis of Manitoba, even if most felt ambivalent towards their Indigenous origins (Silver 1997, 155–6). The Catholic clergy had also defended the cause of the Métis, and campaigned for the pardon of Louis Riel, their leader, who was accused of participating in the murder of Thomas Scott, a Canadian government land surveyor, during the rebellion. Although Riel had been elected to Parliament in 1873, and again in 1874, he ultimately was forced to move to the United States in exchange for amnesty. Riel, however, did not remain in exile for long. He was asked to return to Canada in 1884 to defend once again the territorial claims of the Métis, who by then had resettled west of Manitoba. Riel's involvement in the short-lived North-West Rebellion ended in defeat the following year. The story of his surrender, trial, and execution by a federal court had a profound effect on his supporters in Quebec. Some scholars even suggest that the victory of Liberal Honoré Mercier in this province's 1886 election can be attributed to the resentment felt towards the Conservative Party and Macdonald's handling of the Riel affair (Neatby 1973, 28–9). For many nationalists, the hanging of Louis Riel represented a failure of Confederation to protect the rights of the French-speaking minority outside Quebec. Therefore, when the Manitoba government decided to abolish the separate school system in the province five years after Riel's execution, the outrage was felt even more intensely among Catholics in the province. This was yet another example of flagrant prejudice against the Roman Catholic minority in Canada. Not even Wilfrid Laurier could accept that children be taught in nondenominational schools. For him, the abolition of the separate school system was "a declaration of war against the French race" (Silver 1997, 186).

Unfortunately for the Conservative Party of John A. Macdonald, there was no easy solution to this crisis. A return to the status quo seemed unlikely: "The mere threat of the re-establishment of Roman Catholic schools in Manitoba over the expressed wishes of the Protestant majority in that province was a clarion call summoning Orangemen to their posts" (McLauchlin 1986, 41). D'Alton McCarthy, a prominent MP and Grand Master of the Orange Order, declared in a speech to the Protestant Protective Association in Ottawa that the only way Canada could ever be united was by "obliterating" the French language through English-only education (McCarthy 1889, 4–11). To this end, McCarthy introduced a bill to forbid the official use of French in the Northwest Territories, which further divided the Conservative Party along ethnic and religious lines (Silver 1997, 186).

The Manitoba Schools Question presented yet another problem for the Conservative Party. Since the School Act adopted in 1890 clearly violated the rights of the Catholic minority in the province, this group could formally request that the federal government intervene to repel the law under section 22.2 of the Manitoba constitution. The conflict over separate schools thus eventually was moved to the courts, where it was ruled that the federal government could take remedial actions to provide for the protection of the Catholic minority in the province.[3] After much hesitation, the Conservative government presented a remedial bill to Parliament in 1896. The legislation, however, never made it past second reading; it was blocked by a month-long filibuster orchestrated by the Liberal opposition, which wanted to force an election on this issue (Black 1975, 128). This strategy paid off: Parliament was dissolved, and an election was called for 23 June, five years after the Conservatives had taken office for the fourth consecutive term.

The leader of the Liberal Party, Wilfrid Laurier, took advantage of this situation by campaigning in favour of minority rights in Manitoba and by positioning his party as the defender of Roman Catholics across Canada. The Conservatives in Quebec had a much harder time convincing their traditional allies of their willingness to support the Manitoba minority (Silver 1997, 210). The party, now led by Charles Tupper, had been plagued by internal rivalries between the ultramontane and orangist factions since Macdonald's death in 1891.[4] The Conservatives also entered the election divided after about half of the cabinet (all Protestant ministers) resigned when the remedial bill was introduced in the House of Commons. Even the Catholic bishops in Quebec, who had always been traditional supporters of Macdonald and the Conservative "Bleus" in the province, demanded their followers vote in favour of whichever party promised to restore the rights of the minority in Manitoba (Neatby 1973, 74). Although the clergy did not go so far as to endorse the Liberals openly, the belief at the time among Laurier's supporters was that this would put an end to the Conservatives' "odious exploitation of holy authority" in the province (Silver 1997, 213).

In the end, the conflict over separate schools was a decisive factor in the election of Wilfrid Laurier, the first French-Canadian Catholic prime minister, who went on to resolve this crisis by compromising with Manitoba's Premier Thomas Greenway on the issue of language and religious education in the province (see, for example, Beck 1968, 82; Lower 1961, 396–7; Wade 1956, 436–7). For several scholars, this election signalled the beginning of a partisan realignment in Canada that ultimately led to the domination of the Liberal Party in Quebec for decades to come. Prior to this, the Conservatives and Liberals usually elected a mix of Protestant and Catholic members to Parliament, and each had supporters across both denominational groups. A consequence of this heterogeneity was that ethnic and religious tensions always had the potential to divide parties internally in the legislature, but also to polarize Catholic and Protestant voters in the electorate. As we saw above, several events that occurred before the Manitoba Schools Question already had contributed to enhancing these divisions. The debate over confessional education in New Brunswick, the Métis rebellions in Manitoba and the North-West, and the hanging of Louis Riel were all crises that could have pushed some Catholic voters away from the Conservative Party. The emerging nativism and anti-Catholicism sentiment across Canada, which was in part a reaction to the growing influence of the ultramontane and nationalist movement in Quebec, also contributed to accelerating this trend. All of these factors offer circumstantial evidence to explain the realignment of Catholic voters towards the Liberal Party, one of the most important changes in Canadian politics during the previous century. A lingering question remains, however: was this change driven by political elites or by the voters? In other words, did Catholics abruptly break from the Conservative Party in 1896, or was this transformation the result of a gradual shift that followed from changes first observed in Parliament?

Sorting the Voters

Here I provide empirical evidence to confirm that Catholic voters in Canada increasingly supported the Liberal Party after the election of Wilfrid Laurier in 1896. I rely on aggregate data to measure the association between the proportion of Catholics in the riding and support for Liberal and Conservative candidates in each election between 1867 and 1930 and between 1949 and 1965. The analysis reports the results of linear regressions between the proportion of Roman Catholics and the proportion of Liberal voters in the electoral districts, and assumes that this relationship applies at the individual level as well. Obviously, this approach suffers from an ecological inference problem, because we do not know how each Catholic voter behaved individually during an election. Nevertheless, Blais (2005, 822–7) and Johnston (2017, 120) both confirm, with individual-level survey data, that Catholic voters were more likely to support the Liberal Party between 1965 and 2004, so I am confident that my analysis provides a reliable indicator of this trend.[5] To be safe, the analysis also includes an additional robustness check that considers the relationship between the proportion of Methodists and support for the Liberals and Conservatives in the ridings over the study periods.[6] The idea here is that the Methodist Church – which André Siegfried considered "the centre of anti-French aggressive Protestantism" (Siegfried [1906] 1966, 53) – should support the Conservative Party (McLauchlin 1986, 51), especially after the election of Wilfrid Laurier, when Methodists represented around 17 per cent of the population.

The theoretical expectations of this analysis are pretty straightforward: I hypothesize that the relationship between the proportion of Catholics and Liberal (Conservative) votes in the riding will increase (decline) over time. The reverse should be true for Methodists. Although Johnston (2017, 102) argues that the association between Catholics and the Liberal Party has very little to do with "faith," "morals," or "ecclesiology," I show in the remainder of this chapter that it is precisely these factors that prompted this change.[7]

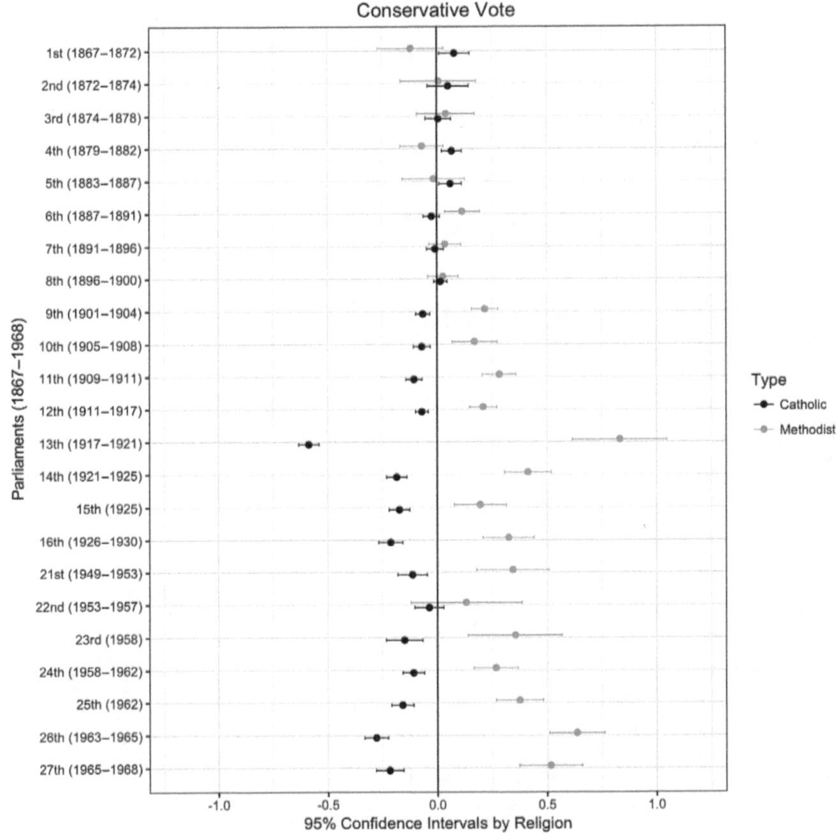

Figure 7.1 Proportions of Catholics and Methodists and Vote Shares of Conservative and Liberal Candidates, by Riding, 1867–1968

In determining the relationship between religion and the vote, figure 7.1 reports the results of a series of linear regression models in which the independent variable represents the proportion of Catholics (Methodists) in each riding, while the dependent variable represents the corresponding vote share for the Liberal (Conservative) candidate in the election. Both plots of figure 7.1 display the values of the regression coefficients, with their 95 per cent confidence interval, for each party separately. I obtained the proportion of Catholics and Methodists in each riding from the decennial Canadian census,[8] and the proportions of votes for Conservative and Liberal candidates from the historical election results of federal ridings found on the Parliament of Canada website.

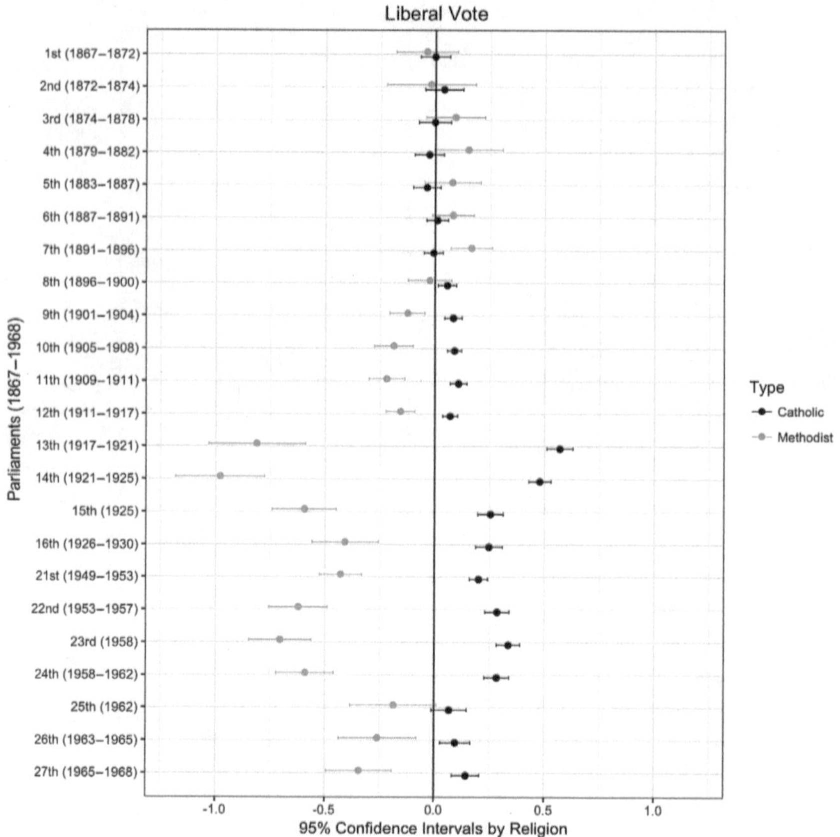

Figure 7.1 continued

The results presented in figure 7.1 confirm that the correlation between the proportion of Catholics and Conservative Party support in each riding was either positive or close to zero until the 1901 election. Similarly, the relationship between the proportion of Catholics and the Liberal vote was positive only after Laurier became prime minister, and somewhat increased thereafter until the 1917 election, when it jumped by more than fifty percentage points. This result is not surprising given the special context of the wartime election, which was centred on conscription. During this election, all Liberal MPs from Quebec – and a handful, mostly Catholic Liberals, from the rest of Canada – joined Laurier to oppose the Conservatives and pro-conscription Liberals, who had formed a national unity government under Robert Borden in 1917. What is perhaps more interesting to see in this case is the long-lasting effect of the

Liberal-Catholic connection, which remained relatively strong throughout the 1920s and was still comparable in scope even after the Second World War.

Figure 7.1 also confirms the negative relationship between the proportion of Methodists and the Liberals' vote share. The First World War appears to have had the same effect on Methodists as on Catholics, but this time support grew for the Conservatives, increasing dramatically after the 1917 election, when the Methodist Church decided to support conscription (Heath 2012, 36). This relationship remained relatively high in the 1920s, but also during the 1950s and 1960s, when it was even stronger than the correlation between Catholics and the Liberals' vote share.

It is interesting to note that, when there was a decline in the relationship between the proportion of Catholics or Methodists and support for the Liberals and Conservatives, the votes do not appear to have gone necessarily towards the opposite party after 1917. For example, in the 1962 election, the correlation between Catholics and the Liberal vote was near zero, but this did not translate into more votes for the Conservatives, as the correlation between the proportion of Catholics and the Conservative vote remained negative. In this case, support of the most Catholic ridings appears to have gone towards a different party, the Ralliement Créditiste, which won twenty seats and 26 per cent of the vote in Quebec.[9]

To summarize, this first analysis confirms that there was a gradual increase in the relationship between the proportion of Catholics and support for the Liberal Party. This finding is apparent in almost all elections after 1896. Furthermore, this relationship seems to have strengthened following the 1917 election. Likewise, we find that the association between the proportion of Methodists and support for the Conservative Party also increased during the same period. Overall, these findings suggest that there was most likely a Catholic (and Methodist) shift towards both major parties at the beginning of the twentieth century, with long-lasting consequences for the Canadian party system. The fact that the two religious denominations moved in the opposite direction implies that faith played an important role in this transformation.

Table 7.2 reports the results of a different analysis to confirm this change and to ensure that the findings were not simply driven by Quebec voters. The table shows the results of three different regression models to measure the strength of the association between the proportion of Catholics and corresponding support for the Liberal candidate in the riding: first, for all the data available between 1867 and 1930; second, for the period between 1949 and 1965; and third, by combining both datasets (1867–1965) into one cumulative file. The analysis also divides voters into three distinct groups. The first one pools everyone together (the second column); the second group considers only Quebec voters (the third column); and the third looks at voters outside that province (the fourth column).[10] The results confirm the strong association between Catholics

Table 7.2 The Relationship between Catholics and the Vote, 1867–1965

Variable	All Ridings	Quebec Ridings	Ridings in Rest of Canada
		Elections, 1867–1930	
% Catholic	0.14 (0.01)***	0.11 (0.03)***	0.02 (0.03)
Parliamentary dummies	✓	✓	✓
N	2,988	862	2,126
		Elections, 1949–65	
% Catholic	0.20 (0.02)***	−0.15 (0.04)***	0.31 (0.02)***
Parliamentary dummies	✓	✓	✓
N	1,825	523	1,302
		Elections, 1867–1930 and 1949–65	
% Catholic	0.16 (0.01)***	0.03 (0.03)	0.11 (0.01)***
Parliamentary dummies	✓	✓	✓
N	4,813	1,385	3,428

***p < 0.001; **p < 0.01; *p < 0.05; ˙p < 0.1.
Note: Ordinary least squares regressions. Standard errors were corrected to control for autocorrelation and heteroscedasticity. The dependent variable is the proportion of votes obtained by the Liberal Party candidate in an election. The variable % of Catholics indicates the proportion of Catholics in the riding, as measured by the decennial census. The table reports only the values of this coefficient.

and the Liberal vote, but this time with an important caveat. Separating the data by periods, we find that this relationship holds in Quebec only between 1867 and 1930, but not during the later period (1949–65). Furthermore, looking at the results outside Quebec, we find the relationship confirmed only in the later period. Finally, combining both periods together into a single model confirms that the link between the proportion of Catholics and the Liberal vote is significant outside Quebec, but not in that province alone.

How can these differences be explained? My own interpretation is that the Catholic shift began in Quebec, where protecting language and religious rights was the most important issue, and later moved to the other provinces, but for different reasons. Given that the proportion of Catholics outside Quebec gradually increased between 1871 and 1961 from 14 to 20 per cent of the total population, the correlation observed between the Catholic vote and Liberal support between 1949 and 1968 could be related to this demographic shift. What motivated this connection is another question altogether. I tend to agree with Johnston (2017, 102) and Smith (1963, 128–9), who argue that the Catholic vote outside Quebec is explained more by the development of a new Canadian identity, championed by the Liberal Party, that was critical of the country's role in the British Empire and its participation in foreign wars. These issues could have played only second fiddle, however, to a realignment process that was already well underway by the time Wilfrid Laurier became prime minister in 1896. Moreover, it remains difficult to explain why Methodists also drifted away from the Liberal Party towards the Conservatives during the same period. The Methodist Church was always a staunch supporter of the Empire, but it was also concerned by what it perceived as a more "aggressive and intolerant [form] of Catholicism," "ultramontanism," and "French-Canadian nationalism" (Semple 1996, 418–19). At the core, the Methodists' opposition to the Liberal Party was linked to a "strong anti-foreign and anti-Catholic sentiment" (348) that "would remain close to the surface in Protestant thinking at least for the first half of the twentieth century" (418).

Finally, this last analysis also highlights the importance of group identity and social context in explaining political behaviour in Canadian elections (Gidengil 2012, 106–7). For decades researchers have been struggling to understand why Catholic voters support the Liberal Party more (see, for example, Blais 2005; Irvine 1974; Irvine and Gold 1980; Johnston 1985, 2017). It is clear from my analysis that there has been some transfer of partisan values across generations over time. Indeed, we now know that former political systems, such as slavery or colonial rule, can affect "both institutional and behavioural outcomes long after the institutions themselves disappear" (Acharya, Blackwell, and Sen 2016, 623; see also Nunn 2009, 70). This argument can be easily extended to the Catholic Church, one of the oldest formal institutions in Canada.

We also know geography plays an important role in explaining political behaviour, and that group-based voting will be stronger in more densely populated and homogeneous areas (Hersh and Nall 2016, 290). Outside Quebec, Catholics were more likely to band together and live in tightly knit communities, such as in the Glengarry district of Nova Scotia for the Scots (MacLean 1976, 96–7), the St Peter's and St Joseph's colonies in Saskatchewan for the Germans (Dawson 1936, 287–8), the northern part of Winnipeg for the Poles and Ukrainians (Perin 1998, 17), or the Parish of Downeyville in Ontario for the Irish (Mannion 1974, 41). This group proximity promoted religious identity and a transfer of partisanship across generations. For Scottish Catholics, loyalty was paramount. "I think the Highland people are more traditional," claimed a farmer in Nova Scotia. "I mean they are more apt to vote for one party the way their parents would" (quoted in MacLean 1976, 109). The correspondence between the party identification of Catholic parents and their children is indeed very high among Liberals: if we combine respondents from the 1965, 1974, and 1979 Canadian Election Studies who resided outside Quebec, we find that the transfer of Liberal Party identification across one generation to another was 78 per cent for Catholics but 63 per cent for Protestants.[11] This socialization process is a credible mechanism to explain the success of the Liberal Party among Catholic voters, especially given that this relationship was already beginning to wane in the 1960s (Johnston 2017, 124–5). One can only assume that the parental transfer of party identification was much stronger in the earlier decades of the twentieth century, when most Canadians lived in rural areas and weekly church attendance was much higher (Clark 2003, 2). The effects of this transfer thus could have been felt decades later, as positive attitudes towards the Liberal Party among Catholics were passed down across generations.

Sorting the Members

The results presented above still leave open the question as to whether the Catholic shift was an elite- or a mass-driven phenomenon. What might have started as a reaction to events reported by the Church or the newspapers in Quebec could have culminated in the realignment of voters away from the Conservatives by the end of the nineteenth century, a view apparently confirmed by historical accounts of the period. The discontent of Catholics had its first major political effect following the victory of Honoré Mercier in the 1886 Quebec election. Although a Liberal, Mercier had created a new party – the Parti National – in reaction to the hanging of Louis Riel by forming a coalition between some Liberals and a handful of dissident Conservative nationalists in the province (Lemieux 2008, 16). For the first time, the Catholic clergy saw the Liberals, historically at odds with the ultramontanes, as an acceptable alternative to the Conservative "Bleus" (Linteau, Durocher, and Robert 1989, 322). The Parti National's 1886 victory provoked unease among the Protestant population, especially after the provincial assembly adopted the Jesuit Estate Act in 1888, which compensated the clergy for land seized by the British Crown after the Conquest. This financial settlement contributed to the growth of anti-Catholic nativism in Ontario, and led to the creation of the Equal Rights Association (a forerunner of the Protestant Protective Association), which spearheaded the movement against separate schools in Canada (Miller 1974, 36). Above all, Mercier's victory signified a change in the Catholic Church's perception of the Liberal Party in Quebec. Indeed, the anti-clerical Liberal "Rouges" previously had opposed all bills for the restitution of the Jesuit Estates (Monet 1966, 48–9). Now they were allied with the Church, perceived as defenders of the Catholic faith in the province. This new alliance also paved the way for the premiership of Wilfrid Laurier a decade later, which in turn was made possible in part by the Conservative Party's handling of the Manitoba Schools Question.

This is the historical account, but what about empirical evidence from parliamentary voting data? We saw previously that the growing conflict between French-speaking nationalists and English-speaking nativists preceded what appears to have been a sorting out of Catholic and Methodist voters towards the Liberal and Conservative parties. Is it possible that this shift also influenced the behaviour of the political elite? In other words, did the sorting process operate similarly within the Liberal and Conservative caucuses in Parliament? Were

Catholics more likely to be elected as Liberals after the creation of the Parti National in Quebec, or after Laurier became party leader in 1887? Although the evidence of the partisan shift shown above does not really indicate a strong relationship between the proportion of Catholics and Liberal support in the ridings before the 1896 election, it is possible that Catholic and Protestant MPs shifted allegiances much earlier. The historical evidence for this type of change, however, is rather thin. The parliamentary records note only five cases of French-speaking Conservatives from Quebec who switched parties after Riel's hanging in 1885, either by becoming independent (J.G.H. Bergeron and Alphonse Desjardins) or by joining the federal branch of the Parti National (Guillaume Amyot, Alexis Desaulier, Firmin Dugas). Of those, only three (Amyot, Bergeron, and Desjardins) kept their seats in the next election, in 1887.

The consequences of Riel's hanging for support of the Conservatives in Quebec were much more dramatic (Lemieux 2008, 18). The party could keep only thirty-one of its fifty seats in the province during the 1887 election, while their vote share dropped by more than twenty points from 70 per cent of the two-party vote in 1882 to 50 per cent.[12] These seat losses either went to the Liberal Party (12), the (federal) Parti National (2), or to independent members of the House (5).

Clearly, the emergence of the Parti National weakened the Conservatives' hold on Quebec voters. Figure 7.2 illustrates this shift by reporting the Liberal Party vote share as a proportion of all votes cast in each federal election in Quebec between 1867 and 2011. As we can see from the graphic, support for the Liberal Party increased dramatically after the execution of Louis Riel in 1885. The upward trend continued when Laurier ran his first campaign as party leader in 1891, but increased even more after he became prime minister in 1896. The decline in Liberal support observed in the first decade of the twentieth century has to do with the emergence of the Conservative-Nationalist alliance of Monk, Bourassa, and Borden, described in chapter 2. Not surprisingly, the conscription crisis of the First World War also significantly increased support for the Liberals in Quebec, which then slowly declined until the 1960s, when Pierre Trudeau became party leader. Finally, the decline observed during the 1980–2000 period can be explained by the election of Brian Mulroney, the arrival of the Bloc Québécois in 1990, and the NDP surge in the 2011 election.

Another way to understand how Catholic and Protestant voters might have shifted parties is to look at the denominational composition of each major party caucus during the nineteenth and early twentieth centuries. This information is found in the Canadian Parliamentary Companions or other biographical notices that list the religion of MPs (Roman Catholic, Anglican, Presbyterian, Baptist, Methodist, Jewish, Spiritualist, and so on).[13] If Catholic voters were more likely to support Catholic candidates, and if the Liberal Party had more Catholic candidates than did the Conservative Party, then we should expect the

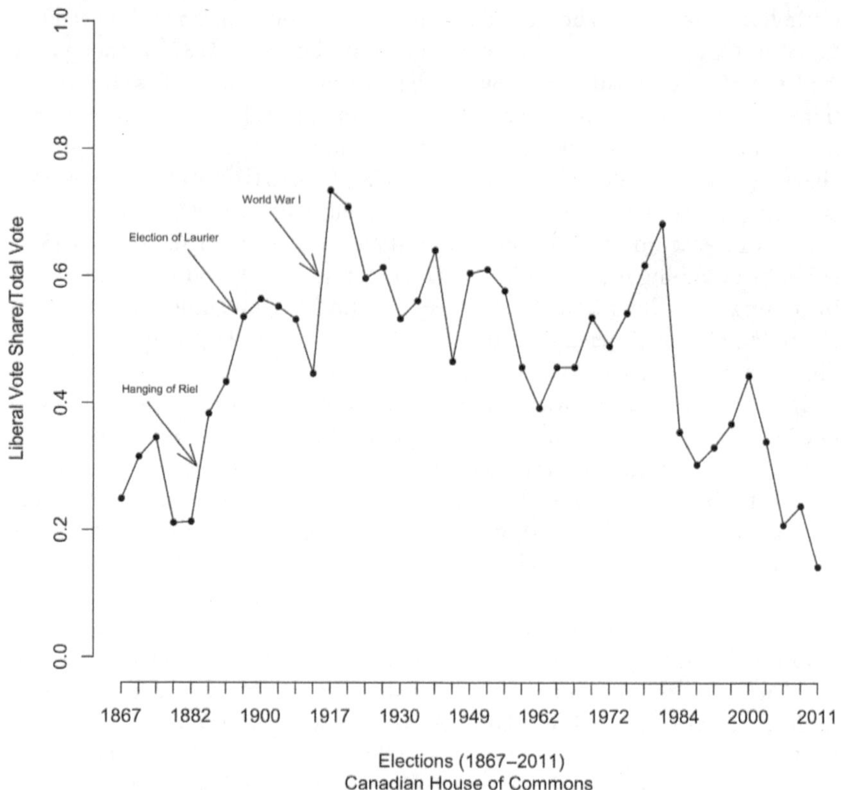

Figure 7.2 Liberal Votes as Proportion of All Votes, Quebec, 1867–2011

Liberal Party to have more Catholic MPs, on average. The reverse trend should be found with Protestants and the Conservative Party. Of course, this type of analysis has certain limitations, especially since we do not know the religion of both major party candidates during earlier elections (only the religion of the winner). We can also look at the distribution of French and English surnames in both major parties to estimate how ethno-linguistic groups shifted towards either of the major parties over time.[14] Although far from ideal, this method is a relatively straightforward approach to identify French-speaking Catholics in the data, since virtually all French speakers were Catholic until the 1960s.

The distribution of Catholics, Protestants, and French speakers in the Conservative and Liberal parties is reported in figure 7.3. Since we do not know the religious affiliation of members after 1925, the graphic reports only the loess curve (local regressions) fits for both Catholics and Protestants in each

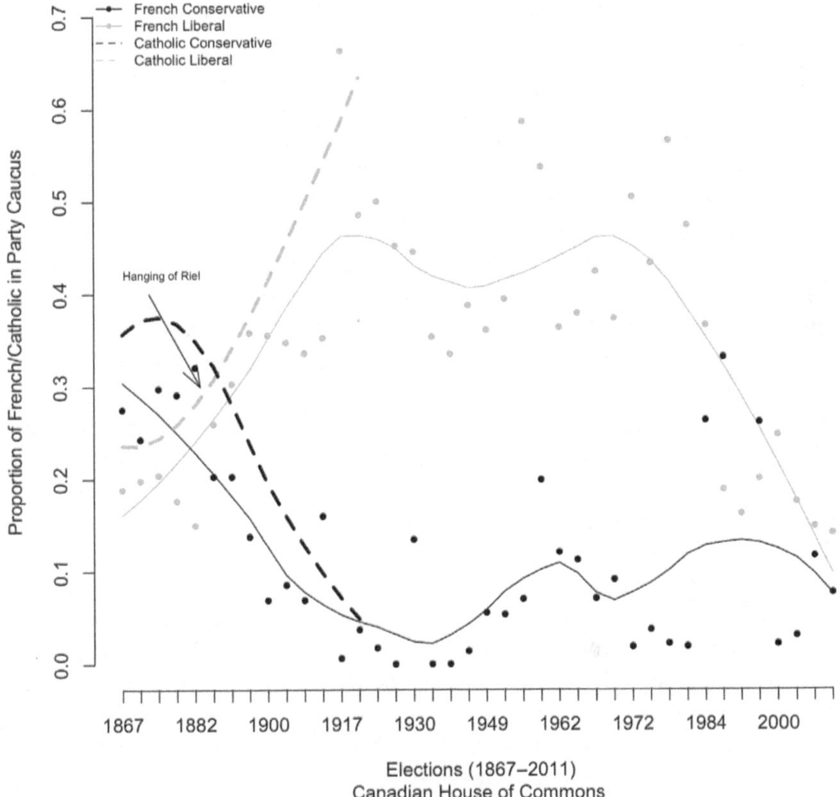

Figure 7.3 Proportion of French-Speaking and Catholic MPs in Liberal and Conservative Party Caucuses, 1867–2011

caucus prior to this date.[15] The points in the figure represent the proportion of French-speaking Liberals and Conservatives elected in each term, with the corresponding trend lines also obtained by local regressions.

The first thing to note from this figure is that the proportion of Catholics in the Conservative Party began to decline after the sixth Parliament (1887–91), which immediately followed the execution of Riel. The same pattern is observed with French-speaking Conservative members. The proportion of Catholics in the Liberal Party eventually reached 71 per cent in the 1917 election (with 65 per cent of French speakers in the caucus). The longer trend also confirms that the Liberals were the party of French-speaking Canadians until the 1980s, with about 40 per cent of the caucus made up of this group (from Quebec, but also strongly elsewhere, such as New Brunswick). The Progressive

Conservatives' victory in 1984 and the arrival of the Bloc Québécois put an end to Liberal domination in Quebec. Still, the figure clearly shows that the Liberal Party is, first and foremost, a Catholic party. The proportion of Catholics in the Conservative Party, high following Confederation, declined steadily during the nineteenth century and had fallen close to zero by the 1920s.

We thus have strong evidence to confirm that Protestant (English) and Catholic (French) MPs were more likely to be elected as Conservatives and Liberals, respectively, through most of the twentieth century. As we saw earlier, this change might have begun with the defection of Quebec Conservatives following Riel's execution in 1885, but these numbered only a handful – not enough to support the long-term shift we see in the data. Rather, the increasing number of Catholic (and French-speaking) Liberals is more likely explained by election losses and the replacement of old members with new ones. This movement away from the Conservative Party might have begun at the elite level prior to the 1887 election, but it was clearly supported by voters after this point.

Perhaps the most informative finding here relates to the distribution of Catholic and Protestant members across both parties in the years following Confederation. Before 1891, each denomination was more or less equally well represented in both the Conservative and Liberal parties: around 25–35 per cent of Catholics in each caucus. This ideological heterogeneity could help explain why party unity was much weaker in this period, especially when ethno-religious issues were debated on the floor of the House. When voting occurred over these questions, members could have been more likely to follow their conscience instead of the party line. We are thus given another piece of the puzzle: that party cohesion increased in parallel with the growing number of Catholics in the Liberal Party and Protestants in the Conservative Party. And since we know the religion of members between 1867 and 1925, we can verify this hypothesis by their parliamentary voting records.

Voting in Parliament

So far I have used individual loyalty scores and the Rice index in chapters 5 and 6 to understand how members have behaved in Parliament. Another way to look at legislative behaviour is to undertake a spatial analysis of parliamentary voting. This method is useful because it identifies which types of issues were more likely to divide parties internally during legislative votes. And unlike regression analysis, the spatial model approach also allows us to determine how frequently members voted together in Parliament. This will come in handy when comparing the voting behaviour of Catholics and Protestants.

The theoretical principle underlying the spatial model of voting is that legislators have ideal points (or preferences) across a set of policy alternatives located on a spatial map that represents the main dimensions of conflicts in the legislature.[16] These vote-based scores are recovered by different scaling methodologies that aggregate the outcomes of individual recorded votes into distinct dimensions. Each dimension corresponds to various issues that generally map votes onto a one- or two-dimensional Cartesian coordinate system.

What these dimensions exactly represent is another question. Much as in factor analysis, scaling techniques identify latent variables ("dimensions," in spatial terms) that are correlated with the outcome of hundreds of recorded votes. Note here that the researcher must infer the meaning of these dimensions. In the context of the US Congress, for example, spatial models of voting generally assume that the first and second dimensions represent two distinct policy spaces (see Poole and Rosenthal 1997, 2007). The first dimension (the horizontal axis in the Cartesian coordinate system) is associated with partisan and ideological conflicts: Democrats and Republicans are clustered together at opposite extremes, while moderates are located near the centre. The second dimension (the vertical axis) corresponds to a different set of policy issues that are mostly linked to regional conflicts in American history, such as slavery or civil rights. Since the first dimension explains partisan divisions in Congress, the second dimension must necessarily be associated with issues that have the potential to divide parties internally.

In the context of the UK Parliament (Spirling and McLean 2007, 8) and the Canadian House of Commons (Godbout and Høyland 2011, 371), one cannot be certain that the location of standard scaling techniques is related to the ideological orientation of MPs. Perhaps in earlier parliamentary terms, when party discipline was weaker, one could interpret the first dimension of voting as representing the left–right ideological continuum. The division, however, might not necessarily have been over economic redistribution – in Canada, this conflict could have been between toryism and radical-liberalism or over protective tariffs and free trade. Given that party unity dramatically increased over time, the analysis presented below does not assume that the coordinates in the first dimension represent the ideological orientation of MPs on these issues. Rather, we can assume that the first dimension of legislative voting represents the level of support for the governing party.[17] The closer members are to one of the two extremes in the first dimension, the more likely they are to have voted with (or against) the government.

The presence of a strong second dimension of legislative voting in earlier Canadian Parliaments is more difficult to interpret. Indeed, votes that fall into this dimension presuppose some level of intra-party divisions. We might suspect ethno-religious conflicts to have had an important influence on the behaviour of certain members, and to have offered some incentives for legislators to defect and support what they assumed were the best interests of their Church or constituents. Thus, we can anticipate that MPs who shared the same religion (Catholic or Protestant) will have formed alliances on certain votes. Such conflicts should be represented by horizontal lines in a two-dimensional spatial model (the vertical lines are partisan divisions), with Catholics from both parties clustering at the top (in the first and second quadrants) and Protestants at the bottom (in the third and fourth quadrants).

Since we know the religion and party affiliation of members, we can visually identify the location of both Protestant and Catholic MPs in the spatial models. To obtain these coordinates, I calculated the locations of all legislators using a binary discrete choice model based on Poole's (2005) Optimal Classification (OC) algorithm.[18] This approach computes the ranking of all MPs from their voting records to maximize the proportion of correctly classified votes in a one- or two-dimensional spatial model.[19] A correctly classified vote implies that the algorithm separates all members according to their vote choice (either yea or nay).

The classification becomes trickier when party unity breaks down. In this context, it is often necessary to add a second dimension to the spatial model, so that the algorithm can move members around in a two-dimensional space to improve its classification accuracy. If all members follow the party line in a two-party system, then a one-dimensional model is sufficient to explain the outcome of most, if not all, legislative votes. Suppose, however, that two factions of members, consisting of Catholics and Protestants from both major parties, sometimes vote together. Then the introduction of a second dimension becomes necessary to improve the performance of the model.[20]

With the basic principles governing the spatial model of voting in hand, how can we use this approach to analyse the composition of different voting coalitions in the Canadian Parliament? First, we can use the OC algorithm to locate all MPs according to their voting records in a one- and two-dimension model. Second, we can use these estimates to determine the importance of the second dimension of voting in explaining the outcome of individual recorded votes. And finally, we can use this approach to identify what types of votes were more likely to be associated with the second dimension of voting in each Parliament – that is, issues that divided both parties internally. The expectations from this model are straightforward. If we follow the sorting argument described earlier in the chapter, we should find that the second dimension of voting is associated with ethno-religious conflicts, and that the importance of this dimension declines over time as the proportions of Catholic and Protestant members shift towards the Liberal and Conservative parties, respectively.

Table 7.3 reports the relevance of each of these dimensions in Parliament between 1867 and 1925, and compares by term the fit of the OC algorithm for a one- and a two-dimensional model.[21] The main finding here is that the explanatory power of the first dimension increases over time. In the first term, a one-dimensional model predicts correctly 88 per cent of all voting decisions, while a two-dimensional model improves the proportion to 91 per cent.

Table 7.3 Proportion of Correctly Classified Voting Decisions in a One- and Two-Dimensional Model, by Parliament, 1867–1925

Parliament	PCC 1st Dim	APRE 1st Dim	PCC 2nd Dim	APRE 2nd Dim	PCC Diff	APRE Diff	> 0.20 Diff
1st	0.88	0.63	0.91	0.75	0.04	0.11	0.22
2nd	0.94	0.85	0.99	0.97	0.05	0.12	0.26
3rd	0.91	0.73	0.95	0.85	0.04	0.12	0.25
4th	0.95	0.84	0.97	0.89	0.02	0.05	0.12
5th	0.95	0.85	0.97	0.90	0.02	0.06	0.08
6th	0.93	0.82	0.96	0.90	0.03	0.08	0.15
7th	0.97	0.92	0.99	0.96	0.01	0.04	0.09
8th	0.96	0.88	0.98	0.94	0.02	0.06	0.15
9th	0.99	0.96	0.99	0.98	0.01	0.02	0.04
10th	0.99	0.96	1.00	0.98	0.01	0.02	0.10
11th	0.99	0.98	1.00	0.99	0.01	0.01	0.05
12th	0.99	0.96	1.00	0.99	0.01	0.03	0.07
13th	0.98	0.96	0.99	0.97	0.01	0.01	0.03
14th	0.91	0.71	0.97	0.90	0.06	0.19	0.38

Note: The fit statistics are: PCC = percentage correctly predicted; APRE = average proportion reduction in error; Diff = difference between the second-dimension statistic and the first-dimension statistic (PCC or APRE); > 0.20 = proportion of votes where APRE 2nd dim; APRE 1st dim > 0.20.

Recall that the first dimension captures government-opposition votes in the legislature, while the second dimension relates to issues that weaken party unity. By the tenth term, the one-dimensional model correctly predicts 99 per cent of all individual voting decisions, while a two-dimensional model improves the classification by less than one percentage point, to 99.6 – an almost perfect fit. At that point, a single-dimension model is sufficient to account for the outcome of virtually all legislative votes.[22] Finally, in the fourteenth Parliament (1922–5), the one- and two-dimensional models drop back to lower values, mainly because the importance of the second dimension increases again with the arrival of the Progressive Party. In this case, the performance of the spatial model is affected by the presence of three party caucuses, so a two-dimension model is needed to account for the shifting dynamics of these voting coalitions.[23]

Figure 7.4 illustrates how the different parties are organized in a series of spatial models between 1867 and 1925. The dots in each plot correspond to the two-dimension coordinates of legislators obtained with the OC algorithm. Every Parliament is represented in two distinct figures that identify members either by their party affiliation (Conservative, Liberal, third party, independent) or by religion (Protestant, English Catholic, French Catholic). These spatial models clearly demonstrate that the first dimension clusters parties into coherent voting groups. We also find, however, that the second dimension polarizes Catholic and Protestant MPs, especially around the fifth Parliament, right when Louis Riel was executed. In this Parliament, all Catholic MPs are clustered on top of the plot (quadrants one and two), regardless of their party affiliation, which indicates that several votes divided each party internally. This clustering remains the same until the eighth Parliament (1896–1900), when Laurier became prime minister and the proportion of Catholic MPs in the Conservative Party began to decline dramatically.

Since I obtained these spatial models from the voting records of members, it is possible to determine which types of votes were more likely to fall in the second dimension of voting and if they were indeed related to ethno-religious conflicts. One procedure to identify these votes is to select all recorded ones where the difference in the aggregate proportional reduction in error (APRE) between a one- and two-dimension model is greater than 20 per cent (see Poole and Rosenthal 2007, 37). By following this rule, we find that 243 of the 1,657 votes recorded between 1867 and 1925 fall into this category (roughly 14 per cent of the data for the whole period).[24] The last column of table 7.3 reports the proportion of second-dimension votes with an APRE greater than 20 per cent in each term. As we can see, these numbers are relatively important in the first three Parliaments and remain high until the eighth Parliament, when Wilfrid Laurier became prime minister.

With this analysis, we can also identify the types of issues most likely to fall into the first and second dimensions of voting. The results confirm that around half of all recorded divisions can be strictly considered in terms of first-dimension votes between 1867 and 1925, with members of the government rallied against the opposition (for example, the APRE difference is zero). Of these votes, 20 per cent related to railroads, which was then official government economic policy. We also find divisions on the budget and tariffs/taxation (18 per cent) and election and democratic reform (19 per cent). In fact, over half of all the first-dimension votes were linked directly to motions introduced by members of the cabinet. If we compare this number with votes that fell strictly in the second dimension (APRE > 20 per cent), the proportion of government business drops to 35 per cent. Therefore, we can conclude with confidence that the majority of first-dimension votes correspond to issues associated with government policies, on which Conservative and Liberal MPs were opposed.

Turning now to the second dimension, we find that one-third of these votes were associated with religious and ethnic questions, such as marriage and divorce, schooling, language, prohibition, temperance, and the North-West Rebellion. Examples of these votes are the motion to incorporate the Orange Association of British America in the fifth Parliament and the motion to expel

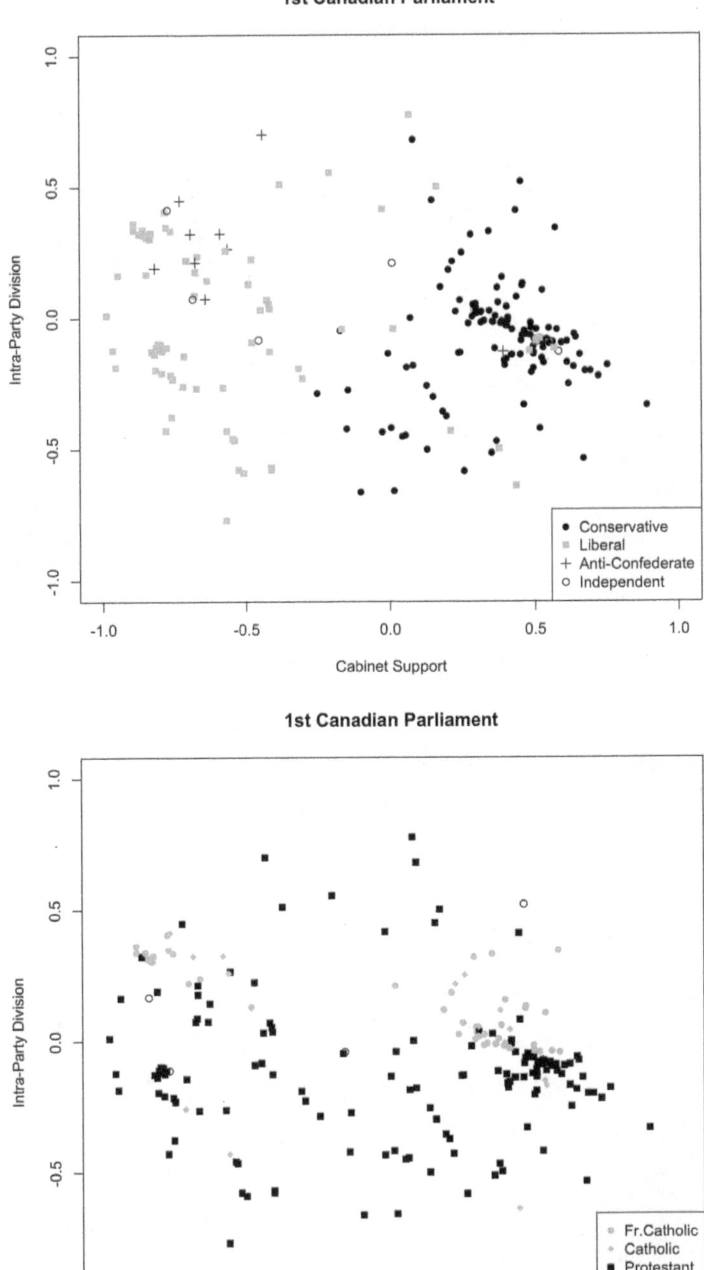

Figure 7.4 Optimal Classification Analysis, by Party and Religion, 1867–1925

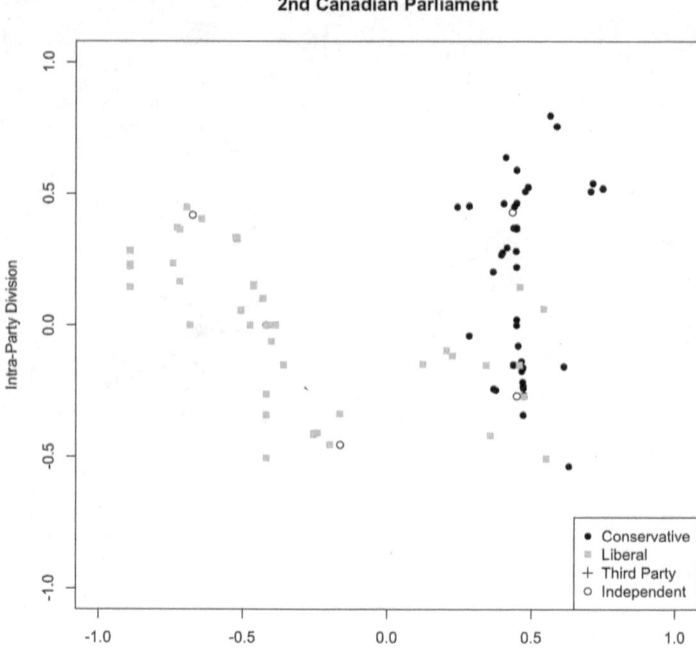

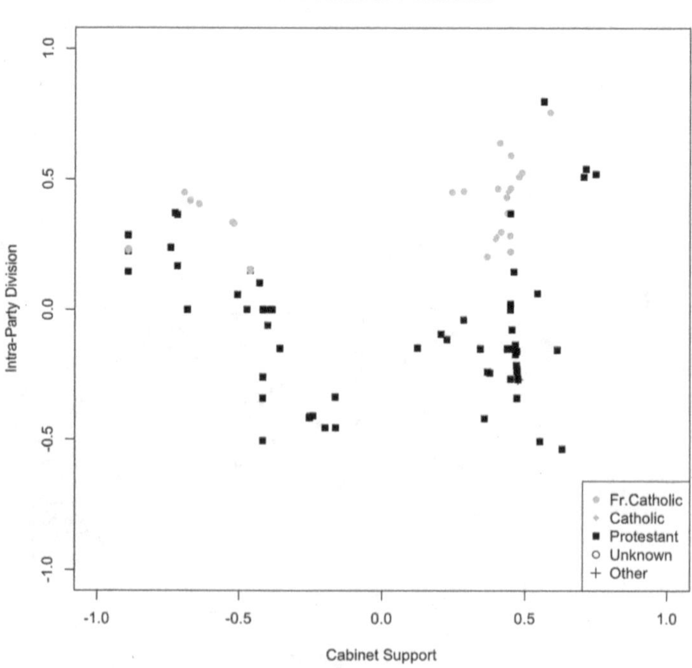

Figure 7.4 Optimal Classification Analysis, by Party and Religion, 1867–1925 (continued)

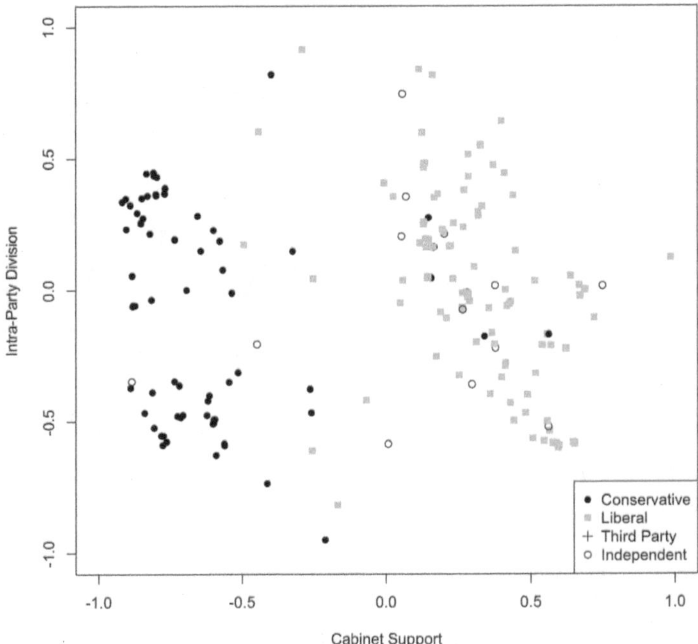

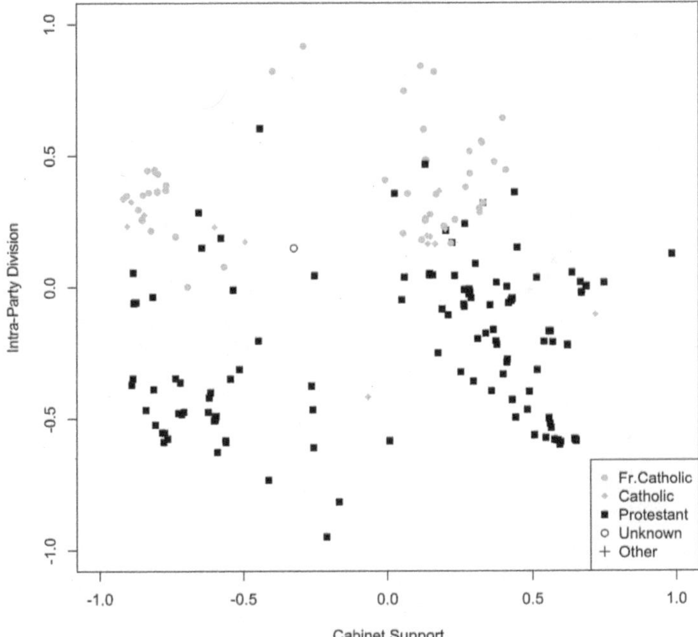

Figure 7.4 continued

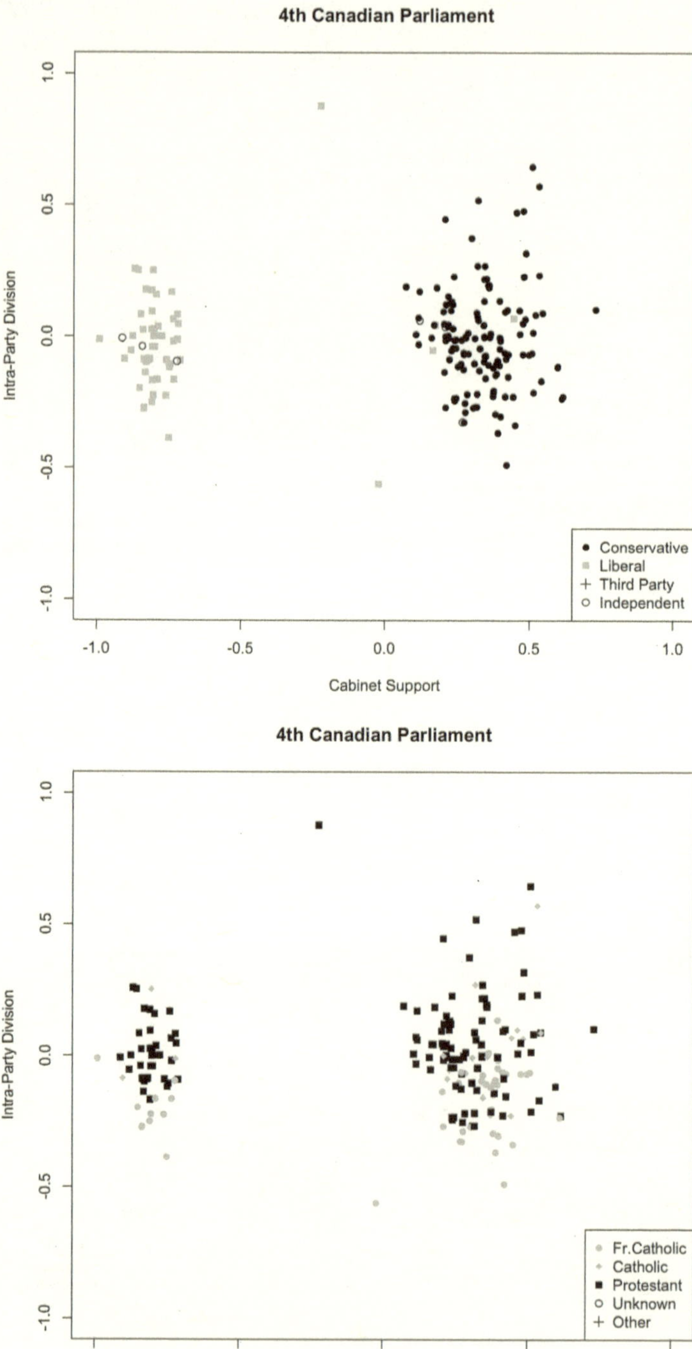

Figure 7.4 Optimal Classification Analysis by Party and Religion, 1867–1925 (continued)

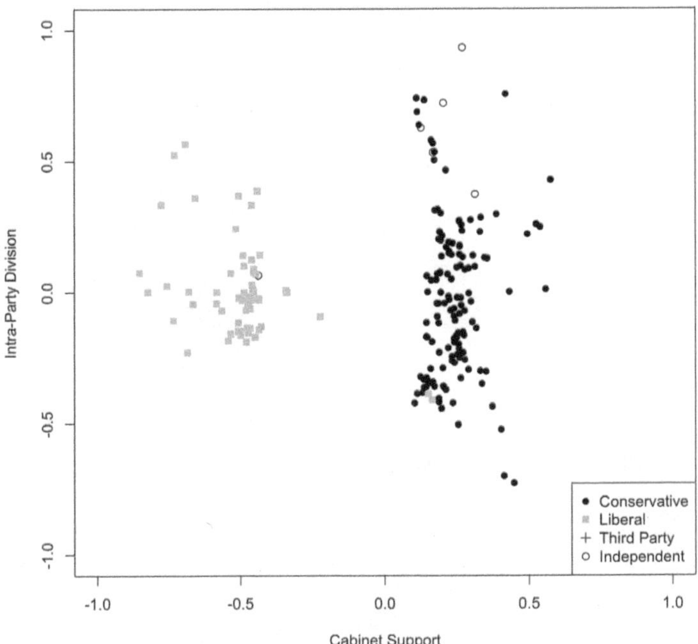

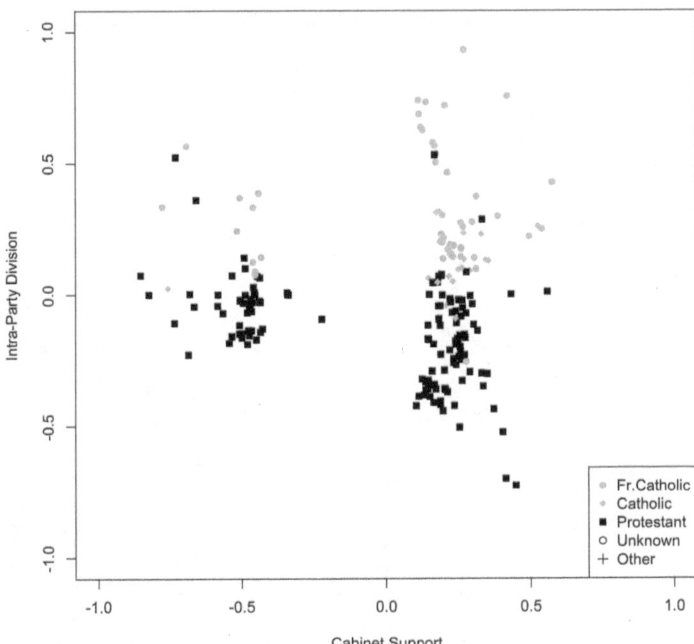

Figure 7.4 continued

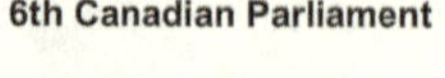

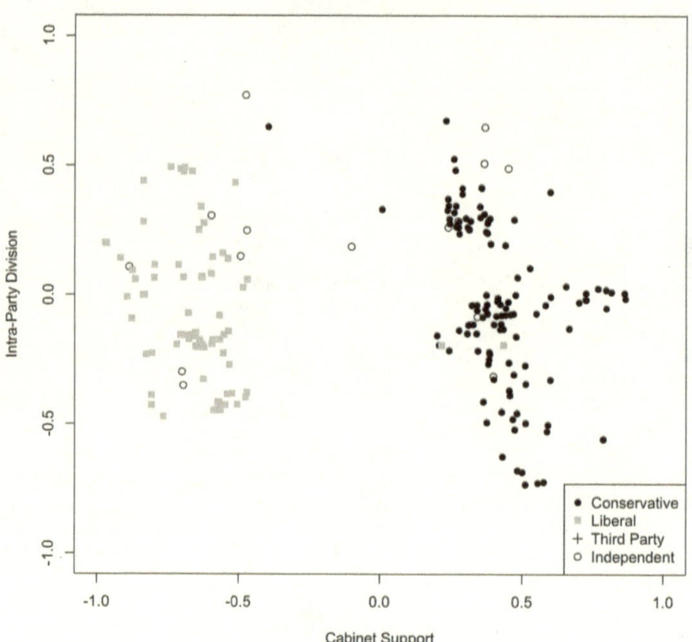

6th Canadian Parliament

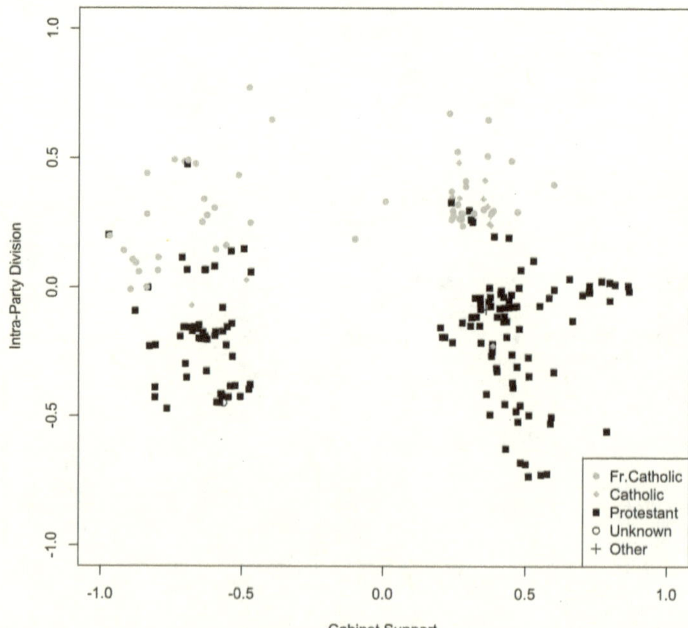

Figure 7.4 Optimal Classification Analysis by Party and Religion, 1867–1925 (continued)

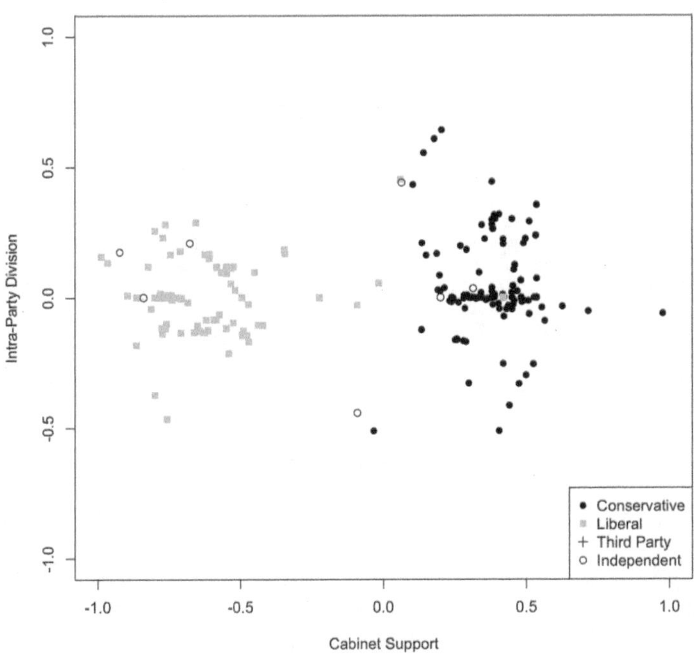

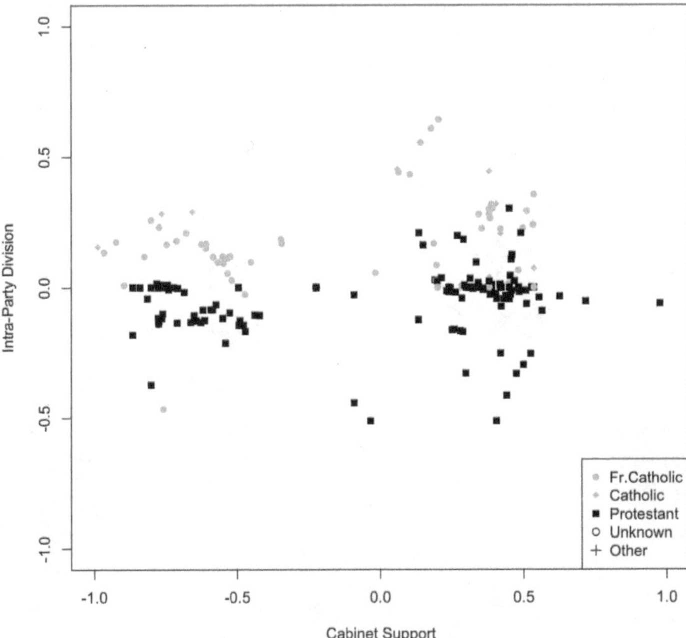

Figure 7.4 continued

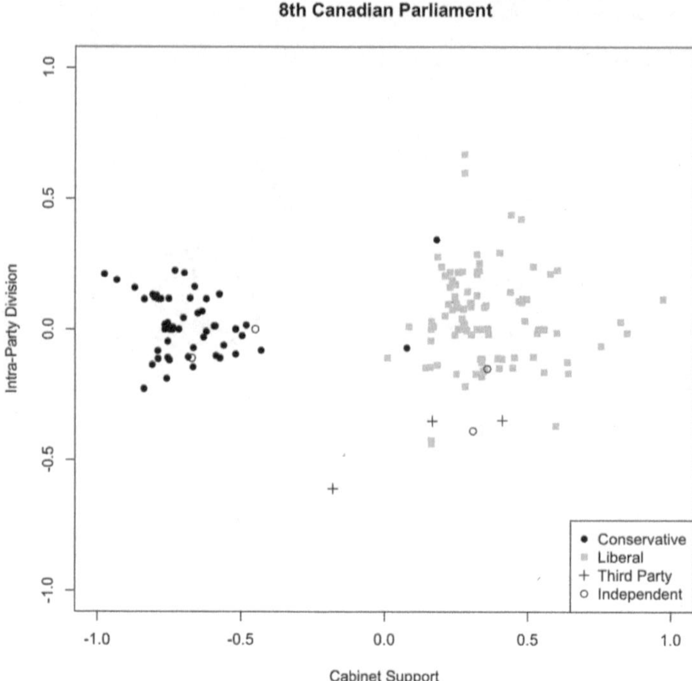

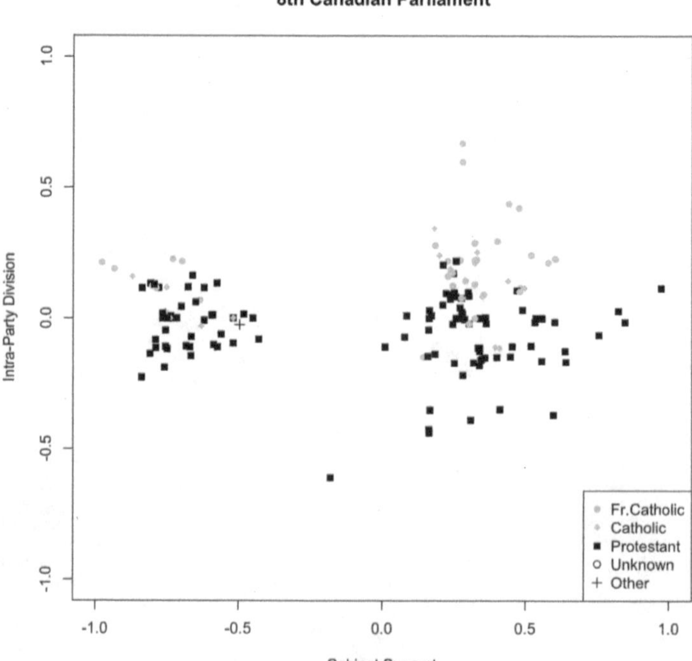

Figure 7.4 Optimal Classification Analysis by Party and Religion, 1867–1925 (continued)

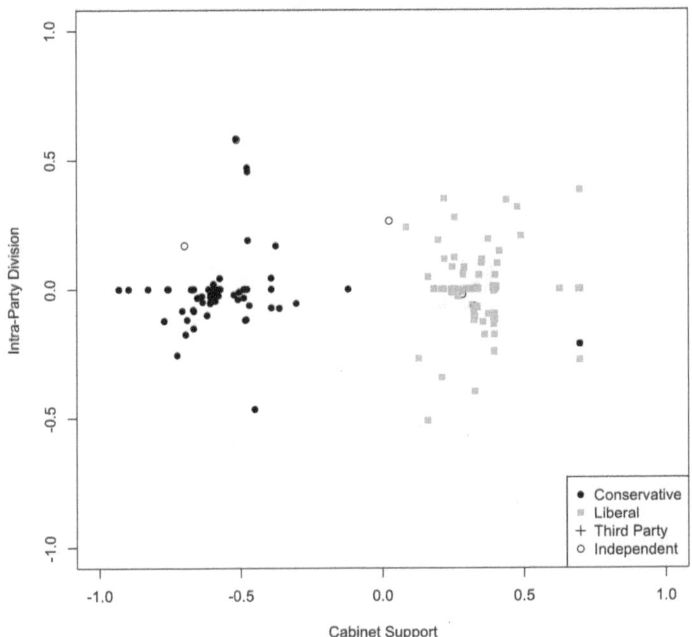

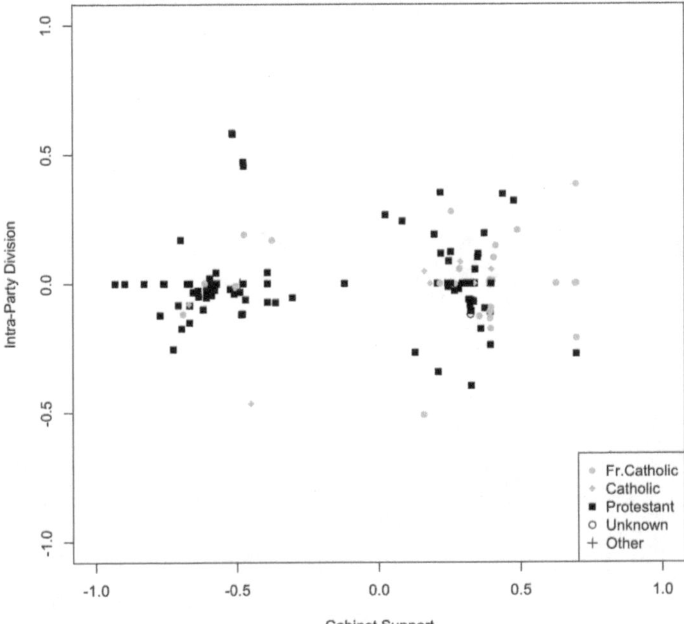

Figure 7.4 continued

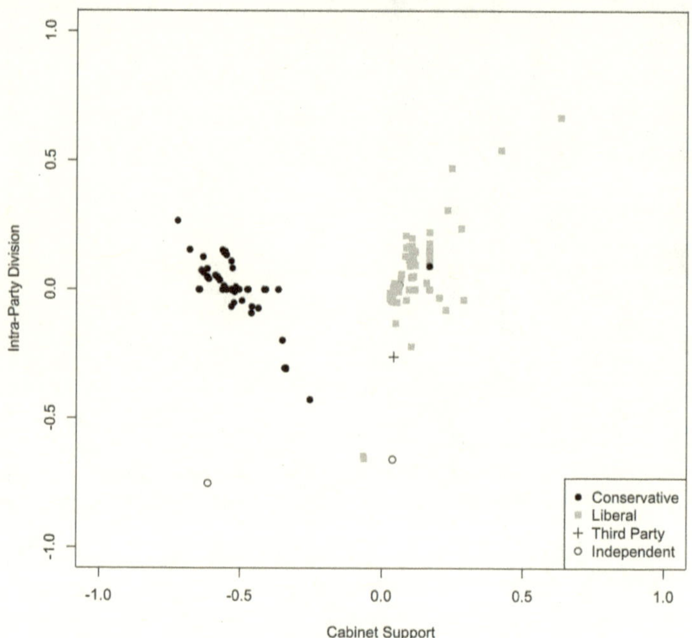

10th Canadian Parliament

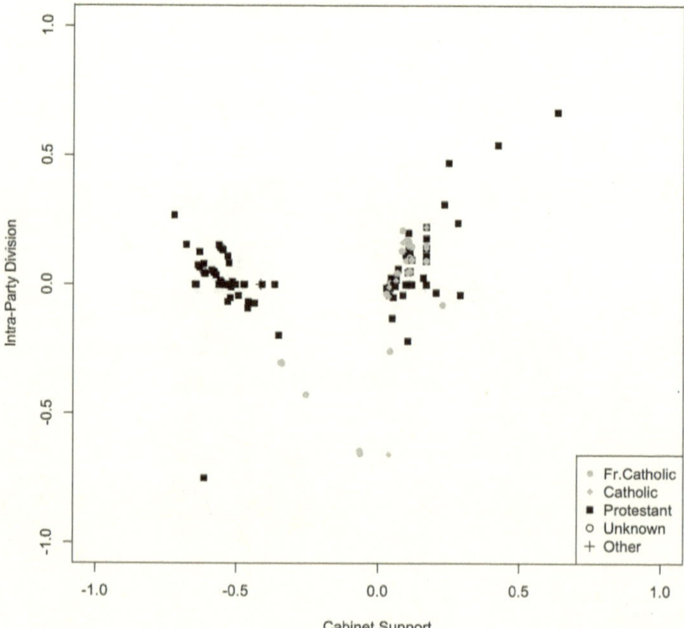

Figure 7.4 Optimal Classification Analysis by Party and Religion, 1867–1925 (continued)

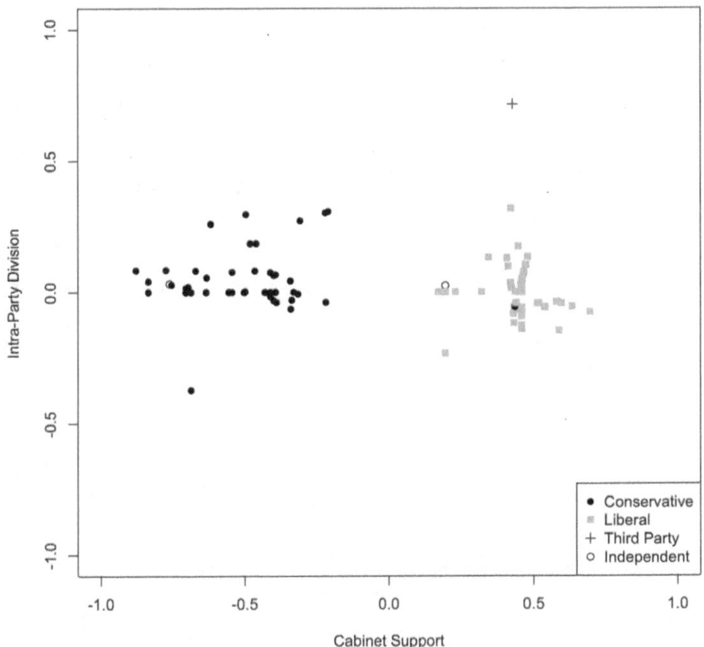

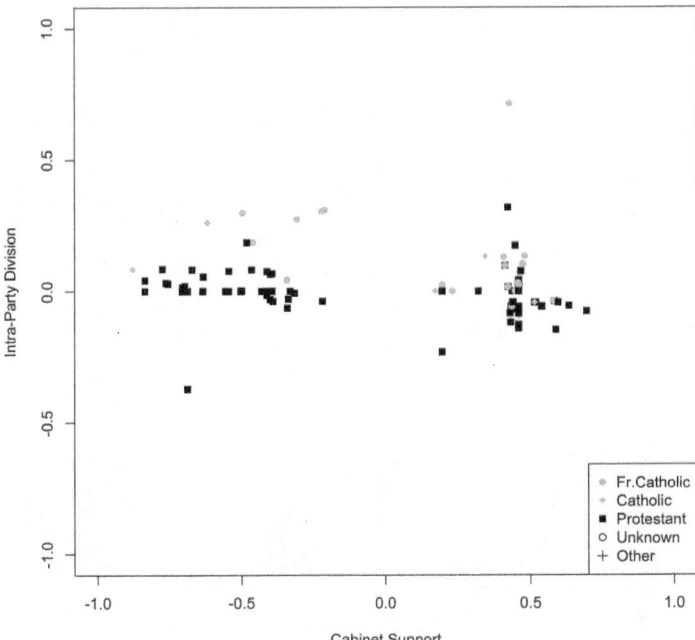

Figure 7.4 continued

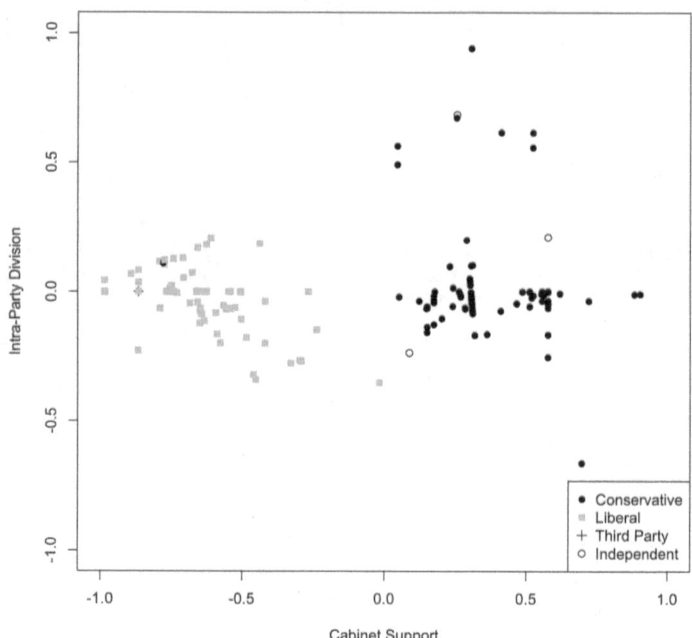

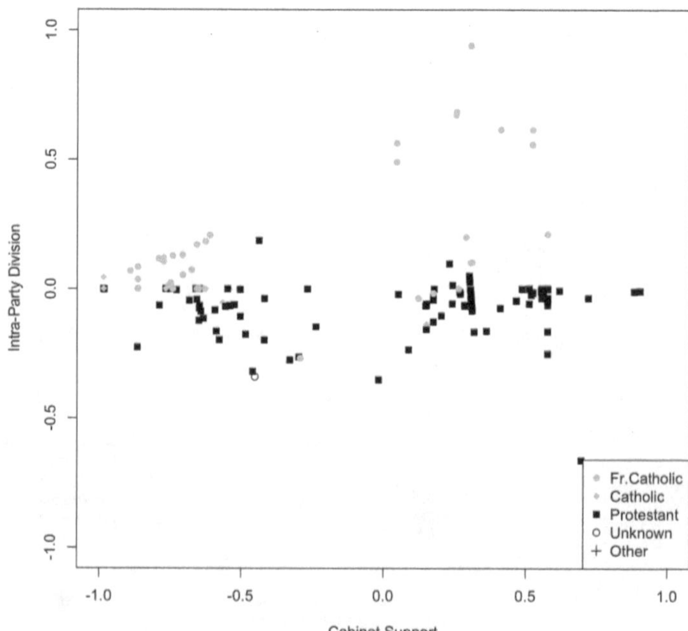

Figure 7.4 Optimal Classification Analysis by Party and Religion, 1867–1925 (continued)

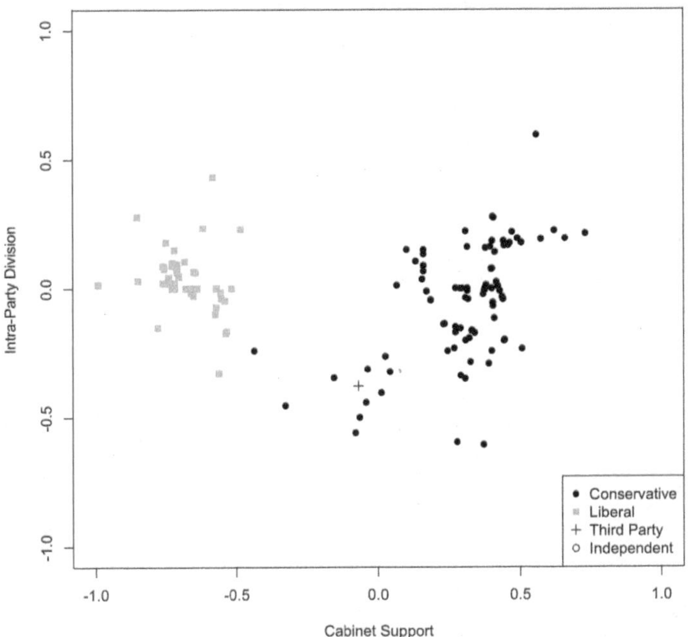

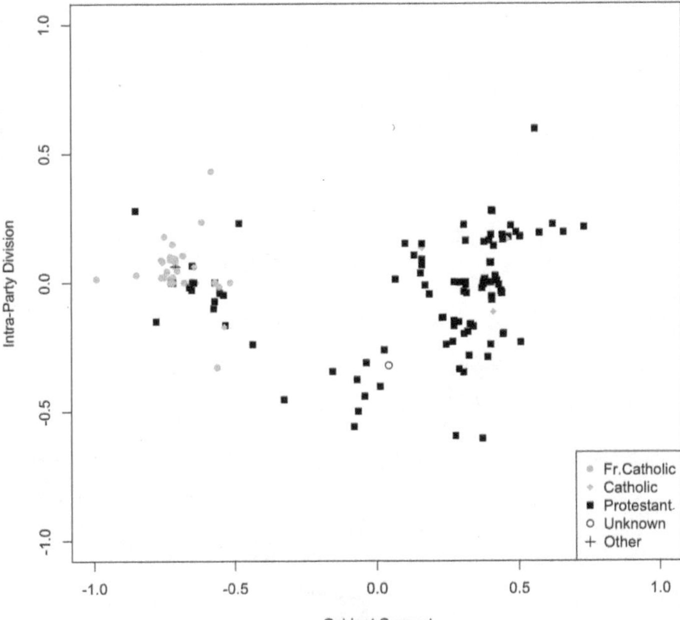

Figure 7.4 continued

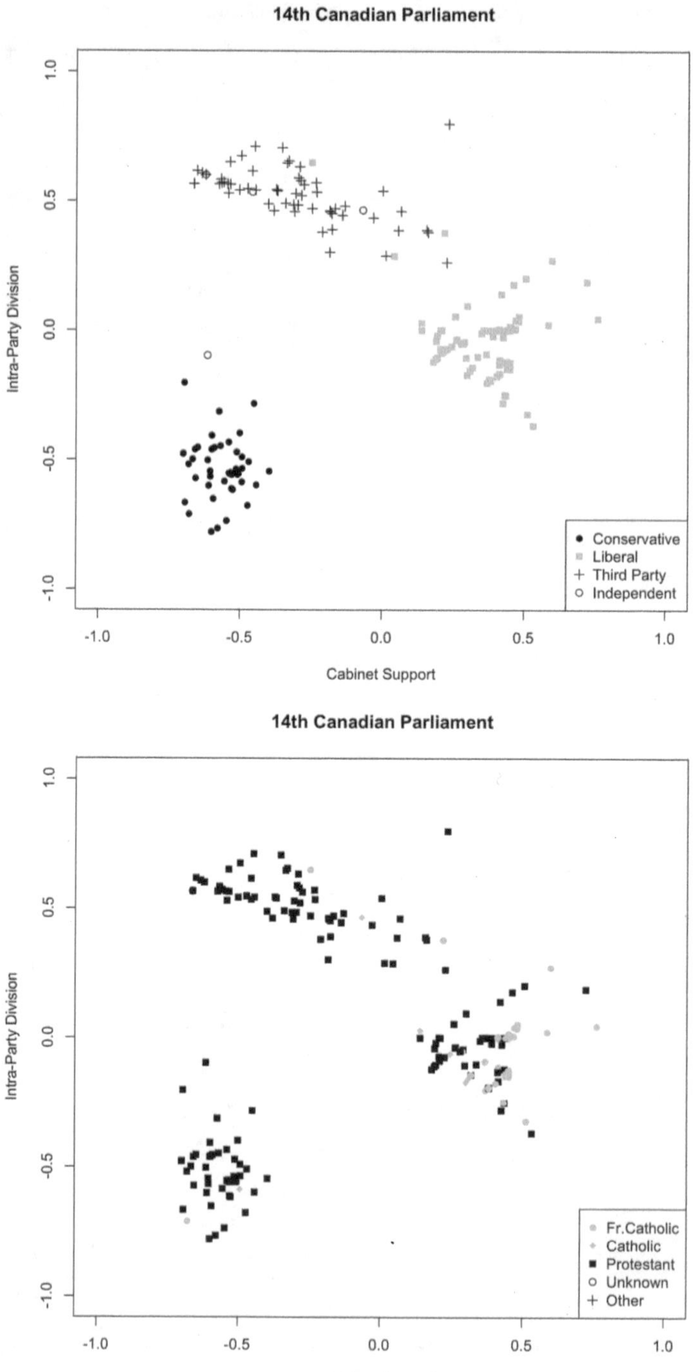

Figure 7.4 Optimal Classification Analysis by Party and Religion, 1867–1925 (continued)

Louis Riel from the House of Commons in the third Parliament. Not surprisingly, motions related to the prohibition of Catholic and French-language education in New Brunswick (1872) and the Northwest Territories (1890) also fall into this dimension. In all of these cases, most Catholic MPs banded together to support their Church against Protestant members of the House. Specific local concerns were also associated with the second dimension of voting, as when the government supported a more aggressive tariff on staples such as corn or tobacco (1893) or transferred payments to Nova Scotia (1868). In each case, the economic interests of different constituencies represented by members of the same party could have weakened caucus unity. The selection of specific railway routes or the location of railway stations could have also weakened cohesion when the choices were between two constituencies represented by the same party (Hamelin 1974, 260). Banking and bankruptcy is another frequent category in this dimension, mainly because it opposed the financial interests of Montreal, Toronto, and Halifax. As indicated earlier, one of the first nation-building tasks of the federal government was to create a common banking and currency system. Since most of these questions were rapidly settled after Confederation, however, they tend to be less frequently associated with the second dimension of voting after the fourth Parliament, when the Conservative government adopted the National Policy.

Another important category of second-dimension votes is democratic reforms, which lumps together proposals to modify the Senate, the voting franchise, the judicial system, and procedures of the House. These together corresponded to around 10 per cent of all second-dimension votes. Democratic reforms always had the potential to weaken party unity within the Conservative Party, since its caucus was formed from a coalition of Tories and moderate reformists prior to Confederation. In the first few Parliaments, several reform bills were introduced, most notably to abolish dual representation in provincial and federal legislatures (1871), to make the Senate an elected chamber (1875), and to create the Supreme Court of Canada (1875). Once again, the interests of members from the same party had the potential to be in direct opposition when, for example, certain members had dual representation and others did not.

Clearly, this analysis confirms that conflicts over religion and language are one reason party unity was much weaker in the years following Confederation. Not only did the number of second-dimension votes decline over time, but the number of ethno-religious votes also declined during the same period – from 53 per cent of all second-dimension votes between 1867 and 1896 to 15 per cent between the election of Laurier in 1896 and 1925. Although party unity appears to have been affected by other issues of local concern, most of these debates were settled in the years immediately after Confederation. The subsequent increase in party unity observed at the beginning of the twentieth century thus can be explained by two successive processes: first, by the sorting out of Catholics towards the Liberal Party after the hanging of Louis Riel; and, second, by the increasing ideological cohesion of the Liberal and Conservative caucuses with regards to language and religious issues.

Conclusion

I began this chapter by arguing that language and religion shaped Canada's first party system. At the time of Confederation, both the Liberal and Conservative parties were composed of a mix of Protestant and Catholic members. This heterogeneity represented a challenge for party leaders, mainly because language and religious questions always had the potential to divide parties internally. Indeed, conflict soon arose in Parliament over the rights of Catholics outside the province of Quebec, which culminated with the hanging of Louis Riel and later, in the last decade of the nineteenth century, the Manitoba Schools Question. This set the stage for the realignment of Catholic voters towards the Liberal Party, but not before several French-speaking MPs from Quebec had left the Conservatives, either to sit as independents or to join the Parti National, which was created the day after Riel's execution.

Although it is impossible to pinpoint the exact moment when this Catholic realignment started, the evidence presented in this chapter suggests that their increasing support for the Liberals began at the elite level and later moved to the electorate. Several results confirm this hypothesis. First, Catholic voters were not the only ones who changed their political allegiance during this period; Methodist voters also moved away from the Liberals, which hints at the importance of religious grievances in this realignment. Although difficult to prove, it seems reasonable to expect that both Catholics and Methodists were reacting to the changing composition of the Conservative and Liberal caucuses, with the selection of Wilfrid Laurier, a French Catholic, as leader of the Liberals in 1887 and of Mackenzie Bowell, a former Grand Master of the Orange Lodge, as leader of the Conservatives in 1894. Second, as we saw, the proportion of Catholics in the Conservative Party started to fall before Wilfrid Laurier became prime minister: between 1886 and 1890, the number of French Canadians in the Conservative caucus declined by 35 per cent. In addition, the analysis showed that the correlation between Liberal support and the number of Catholics in the riding increased significantly only after 1900, when the religious composition of each caucus had already begun to change. Cochrane (2015, 172–3) observes a similar process in his analysis of the ideological content of Canadian party platforms in more recent times. He notes that the Conservatives shifted towards the right during the 1980s, almost two decades before the electorate began to polarize towards the left and the right. Thus, the ideological sorting observed among voters in the 2000s was mostly an elite-driven phenomenon because it lagged behind the emergence of policy differences first observed between parties.

To be fair, religion and language questions were not the only issues that could have affected the behaviour of MPs in the years following Confederation. Other nation-building projects, such as transportation infrastructure, tariffs, and the financial system, also had the potential to divide parties internally. Although most of these issues were quickly resolved in Parliament soon after Confederation, conflicts over religion and language remained controversial for several decades to come. The spatial analysis confirms that these issues were likely to have weakened party unity until almost all Catholics were elected under the Liberal banner. Although questions of religion and language rights somewhat abated after the 1896 Laurier-Greenway compromise, other issues quickly emerged to replace them and to threaten once again the unity of both major parties. At the beginning of the twentieth century, these new controversies were primarily related to Canada's role within the British Empire, western expansion, and the country's trade policy.

Since earlier parliamentary rules gave members numerous opportunities to decide the topics of debates, any potential issues could be raised in the House, even at the expense of party unity. The nationalist and farmer factions represented by Henri Bourassa and Thomas Crerar illustrate how two loosely organized groups could take advantage of this situation to promote their own agenda. Borden, who replaced Laurier as prime minister in 1911, knew the importance of controlling the debates. He believed that certain questions, such as language and religion, "were of such national significance that partisan debate was inappropriate" (Brown 1975, 61). Clearly, something had to be done to control the legislative agenda in Parliament. The rules had to be changed to promote party unity.

Chapter Eight

Western Discontent and Populism

What has been the influence of parliamentary procedures on legislative behaviour, and how has the modification of these rules affected the structure of the party system more broadly? So far, I have argued that party voting unity increased dramatically in Parliament after Canada adopted its first nation-building projects in the years following Confederation. I also argued that ethno-religious conflicts continued to divide both major parties internally, until most Catholics began supporting the Liberal Party around the turn of the previous century. This wave of partisan sorting consolidated the ideological cohesion of the Liberal and Conservative caucuses. It also occurred around the time when the rules of the House of Commons were modified to strengthen the influence of party leaders in the legislative arena.

This coincidence is not accidental: both Aldrich (2011, 204–5) and Rohde (1991, 31–4) have observed the same type of changes in the US House of Representatives. This is because the rules governing legislative organization are more likely to be modified if there is widespread ideological consensus among party members. When this condition is met, the rank and file of a party will be more willing to accept strengthening the power of their leadership to facilitate agenda control. In the US Congress, the relationship between ideology and parliamentary rules explains why parties became more polarized under Speakers Thomas Reed and Joseph Cannon more than a hundred years ago (Rohde 1991, 4), and again after Newt Gingrich became speaker in 1995 (Rohde 2013, 854). In both cases, new rules were adopted to decrease the autonomy of standing committees, primarily because Republicans and Democrats had "become more divergent and more homogeneous ideologically" (854). These procedural reforms became possible because members were willing to delegate strong legislative powers to party leaders, who were less likely to pursue goals incompatible with their own interests (850). Aldrich and Rohde call this the theory of conditional party government, because the influence of parties is conditional on the distribution of policy preferences in the legislature.

One must be careful, of course, in applying this logic to the Canadian context. Unlike in the US Congress, MPs always have strong incentives to support their party in Parliament because of the confidence convention. Nevertheless, the behaviour of MPs is still influenced by legislative procedures, and I believe that the Aldrich and Rohde theory can help us understand why the rules of the House were modified in the first two decades of the twentieth century, when both the Conservative and Liberal caucuses became relatively ideologically homogenous for the first time.

The primary goal of this chapter is thus to validate the claim that the modification of legislative rules contributed to the consolidation of party voting unity in Parliament. Although the House of Commons saw some procedural modifications in the years following Confederation, it was only on the eve of the First World War that the government won the right to fully control the agenda (O'Brien and Bosc 2009, 1103). Prior to this, the House could operate under an open rule for a majority of the sitting days, which permitted any number of amendments to be proposed once a bill – public or private – reached the floor. A series of procedural changes was thus introduced between 1906 and 1913 to reflect the increasing legislative workload of the executive, and giving party leaders the tools necessary to impose their will on the assembly (Dawson 1962, 23). I argue that these modifications had three major consequences for legislative organization. First, they increased the amount of government business on the agenda; second, they reduced the opportunities for members to intervene during debates; and third, they limited both the range of topics and the number of divisions recorded in the House.

In this chapter, I show that party unity increased after the government took full control of the legislative agenda and members lost most of their opportunities to express their grievances in the House. Not only did this newfound rigidity create pressure to conform to the views of the two dominant parties; it also greatly increased the costs of loyalty for some members, especially after the Civil Service Reform Act was adopted in 1918. My argument is that patronage reform, combined with more restrictive parliamentary procedures, can help us understand why the two-party system broke up in 1920. I explain why a handful of members, mostly from the West and facing increasing demands by the electorate for more independence and better representation, decided to create their own separate caucus in the House.

It is no coincidence that the emergence of third parties occurred during a period when party voting unity became, for the first time, extremely high in Parliament. Indeed the increasing ideological polarization in Parliament resulted in part from the removal of two important factions within the Conservative and Liberal caucuses, Quebec nationalists and western progressives, who later found niches inside several distinct regional parties. Below, I explain how these changes were related to parliamentary procedures.

The chapter is organized as follows. I begin by describing how the rules of the House of Commons were modified to increase the influence of party leaders, both government and opposition. I then outline the circumstances leading to the adoption of the Civil Service Act, and explain how this legislation affected incentives to support the parties in the legislative arena. I show how these two changes helped create new parties in Parliament, mainly, as noted, by forcing some western and Quebec MPs to leave the Liberal and Conservative caucuses. I conclude by explaining how the removal of these factions helped increase party unity even more, making it almost impossible for backbenchers to reclaim their influence in the legislative process.

Procedural Changes in Parliament, 1906–1913

The right of MPs to express grievances and obtain concessions from the Crown was greatly limited in the House of Commons at the beginning of the twentieth century. During this period, new procedural rules were adopted to increase the government's control over the legislative agenda. These changes also enhanced the powers of opposition party leaders: since members now had fewer opportunities to intervene during the debates, the leadership gradually took over the remaining time available for private members to conduct their own business in the House (Stewart 1977, 208–13).

Although the weekly legislative program was evenly divided between government and private members' business in the years following Confederation, the rules were often temporarily modified to give ministers special rights to control the agenda. This arrangement rapidly became impractical, however, as the nation expanded and the economy developed. To recognize this new reality, the rules were formally changed in 1906 so that most days of the week would now be spent on business initiated by the executive. According to Dawson (1962, 96), this revision "marked the beginning of the period of Government control of the time of the House." But this was not the only major procedural transformation during this period: three additional rules were introduced to facilitate the government's takeover of the legislative agenda. First, procedures were modified to reduce the time spent considering private members' bills.[1] Second, the rules were changed to limit the number of opportunities to introduce amendments during debates. And third, the rules were modified to reduce the length of parliamentary speeches. Taken together, each of these new procedures was designed to limit the influence of backbenchers in the legislature.

Prior to 1906, only a limited number of motions could be adopted without a debate, and members had countless opportunities to introduce amendments that could delay parliamentary proceedings. A frequently used method to disrupt debates was to propose the adjournment of the House, which gave members the opportunity to discuss specific and urgent problems that normally would have been considered out of order by the speaker. This practice changed when it was decided that the majority of adjournment motions would no longer be debatable (Dawson 1962, 172). Although minor in appearance, the introduction of this new rule in 1906 was deemed by the members of the opposition to be "restricting the rights of private members of this House beyond what is reasonable" (Debates 1906, 7608). The category of nondebatable motions subsequently increased in 1910, when motions for the production of papers were added to the list (Dawson 1962, 169). The biggest change came in 1913, when the Standing Orders were modified to allow for the adoption of all motions "without debate or amendment," unless otherwise specified by the rules (24).[2]

Since a nondebatable motion cannot be amended, the opportunities to debate bills as they passed through the House greatly declined after this point. Not surprisingly, the new procedures also led to an important reduction in the number of amendments proposed by members. Figure 8.1 confirms this trend (solid line) by showing that the proportion of recorded divisions specifically related to amendments dropped abruptly between 1906 and 1913, when the three new rules were put in place.

The same pattern of disruption can be observed with the adoption in 1913 of closure, a rule specifically tailored to reduce the length of parliamentary debates. Prior to this, there was no real time limit on the duration of speeches in the House. As such, it was not uncommon for members to bring the legislature to a standstill by initiating filibusters. Few rules existed to prevent this type of obstruction, since members had almost "illimitable discussion" opportunities (Debates 1911, 8038). Although the idea of introducing a closure mechanism to prevent the further adjournment of debate was supported by Laurier himself (Laurier 1908), so far nothing had been done to restrict the length of speeches in Parliament, since "the conduct and duration of proceedings ... were based largely upon a spirit of mutual fair play ... or 'closure by consent'" (O'Brien and Bosc 2009, 648). This informal arrangement reached its limits, however, when the House considered the adoption of the Naval Aid Bill in 1913. As we saw in chapter 2, this issue was highly contentious because it divided supporters of the Empire and Canadian nationalists in both the Liberal and Conservative parties (English 1977, 86–7). To prevent the adoption of this bill, Laurier orchestrated a filibuster that "culminated in the Committee of the Whole," where the Liberals "kept the House in virtually continuous session for two weeks" (Dawson 1962, 122). The House eventually passed the bill, but only after closure was adopted and later used by Robert Borden's Conservative government.

Before the introduction of closure, the opposition had been able to obtain concessions from the cabinet by systematically obstructing the passage of such controversial bills. On two occasions – the Reciprocity trade agreement of 1911 and the Manitoba Schools Remedial bill of 1896 – prolonged filibusters even led to early elections. It was precisely this threat of dissolution that forced

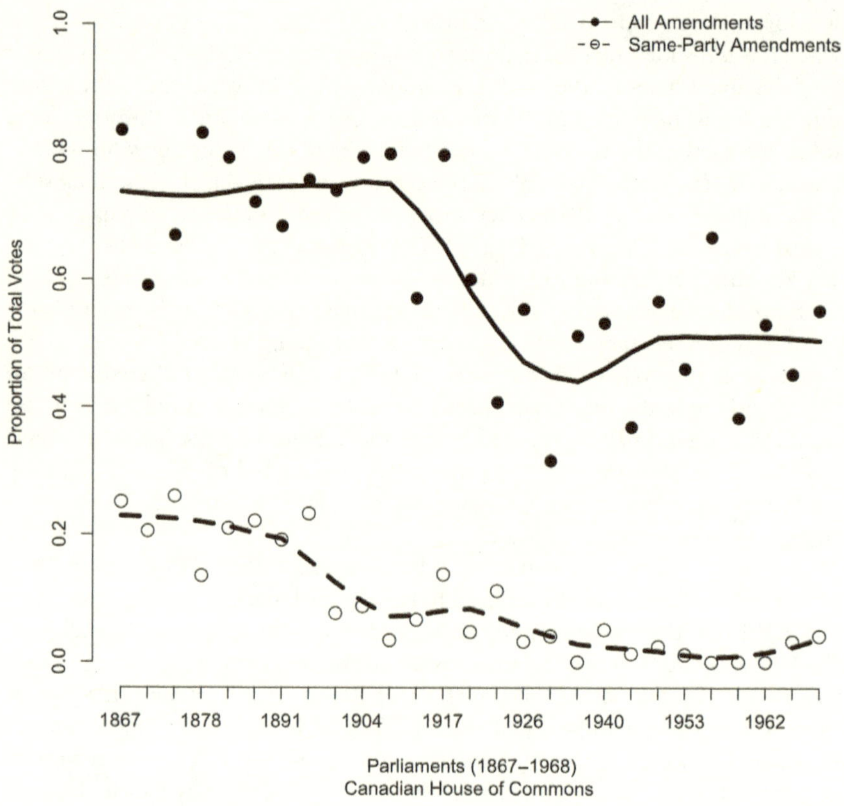

Figure 8.1 Amendments as Proportion of Recorded Divisions, by Parliamentary Term, 1867–1968

Borden to modify the procedures of the House and adopt closure in 1913. This was the first time that the Standing Orders were modified without consulting any members of the opposition (Borden 1938, 415; Dawson 1962, 19).

The introduction of closure, almost seven years after the executive began encroaching on private members' rights, marks the moment when the government won almost total control over the legislative process. It is also during this time that Borden expanded the list of nondebatable motions in the Standing Orders (Rule 17A), and introduced a new rule to restrict the opportunities for debate when the House examined public expenditure and taxation (Rule 17C). This last change represented a more serious infringement on the sacrosanct rights of backbench and opposition members to air their grievances before considering the government's budget (O'Brien and Bosc 2009, 842). Under previous practice, MPs had several opportunities during the week to propose an amendment to the motion "that the Speaker do now leave the chair" before going into the committees of supply or ways and means to study public expenditures and revenues. Both opposition and government backbenchers usually took this time to voice their concerns, since amendments of this nature could be made on any topic – local, national, or even international – and debated at length in the House (Dawson 1962, 212). A handful of members, sometimes only one or two, thus could "delay, or even prevent, the work planned for a sitting" (Stewart 1977, 211). Examples of such amendments include motions on postage fees, duties on farm machinery, railroad freight rates, immigration, and veterans' benefits. With the introduction of rule 17C, the cabinet could now conduct its business without fear of interruption: the motion of going into committees of supply or ways and means would no longer be debatable on Thursdays and Fridays. Not only did this change reduce the power of backbenchers, it also further centralized control of the agenda in the hands of cabinet ministers. But perhaps more important, it enhanced the influence of opposition party leaders, who now had greater incentives to regulate access to the floor during these debates. Indeed, before going into the committees of supply or ways and means, the speaker generally recognizes for debate any member who first rises from the bench. As O'Brien and Bosc explain, however, "by tradition, some Members of the House such as party leaders, Ministers when appropriate, and often opposition critics or spokespersons are given some priority to speak" (2009, 595). Party whips also began to give the speaker a list of members who should speak first, so floor access became even more constrained after this point.

What can the legislative voting data tell us about the influence of these rule changes on the development of party unity in the House of Commons? Did Laurier and later Borden intend to strengthen executive agenda control and increase party unity by using new procedural tools to "rationalize" Parliament, as in the French Fifth Republic (Huber 1996, 4–5)? Below, I argue that two of these modifications – those that placed limits on the number of amendments and the amount of private members' business – were designed specifically to achieve these goals.

The Influence of Procedures on Party Unity, 1867–1968

One way to estimate the effects of rule changes on legislative behaviour is to look at the distribution of amendments and private members' motions in the voting data. As in chapter 6, we can build a model to measure how the type of motion under consideration (government versus private members') or the provenance of an amendment (introduced by the opposing party or by a member of the same party) affects party unity. Not surprisingly, we should find a negative relationship between private members' business – including the more controversial categories of adjournment, supply, or ways and means motions – and party unity.

We should also find a reduction in party unity when members propose to amend bills sponsored by someone from their own party. The logic here is that anyone who attempts to change his or her own colleague's bill or motion does so because they are opposed to its principles. I expect this to be true, since until 1968 the detailed study of bills was almost always done in the committee of the whole, where divisions were not recorded in Hansard. It is in this context that members usually introduced friendly amendments to improve legislation (Dawson 1962, 177). Other types of amendments, related to the broader principles of a proposed bill, or its adoption, were usually put directly to the House. As such, they were more likely to generate partisan conflicts (O'Brien and Bosc 2009, 748–9).

Note that government backbenchers frequently introduced amendments to the throne speech, the budget, or even bills sponsored by cabinet members. Sometimes these amendments could have a great effect on party unity, such as when government backbenchers Armand Lavergne and Henri Bourassa attempted to modify Laurier's autonomy bill in 1905. This bill aimed to introduce a common school system in the newly created provinces of Saskatchewan and Alberta. At the time, Liberal and Conservative nationalists who preferred separate schools proposed three amendments to protect the Catholic minority. None was adopted, and as a consequence Laurier's popularity began to wane in Quebec while the nationalist movement shifted towards the Conservative Party (Neatby 1973, 166).[3]

The evidence presented in figure 8.1 confirms the latter part of this argument: the bottom (dotted) line clearly shows a decline in same-party amendments after 1900. Likewise, we can infer that the reduction in the amount of private members' business will have had a positive effect on the level of party unity. This trend, too, is confirmed in figure 8.2, which shows an important reduction in the number of motions introduced by private members as a proportion of all the divisions recorded during a given parliamentary term. Note that this decline is most noticeable between 1911 and 1921, when more restrictive parliamentary procedures were in place, but less so after 1923, when concessions were made to reinstate some of the lost privileges of backbenchers in the legislative arena (Dawson 1962, 24–6). And since we know from the analysis presented earlier that private members' business reduces party unity, I expect this decline to be associated with more partisan voting as well.

Turning now more directly to the task of measuring the influence of same-party amendments and private members' business on party unity, figure 8.3 presents the results of a series of linear regressions where the dependent variable is the Rice index for both the Liberal and Conservative parties, and where the variable of interest is whether the motions/bills were sponsored by private

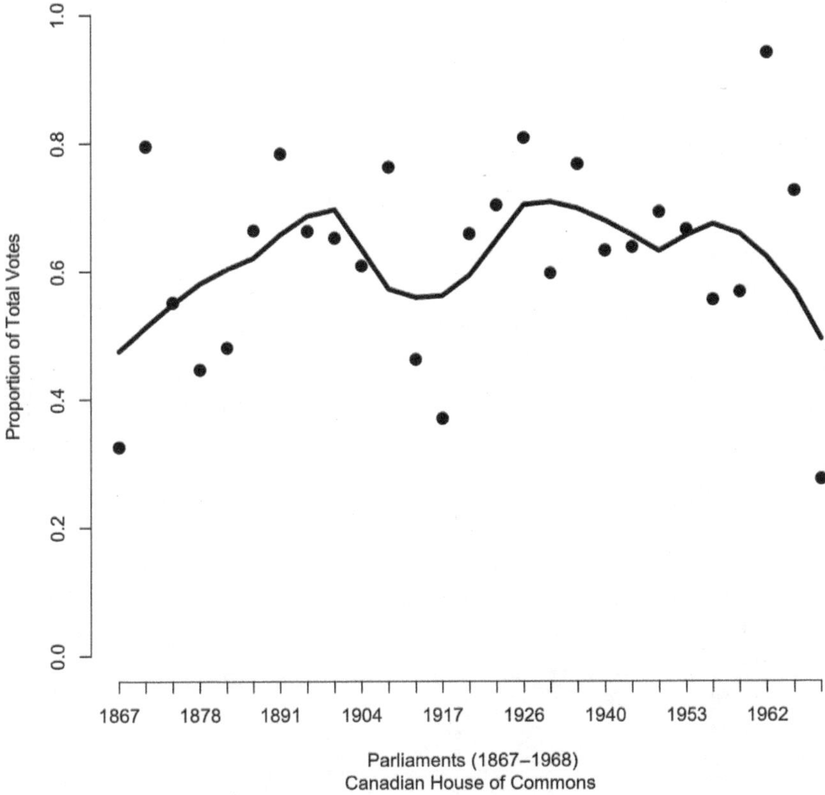

Figure 8.2 Private Members' Business as Proportion of All Recorded Divisions, by Parliamentary Term, 1867–1968

members (as opposed to government-sponsored motions/bills) and same-party amendments (as opposed to opposite-party amendments). Each superimposed dot in the plots represents the unique effect of these variables on party voting unity between 1867 and 1968.[4] These estimates are from the regression coefficients obtained for each parliamentary term, where I also control for the origin of the motion (for example, whether or not the vote was taken over a motion introduced by a member of the party).[5]

As before, the findings confirm that motions/bills sponsored by private members are associated with lower levels of party unity in earlier parliamentary terms, when they were more likely to be debated in the House. A similar finding is observed for same-party amendments, which have a strong negative

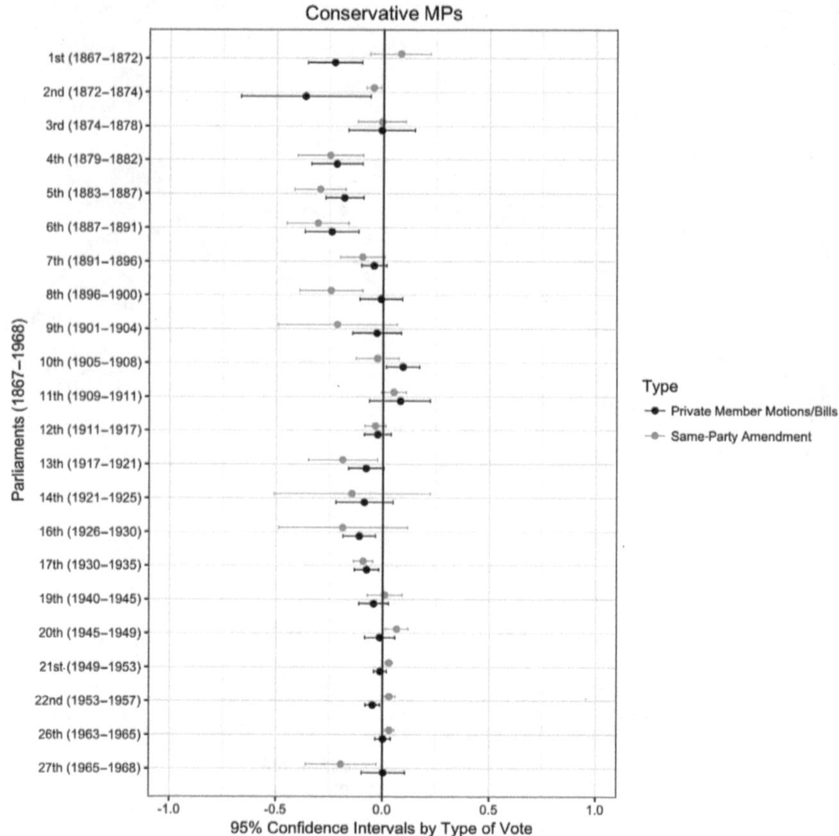

Figure 8.3 Influence of Private Members' Motions/Same-Party Amendments on Party Unity, 1867–1968

effect on the Rice index, mostly prior to 1900. Thus the previous results suggest that restricting both the amending procedure and the opportunities for introducing private members' bills/motions (including amendments to enter the committees of supply and ways and means) played an important role in promoting partisanship in the House. To be sure, party unity also increased in part because the rules were changed to limit the number of amending opportunities. It follows that, with fewer such opportunities, debates were much more likely to be related directly to government business, which now dominated the daily legislative program. In turn, this change enhanced the adversarial nature of the House by limiting the expression of opinions not directly supported by either one of the two main parties.

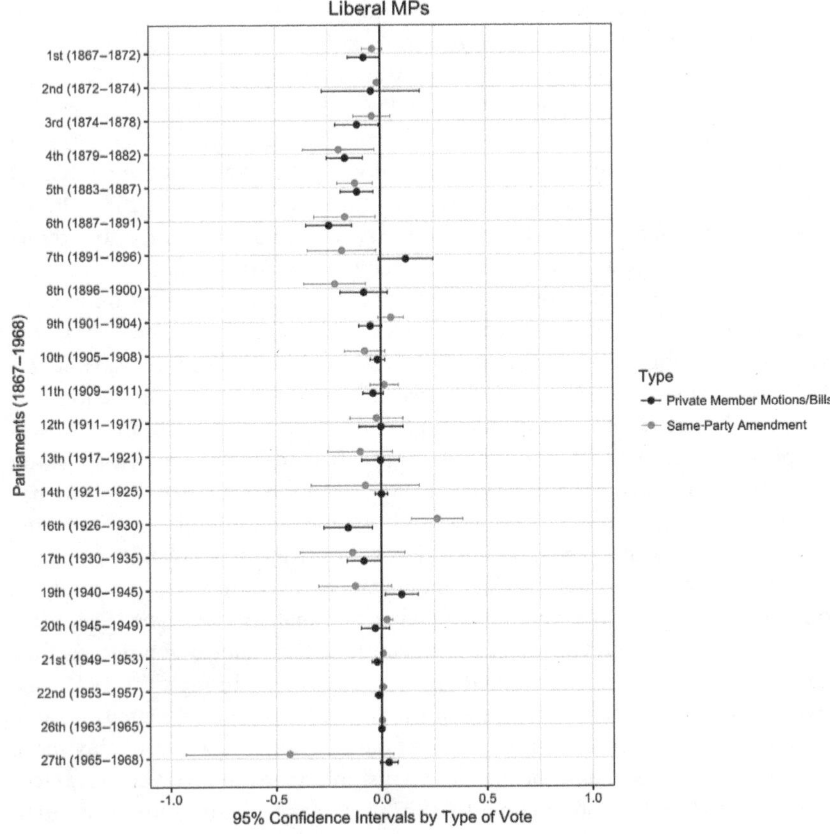

Figure 8.3 continued

Overall, then, the results confirm that modifications of the legislative rules between 1906 and 1913 had a profound effect on the representation of interests in Parliament. Although closure played an important role, it was really the permanent increase in the number of government business days, the reduction in the number of amendment opportunities, and the transformation of the supply procedure, that limited the opportunities for backbenchers to intervene during the debates. These changes not only strengthened the government's control of the agenda, they also increased the influence of opposition party leaders. For instance, the proportion of amendments to the motion of going into the committee of supply introduced directly by the leader of the opposition party grew from 18 per cent when Borden was leader of the opposition Conservative Party between 1901 and 1911 to 63 per cent in the term immediately following the introduction of rule 17C (1918–21).[6]

At this stage, it is important to understand the motivation behind the adoption of these new rules. The increase in the number of allotted days to consider government business is not really surprising. Dawson (1962, 212) notes that, as early as 1876, some ad hoc arrangements were made to increase the amount of time to discuss government business in the House. Although the 1906–13 modifications were important, they were probably inevitable in the context of the political and economic development of Canada (Stewart 1977, 203). On the other hand, the adoption of closure and the reduction in the number of opportunities to introduce amendments are perhaps more surprising.

As we saw earlier, conventional theories of legislative organization lead us to expect that such important rule changes will only occur if the majority is ideologically cohesive (Aldrich and Rohde 2005, 265). Indeed, Stewart (1977, 203) finds a historical relationship between "intense political contention and procedural reform" in Canada. Although the Conservative Party in 1913 was composed of two distinct factions – a larger one made up of English-speaking supporters of the Empire and a smaller one composed of French-speaking nationalists – Borden could change the rules precisely because, for the first time, he had enough English-speaking members to control a majority of the seats in the House. In fact, Bourassa himself publicly recognized that the Conservatives could govern without the support of Quebec nationalists (Bélanger 1983, 136). In other words, French Canadians no longer held the balance of power as they did under the different Macdonald governments. Even though the 1913 rule change was made with the blessing of the whole Conservative caucus – there was only one dissenting member on the final division – it was probably more important for Borden, and for the Nationalist members, to avoid an early election over the naval question (English 1977, 82). Hence the usefulness of introducing closure.

This does not mean that all was well within the Conservative caucus. The party still remained highly polarized over the question of Imperial relations. A prominent nationalist member of the party, Frederick Monk, even resigned from the cabinet because he could not support Borden's naval policy. "Everything is chained in the shackles of party discipline," he had claimed two years earlier in a speech to voters in Quebec, since "the deliberative nature of the House of Commons is a thing of the past, especially among the members of the majority" (*Le Devoir* [Montreal] 1911).

In the end, only seven of the nineteen Nationalist Conservative members voted to oppose the Naval Aid Bill in 1913 (English 1977, 82). Note that the split occurred despite the adoption of rule 17. It is clear that procedural changes could only go so far in reducing the opportunities for intra-party dissension. As long as the government's program had the potential to divide both French and English factions, issues such as the naval policy or conscription could always weaken party unity in Parliament.

Civil Service Reforms, 1918–1921

The government's decision to adopt more restrictive parliamentary procedures coincided with an important transformation of the Canadian party system. This change, which began with the establishment of a formal Progressive caucus in 1920, can be traced back to patronage reforms and agrarian discontent in the West. Although the introduction of third parties in the House of Commons cannot be explained entirely by the government's attempt to control the legislative agenda, I argue that institutional rules played a crucial role in this process. In the remainder of this chapter, I demonstrate how patronage reform raised the costs of party loyalty and how this situation became untenable for certain members – mainly from the West – who opted to exit the party system. I also discuss how this transformation was compounded by legislative rule changes.

As we saw in chapter 6, members of the governing party controlled patronage at the constituency level for many years after Confederation (Simpson 1988, 107). John A. Macdonald himself introduced the practice of sharing the spoils of office with his supporters in the House, regardless of whether his party won the election in the riding or not. As long as they were in power, Conservatives – or their riding association if the opposition represented the riding – had the authority to offer local federal jobs to voters. The Liberal Party adopted the same practice between 1896 and 1911, so that, in effect, the spoils system gave backbenchers the opportunity to reward loyal party supporters until the onset of the First World War. At the time, this represented probably one of the most effective tools to promote the election of a party candidate at the constituency level (Reid 1936, 37).

Although there were earlier attempts to change the appointment process of federal bureaucrats (Brown and Cook 1974, 192–4), it was only after the election of the Unionist Liberal-Conservative government of Robert Borden that this system was permanently modified with the adoption of the Civil Service Reform Act in 1918. Patronage had become an important issue during the 1917 election campaign because voters now "demanded a more efficient prosecution of the war effort" (Simpson 1988, 131). Borden himself saw this reform as a progressive policy that would modernize Canada and "destroy every vestige of patronage" in "every possible aspect," while at the same time improving the competence of civil servants by favouring merit-based recruitments (Borden 1938, 804). Two other events are worth mentioning about the 1917 election. First, the campaign was primarily fought over the issue of conscription, a measure adopted by the Conservative government towards the end of the previous Parliament. Although this policy was already in place by the time of the election, Borden wished to increase support for mandatory military service across the country, mainly because the conscription bill had created a split within both major parties. As with the naval question, the House of Commons once again had divided along ethnic and religious lines, with, on the one side, French Canadians in favour of maintaining a voluntary force and, on the other, Canadians of British origin who primarily favoured mandatory service. This time, however, the conscription crisis created a permanent schism within the party system, since most Protestant and English-speaking members of the Liberal Party joined the Conservatives to campaign in favour of conscription. As a consequence, both pro-conscription Liberals and Conservatives ran under a common Unionist banner, while the opposition rallied behind former prime minister Wilfrid Laurier, who ran as a Liberal. The second important event of the 1917 election had to do with the extension of the electoral franchise. In order to increase its chances of securing a majority in the House of Commons, the Conservative government changed the law to grant all female relatives of military personnel the right to vote in this election. The gamble worked. The Unionists won, and the new franchise rule was subsequently broadened to give most women the right to vote in 1918.

Taken together, the massive increase in the number of voters, patronage reform, and the creation of a Conservative-Liberal wartime coalition suggest that there was an important change in the relationship between voters and their representatives in the House of Commons between 1918 and 1921. These changes ultimately raised the cost of party loyalty for supporters of the government. Indeed, because of the adoption of the Civil Service Reform Act, Unionist MPs could no longer rely on federal patronage to consolidate support in their riding, as previously had been the norm. According to Simpson (1988, 131), one of the motivating factors for Liberals to join the Conservative Party in 1917 had been to benefit from future government support. Thus, for many Unionists, Borden's decision to remove patronage at the constituency level was seen "as sheer robbery" (English 1977, 224). Further compounding the problem was the fact that members of the government could no longer rely on the machinery of Liberal or Conservative provincial parties to help them get re-elected; unlike their federal counterpart, the provincial parties did not merge but remained somewhat independent from the Unionists (226). Finally, the sudden increase in the number of voters further weakened supporters of the government in the House, since they now had fewer opportunities to distribute patronage to an increasingly larger electorate. Unfortunately for Robert Borden, the combination of electoral, patronage, and legislative reforms had disastrous consequences for Unionist candidates (now called the National Liberal and Conservative Party) in the 1921 election, mostly because they set the stage for the establishment of a permanent multiparty system in Canada.

In order to understand more fully how these changes affected the organization of parties in the House of Commons, we must return to the theoretical argument I presented in chapter 3. Recall that this theory accounts for the decision to support the party during a legislative vote by considering three different career objectives of MPs: being re-elected, having influence in the legislature, and adopting good public policies. Recall also that the theory predicts that members will support their party as long as it helps them achieve these goals. We can add to this decision mechanism by considering the classical theory of Hirschman (1970). In this simple model, dissatisfied members have a choice between exiting an organization and voicing their discontent towards its leaders. One easy way to understand this dilemma is through a cost-benefit analysis associated with the options of leaving and the opportunities of remaining loyal (Gehlbach 2006, 397). In the Canadian Parliament, this argument rests on the assumption that the modification of the legislative rules between 1906 and 1913, which increased the agenda-setting powers of party leaders, limited the opportunities for MPs to voice their discontent in the House of Commons. This change was not sufficient, however, to bring about a massive transformation of the party system. Indeed, the loyalty of party members could still be maintained because of the high costs associated with running an election campaign, as either an independent or a third-party candidate. As long as the government could lower these costs (through patronage, for example), incentives to exit the party system remained relatively low. The same logic can be applied to members of the opposition, who could stay loyal to the party and wait to form the next government or, more important, benefit from provincial patronage, as long as their own party controlled the local government (English 1977, 226).

The adoption of the Civil Service Reform Act profoundly modified this incentive structure. From that moment on, members could no longer expect federal patronage to influence voters in their riding. They either had to depend on the party's program or get help from the provincial government. As Chubby Power explained, "the provincial people supplied material rewards for faithful service to the party by the skilful exercise of patronage, which could be practised provincially without the legal restraints in effect on the Ottawa administration" (quoted in Ward 1966, 312–13; see also Reid 1936). This change, in combination with the now more limited influence of backbenchers in the House, proved too much for some members, mainly western representatives of the progressive movement, but also French-Canadian nationalists. For them the costs of loyalty eventually outweighed the benefits of party membership, and so they decided to leave the Liberal and Conservative caucuses.

Exiting the Party System

The Unionist government's difficulty addressing agrarian discontent and constructing regional ties with the old provincial party structure explains why the Progressives won 25 per cent of the seats in the 1921 federal election. The roots of this Unionist failure can be traced to the imposition of conscription during the war, which ended the alliance between Borden's Conservatives and Quebec nationalists. As a consequence, Monk and several other nationalists resigned from the Conservative caucus during the course of the wartime Parliament;

of the handful who remained loyal to Borden, none was re-elected under the Unionist banner in 1917 (Beck 1968, 143). The newly formed Unionist government was to be exclusively controlled by English Canadians (English 1977, 207): 62 of the 65 seats in Quebec went to Laurier's Liberal caucus, while 150 of the remaining 170 seats outside that province went to Borden's camp. The 1917 election results also marked the first time that a united western group was elected to the House: only 2 of the 54 seats in the Prairies and British Columbia went to the Liberal opposition (Morton 1950: 68). Most of these new members remained indifferent towards existing party lines. They had campaigned for conscription, but also to reduce tariffs and maintain the fixed wartime price of wheat set by the newly established Board of Grain Supervisors (108). Above all, westerners saw in the formation of a Unionist government a solution to rampant patronage, corruption, and partyism. The most radical elements even believed that national problems no longer would be dealt along partisan lines, since Parliament now would consider government business on its own merit and in an impartial way (Macpherson 1953, 26).

Unfortunately for Borden, the newly formed coalition of Conservatives, pro-conscription Liberals, and Prairie reformers proved short lived. It quickly became apparent in the first post-war budget that the government was incapable of accommodating farmers' demands. The minister of agriculture himself, Thomas Crerar, was the first to resign over this issue. Nevertheless Borden's troubles were just beginning. Several months later, Liberal A.R. McMaster proposed an amendment to the budget (through a supply motion) by requesting a reduction in tariff rates, a measure supported by nine western Unionists, including Crerar (Morton 1950, 69). In 1920 these members would split entirely from the government ranks to form their own National Progressive caucus inside Parliament.

What, then, can the theory tell us about the decisions of these members to leave the Conservative Party? Why did this group of MPs refuse to join the Liberals and instead choose to form a distinct opposition caucus in the legislature? Part of the answers to these questions has to do with parliamentary rules. As we saw earlier, there was a significant reduction in the number of opportunities for dissenting members to express their grievances in the House of Commons. These new constraints put pressure on members to conform to the views of their leaders, who also increasingly controlled access to the floor. Such changes were in direct opposition to the nonpartisan beliefs of agrarian reformers who valued their independence above all and who had been elected to represent western interests in Parliament. As Denis Smith (1963, 131) explains, third parties arose precisely because it became increasingly difficult to express dissent within the two-party system. For western reformers, political debates had to take place instead in other venues, where different views could be heard, such as the grain growers' associations. Many reformers chose to leave the Unionist government precisely because it was becoming increasingly difficult to speak up inside the caucus – let alone in the cabinet. These members also had little incentive to join the Liberal opposition, which was "corrupted by party discipline" and included very few low-tariff supporters (Morton 1950, 70).

So far, the evidence presented to support the hypothesis that parliamentary rules help explain the rise of third parties in Canada is rather thin. Through archival research, Smith (1963, 130) confirms that Crerar left the Unionist government because he believed that the views of western politicians failed to be accepted in the House. Smith explains that Crerar, along with other members of the Progressive caucus, realized that the parliamentary system imposed too many constraints on regional factions, which could no longer be brokered within the existing party system. Epstein (1964, 57) makes a similar claim by arguing that, contrary to the US case, strong party discipline in Canada, combined with the absence of primary elections, log rolls, presidential vetoes, or opportunities to filibuster, limits the influence of regional factions in the legislature. Both Smith and Epstein argue that these institutional features explain why we now find third parties in Canada, but not in the United States, since American political parties historically have given members more opportunities to air their grievances in Congress. "If they do not always succeed, American regional groups can at least talk freely within the existing party framework" (Smith 1963, 131).

To be sure, we must also consider the fact that the proportion of MPs from the Prairies increased from 5 per cent to 12 per cent of the House in 1904, and to 18 per cent in 1917. This newfound numerical importance clearly put the interests of western farmers at the forefront of parliamentary debates. For a time, it seemed that MPs from Manitoba and the Northwest Territories did indeed use parliamentary procedures to their advantage. For example, James Douglas, a Liberal member from Assiniboia, proposed several private bills in 1898–9 to allow farmers to load grain directly from platforms to Canadian Pacific Railway (CPR) wagons (Rennie 2000, 17). Others used petitions, such as the one presented to Parliament in 1893, requesting that the government lower freight charge and duties on farm machinery and binder twine (16). Many more frequently moved for the adjournment of the House to discuss different issues of interest to farmers, such as the seed grain shortage in the Northwest Territories in 1904 (Stewart 1977, 208). And some western members proposed amendments to the motion for the speaker to leave the chair during supply debates to ask questions about issues that directly affected their community, such as the government taxation of CPR land (Debates 1901, 5417). In fact, members from the Prairies sponsored more than 22 per cent of supply motions between 1901 and 1911, while, as a group, they represented less than 12 per cent of House members.[7] It is worth nothing that most of these members were Liberals serving on the government side at the time. As we saw earlier, the different opportunities for western MPs to represent the interests of farmers dried up when Parliament adopted a series of reforms to limit the amount of petitions, private members' bills, motions to adjourn, and supply debates. All of these changes contributed to reducing the capacity of the two-party system to broker the interests of a now much more diverse group of members in the House.

The declining power of MPs was even noted in the 1919 farmers' platform of the Canadian Council of Agriculture, the national organization of the provincial Grain Growers of Manitoba and Saskatchewan and the United Farmers of Alberta and Ontario, whose program was to promote the interests of farmers in Parliament. Between 1910 and 1919, the Council adopted three different platforms, each discussing tariffs at length, but the 1916 and 1919 versions also proposed democratic reforms such as direct legislation, recall elections, the abolition of the patronage system, and campaign finance reform. One additional proposal related to parliamentary procedures, however, is found only in the 1919 platform. This plank clearly shows that farmers wanted to restore some of the lost influence of their representatives by demanding "an immediate check upon the growth of government by order-in-council, and increased responsibility of individual members of parliament in all legislation" (Morton 1950, 305). Although all parties and candidates were encouraged to adopt and defend this position in Parliament, western farmers ultimately realized that direct political action was needed to protect their interests.

Unsurprisingly, the arrival of third parties in Parliament, which coincided with the removal of an important faction of dissenters from the Unionist caucus, led to a dramatic increase in party unity after 1921. So far in this chapter, I have established that the government's ability to control the legislative agenda played an important role in explaining this outcome. However, I have not yet considered the possibility that ideology and partisan sorting also affected this transformation. As we saw earlier, the presence of French-Canadian nationalists and western progressives inside both the Conservative and Liberal caucuses could always weaken party unity, even if parliamentary rules limited their opportunities to intervene during debates. Indeed, some controversial issues, such as conscription and tariffs, were impossible to ignore and difficult to resolve without risking intra-party strife. The difference is that, under the old rules, members had more opportunities to discuss, amend, or filibuster motions of this nature. It became much harder to do so with the new rules in place.

We can measure directly how the presence – and subsequent removal – of these two factions influenced the level of party unity in the Conservative and Liberal caucuses.[8] Recall that, in the context of a parliamentary system, it is difficult to disentangle the preferences of legislators (which can vary across time) and the ability of party leaders to enforce discipline within their ranks (which can also vary across time). In the previous chapter, I used religion as a proxy to measure the preferences of party members and to explain why the Liberal and Conservative parties became more cohesive after the election of Wilfrid Laurier. In this chapter, I use two other proxy variables – language and geography – to determine how the presence of westerners and French-Canadian nationalists affected party unity after 1900.

The first group of MPs in this analysis is composed of French-speaking nationalists, who constitute only a small proportion of all French-Canadian representatives elected to Parliament.[9] It is relatively easy to identify the preferences of these members on several important issues that have created internal divisions within the two major parties over time. These conflicts are related to language and religious rights. In the years following Confederation, French-Canadian MPs were more or less equally distributed between the Liberal and Conservative parties. But, as we saw in the previous chapter, the Liberals became known as the defenders of the French language and the Catholic religion after the election of Laurier. Still, many members of the French-Canadian elite perceived the Liberals' positions on several related issues, such as Imperial relations, conscription, and education, to be insufficient compromises for protecting their rights in the federation. As a consequence, Quebec voters often elected nationalist representatives when conflicts over culture and language became salient, such as in the 1911 election. These candidates usually ran under the Conservative Party banner until the end of the First World War. Once in parliament, however, they regularly failed to support the party platform during important legislative votes (English 1977, 64).

The second group of dissenting MPs was found within the Liberal Party. Like Quebec nationalists, western farmers were at odds with the position of the two main parties on several important issues. The first split was over economic policies: farmers were more likely to favour lower tariffs and free trade, a position championed by the Liberals, but opposed by the Conservatives until the 1980s. On the other hand, western farmers were also more likely to be socially conservative on issues such as prohibition and temperance, and to oppose the Liberals on questions of French language rights and confessional education.

In the first decades following Confederation, western farmers frequently elected their own candidates within the Liberal Party structure. As we saw earlier, the goal was to influence politics from within the existing two-party system. Several of these representatives, however, eventually were co-opted by the Liberal leadership, while others decided to join the Unionist government during the First World War. It is this last group that rebelled against the two main parties and further organized into the Progressive Party. Note that Progressive leaders refused to impose party discipline within their ranks because they believed it prevented a fair representation of the interests of westerners and farmers in the legislature (Morton 1950, 176).

We should expect the presence of these two factions to have lowered party unity within the Liberal or Conservative caucuses. Figure 8.4 confirms this hypothesis by showing the results of an analysis of the determinants of individual loyalty scores, where western and French-speaking MPs are identified in the data. The model used in this analysis is fairly simple.[10] I separated Liberal and Conservative members and estimated how language and geography influenced the member's individual loyalty score (I used the same dependent variable in

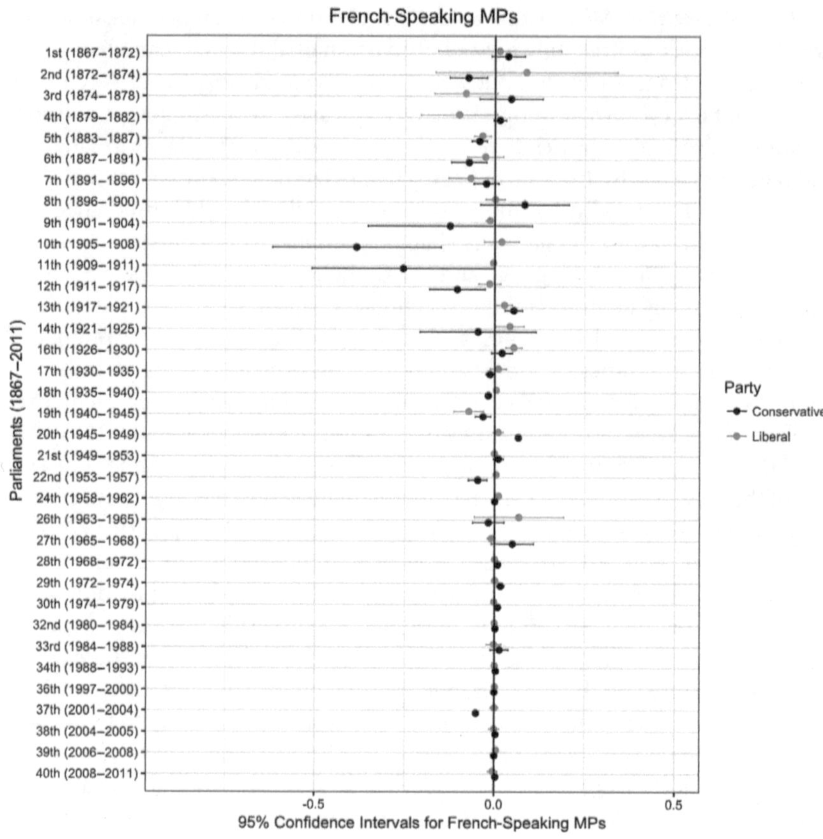

Figure 8.4 Influence of French-Speaking and Prairie MPs on Party Loyalty, by Party, 1867–2011

chapter 5). I identified French speakers by name and biographical information, and determined the identity of westerners by the province of their riding (Prairies versus British Columbia, Quebec, the Maritimes, or Ontario). I opted to separate British Columbia from the Prairies because of the high number of farmers elected in the latter region (English 1977, 202). Beyond these two variables, the model also controls for cabinet membership. The results in figure 8.4, however, include only the regression coefficients for French speakers and Prairie members. Note that each dot corresponds to the unique effect of variables on individual loyalty scores, holding all other variables constant in a given parliamentary term. Note also that the bars on the left- and right-hand sides show the 95 per cent confidence intervals.

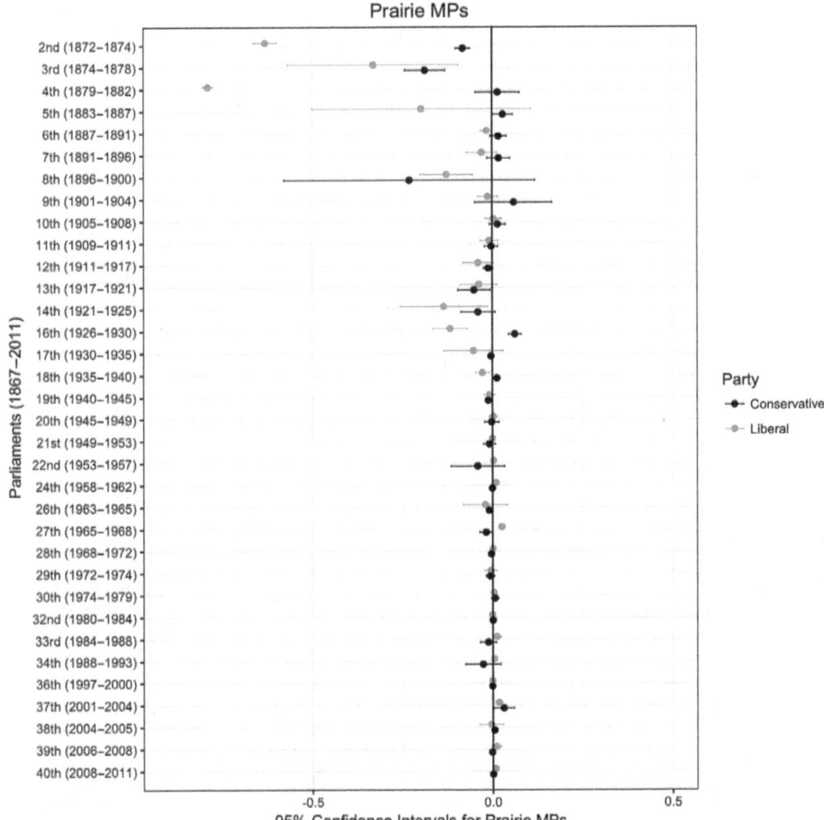

Figure 8.4 continued

Since we are interested in estimating the effects of factions on party unity after 1900, my analysis focuses mainly on this period. To begin, we find that French-speaking members of the Conservative Party had lower levels of party loyalty between 1905 and 1917. This is not surprising, as these members were mostly nationalists at the time. Westerners, for their part, were less likely to support the Liberals between 1909 and 1930; note that this effect is not significant at the beginning of the twentieth century but increases over time. Likewise, the foray of Crerar and his supporters into the Unionist government during the 1917–21 Parliament is also marked by a negative and significant coefficient, which implies that MPs from the Prairies were less likely to support the government during that term.

This last analysis also confirms that Prairie MPs who were elected under the Liberal Party banner during the 1920s had lower levels of party loyalty on average. The same negative relationship is evident between French-Canadian

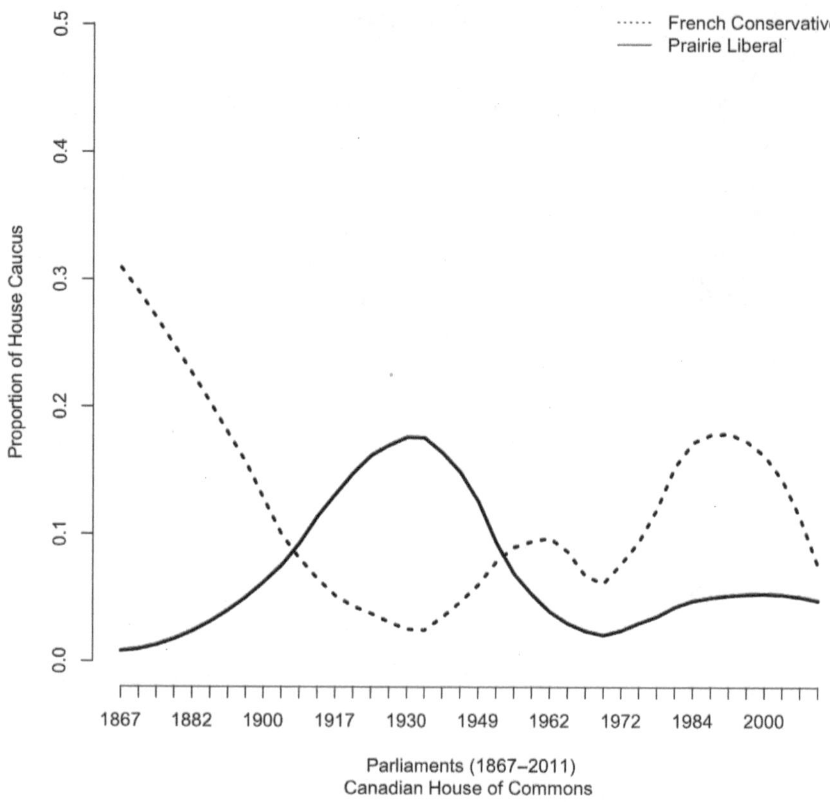

Figure 8.5 French-Speaking Conservatives and Western Liberals as Proportion of Their Respective Parties' MPs, 1867–2011

members and the Conservative Party, with the effect much stronger before conscription, when the nationalists joined Borden's coalition. Both of these findings show that members of these factions were always more likely to be independent from their party, not just in the years leading up to the breakup of the two-party system. As was the case with private members' business, this analysis suggests that the overall level of party unity increased whenever the proportion of western farmers or French-Canadian nationalists declined within the Liberal and Conservative caucuses.

Figure 8.5 offers some evidence to confirm this trend by comparing the proportion of French-speaking Conservatives and western Liberals elected in each party by term.[11] As we can see, the reduction in the number of French-speaking Conservatives, especially after the First World War, occurred at the same time that loyalty increased within the party. The effect of the presence of a western

Liberal faction is slightly more difficult to gauge. Although the Progressive Party emerged at the beginning of the 1920s, the number of western Liberals actually increased during this decade and began to drop again only after 1930.

The finding that the 1921–30 period was marked by weaker party loyalty by westerners supports the idea that the emergence of third parties occurred when party voting unity became, for the first time, extremely high in Parliament. This was made possible by the removal of two important dissenting factions from the Conservative and Liberal caucuses. Those factions later found niches in several different parties with strong regional ties, such as the Bloc Populaire (1942–7), the Progressive Party (1921–30), the Social Credit Party (1935–79), the Reconstruction Party (1935–8), the United Farmers of Alberta (1921–30), and the Co-operative Commonwealth Federation (1932–61).

Conclusion

The empirical evidence presented in this chapter supports the hypothesis that the modification of the rules to increase the government's control over the legislative agenda promoted the rise of third parties in the Canadian Parliament. Because initiatives sponsored outside the cabinet are associated with weaker party unity, it is not surprising to find that majority party leaders, over the years, have changed the rules to reduce the influence of backbenchers. The most important reforms to this effect were adopted between 1906 and 1913, when successive governments restricted the amount of private members' business and adopted closure. Another important change during that period was the abolition of federal patronage appointments. The consequence of these transformations was to limit both the opportunities for backbenchers to air their grievances in the legislature and to raise the costs of conducting elections at the riding level. With the removal of federal patronage opportunities, members could no longer make clientelist appeals to voters. They also had fewer opportunities to represent their interests in Parliament. The combined effect of these reforms was to reduce significantly the incentives for members to support the two main parties in the House of Commons. For a number of dissatisfied members, then, exiting the party system became a feasible option. These defections came mostly from representatives from the West, who left the government ranks to create their own separate Progressive caucus with the aim of abolishing party discipline (Morton 1950, 147–8).

Until now, the emergence of the Progressive Party in the House of Commons has been explained in terms of the electoral realignment thesis proposed by V.O. Key (1955, 3–4). According to this view, a change in the party system is caused by a fundamental shift in the preferences of voters during an election, and this new alignment of interests should persist for several future elections. In the case of the first transformation of the Canadian party system, observed after the First World War, scholars such as Carty, Cross, and Young (2000, 5) and Johnston et al. (1992, 36) have argued that the end of the historic era of two-party dominance was caused by a fundamental regional realignment that followed the landslide victory of Borden's Conservatives in 1917. This pattern of "Conservative boom and bust," Johnston (2008, 828) notes, is also observed in the collapse of the two subsequent party systems in the 1960s and again in the 1980s. The continuing presence of a multiparty system in the House since then has puzzled researchers – both Duverger's law and Anthony Downs's median voter theorem predict that Canada should have (re)converged towards a two-party equilibrium. Yet the Canadian party system has never returned fully to its pre-1921 configuration.

Starting with the work of Cairns (1968), followed by that of Bakvis and Macpherson (1995) and later Gaines (1999), researchers have accounted for this "Canadian exceptionalism" by focusing on the plurality electoral system and its effects. According to this view, the combination of first-past-the-post elections and strong sectionalism has produced small regional parties that have competed at the local level over time. Thus, Canada's "multipolar system in the aggregate" can be explained by the "bipolar competition [observed] region by region" (Gaines 1999, 855). What is missing from this account is the role played by Parliament, especially with regards to the end of the first party system in 1921.

In this chapter, I argued that the original procedural rules adopted after Confederation allowed for a more diverse representation of interests in the national legislature. As a result, two important regional factions of members – represented by Quebec nationalists and western farmers – were able to find a place within the Conservative and Liberal parties, respectively; they were also more likely to break from the party line during legislative votes or to introduce controversial bills and amendments. When the government adopted more restrictive procedures to centralize agenda control between 1906 and 1913, it became much more difficult for these members to take such actions. As a consequence, the House became increasingly adversarial because more time was spent on government business (Stewart 1977, 202). The collapse of the first party system was not so much the result of a fundamental realignment of the electorate or of the effects of the electoral system – which was already present at the time of Confederation. Rather, it was the incapacity of the existing parliamentary structure to accommodate the interests of certain members who now represented a much more diverse electorate.

In this chapter, I attempted to explain the adoption of these new restrictive parliamentary rules by using the conditional party government thesis of Aldrich and Rohde (2005), which posits that the organizational strength of legislative parties is related to their ideological cohesiveness in the legislature. In the Canadian context, parliamentary procedures were indeed modified around the time when the ideology of both major parties became relatively homogeneous. Excluding the nationalist faction of the Conservative Party – which was not large enough to hold the balance of power – Borden could count on the support of enough English-speaking Protestant members to modify the rules of the House unilaterally and introduce closure in 1913. Likewise, Laurier could rely on the support of more than 90 per cent of Catholics elected to the House when he introduced the first major modifications to parliamentary rules in 1906. These changes contributed significantly to the collapse of the first party system and the rise of third parties in Parliament. This is in sharp contrast to the US Congress, where, in the past, ideologically cohesive majorities have tended to grant additional agenda-setting powers to the majority, while less cohesive ones have favoured instead a more decentralized form of legislative organization. In Canada, it has not been possible to reverse this trend – the adoption of more restrictive parliamentary rules further contributed to the fusion of executive and legislative powers, to the point where we now speak of the presidentialization of the government (Marland 2016, 15). It is precisely the emergence of third parties in the House of Commons that made this centralization possible. With more ideologically cohesive caucuses, the majority had far fewer incentives to return to a more decentralized management system of the legislative process. It is also not surprising to find that the most important parliamentary reforms aimed at increasing the influence of backbenchers occurred between 1984 and 1988, when the majority controlled almost three-quarters of the seats in the House (Canada 1985).

I wish to conclude this chapter with a caveat. So far, the evidence presented to support the claim that members of the Unionist Party left the government because of more restrictive parliamentary procedures is rather limited. When we consider the adoption of closure in the previous Parliament, there is no doubt that Borden introduced this rule to silence both the opposition and nationalist members of his own party. The data are circumstantial at best, however, to support the claim that Crerar and other members of the progressive faction left the Unionist party in 1920 because they were prevented from expressing their views in the House. The only evidence I provided in this chapter is found in some of Crerar's correspondence. There is strong support for this claim, however, from the following: (1) party discipline and cabinet control was such an important object of critique of the progressive movement, that (2) the newly formed Progressive caucus did not impose party discipline within its own ranks, and that (3) prior to the introduction of closure and patronage reforms, both Quebec nationalists and western farmers could find a place inside the two dominant parties. I return to this issue in the conclusion of the book, where I present evidence from the *Grain Growers' Guide* and other farmers' publications that parliamentary procedure mattered in the decision to form a separate Progressive Party.

Chapter Nine

Partisanship in the Senate

What do we know about partisanship in the Canadian Senate? Originally conceived as a chamber of "sober second thought" with a mandate to represent Canada's sectional and class interests, the Senate always has had a reputation for being more independent than the House of Commons (Smith 2003, 110). Since senators are appointed by the governor general on the advice of the prime minister, they are isolated from partisan and electoral pressures. They also have more career stability than House members, since they can hold their seat until mandatory retirement at age seventy-five. Many believe this special status allows senators to spend more time studying and improving legislation adopted by the House, much as the House of Lords does in the UK Parliament (MacKay 1963, 90). Indeed, the examination and revision of bills requires a more consensual and less partisan view than that generally expressed in the lower chamber (Thomas 2003: 191). Unfortunately, over the years the Senate has become highly partisan and plagued with scandals, so much so that in 2015 the Liberal government of Justin Trudeau introduced a reform to change the process of appointing senators with the explicit goal of reducing the level of partisanship in the upper chamber.

Supporters of this reform have claimed that nonpartisan nominations should produce "better quality senators," "a more independent Senate," and ultimately lead to a "post-patronage era" in Canadian politics (*National Post* 2015a). This raises the questions, though, of the extent to which partisanship is a problem in the Senate today, and how much this has changed over time. In this chapter, I provide an answer to these questions by analysing the legislative voting records of senators from the first to the forty-first Parliaments. This analysis shows that partisanship in the Senate was relatively high for most of the twentieth century, and comparable in scope to what was observed in the lower chamber after the 1950s.

The chapter is organized as follows. I begin by briefly discussing some of the past attempts to reform the Senate. I then review the existing work on partisanship in the upper chamber. This is followed by a discussion of the different methods used to measure party unity and party discipline, and an analysis of the outcome of legislative votes in the Senate from the first to the forty-first Parliaments. I use the last Parliament of the study period (2011–15) to conduct a counterfactual analysis that compares the voting behaviour of Liberal senators before and after their expulsion from their party's caucus. I also look at some of the most recent votes in the forty-second Parliament to evaluate the effect of this reform following the first nonpartisan nominations of the Trudeau government and the creation of the Independent Senator Group in 2016. In the final section, I discuss the potential effect of the newly adopted reform of senatorial appointments on partisanship in the upper chamber.

Reforming the Senate

Only a handful of studies explicitly focus on explaining the legislative behaviour of Canadian senators (see, for example, the work of Kunz 1965; and MacKay 1926, 1963). This is perhaps surprising considering the large amount of scholarly work that has taken a more normative approach in analysing the composition and legitimacy of the Senate (see, for example, Campbell 1978; Joyal 2003; Smiley and Watts 1985; Smith 2003).

Three broad criticisms are usually levelled against this chamber. The first is that the Senate is not really a federal institution, and does not represent the interests of the provinces in Parliament (Hicks and Blais 2008). This is because senators are nominated by the prime minister – rather than elected, as in Australia, or named by the provinces, as the *Länder* do in Germany – and thus cannot truly serve as as a regional chamber in the federation. The second criticism is linked to the unequal distribution of Senate seats across the provinces. Many have claimed that the chamber is undemocratic because Ontario and Quebec both have the same number of senators (twenty-four) as the four western provinces combined (six in each province). The third criticism is the partisan orientation of the Senate and the fact that its members are not representative of the broader Canadian population. The selection of senators has always been a highly politicized process, and historically has been used to reward party supporters (see chapter 5). These patronage nominations are not easily reconcilable with the idea of the Senate as an independent body responsible for overseeing the government's legislative program. In addition, although the Senate is composed today of more women and Aboriginal members than is the House of Commons, it historically "remains largely a chamber of former lower-house legislators and partisan loyalists" (Docherty 2002, 33).

Given these criticisms, it is not surprising that Senate reform has been on the constitutional agenda for some time, most notably since the Constitution was patriated in 1982. Several proposals have been discussed to make the upper house more representative of provincial interests, more equal in size, and less partisan, but because most of these changes would require formal constitutional amendments, such proposals have failed. Even proposals to modify the appointment process of senators by nonconstitutional means – such as Bill C-7, the Senate Reform Act, introduced by the Conservative government in the thirty-ninth Parliament to elect senators directly and impose term limits – have been declared unconstitutional by the Supreme Court of Canada. Here, the Court reiterated that such changes could be made only under the general amending procedure (Supreme Court of Canada 2014).

The constitutional requirements imposed by the Supreme Court to alter the nomination process of senators have placed important limitations on any future attempt to change the Senate appointment process. This explains why the reform introduced by the Liberal government of Justin Trudeau in 2015 was explicitly designed to avoid amending the Constitution. The objective of this proposal was to make senators more independent from their party in order to reduce the level of partisanship in the upper chamber and to improve provincial representation. Under this latest scheme, each new senator will be selected from a short-list created by a five person advisory board "whose mandate is to provide non-binding, merit-based recommendations to the Prime Minister on Senate appointments" (Canada 2019). These new senators will be expected to sit independently from the Liberal caucus and work in a nonpartisan manner in the chamber.[1]

Critics have been quick to point out the important limits of this practical change – most notably, that unequal provincial representation continues and senators remain unelected. Furthermore, that there is no constitutional guarantee that future prime ministers will follow this procedure greatly limits the scope of the reform.[2] Perhaps more important, what has been labelled "Trudeau's fix" is expected to alter, at least temporarily, the legislative organization of the Senate, since there is now no formal caucus to support government bills in the chamber and only three senators to defend the cabinet's agenda before the opposition.[3]

This latest attempt to transform the Senate into a more independent chamber of "sober second thought" – where the government does not control the agenda – raises two important questions about the absence of political parties in the legislative arena. First, what do we actually know about the partisan behaviour of Canadian senators? Is partisanship in the upper chamber higher than in the House of Commons? Is this really a greater problem today than it was 150 years ago? Second, what should we expect from a Senate divided between an organized opposition party and a majority of independent members? Because the rules and procedures of Westminster-style parliamentary systems were primarily designed to facilitate agenda control by the government (Campion 1955, 144), it is unclear what will happen to its legislative program if no party controls a majority of seats in the Senate.

Partisanship in the Senate: What We Know

As we saw in the previous section, the most recent attempt to reform the Senate was made under the assumption that partisan divisions are problematic in this chamber, and that these conflicts prevent senators from effectively representing the interests of Canadians in Parliament. But exactly how influential are parties in the Senate? Is this more a problem today than it was in the past?

To answer these questions, we must first ask if an independent Senate is a requirement for providing "sober second thought" as a complement to the elected House of Commons. The original intention of the Fathers of Confederation was to have an upper house representative of the regions and of certain minorities in Parliament, with the purpose of protecting the interests of property owners (Smith 2003, 77). Very little was said about impartiality, except perhaps that the appointment of new senators was expected to be made by government party leaders (MacKay 1963, 44). Still, several organizational features of the Senate should lead us to expect lower levels of partisanship than in the House. First, senators are appointed, not elected. As we saw in chapter 3, this guaranteed tenure removes an important number of incentives that usually explain why House members rarely break party lines during legislative votes. As a consequence, senators are isolated from electoral oversight. They are also less likely to be pressured in supporting the government because the confidence convention of responsible government applies only to the lower house. The "corporate" environment of the Senate has also been known to have a moderating influence on its members. This culture of cooperation has provided a counterbalance to the potential partisan effects of the appointment system by promoting a "unique sense of political self-restraint" among senators (Kunz 1965, 115).

Given that these organizational features have existed in the Senate for the past 150 years, we should expect senators to remain on average more independent from their party than are House members. Still, other factors could also have contributed to increasing partisanship over time. For example, the gradual replacement of the first cohort of senators – who were selected from the different colonial assemblies in 1867 – by new members directly appointed by the governing party (either Liberal or Conservative) most likely influenced partisan divisions in the years following Confederation. The introduction in 1965 of mandatory retirement at age seventy-five also could have played a role in increasing partisanship by forcing the departure of older senators who were on average less likely to be influenced by party leaders (Mackay 1963, 156). Finally, the nomination of a different and more ideological breed of senators in the 1960s and 1970s might have had an effect as well, especially towards the end of the century (Franks 1999, 140).

Thus, changes in the membership and organizational features of the Senate offer conflicting views on the potential influence of parties in this chamber.

Unfortunately, only a handful of studies have explicitly attempted to measure how political parties affect the legislative behaviour of senators in Canada. The most complete analyses to date are found in the work of MacKay (1926, 1963) and Kunz (1965), who devoted special attention to the study of partisanship in their broader treatment of the institutional features of the Senate. By looking at the number of bills blocked (or what I call vetoes) and amendments of House bills, for example, the two authors find that the upper chamber was much more active in the decades following Confederation. They also confirm that partisan opposition was always strongest when Parliament was divided and a different party controlled each chamber (in other words, when the majority in the House was from a different party than the majority in the Senate). Although the number of bills blocked by the Senate is extremely small (a total of 133 between 1867 and 2015), conflict between the Senate and the House is more likely to occur under these circumstances, such as during the periods 1873–8, 1896–1903, 1911–16, and 1921–30 (MacKay 1963, 96). A similar relationship exists with House bills amended by the Senate, which are more frequent in a divided Parliament (Kunz 1965, 116–17).

From these authors, we learn that partisan conflicts became less frequent during the inter-war period as the Senate began to experience unprecedented changes in its organization and membership. The Senate entered a phase of nonpartisan collaboration between the 1940s and 1970s, when Conservative and Liberal senators became more independent of their parties. For instance, Kunz (1965, 118) shows that the frequency of cross-party voting increased during the 1940s through the 1960s, while Mackay demonstrates that the number of House bills blocked by the Senate decreased significantly over the same period (Mackay 1963, 96). These changes can be attributed partially to the introduction of new procedures in Parliament for the drafting and pre-study of bills, which greatly reduced the number of conflictual amendments between the two chambers (156). The other reason put forward to explain this less conflictual tone is the leadership of senators Raoul Dandurand and Arthur Meighen, who prided themselves on remaining independent from their respective caucuses (Kunz 1965, 92–5; Mackay 1963, 157–8). Both of these Liberal and Conservative leaders contributed to making the Senate less partisan by firmly establishing a culture of collaboration, which rejected party discipline and the whip system. Chubby Power, who was appointed to the Senate in 1955, also noticed its less partisan tone: although the "debate often does finish up on party lines" he explained, "there is really not much partisanship" (quoted in Ward 1966, 400). One has also to remember, however, that the Liberals controlled most of the governments between 1935 and 1983, and were thus less likely to be in conflict with an upper chamber dominated by their peers.

This four-decade-long period of senatorial collaboration came to an abrupt end in 1984, when the Progressive Conservative Party won a majority government in the House. It was after this election that the Liberal Party began to rely on its majority in the Senate to oppose Brian Mulroney. This new era of unprecedented partisan division followed the nomination of Allan MacEachen as opposition leader in the Senate from 1984 to 1991 (Franks 1999, 124). During MacEachen's tenure, the Liberals often used their majority in the upper house to advance partisan considerations, either by blocking legislation from the House or by filibustering Conservative initiatives. Two good examples of such activities are the Senate's failure to pass the free trade agreement with the United States in 1988, and the nomination of eight additional senators to break the gridlock over the adoption of the goods and services tax in 1990 (129–35). According to Franks, this new era of partisan conflict can be explained by the influence of several important senators appointed by Pierre Trudeau who were opposed to the dismantlement of the welfare state and were more likely to engage in legislative activism to defend their views (140).

The Liberals' victory in the 1993 election marked the return of less conflictual relations in Parliament, even if for a short time the Senate was still controlled by a Conservative majority. Given that the three subsequent governments were also Liberal (1997–2006), the likelihood of conflicts between the two chambers of Parliament remained relatively small. This all changed, however, with the election of back-to-back Conservative minority governments in 2006 and 2008. Once again, Parliament was divided for almost four years, and the Liberal Party used its majority in the Senate to obstruct the government's program, most notably by slowing down the adoption of more contentious government bills. Ironically, the only House bill blocked during this period was shortly after the Conservatives regained control of the Senate in 2010. In this case, the Harper government used its majority in the upper chamber to block the adoption of the Climate Change Accountability Act, a private member's bill it was unable to defeat in the House.

From this brief review, we can identify three distinct eras of legislative activism and partisanship in the Canadian Senate. The first can be said to have begun at the time of Confederation with the nomination of the first cohort of senators, who remained highly independent of the newly created federal parties. This phase lasted until the end of the nineteenth century, when party nominees gradually had replaced all of these appointments. The second era was marked by a series of partisan conflicts brought about by intermittent periods of divided governments. This lasted until the 1940s, when Parliament entered a new era of Liberal domination and cross-party collaboration that endured for almost forty years. The third conflictual era marked a return to partisan conflicts, first during the 1980s and then in the 2000s, when Parliament was once again divided between Conservative and Liberal majorities in the House and Senate.

It was also during this last period that one began to hear claims that Parliament was becoming too partisan, dysfunctional, and unresponsive to public opinion, and that the Senate was in part responsible for this problem. Unfortunately, if we exclude the studies of Mackay (1963) and Kunz (1965), the most recent empirical evidence supporting these assertions remains anecdotal at best. In the next two sections, I propose to update this work by providing a new systematic analysis of legislative behaviour and partisanship in the Senate over the past 150 years.

Measuring Partisanship in the Senate: What We Don't Know

To evaluate the level of partisanship in the Senate between 1867 and 2015, I use two different approaches: the first considers the number of vetoes and amendments to House bills in the Senate; the second analyses the number of recorded divisions and cross-party voting over time. In the next section, I present a more detailed analysis of the most recent completed Parliament (2011–15) at the time of writing by considering how the removal of Liberal senators from the caucus affected their legislative behaviour.

To begin, figure 9.1 shows the proportion of government bills blocked in the Senate between 1867 and 2015. I calculated these numbers in each term as a proportion of the 11,738 government bills passed by Parliament during this period. The data are directly from the Library of Parliament website and include government House bills that were either blocked (not adopted) or amended by the Senate, but rejected by the House (killer amendments). In the figure, a light-grey or dark-grey background indicates whether Parliament was divided – either by a Liberal/Conservative House or an opposing Senate.

We can see that there were indeed more government bills blocked prior to the 1940s – as much as 8 per cent of all government legislation passed in the fifteenth Parliament (1925–6). The figure also confirms the relatively long period of collaboration between the two chambers from the 1940s to the mid-1980s, when only three bills were blocked by the Senate in 1958. Finally, we see a slight increase in the amount of blocked legislation in the most recent period, when Parliament was divided between Conservatives and Liberals and the upper house became more partisan.

These data confirm that the proportion of vetoed government bills was significantly higher during periods of divided governments. The average proportion of bills vetoed was 0.012 across all Parliaments, but only 0.007 when the government was unified and 0.018 when Parliament was divided (z-test < 0.001). We also find that government bills were more likely to be blocked when the government was Liberal and the Senate was controlled by a Conservative majority (0.032 for a Liberal/Conservative majority versus 0.005 for a Conservative/Liberal majority). Of course, this difference is mostly explained by the fact that a majority of these divided Parliaments occurred in earlier terms, when the Senate was much more active in the legislative arena.

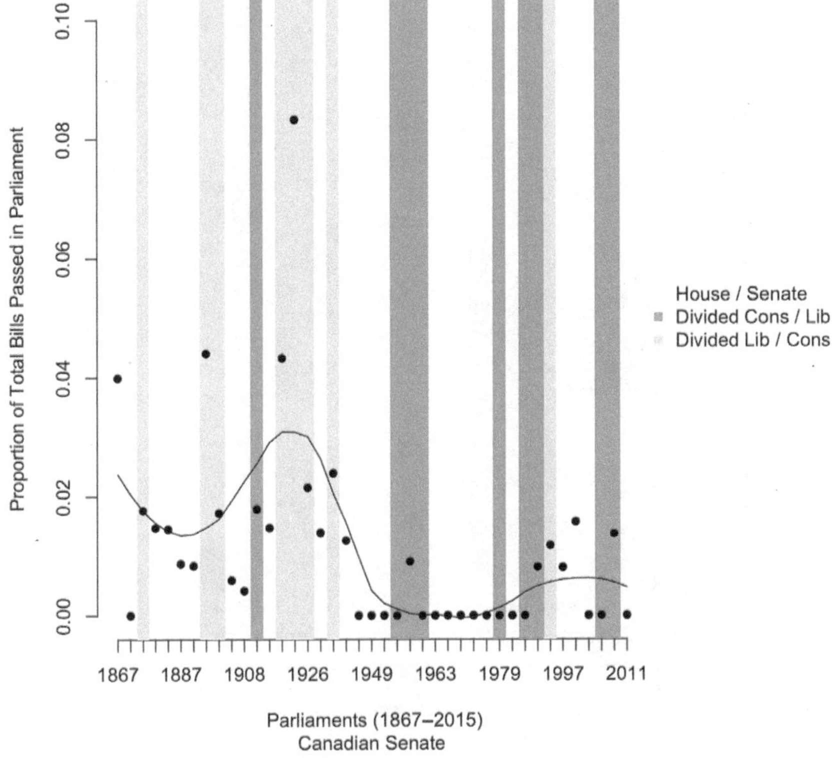

Figure 9.1 Proportion of Bills Vetoed by the Senate, 1867–2015

Since vetoes are relatively rare events in the Senate, I also present, in figure 9.2, an analysis of the proportion of government House bills brought up from the House that were amended by the upper chamber (a total of 4,442 bills). I collected these data for each of the eighty-one parliamentary sessions between 1926 and 2015 from two different sources: for the 1926–63 period, I used the amendment data collected by Kunz (1965, 378); for the period from 1963 onward, I used data from the Library of Parliament website. As before, the figure reports instances of divided governments in light-grey (Liberal House/Conservative Senate) and dark-grey (Conservative House/Liberal Senate) bars throughout the different parliamentary sessions.

Once again, the figure confirms that there was a sharp decline in Senate legislative activism over time. The number of amendments seems to have peaked during the 1930s, and to rise again in more recent parliamentary sessions. Note that Mackay (1963, 199), computing a similar measure for the earlier period,

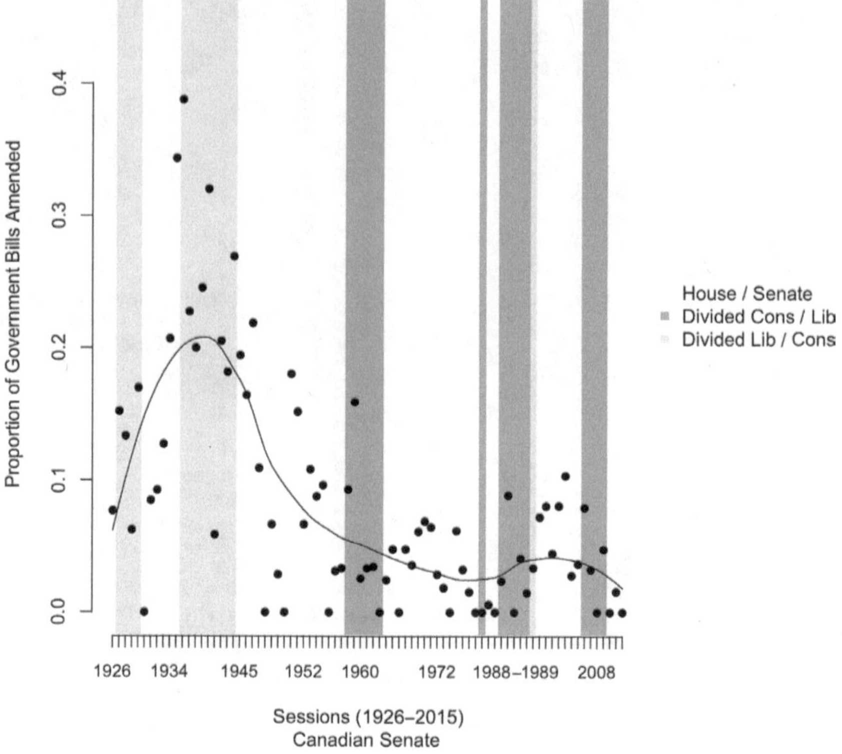

Figure 9.2 Proportion of Government Bills Amended by the Senate, 1926–2015

finds a comparable level of amendments, with about 20 per cent of public bills modified by the Senate prior to 1921. A cursory statistical analysis suggests that amendments were more frequent in divided Parliaments: 11 per cent of bills introduced by the government were amended in the Senate when the two chambers were controlled by different parties, and 7 per cent when they were unified (z-test < 0.001). As well, more amendments were made under Liberal governments, when the Senate was controlled by a Conservative majority (0.19 versus 0.04). Once again, this difference is explained by the fact that most of the divided Liberal Parliaments occurred in earlier terms, when the Conservative Senate was much more likely to be active.

In the remainder of the analysis, I turn away from partisan conflicts between the House and the Senate and look more directly at the legislative behaviour of senators. The analysis includes the voting records of 925 individual senators who participated in one or more of the 1,423 divisions recorded between 1867 and 2015; the data were collected directly from the legislative records of the Senate.

Figure 9.3 shows the level of cross-party voting in each Parliament between 1867 and 2015 by reporting the average Rice index for all legislative votes recorded for both the Conservative and Liberal parties.[4] The analysis reveals two interesting trends. First, there was a more or less linear increase in the level of party voting unity in the Senate for both parties across the whole period. On average, party unity was slightly lower for the Liberals, with a Rice score of 70 per cent, than for the Conservatives, at 76 per cent. Second, there was a clear decline in party unity for the Liberals during the 1940s. For example, between 1945 and 1953, the Rice index for the Liberals was lower than 50 per cent, which implies that, on average, one-quarter of Liberal senators opposed their own caucus during legislative votes; however, this cross-bench collaboration was short lived. Note that partisanship increased sharply in the 1960s and appears to have levelled off after the 1980s, when unity levels reached over 90 per cent for both parties, which is comparable to what we saw in the House of Commons during the same period (chapter 3). Indeed, the average Rice index in the House was 97 per cent for the Liberals and 98 per cent for the Conservatives after 1980. It is important to remember here that this increase in party unity cannot be explained by electoral pressure, as senators are appointed to this chamber.

How, then, can we explain this transformation over time? It is difficult to pinpoint exactly what was responsible for these changes, since several factors might have contributed simultaneously to promote partisanship. The upper chamber usually has been more active during divided governments, but the increase in partisan voting does not seem to have been affected by this because party unity was not necessarily higher when different parties controlled the House and Senate. Another possible explanation relates to the ideological leanings of senators themselves. Scholars have suggested that the introduction of mandatory retirement and the subsequent nomination of more partisan senators during the 1960s and 1970s could have increased ideological polarisation, especially after Parliament was divided between Conservative and Liberal majorities in the 1980s (see, for example, Franks 1999; Lynch-Staunton 2000). The analysis of more recent data confirms that this opposition remained high during minority governments.

Finally, a series of changes in the rules and proceedings of the Senate could also have affected the level of partisan conflict in the chamber. Some of these modifications were intended to reduce the amount of friction with the lower house. For instance, the need to amend legislation formally in the Senate was greatly reduced after 1947, when the Department of Justice became involved in the drafting of all government bills (Mackay 1963, 88). Another example is the practice of studying certain government legislation in the Senate while it is still being considered in the House. This pre-study procedure – introduced in the 1940s and formalized in 1971 – reduced the need to make formal amendments

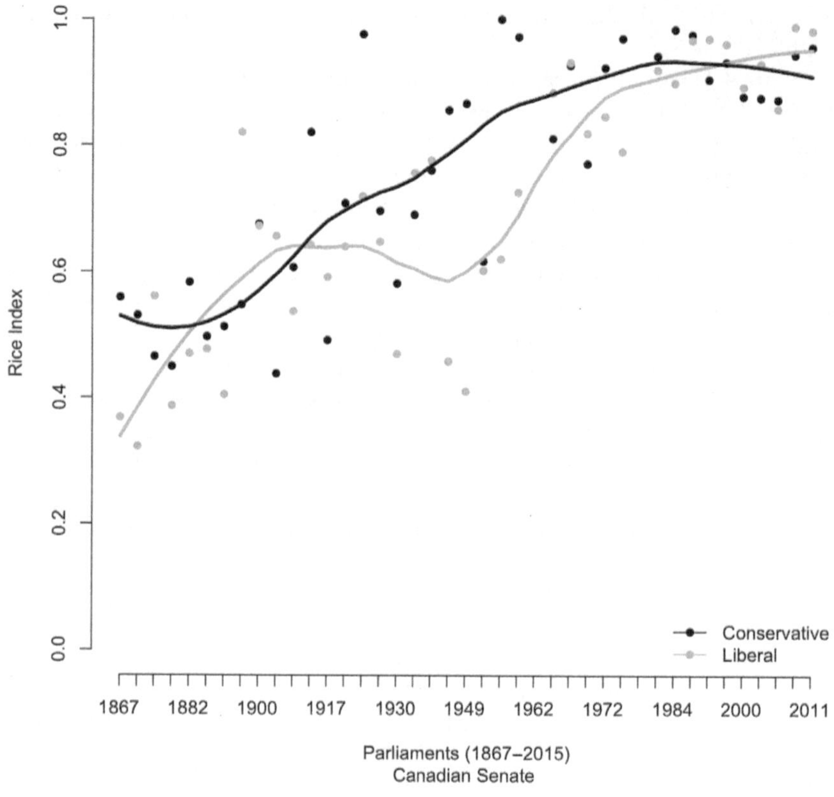

Figure 9.3 Party Unity in the Senate, 1867–2015

since senators could now propose changes before bills were brought up from the House (Kunz 1965, 156; Smith 2003, 114).

On the other hand, several rules and procedures were introduced with the explicit goal of transforming the Senate into a more partisan chamber. Although for many years senators had adopted a more collaborative approach to law making – closer in spirit to an assembly of judges (Kunz 1965, 92) – the 1980s marked the end of this era. First, in 1984, the Liberal majority abandoned the practice of bill pre-study (Franks 1999, 125). Then, in 1991, the Conservative majority adopted a series of new rules to increase the government's control of the legislative agenda – most notably by introducing closure and other procedural tools to prevent the use of dilatory motions (136). Just as in the House of Commons around the turn of the twentieth century, these changes contributed to altering the dynamic of debates in the upper chamber by promoting divisions between Conservative and Liberal senators.

To summarize, partisan conflict is more prevalent in the Senate today. This situation, though, is not new: it began in the 1980s, when Parliament was divided between Conservative and Liberal majorities, and has remained high since then. Recall that one of the primary objectives of the most recent Senate reform proposed by the Liberal government of Justin Trudeau was to reduce partisanship by appointing more independent senators. What effect will this change have on legislative behaviour? Will this new group of members be as cohesive as Liberal and Conservative appointed senators? Will they remain independent, or work with the Independent Senator Group to form a new "governing" coalition in the Senate? Finally, will a more "independent" Senate become more active and confrontational? Will senators be tempted to amend or block government legislation as they did a hundred years ago?

A Senate without Parties? An Analysis of the Forty-First and Forty-Second Parliaments

It is difficult to predict how newly appointed senators will behave in the post-reform Senate. Perhaps the only time in history when we had a comparable group of independent members was following Confederation, when senators were appointed by their respective colonial assemblies. As we saw, the upper house was much more independent from parties during this period, as was the House of Commons (see chapter 4).

The counterfactual in this case would be to imagine a Senate without parties. This is difficult to do, as we have no other contemporary point of comparison. Indeed, the comparative literature offers no other example of a similar change in partisanship in an upper house. Most of the historical changes in party attachment in the legislative arena so far have moved away from a chamber dominated by independent members to one dominated by parties – see, for example, Sircar and Høyland (2010) for the Irish Senate; Aldrich (1995) for the US Congress, Jenkins (1999) for a return to an independent chamber in both the US and Confederate Houses at the time of the Civil War; Wiseman (1973) for the non-partisan league of Manitoba and the independent government of 1940; and White (1991) for the nonpartisan adaptation of British parliamentarism in Canada's Northwest Territories.

Perhaps we should begin our investigation in the forty-first Parliament (2011–15). Indeed, Justin Trudeau formally excluded Liberal senators from the party's caucus in the middle of this term. Although these senators were in the opposition at the time, we can assume that they acquired a greater level of independence from their party, especially if they were no longer required to follow the direction of Liberal leaders in the House.

Figure 9.4 compares the voting records of senators in the last Parliament before and after the Liberals were expelled from their caucus (represented by the

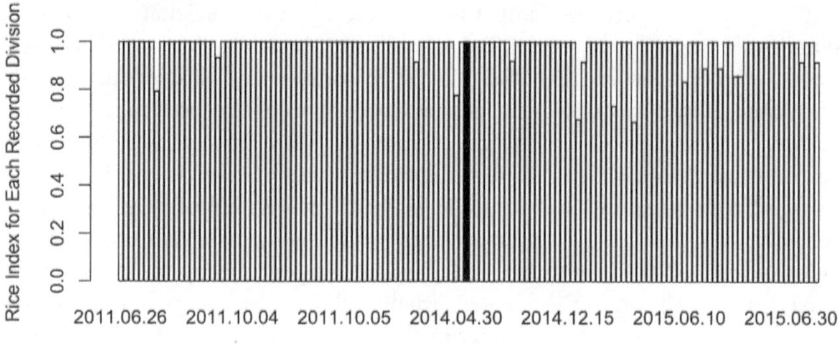

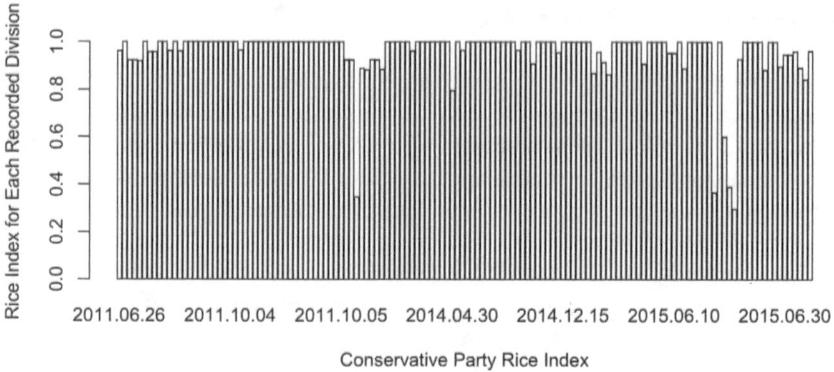

Figure 9.4 Party Voting Unity in the Senate, Forty-First Parliament, 2011–2015

black vertical bar) by plotting the Rice index for each legislative vote recorded in the forty-first Parliament. A comparison of proportion test (z-test) shows that average party unity remained unchanged for both the Liberal and Conservative caucuses during these two periods. In other words, expelling Liberal senators from their caucus did not reduce the overall level of partisanship in the chamber. In fact, the level of party unity observed among Liberal-Independent senators was actually higher than that observed in the Conservative caucus in the second half of the term.

Of course, there are serious limits to this analysis. First, these sitting Liberal senators were not nominated following the recommendations of the newly established independent commission. And second, these senators were also in the opposition when these data were recorded, so they perhaps were more likely to oppose government bills for ideological reasons. Although we should expect party voting unity to remain high among the remaining Conservative senators, it is more difficult to predict how independent senators will behave in the future. Without a formal whipping system, the government might be required to build a different winning coalition of members for each bill introduced in the Senate. In return, these temporary, ad hoc coalitions might generate a great deal of legislative instability over time. Indeed, social choice theory predicts that the absence of cohesive and unified political parties in the legislative arena will lead to "coordination, bargaining, and collective action problems" (Rask 2014, 462).

In order to understand why parties are essential for promoting political stability in modern representative assemblies, we have to return to the legislative "state-of-nature" when parliaments were not organized along partisan lines. In the absence of parties, collective action problems are more likely to arise in an assembly (Aldrich 2011; Shepsle and Weingast 1981). This is because there will be no formal means to control the legislative agenda and no restrictions on voting. Consequently, lawmakers will have the ability to change any existing piece of legislation with a simple majority. Under these conditions, social choice theory predicts that there will always be a winning coalition of members to defeat the status quo (McKelvey 1976, 480). In other words, without parties there is no majority-rule equilibrium. This ultimately might lead to voting cycles, which implies that the most recently adopted piece of legislation can be amended successfully by a different winning coalition of members. Unfortunately, no agreement between legislators, not even temporary ad hoc voting coalitions, can overcome the instability caused by the absence of majority-rule equilibrium, except perhaps political parties (Shepsle and Weingast 1981, 505).

Thus, political parties are important because they have the power to decide which bill or amendment can reach the floor when their caucus controls the majority of seats in Parliament (Shepsle and Weingast 1981, 507). As mentioned earlier, this is done mostly through agenda control. For this to work, the majority party must organize members into permanent coalitions – that is, members should "empower a boss (party leader) to discipline and coordinate them, so that they all can achieve the benefits of fuller cooperation" (Cox and McCubbins 2004, 11). In the case of the post-reform Senate, we can assume that most of the bills introduced in this chamber will originate from the government side of the House. However, without an organized majority party to support these proposals, it is difficult to predict how senators will behave, or whether or not they will vote to approve bills sponsored by the cabinet.

In March 2016 the Liberal government appointed Peter Harder to be its representative in the Senate (Trudeau 2016). Harder was mandated to be in charge of introducing government legislation in this chamber, "while still avoiding the official partisanship required of a government leader," and Senate rules and procedures eventually will be amended to better reflect "a more independent and less partisan government leadership" (*Toronto Star* 2016). New senators will be required to defer to the House of Commons, and limit themselves to amending only government legislation. The former leader of the government in the House of Commons, Dominic LeBlanc, declared in an interview that he expects senators to support the Liberal agenda, primarily because it is based on the party platform of a democratically elected government (*National Post* 2015b). It is extremely unlikely, however, that Harder will have the ability to control all aspects of the government's agenda in the upper chamber. Without the constant support of a cohesive majority of members, independent senators will be tempted to form temporary voting coalitions to block or amend controversial bills from the cabinet. Likewise, remaining disciplined Conservative senators will have strong incentives to build ad hoc majority coalitions with other like-minded independent senators to stall the Liberals' agenda, especially as new or divisive issues take the national stage.

Although at the time of writing this book, the forty-second Parliament was still in session, we can compare the voting records of the twenty-five independent senators appointed by the Trudeau government with those of the twenty-two former Liberals, fourteen independents, and forty-two Conservatives senators.[5] To determine how frequently these members voted together, I counted the number of times each sided with either one of the government's representatives (Senators Peter Harder and Diane Bellemare) during a recorded division.[6] I thus obtained an index of government support by calculating the proportion of individual votes matching the votes of Harder and Bellemare. By averaging these "government" loyalty scores for each parliamentary group, I find that Trudeau's appointees supported the government in 93 per cent of the divisions, followed by Independents (85 per cent), former Liberals (75 per cent), and Conservatives (27 per cent). Clearly, these preliminary findings suggest that the absence of a formal government parliamentary caucus is associated with lower levels of party unity among (former) Liberal senators. Should we be surprised to find that, as a group, the independent senators are more likely to support the government's agenda than those who were expelled from the Liberal caucus in the previous Parliament? Perhaps it is more interesting to note that senators appointed by Trudeau have been the most ardent supporters of the government so far. Ironically, these "crypto-Liberals" were supposed to be more independent.[7]

Ultimately, there is a distinct possibility that the absence of a cohesive voting majority to support government proposals in the Senate might create legislative gridlock in Parliament, especially since there will be a majority of independent members in this chamber beyond the forty-third Parliament. In return, this situation is likely to have a negative effect on the Liberal Party brand. House members, who rely mostly on the party's reputation to get elected, will be tempted to increase pressure on the leadership to rein in those recently appointed unelected "maverick" senators. In turn, this should increase the incentive of party leaders to promote voting unity in the upper chamber, either by nominating "Liberal ideologues" or by reintroducing party discipline and reinstating independent senators to their caucus. Theories of parliamentary organization predict that this is likely to occur and that partisan divisions will continue to be the norm, regardless of whether or not senators are formally affiliated with a party. History confirms that legislative factions eventually organize into formal caucuses to grant party leaders special agenda-setting powers to promote their interests in the legislature. The post-reform Canadian Senate most likely will prove no exception. Indeed recent developments seem to confirm that the new Senate reforms have already created problems for Trudeau's cabinet, as it attempted to push its agenda through both houses of the forty-second Parliament. As reported in the *Toronto Star*, Senator Stephen Greene of Nova Scotia summarizes the problem: "We have essentially an opposition, which is a political caucus, and no political caucus on the (government) side" (*Toronto Star* 2017). No surprise, then, that there is growing unease among government backbenchers "frustrated" by the government's "inability to move its legislative agenda forward" (ibid.).

Conclusion: A Crypto-liberal Senate?

Partisan divisions are high in the Senate today, but this is nothing new. We have seen that party conflicts have been on the rise since the middle of the 1980s, when Parliament was divided between a Liberal and Conservative majority in the House of Commons and the Senate. There was indeed an era of relative collaboration between the two chambers from the 1940s to the early 1980s, but this period was unusual in many respects, mostly because the Liberals were in power for almost forty years. The absence of a strong Conservative opposition in the House, combined with the nomination of like-minded Liberals as senators, almost guaranteed that the government would face no real opposition from that chamber.

This is akin to the "absorption" rule of the veto player theory of Tsebelis (2002, 26, 45), which demonstrates formally that a second chamber will have no real influence on policy outcomes if a majority of members share the same ideological preferences. In the Canadian context, the absorption rule implies that the Senate will support the government's agenda as long as newly appointed senators support the views of the cabinet in the House. Under these conditions, we might observe voting cohesion among legislators, not because of party discipline, but because they share a common ideology and are thus more likely to cast similar votes (Kam 2014, 406). In Canada, this equilibrium is likely to hold if the upper chamber is dominated by a majority of like-minded independent senators. Evidence from the most recent forty-second Parliament seems to confirm this view: independent senators appointed by Trudeau were indeed the most likely to support the government.

Of course, this preference-induced equilibrium can be maintained only if future governments follow the same appointment process and if all subsequent nominees share a common ideology. This is likely to be the case if the Liberal Party dominates the next few election cycles, as it did between 1940 and 1980. However, even if subsequent Liberal governments reverted to partisan nominations, we should still find that those new senators would have more or less the same preferences as the independent senators – unless Justin Trudeau's nominations were truly nonpartisan. But this implies, for example, that the Liberal government would appoint Charter critics or Quebec nationalists to the Senate, which is highly unlikely given that the final decision rests with the prime minister.

In the meantime, the presence of a cohesive group of Conservative senators, former Liberals, and independent senators (not affiliated with the Independent Senator Group) has the potential to create gridlock in the future, especially when the government has to make unpopular decisions. This has happened before: in 1911 with the Naval Aid Bill, and in 1988 with the Free Trade Agreement. More recently, Conservative senators have vowed to block any attempt to modify the electoral system without a referendum. And incentives to obstruct the government will be even higher in the Senate when all major opposition parties are unanimously opposed to the Liberals in the House.

But if we assume for a moment that, in the near future, partisan labels are removed from the Senate and a truly independent commission makes all new appointments, how will the legislature organize? The closest examples to a parliamentary system with weak party structure dominated by independent members can be found in the French Third and Fourth Republics. Unfortunately, these legislatures were highly unstable, characterized by government failures and legislative gridlock (Huber 1992, 675). The main consequence of this chronic instability was the adoption of a rationalized form of parliamentarism in the Fifth Republic, which was designed primarily to reduce the influence of members in the legislative process (Godbout and Foucault 2013). What makes the French case relevant here is that these changes were achieved through the introduction of restrictive parliamentary procedures aimed at inverting the balance of power between the government and the Assembly (Elgie and Griggs 2008, 27; Hayward 2004, 80).

Perhaps the Liberal government should consider introducing similar changes in the Senate in order to limit the blocking or amending powers of the upper house. This was the approach the UK government took in 1911 to reduce the influence of the House of Lords by removing that chamber's right to veto money bills and limiting its veto power over other government public bills (see Sharman 2015, 166–7). As mentioned earlier, the real danger here is that a majority of senators might prevent the adoption of the government's agenda, which would create a strong incentive to organize more permanent voting coalitions to support the government in this chamber. Political parties and party whips were created precisely for this reason: to control legislative procedures and to prevent government defeats in the legislature (Cox and McCubbins 2005, 6).

Although the new appointment process of senators is a definite improvement over the previous practice centred on partisan rewards and patronage, it is highly unlikely to reduce partisanship in the long run, unless perhaps the Senate is stripped of most of its legislative power. The government-versus-opposition nature of the Westminster-style parliamentary system creates strong incentives for opposing factions to organize and seize control of the legislative agenda. Even without electoral pressure and the responsibility to support the government, senators still have a constitutional mandate to adopt or reject bills sent from the House of Commons. Unelected independent senators might proactively decide to constrain their own behaviour to avoid engaging in legislative activism. House members might feel differently, however, especially if they see an advantage in waging a partisan war with the Senate to advance their (re)election goals.

Chapter Ten

Conclusion

Party discipline dominates Canadian politics. Almost everyone who studies Parliament agrees that this is one of the most important problems facing the nation today, mostly because it contributes to increasing the democratic deficit in government. When asked about their job and the work they do, Members of Parliament systematically identify party discipline as the greatest barrier to legislative responsiveness, something that weakens the relationship between constituents and their representatives (Samara Centre for Democracy n.d.). This sentiment is shared by the broader public. In a national survey, more than 85 per cent of Canadians agreed with the statement that "we would have better laws if Members of Parliament were able to vote for what people in their riding thought was best rather than having to vote the same way as their party" (Howe and Northup 2000, 22). This is not really surprising. Canada's political institutions were originally designed to promote the representation of local interests. The combination of a Westminster-style parliamentary system and geographically based electoral districts did indeed provide a strong link between voters and their representatives, at least in the first few decades following Confederation. But this relationship has weakened over time. Members who once enjoyed a great deal of liberty in the legislative process now willingly submit themselves to party discipline.

What caused this sudden change of heart among Canadian parliamentarians? What factors explain the growth and dominance of parties in the legislative arena today, and, perhaps more important, how has this transformation affected party competition? The main goal of this book has been to provide comprehensive answers to these questions by analysing all of the recorded votes in Parliament since Confederation. So far, several different theories have been put forward in the political science literature to account for the emergence of modern political parties in legislative assemblies. To date, the most common of these have focused on the US Congress or the UK Parliament, where the growth of partisanship is usually explained by a mix of external and internal factors, such as the expansion of the franchise, electoral pressure, the socialization of members, or the professionalization of legislative careers. Other factors, such as the fusion of the executive and legislative branches in the UK Parliament, the leadership's struggle to control the legislative agenda, or the ideological sorting of members in the US Congress, have been shown to matter as well.

In the preceding chapters, I revisited each of these explanations to try to determine what best accounts for the development of partisanship in the Parliament of Canada. In order to understand how parties might have changed over time, I identified three main sources of influence: historical context, the ideology of members, and the evolution of parliamentary procedures. I argued that the dramatic increase in voting unity observed in Parliament could be linked to three successive changes in the organization of the House of Commons: first, by the sorting out of Catholic and Protestant members within the Liberal and Conservative parties, which occurred after most of the major nation-building projects were settled in Parliament; second, by a reduction in the influence of backbench members following several modifications of the rules of the House intended to increase the government's ability to control the legislative agenda; and third, by the breakup of the party system and the realignment of dissenting factions towards alternative regional parties. Each of these changes was strongly influenced by the institutional context of the House of Commons and the behaviour of its members.

My intention in this last chapter is to review these conclusions in detail by taking a more comparative approach to see how my findings can be linked to the development of parties in other countries as well. I also take a closer look at how this parliamentary-centred explanation of third-party development holds up against existing theories of party system change. In the final two sections, I discuss some of the limits of my analysis, and offer some thoughts on the more recent proposals to reform Parliament, which aim to reduce the influence of the prime minister and the cabinet by weakening party discipline.

Comparing the Canadian Experience

The first objective of this book was to evaluate competing theories to explain the development of legislative party unity in Canada over time. The principal argument can be summarized as follows. First, my analysis determined that the most common explanations in the literature to account for the emergence of party loyalty – such as electoral pressure, the expansion of the franchise, or the professionalization of political careers – had only a limited influence on the voting behaviour of MPs. Rather, as shown in chapters 5 and 6, this change most likely was linked to institutional rules and the content of the legislative agenda. By analysing the outcome of every single recorded vote since Confederation, I established that motions introduced by cabinet members were associated with higher levels of party unity compared to motions sponsored by members of the opposition or even by government backbenchers. The conclusion is that the observed consolidation of party unity in Canada resulted primarily from the government's ability to control the legislative agenda, especially after the 1906–13 period, when the rules were modified to reduce the influence of private members in the House. Since the confidence convention provides a strong incentive for members to support their party in a parliamentary system, it is not surprising to find that voting unity increased after government-related motions took precedence over private members' initiatives. My contention here is not to suggest that the legislative agenda explains everything. Rather, I believe that variations in the data observed in the House of Commons are more closely associated with the reduced influence of backbenchers in the legislative process, as the analysis in chapter 8 confirms. This seems to be a much more reliable mechanism for promoting party unity than external factors that could affect the behaviour of members, such as election results or the expansion of the franchise.

A similar trend was observed in the Senate, where members are appointed and thus isolated from electoral pressure. The analysis of voting presented in chapter 9 confirms that partisanship gradually increased in this chamber, albeit at a slower rate than in the House of Commons. Most of this increase occurred when senators had life-long tenure and when almost half of the open seats were offered to retired members of the House (Kunz 1965, 41). Under these conditions, arguments that the professionalization of senators or legislative ambition explain the rise of partisanship in the Senate seem doubtful. We thus are left with only two plausible explanations for this transformation: the changing content of the legislative agenda and the ideology of senators. Although the Senate's procedures have remained mostly the same since Confederation, the number and types of bills moving up from the House have changed dramatically over time, reflecting in part the transformation of the legislative agenda in the lower chamber. As a consequence, there was an increase in the number of divisions between government and opposition members in the Senate. Likewise, the partisan sorting observed in the House around the turn of the twentieth century most likely modified the pool of potential senators available for promotions to the upper chamber. Hence, as parties became more ideologically cohesive in the House, so did newly appointed senators.

My analysis also confirms that limiting the influence of backbenchers in a parliamentary system can exacerbate intra-party divisions, which, in turn, can push members to leave their caucus. In chapters 7 and 8, I argued that this was most likely to occur when party leaders controlled the legislative agenda, but also when members had heterogeneous preferences on several important political issues. I identified two such cleavages – one related to language and religious rights, the other linked to agrarian and frontier ideology – but other issues, including immigration, economic development, and foreign policy, also had the potential to divide parties internally or realign political forces in the legislature.

For such a dramatic change to occur, however, members had to weigh the costs and benefits of belonging to a caucus. I argued in chapter 8 that the modification of House rules during the first two decades of the twentieth century altered this calculus. Reduced opportunities to air grievances, in combination with patronage reforms, raised the costs of party support for certain members, who opted to leave their caucus and form their own party in the legislature.

From this summary, we can draw three main conclusions. First, both electoral incentives and the replacement of members have had a relatively limited effect on party-line voting in the Canadian House of Commons. Second, there is strong evidence that motions or bills introduced by noncabinet members are associated with lower levels of unity, and that there has been concerted efforts by the executive to reduce the amount of these initiatives on the legislative agenda over time. And third, the presence of distinct regional factions within the two main parties is associated with lower levels of unity, an effect that was significantly reduced with the modification of parliamentary rules and the arrival of regional parties during the first half of the twentieth century. How do these three implications compare with what we know about the development of legislative party unity elsewhere?

To begin, the expansion of the franchise and the emergence of a more partisan electorate have both been identified as central components to explain the development of modern, unified, and programmatic political parties in the United Kingdom and the United States.[1] In both these cases, the appearance of parties in the legislature preceded the introduction of franchise reforms. In contrast, suffrage in Canada was always comparatively higher than in the United Kingdom during the nineteenth century, while the size of electoral districts remained relatively small until the end of the First World War (Garner 1969, 4).

It follows that the traditional sequential model proposed by Duverger (1954, 65) and Sartori (1976, 21) to explain the development of the first political parties – which begins with the formation of parliamentary groups, followed by franchise reforms, greater electoral competition, and, finally, the establishment of permanent party organizations – is not supported by the Canadian case (see also Boix 2009, 511). Rather, as my analysis in chapter 5 confirms, the increase in the number of voters failed to have a significant effect on the development of party unity. This finding is in line with the experience of several other European countries throughout the nineteenth century, where the introduction of the first major franchise reforms occurred only after the emergence of strong legislative party organizations (Scarrow 2006, 17–19).

Furthermore, my analysis confirms that the gradual replacement of older cohorts of MPs had a relatively limited effect on the development of party unity over time. This is also what Eggers and Spirling (2016, 586) found in their analysis of legislative voting in the UK Parliament during the Victorian era. These authors also suggest that the enticement of ministerial promotion could be an alternative explanation for the growth of partisan support in that legislature. In the Canadian context, as I showed in chapter 5, party loyalty had no effect on the likelihood of being promoted to the Senate, but party loyalty did increase a member's chance of being appointed to the cabinet. Still, it seems doubtful that this factor alone explains the growth of partisanship over time. Promotions to earlier cabinets conformed to certain norms of representation – regional, linguistic, confessional – and a large number of outsiders without any prior parliamentary experience have been appointed as ministers (Kam 2009, 19). Perhaps more interesting, there is also some evidence that faithful government supporters received additional patronage appointments in their riding. Although the analysis was limited to postmasters, it offers some proof that the bureaucracy was for a time an important tool for the promotion of loyalty among government backbenchers. Taken together, both of these results might explain the increase in party unity observed in Canada since Confederation. However, given that party unity was at its weakest when patronage appointments were the norm, and that cabinet appointments are infrequent and subject to regional constraints, these factors on their own cannot account for the changes observed in the data. For these reasons, the lure of legislative promotions and patronage could have had only a marginal effect on the growth of partisanship in Canada.

The second implication relates to the influence of the legislative agenda. My analysis shows that, once the government took control of the proceedings in the House between 1906 and 1913, recorded divisions became increasingly related to government business, where party unity was expected to be higher. Of course, the importance of the legislative agenda in explaining the emergence of cohesive parties has been known for some time in the context of the UK Parliament (Berrington 1968, 363–4). Studies of partisan behaviour in the United States have also reached a similar conclusion – namely, that the agenda or the rules and procedures play a fundamental role in accounting for partisan polarization in Congress (Finocchiaro and Rohde 2008, 56; Lee 2009, 131–3).

This finding is perhaps the most direct evidence that a set of common denominators explains the growth of partisanship in the Canadian, UK, and US contexts. Each case demonstrates that majority party leaders were granted special agenda-setting powers to prevent systematic obstruction in the assembly. For example, both closure in the UK House of Commons and Reed's rules in the US House of Representatives were adopted during the second half of the nineteenth century to reduce the influence of members of the Irish Home Rule League and populist silverites, respectively (Cox and McCubbins 2005, 58; Dion 1997, 191). Likewise, the adoption of closure in Canada on the eve of the First World War was in part to prevent an organized minority of French-Canadian MPs from blocking the granting of emergency funds for the defence of the British Empire.

The third implication concerns the partisan sorting argument and the structure of the party system more broadly. Recall that Canada is composed of several regional, linguistic, and ethnic groups whose interests have not always been represented adequately within the traditional Westminster model of two-party competition. As we saw in chapter 7, conflict over certain issues, such as religion and tariffs, have at times divided the two major parties internally, but they also can be linked to the creation of third parties in the legislature. This is by no means exceptional. A similar pattern was observed in the UK Parliament following the split of the Conservatives during the Corn Law debates, and in the United States following the division of the Whigs over the issue of slavery (McLean 2001, 37; Poole and Rosenthal 2007, 124). In both cases, the presence of strong regional factions weakened the unity of the dominant parties – until the electorate realigned and the remaining members of these factions banded together to form a new political party (Liberals and Republicans, respectively).

The Canadian case is exceptional, however, in that once third parties entered the House of Commons, they never fully disappeared, nor did they manage to replace either one of the two dominant parties. Canada's long-standing "two-party-plus" system has been sustained by the presence of strong regional political parties (Blondel 1968, 188), which have prevented the government from obtaining a majority of seats in fourteen of the thirty Parliaments elected since the First World War. The continued presence of third parties has also allowed for a more diverse representation of interests in the House of Commons. By extension, this has created more homogeneous and unified party caucuses in the legislature (Malloy 2003, 122), a finding that highlights one of the limitations of the Westminster model of government: the combination of high levels of party discipline and regionally/ethnically diverse populations increases the incentives to create third parties. It would be interesting to explore whether this relationship exists in other former British colonies – such as New Zealand, Australia, India, or South Africa – to see if the introduction of stricter parliamentary rules also has led to the fragmentation of their respective party systems.

Party System Change

The second objective of this book was to determine if parliamentary institutions and procedures have affected the structure of the party system. Although Lipset (1954, 197) and Epstein (1964, 57) made a similar argument decades ago, my study represents the first attempt not only to validate this claim empirically, but also to understand the mechanism behind it. The data and analyses in chapter 8 provided unique evidence supporting the hypothesis that stricter parliamentary rules can push some members to leave their own party and form an independent caucus in the legislative arena.

This finding might seem surprising, since, until now, the conventional wisdom in the Canadian political science literature generally has been that election results explain the transformation of the party system (see, for example, Carty, Cross, and Young 2000, 7). In chapter 8, I argued that to understand more fully how Parliament could promote the creation of new political parties, it was necessary to consider the effect of several institutional rule changes on the behaviour of members early in the twentieth century. The first of these relates to the modification of parliamentary procedures between 1906 and 1913, which centralized agenda control in the hands of the government. The main consequence of this change was to reduce the influence of private members in the legislative process. Add to this the effect of the Civil Service Reform Act of 1918, and we find there was a significant reduction in the incentives for members to support the two main parties in the House of Commons. This second institutional change removed an important benefit associated with party loyalty – namely patronage, which for many members was a central component of their decision to join a party. Under these new conditions, leaving the two main parties became a feasible option for dissatisfied MPs. These defectors were mostly representatives of rural ridings in the West, who created their own separate caucus in Parliament with the aim of abolishing party discipline and giving members more independence (Morton 1950, 229).

This interpretation stands in sharp contrast to the existing literature on party system change. First, in comparative studies, scholars usually explain the emergence of new parties by the heterogeneity of voter preferences (Lipset and Rokkan 1967). This sociological account stipulates that the number of parties in the legislature should reflect the primary dimensions of conflicts found in society, such as those associated with economic redistribution or religion. In the Canadian context, we know that the Conservative and Liberal parties originally were formed to support or oppose Confederation and later free trade, which were the main dividing lines in the first three Parliaments. Later on, the two parties further organized along religious and ethnic lines, a centre-periphery divide, and perhaps over socio-economic issues. As in Europe, we should have witnessed the emergence of several different new parties focused on defending the religious or agrarian interests of voters (Boix 2009, 514). But this is not what happened. Although Quebec nationalists came close to forming their own federal party after the hanging of Louis Riel in 1885, most of the successful candidates who ran under this banner in the 1887 election ended up sitting with the Conservative caucus in the House of Commons. It was not for want of trying, however. Neatby (1973) notes that the creation of Saskatchewan and Alberta in 1905 almost disintegrated the two-party system over the issue of separate schools. "As far as the autonomy bill was concerned," notes Neatby, "the French-Canadians ... might be called a third party" (157). Unity was ultimately maintained because Laurier could secure the passage of the autonomy bill and thus prevent the creation of a permanent "nationalist third party" in the House made up of Conservatives and Liberal Roman Catholics (160). The Progressives, on the other hand, chose a different path almost two decades later by forming their own independent caucus inside Parliament.

While separate farmers' parties already existed at the provincial level in Alberta and Ontario following the end of the First World War, it took much longer for supporters of the farmers' movement to agree to present their own candidates in federal elections – and this only after their leader, Thomas Crerar, left the Union government.[2] Until the 1921 election, the farmers' movement had hesitated between supporting a third party and trying to influence the two main parties from within. The *Grain Growers' Guide*, for example, noted that the time was "not ripe to form an independent farmer's party."[3] It was safer to make "both parties responsive to the will of the people" by "electing men pledged to work in their interest" who would support the farmers' platform (22 February 1911, 6). The movement would also be better served by having members sitting with either the government or the opposition, as long as some would "get into power" (*Grain Growers' Guide*, 7 June 1911, 5), since farmers elected to Parliament could "be trusted to get into line and vote right when any important issue was before them, irrespective of party" (*Grain Growers' Guide*, 18 February 1914, 14).

It quickly became apparent, however, that the rigidity of parliamentary procedures prevented farmers from having their voices heard in the House of Commons. Although the number of representatives from the West more than doubled between 1900 and 1911, their influence in the legislative process seemed to wane. The problem remained partyism, which allowed "a few men to control all the legislative machinery in the country" (*Grain Growers' Guide*, 22 February 1911, 6). And this situation did not improve with the introduction of new rules and procedures to limit the influence of private members after 1913. According to the *Globe* newspaper, adopting closure "greatly and probably permanently changed for the worse the old time House of Commons" by lessening "the dignity and usefulness of the private member" (quoted in Liberal-Conservative Party 1913, 11). "If the opportunity is not to be given to members of the House to discuss [government legislation]," commented Georges Henri Boivin in 1913, "we might as well turn ourselves into voting machines and be gagged entirely, never to speak in this Parliament again" (Debates 1913, 9583). The adoption of higher tariffs in 1915 and unfavourable railway bills adopted during the First World War offered many farmers additional proof that the Conservative Party was "ready to serve the governing class," just as the Liberals had done between 1896 and 1911 (*Grain Growers' Guide*, 27 December 1916, 7). After all, the farmers elected to Parliament remained "party men" who had to "vote as their party machine dictated" (*Alberta Non-Partisan*, 27 September 1918, 9). The war had accelerated this trend: the new procedures prevented members from introducing their own pieces of legislation, which were now "strangled according to parliamentary rules" (*Edmonton Capital*, 26 February 1914, 4). The cabinet increasingly dominated the legislative process as well, since, as the *Alberta Non-Partisan* (21 June 1918, 7) commented, "the time allocated to private members was gradually curtailed" and "[g]overnment matters [now] occupied most of the House's time ... [such that private members ended up as] mere rubber stamps for recording decisions."

Although the creation of a wartime Unionist coalition had led many farmers to believe that a nonpartisan era had dawned in Canadian politics, they quickly realized that this party would be no different than the others. Many now thought that the formation of a national farmers' party was the only way to secure fair representation (Morton 1950, 73–4). Farmers were organizing at the provincial level, the labour movement was uniting, and a large number of electors seemed to "have lost all illusions in regards to party politics" (*Alberta Non-Partisan*, 13 July 1918, 9). Even the *Grain Growers' Guide* now felt that "steps must be taken to launch a new party which would be free from the old centralized autocratic influence of the two old parties" (10 December 1919, 8). This agrarian party would support the Canadian Council of Agriculture's platform, by endorsing a new national policy to defend the interests of farmers in Ottawa. Thus, the formation of the Progressive caucus in Parliament occurred at a time when discussions were already well under way to create a new national farmers' party. Although the Canadian Council of Agriculture formally acknowledged in 1921 that members of the Progressive parliamentary group were now their official representatives in the legislature, there was no real attempt to create a national party campaign in the subsequent election (Morton 1950, 118). Nevertheless, it is fair to assume that the rejection of partyism and of old parties served as a basis for the development of third parties in the House of Commons.

As this brief account shows, the introduction of a new salient political cleavage does not necessarily lead to the formation of third parties or to the replacement of older parties by newer ones. Such a transformation is not simply a question of electoral pressure and social groups – clearly, there is an interaction between institutional rules and legislative representation. It is surprising to find how much parliamentary procedures played a role in the organization of the farmers' movement: first, by favouring the election of their candidates inside the old parties in order to influence the government from within, and second, by promoting the election of their own third-party candidates after they realized that individual members had very little power over the legislative process.

Another popular institutional account in the comparative literature to explain the emergence of new parties suggests that electoral rules affect the number of parties in the party system (Duverger [1951] 1958, 246–8). This view states that, in a plurality electoral system, voters and elites have a strong incentive to coordinate their support for the two candidates with the best chances of winning the riding so as to avoid wasting their votes. In proportional systems, however, this incentive is smaller and new parties are much more likely to be created, since the threshold for representation in the legislature will be lower. Although Canada has a single-member-plurality electoral system, the number of parties represented in Parliament has been higher than two for a long time – at least since the emergence of the Progressive Party. Unlike in other British-derived democracies, there was never a strong party on the left that forced the consolidation of parties on the right. In other words, the Liberals never had an incentive to merge with the Conservatives to prevent the election of the New Democratic Party, as was the case with similar situations in the United Kingdom, Australia, and New Zealand (Cox 1997, 256).

To better understand the emergence of third parties in Canada, we must move away from comparative analyses and focus more on the specificities of this case. For scholars of Canadian politics, the arrival of the Progressive Party, and later of the United Farmers and Social Credit parties in Alberta, also resulted from the plurality electoral system, which tends to "favour minor parties with sectional strongholds and to discourage minor parties with diffuse support" (Cairns 1968, 59). Under these conditions, the mechanism of the electoral system favours "local bipartism," which can vary across districts and produce a multiparty system in the aggregate (Gaines 1999, 837). Thus, smaller parties that have a geographically concentrated base of support benefit from the electoral system by concentrating their appeals in the districts where they are most popular. In this context, the emergence of third parties most likely will be linked to regional or local grievances, which is precisely what we find in the cases of the Progressive, United Farmers, Social Credit, Bloc Populaire, and Bloc Québécois parties.

A different explanation is necessary to account for the emergence of the CCF (and later the NDP), which represented a truly national party, though one with diffuse support. As we saw in chapter 2, the CCF was created as an alliance between labour and farming organizations in 1932 with the ambition of becoming a national party. For much of its history, however, the party has performed better in the West, less well in Ontario, and received relatively little support in Quebec and the Atlantic provinces (Gaines 1999, 854). The NDP's inability to become the party of labour in Canada is usually explained by the country's weak class system and "brokerage politics," which tends to minimize social group differences and conflicts (Brodie and Jenson 1988, 4; Carty and Cross 2010, 193). But this explanation does not really tell us much about why third parties emerged in the first place, nor does it offer additional insights into why they became increasingly important only after 1920. For many years, then, the simultaneous presence of two and later three national parties, in addition to several distinct regional ones, has continued to puzzle scholars of Canadian politics.

Perhaps the most complete effort to explain the emergence of third parties in Canada can be found in Richard Johnston's (2017) analytical history of the party system. Johnston argues that the rise of the first third parties – or what he labels "insurgent parties" – in Parliament was most likely the result of federalism (247–8). He maintains that it is much easier to create new parties at the provincial level, especially in Alberta and Quebec, where regional grievances have a long history. These can take many forms, such as economic hardship (Pinard 1971, 94–5), fiscal issues (Chhibber and Kollman 2004, 114–15), ethno-linguistic questions (Johnston 2017, 159), and tariffs (Morton 1950, 113–14). In this context, federalism provides numerous opportunities for the development of insurgent parties, thanks to the logic of the electoral system, which rewards concentrated regional appeals (Johnston 2017, 244). And because the size of provincial electoral ridings is smaller than federal ones, such appeals are much more likely to resonate among voters, especially when the vote is divided among three or more parties. The presence of a United Farmers provincial government in Ontario and Alberta before the 1921 federal election thus could explain the electoral successes of the Progressives, since farmers in these provinces controlled local patronage and had an existing party organization to facilitate the election of their own federal candidates. Historical data seem to confirm this hypothesis: we find that whenever a provincial government was controlled by a third party, a majority of MPs from the Progressive Party was returned to the House of Commons in the four federal elections between 1925 and 1935.[4]

What role, if any, did parliamentary institutions play in all of this? If regional and economic grievances led to the development of insurgent strongholds at the provincial level, the influence of Parliament in the creation of third parties should have been only marginal at best. There are two ways, however, in which the institutional features of Parliament also could have contributed to this change. First, before any talk of constituting a farmers' party at the federal level and before insurgent parties even elected their first members to provincial legislatures, insurgent candidates had run as Liberals or Conservatives. For instance, the Liberal Farmers Association of the Battleford constituency in Saskatchewan supported its own candidate against the Liberal Party incumbent in a nomination contest for the 1911 election.[5] "I am, and always have been a Liberal, and am strongly in favor of Reciprocity and the general policy of the Liberal Party," declared S.E. McManus to voters of his riding. However, he went on to criticize Laurier's handling of the construction of a railway branch in the West. He also stated that he was "in favor of a greater measure of reciprocity," and believed "that agricultural implements should be on the free list" (Liberal Farmers Association 1911, 2). As we saw earlier, this somewhat unusual Liberal candidacy is explained by the reluctance of the different farmers' associations to oppose the two traditional parties, as they did not originally seek power, but rather representation in Parliament through the two-party system (Morton 1950, 112).

The second way in which Parliament played an important role in the emergence of third parties relates to Prairie farmers' belief that their growing numbers would also increase their influence in government. To many of these farmers, however, it rapidly became clear that party discipline and partyism were reducing their influence in the legislative process, and thus preventing the effective representation of their interests in the House of Commons. Perhaps Lipset (1954, 176) is correct in arguing that the emergence of regional parties is in part explained by the fact that "Canadians are forced to find a way of expressing their regional needs and at the same time supporting national parties" in a context where tight party discipline is the norm. The solution has been to "support different parties on a provincial level than those which they back nationally" (176). And when these regional needs could not find appropriate representation within the Conservative or Liberal parties, new parties were created, such as the United Farmers in Alberta or Union Nationale in Quebec.

I suggest, therefore, that we add parliamentary rules to the repertoire of variables used to study party system change. Just as with the modification of electoral rules, restricting the influence of individual members in the legislative process could increase the incentives to create new parties in the legislature. Indeed, over the years, a large number of new parties have been founded by disgruntled MPs, including the Reconstruction Party, the Bloc Populaire, the Ralliement Créditiste (not to be confused with the Social Credit Party), the Bloc Québécois, and, more recently, Maxime Bernier's People's Party of Canada. Although I have provided some evidence to validate this endogenous account of party system change in the case of the Progressive Party, it is necessary to investigate further what factors explain the creation of new parties in Canada and in other institutional contexts as well, such as presidential versus parliamentary democracies or proportional versus plurality electoral systems.

Caveat Lector

Having reviewed some of the theories to explain the development of party voting unity in Canada and, more broadly, its effect on the structure of the party system, I now want to discuss some limits of the methodological approach I have used in this study. As noted earlier, this book represents the first attempt to explain the development of political parties in Canada from a parliamentary-centred perspective. In doing so, I analysed an original dataset of more than twelve thousand recorded votes to understand why party unity increased so much in the House of Commons and Senate between 1867 and 2015. Such a massive data analysis presents numerous challenges, most notably in attempts to study the relationship between the different factors influencing party unity or in the operationalization and coding of the variables used in the different models, but also because lumping together 150 years of parliamentary data to measure party unity runs the risk of "conceptual stretching" (George and Bennett 2005, 19; Pierson 2004, 21). Whenever possible, I attempted to keep these models simple by using only a small number of variables, or by avoiding analysing the data in time series spanning several decades. Although most of my findings were confirmed in the cumulative analysis of the individual determinants of party loyalty (chapter 5) and party unity during parliamentary votes (chapter 6), I put more faith in the results of the short-term analyses I conducted prior to the 1920s, mostly because the structure of the data changes so much over time. Indeed, this period marked the end of the dominance of private members in Parliament, as well as a dramatic increase in the overall level of party unity for both the Conservative and Liberal parties. After this point, there is little variance left to be explained in the data.

Another important issue relates to the validation of the different theories and hypotheses I outlined in chapter 3. Recall that the analysis confirmed that several of the most likely causes of party development identified in the Canadian and comparative literatures, such as the effects of electoral pressure or franchise expansion, did not have a systematic influence on individual determinants of party loyalty. It is important to mention, however, that failing to reject the null hypothesis – for example, that electoral margins or cohorts have no effect on party line voting – does not imply that it is true (Vaus 2002, 168). In other words, lack of statistical significance here does not mean that the theory is "wrong" because it is impossible to establish the validity of the null with a hypothesis test. Even though I used confidence intervals throughout most of my analyses to show the range and direction of likely values for the parameters under study, this is not the same as an equivalence test, where hypothesis testing can be used to determine if the absence of an effect is statistically meaningful (for a discussion see Salkind 2007, 315). In the end, since confidence intervals report the range of coefficient values in the model, I leave it to readers to form their own opinion about the potential influence of the variables tested in the analysis. One thing is certain: I found much more evidence that the content of the legislative agenda affected legislative party unity than was the case for external parliamentary factors.

Fault might also be found with the approach I used to test the validity of the different factors found in the Canadian and comparative literatures to explain how parties transformed over time. Readers might have noted that the bulk of these variables were borrowed from the UK and US experiences, mainly because they represent the only two cases where comparable legislative voting records exist and where comprehensive empirical studies have been conducted to explain the growth of party voting unity during the nineteenth century (see, for example, Brady, Cooper, and Hurley 1979; Eggers and Spirling 2016; Poole and Rosenthal 1997). Since no comparable dataset existed in Canada, it was difficult for me to find a clear set of widely accepted variables to be tested in this context. Nonetheless, I was still able to find several "domestic variables" to explain how parties transformed following Confederation. These variables range from the staggered election argument (Underhill 1935) to the effect of changes in party membership or in the parliamentary rules of the House of Commons (March 1974; Stewart 1977). Other potential explanations come from the historical description of the first Canadian party system, a period characterized by a limited franchise, public voting, "loose fish" candidates, and elections focused more on local concerns and patronage (Patten 2017, 5–7). Note that, until now, which of these factors, if any, actually affected the legislative behaviour of Members of Parliament remained somewhat of a mystery. Was it the expansion of the franchise or same-day elections that ultimately reined in these "loose fish"? Was it the nature of conflicts in the legislature or changing procedures in the House of Commons? In this book, I have attempted to establish or refute the validity of these claims through an empirical analysis of legislative votes. Challenging this conventional wisdom of party system change was, in my view, a necessary step to determine what we know and what we do not know about parliamentary behaviour in Canada.

Finally, even if archival work, newspaper stories, parliamentary records, and biographies confirm the results of some of my empirical analysis, this type of historical evidence remains highly selective. Nonetheless, this research approach allowed me to focus on the causal mechanism behind the changes observed in the data. In other words, the analysis confirmed that three conditions were necessary for the consolidation of parties in the Canadian House of Commons: first, the sorting out of Catholics and Protestants towards both major parties; second, the modification of parliamentary rules to reduce the influence of backbenchers; and third, the emergence of third parties, which further contributed to creating ideologically cohesive caucuses over time. This "chain of evidence" represents the central argument of my book. It also highlights the reciprocal relationship between party discipline and party system change.

For most of this project, my purpose was to move beyond simple statistical analysis of the determinants of party loyalty by focusing on the different pathways to party consolidation in Canada. That being said, there certainly exists more than one causal path to the same outcome, as shown by studies in the United States (Cox and McCubbins 2005, 221), the United Kingdom (Cox 1987, 169–70; Eggers and Spirling 2016, 586), or Australia (Godbout and Smaz 2016, 493). However, the traditional sequential story to account for the emergence of organized political parties, which always begins with franchise reform, failed to be confirmed in the Canadian case. It is possible that, in other legislatures, the presence of ideologically homogeneous caucuses is sufficient to explain high levels of party cohesion. Absent this condition, however, agenda control becomes necessary to maintain party unity. In the parliamentary context, this has corresponded to a reduction in private members' business and to an increase in the time allotted for government affairs.

If we follow this logic, one might expect the House of Commons eventually to return to a more decentralized style of decision making, as predicted by the conditional party government thesis (Aldrich and Rohde 2005). Recall that this theory presupposes that the legislative influence of party leaders is conditional on the ideology of members: when the majority is composed of a more diverse coalition of members, the legislature should become more decentralized. This condition has translated into a clear movement between periods of centralization and decentralization in the US Congress. In this case, party leaders first increased their influence between 1890 and 1910, when partisan conflicts intensified. This was followed by a revolt against Speaker Joseph Cannon in 1910, which marked the beginning of a period of relative decentralization and low party unity (1911–68) until the 1970s, after which there was another series of reforms to centralize agenda control in the hands of party leaders.

Canada's Parliament has no comparable dynamic. There was a period of weaker party unity after Confederation, which ended with a series of rule changes between 1906 and 1913 to increase the amount of government business on the agenda. This was followed by almost seventy-five years of strict party discipline, until the recommendations of the McGrath Report (Canada 1985) were adopted in 1986 to give a certain amount of power back to private members. But prior to this, no other major rule changes were adopted to reduce the influence of party leaders, although there was a failed attempt by the John Diefenbaker government in 1962 to abolish closure (Debates 1962, 2163). The 1986 reform was adopted when the Progressive Conservative Party controlled almost 75 per cent of the seats in the House and when its caucus was composed of around 25 per cent of members from Quebec and 30 per cent from the West. The 1962 attempt to abolish closure was done when Diefenbaker's party controlled 79 per cent of the seats, with the same proportion of western and Quebec MPs. In both cases, it is easy to assume that the ideological composition of the Conservatives was heterogeneous. But why were the rules modified only in 1986?

We can also ask why other rules were adopted to further weaken the influence of private members, even though the government already dominated most of the legislative process after the First World War (Stewart 1977, 208). For example, the Liberals introduced time allocation in 1968, when the party controlled 58 per cent of the seats (with 36 per cent from Quebec and 18 per cent from the West), yet this rule was approved with the consent of all opposition parties. Why did the most important reforms of the House of Commons adopted in 1906, 1910, 1913, 1955, 1962, and 1968 always move towards a greater centralization of legislative powers? Does that mean the theory of conditional party government does not work in the Canadian context?

There are no easy answers to these questions. I suspect that the presence of third parties changed somewhat the incentives for party factions to demand more input into the legislative process after 1921. Unlike in the US case, third parties have gained increasing influence over time in Canada. Since they have a lower chance of forming the government, their leaders are more likely to demand additional powers in the House of Commons, as opposed to working towards decentralizing the decision-making process in the hands of backbenchers. Another important element to consider is that, in Canada's parliamentary system, the number of veto points is lower than in a presidential system. Throughout most of the twentieth century, Canadians demanded a more active government. The return to a House of Commons in which a minority of members could block the government's agenda seems unlikely today (Stewart 1977, 234) – although the new Senate could prove otherwise. Most parliamentary reforms adopted since Confederation have moved in the direction of increasing the power of the government in the legislative arena. This can be conceptualized as path dependency, where shifting back to a more decentralized form of legislative organization becomes increasingly difficult over time (Pierson 2004, 149). Perhaps the fusion of executive and legislative powers in a parliamentary system contributes to making such a reversal almost impossible today, but more work is required before we can fully understand this puzzle.

Ultimately the transformation of political parties is a complex phenomenon with a multitude of possible causes. What matters is the sequence in which they occurred. In the Canadian case, we first saw that religion played an important role in changing the party system. We also saw that parliamentary rules, not just elections, could affect the structure of the party system. Indeed, the establishment of the Progressive Party was postponed by western farmers' belief that they would have more influence by siding with whichever party controlled the government. Later, when it became apparent that their representatives had very little influence in the legislative process, the movement chose to support its own candidates, but only after the establishment of a Progressive caucus in Parliament. It is perhaps ironic that the arrival of a farmers' party contributed to raising party unity even further, precisely because it removed an important faction of dissenting members from the two major parties, which now became even more ideologically cohesive.

Is Parliament Still Relevant?

Parliament has a reputational problem in Canada. This is nothing new. Politicians and scholars have been complaining about the lack of influence of MPs and the centralization of legislative powers in the hands of the executive for what seems like an eternity (see, for example, Savoie 1999, 7; Stewart 1977, 282–3). For many, the main culprit is party discipline. The story goes as follows: there was a time when MPs had much more influence in the legislative process. They could enact their own legislation and hold the government to account. At some point during the twentieth century, this independence was lost, as party leaders won the right to impose their will on the assembly. Today, more than ever, MPs are at the mercy of party discipline, and this lack of independence greatly affects their ability to represent the interests of their constituents in Parliament.

For many, weakening party discipline is seen as a panacea to Parliament's representation problem. Docherty (1997, 256), Franks (1987, 144–5), Skogstad (2003, 970), and Smith (2007, 124) have all suggested that reducing the scope of the confidence convention would improve democratic responsiveness, empower backbenchers, and diminish partisanship in the House of Commons. As we have seen, however, most MPs gladly agree to follow their leaders in the House, and there is hardly ever any dissension on votes related to government motions. Although I have focused in this book mainly on understanding how Parliament got to this point, one can think of many reasons party unity remains high today. This could be, for example, because of career ambitions, re-election goals, ideological preferences, the socialization of members, or the control exercised by House leaders (Kam 2009, 14–15). Paradoxically, it is mainly this subordination that weakens the link between citizens and their representatives. That said, a return to greater independence on the part of MPs, as in the years following Confederation, would be impractical today. Indeed the executive now dominates the content of the legislative agenda, which used to be evenly divided between government and private members' business. Besides there have been more than two parties in the House of Commons for almost a hundred years now, which allows for a more diverse representation of interests.

Nevertheless, several reforms have been proposed over time to increase the influence of parliamentarians in the House of Commons. The most important of these was the McGrath Report (Canada 1985) – named after committee chairman James McGrath – which resulted in a modification of the Standing Orders to facilitate the consideration of private members' business. More recently, there was the Reform Act (An Act to amend the Canada Elections Act and the Parliament of Canada Act), a 2015 private member's bill introduced by Conservative Michael Chong (Halton Hills, ON), which proposed to increase the influence of party caucuses by establishing a formal process to expel members, trigger leadership reviews, and elect caucus chairs. Both of these initiatives have been met with mixed success. Although the amount of private members' business has indeed increased significantly since the McGrath Report was adopted, the influence of parties seems to have crept in there as well, so that such business is becoming increasingly partisan in the House of Commons (Blidook 2012, 118). It is too early to judge the effect of the Reform Act, but if the goal was to "lighten the whip," as Chong stated in an interview, we should have witnessed a significant decline in party unity. The record shows otherwise: the level of party unity for the Conservative, Liberal, and New Democratic parties has so far been equal or greater than 99 per cent in the forty-second Parliament.[6]

Ultimately the combination of a Westminster-style parliamentary system and a single-member-plurality electoral system in Canada was always going to create tensions between the representation of local interests in Parliament and the need for unified caucuses to support or oppose government: one legislative approach promotes responsiveness, the other accountability (Carey 2008, 6–7). It all comes down to what kind of role we think MPs should play. Should they be trustees or representatives of the whole nation, as argued by Burke ([1770] 1892, 75), Mill ([1861] 2004, 237), and Schumpeter ([1942] 1975, 269)? Or delegates or agents who follow the preferences of their constituents, as viewed by Madison ([1787] 2003, 55), perhaps Rousseau ([1762] 1992, 122–3), and later promoted by the progressive movement in the United States and Canada? To be sure, the separation between the legislative and executive branches in the United States gives members of Congress much more freedom to vote according to their own preferences, or to represent their district. Yet, even in the United States, weak party unity can lead to political instability, as argued by McKelvey (1976, 480) and Riker (1982, 186–8), and demonstrated empirically by Jenkins (1999, 1163) in the case of the Confederate Congress. Allowing more free votes in the House of Commons or following the "three line" whip voting system, which was introduced in 2004 (and only really pursued by the Liberal Party) are two mechanisms that might increase the influence of MPs. Yet, as the most recent data show, party unity has not declined significantly over the past decade, which brings us to the question of the Senate.

It is perhaps ironic that the most significant reform introduced in Parliament to revitalize the role of members has been in the upper chamber. As appointees of an unelected body, senators have much more influence today than do House members: they can introduce their own bills, amend government legislation, and are free to vote as they please. As I argued in chapter 9, this newfound independence is bound to create problems in the long run. As much as I like studying parliamentary voting, party unity plays an important role in promoting legislative accountability and political stability and in preventing logrolls. It also limits the power of lobbyists, who might find it harder to influence individual lawmakers. Perhaps the recent increase in the number of contacts between lobbyists and independent senators suggests that this is not far from the truth (*Hill Times* 2018).

Now we come to the part where I would normally suggest a series of proposals to reform Parliament. I will spare readers such a discussion, however, since the literature already has more than its fair share of recommendations to increase the relevance of the legislative branch. If anything, plans to make Parliament a little more like Westminster or the US Congress are misguided. As my results show, more free votes or more private members' business will not necessarily weaken party unity (Canada 1985, 9; Docherty 1997, 257). Nor will raising the number of MPs promote their independence, as it has in the United Kingdom (Docherty 2005, 179; Franks 1987, 140). The increasing amount of private members' business and the 20 per cent growth in the number of House members since the 1980s have not made much of a difference. In the end, parties will always find a way to maintain their influence in the legislative process.

Conclusion

Why are parties so disciplined in Canada today? Multiple lines of conflict have always existed over language, religion, and geography, yet parliamentary caucuses have remained relatively cohesive throughout the country's history. As we have seen in this book, the stability sought by the union of British North America in 1867 was not easily achieved. One of the main goals of Confederation was to remove the most divisive issues from the national agenda by transferring them to provincial assemblies, where risks of intra-party strife were much lower. For a time, this strategy seemed to work: the party system was consolidated, and the dangers of legislative instability avoided. Unfortunately the Fathers of Confederation could not foresee that the addition of new provinces and territories, which required legislating over language and religious questions, would end up moving some of these local matters back to the fore. The first debates occurred over the New Brunswick and Prince Edward Island school controversies. This was followed by discussions surrounding the creation of Manitoba and the Northwest Territories and, later, the Riel affair. Other matters, such as temperance, divorce, or Catholic and Protestant practices, also periodically took centre stage in the federal Parliament, and thus slowly contributed to eroding the foundation of John A. Macdonald's Liberal-Conservative coalition. Such questions could not be easily avoided; not surprisingly, they created divisions within both parties, which were forced to take sides on these issues.

Religious and language debates ultimately led to the realignment of French-speaking and Catholic voters towards the Liberal Party at the end of the nineteenth century. But the transformation of the party system was not over yet. The westward expansion of Canada brought a new set of local concerns to the national agenda, since the issues that were most relevant to homesteaders – such as tariffs, freight rates, and export prices – were also the responsibility of the federal government (see Sanguinetti 1969, 21). Although farmers attempted to make their views heard, the two-party system was incapable of accommodating their interests as well.

There are not many ways in which the Liberal and Conservative coalitions could have realigned to reflect all the potential divisions in Canadian politics. Farmers and westerners, who favoured free trade but were weary of the corrupting effects of partyism, at first tried to fit within the existing party system.

As their number and importance grew, however, the pressure to create new parties mounted. There was originally some resistance to the idea of forming an independent farmers' party, but patronage reform and changes in the legislative organization of the House of Commons, which resulted from the modification of the rules, the adoption of closure, and a restriction of parliamentary rights, provided sufficient incentives to move in that direction.

It is interesting to see how similar circumstances produced opposite outcomes in the United States. In this counterfactual case, a presidential system with weaker incentives for party discipline, in combination with primary elections, has allowed for a much more diverse representation of interests in the legislature (Lipset 1954, 176). In essence, different party factions, such as conservative Democrats in the South, or progressive Republicans in the Midwest, could rely on the primary electoral system to win party nominations in otherwise noncompetitive congressional districts. Once in Washington, these members were free to vote as they pleased, unbounded by party discipline and the conventions of responsible government. If all else failed, parliamentary rules could always be changed so as to weaken the influence of party leaders and increase the power of backbenchers in the legislative process. Under these conditions, different factions could coexist in relative harmony within the Democratic and Republican parties. This compromise also allowed American voters to remain loyal to the two older parties, even when there was a mismatch between local and national party interests, since their representatives could still differ over certain policy questions, such as tariffs or civil rights (Lipset 1954, 176).

The Canadian Parliament was not as accommodating. Following the end of the First World War, the stage was set for the first major transformation of the party system. Having realized that their views could not be heard effectively in the legislative arena, several members who represented rural districts decided to form their own separate caucus in the House of Commons, which became the Progressive Party in the 1921 election. Several other new parties have come and gone since then, while at least one (the New Democratic Party) has remained more or less permanent. In the end, however, we can explain the emergence of this multiparty system by a simple argument – namely, that the combination of strict party discipline and heterogeneous preferences is not conducive to the representation of groups with distinctive sectional interests in Parliament. The potential lines of division are simply too numerous for a stable two-party system. This institutional arrangement – in combination with conflicts over trade policy, language, religion, and the centre versus the periphery – has created a permanent multiparty system with frequent minority governments. Nevertheless, the Canadian experience has also confirmed the adaptability and resilience of the British constitutional model. Only one government has ever fallen as a result of intra-party division (Macdonald's first ministry in the second Parliament), mostly because the high levels of party unity observed in the legislature have promoted legislative accountability and cabinet stability over time.[7] This would have been much more difficult without the presence of third parties in the legislature.

This book, it is hoped, represents an important step towards the development of a genuine comparative assessment for understanding the emergence of legislative party organization outside the British and US contexts – comparable in scope and detail to those that have invigorated the historical study of the US Congress and the UK Parliament (for example, Katznelson 2011; Spirling 2014). From a comparative perspective, my analysis has emphasized some of the challenges of exporting the Westminster model of government to a geographically and ethnically diverse population. The analysis also revealed the limits of the British North America Act, which was created in part to harmonize the relationships between religious and linguistic factions in Canada through a federal separation of powers and the creation of provincial assemblies with control over local matters. However, the westward expansion of Canada, which made the union complete, posed a challenge to the national legislature, since it could no longer keep some of the more controversial nation-building projects off the agenda. This set in motion a chain of events that resulted, first, in the reorganization of the party system into more ideologically cohesive groups; second, in the introduction of new restrictive parliamentary rules; and third, in the emergence of third parties in the legislative arena.

Central to this account is the role played by parliamentary rules in explaining party system change. Until now, no study has attempted to understand how the modification of parliamentary procedures could favour the development of third parties in the legislative arena. Epstein (1964), Lemco (1988), Lipset (1954), and Smith (1963) have all suggested that party discipline played a role in accounting for the presence of minor regional parties in Canada, but not in the United States. My study has moved beyond this simple comparison to explain the mechanisms behind this relationship.

It is most likely the case that third parties eventually would have emerged in the Canadian Parliament, even if the House of Commons had not adopted more restrictive legislative procedures. As I have argued throughout this book, the development of legislative party unity can be explained by numerous causal pathways. The same could be said about the rise of third parties. Perhaps looser party discipline could have postponed this transformation, but it is difficult to say for how long. One thing is certain: the US Congress offers a good example of a set of institutional arrangements in which dissenting factions can be absorbed easily by the existing two-party system. To get a better sense of how party unity, legislative procedures, and factions interact within Parliament, we must move away from a case-study design to compare Canada with other Westminster systems, where third parties could have emerged before or after the adoption of more restrictive parliamentary rules. With this analysis, it will become possible to determine under what circumstances greater party discipline can lead to party system change.

By introducing a new dataset of parliamentary votes in Canada, I hope this book opens a new era in the study of political institutions, in which historical empirical evidence – such as members' speeches or votes – is used to revisit some of the most important questions about the nature and development of the Canadian state. For far too long, researchers have been unable to do this because of data limitations. The time is thus right to move beyond the traditional approach to studying parties in Parliament and incorporate these new voting records into our research agenda.

Notes

1. Introduction

1 There are usually four periods, ranging from 1867 to 1917, 1921 to 1957, 1963 to 1988, and 1993 to today. Some authors, such as Walchuk (2012), argue that a fifth party system started in 2003, while Koop and Bittner (2013) argue that it started in 2011.

2 See, for example, Forsey (1963) on analysing ten government defeats in the first Parliament, or Williams (1956) on analysing a sample of twenty-eight divisions for the Conservative Party between 1921 and 1948.

3 Asian Canadians and First Nations people obtained full voting rights in federal elections only in 1948 and 1960, respectively.

4 For a discussion of the importance of timing and sequence in institutional analysis, see Pierson (2004).

2. The Emergence of Parties in Parliament

1 Following the Pacific Railway scandal, Macdonald's first ministry resigned in the second Parliament before a vote of confidence could be taken in the House.

2 Part of the text in the next four paragraphs is taken from the article "The Emergence of Parties in the Canadian House of Commons (1867–1908)" (Godbout and Høyland 2013, 778–9). Copyright Cambridge University Press. Reprinted with permission.

3 The courts later ruled that denominational schools in New Brunswick and Nova Scotia were not protected under the British North America Act (Fay 2002, 128).

4 Note that English and French opposition was considered to be an ethnic conflict during this period of Canadian history.

5 Author's translation; the original reads: "Nos partis ne sont que des troupeaux d'esclaves ignorants ou vénaux que les chefs mènent à leur guise. La discipline abrutissante des partis et, plus encore, les subsides électoraux font de la plupart des candidats et des députés les instruments dociles, les bêtes de somme des maîtres

qui les achètent, les mènent à l'abreuvoir, entretiennent leur litière et leur laissent entrevoir pour leurs vieux jours d'opulents pâturages."

6 During this election, pro-conscription Liberal and Conservative candidates ran under a common Unionist party banner, while the opposition (mainly French-Canadian MPs) rallied under former prime minister Wilfrid Laurier's Liberal Party, which was opposed to conscription.

7 No national Labour party existed at the time.

8 The Canadian Reform-Conservative Alliance in the 2000 election comes close, but did not elect any candidates east of Ontario.

9 The only exceptions were the Progressive Conservative governments of John Diefenbaker (1957–63) and Joe Clark (1979–80).

10 This is the index of Laakso and Taagepera (1979). The index is calculated by dividing 1 by the sum of the squared proportion of votes obtained by each candidate in each local riding election. Thus, the index weights the value of the votes in the district by the percentage of support received by each candidate.

11 Author's translation; the original reads: "Depuis trop longtemps la corruption électorale a permis aux hommes de proie de la finance de conduire sournoisement les vieux partis."

3. Theories of Party Development

1 Parts of the text in this chapter are taken from the articles "Unity in Diversity? The Development of Political Parties in the Parliament of Canada, 1867–2011" (Godbout and Høyland 2017) and "The Emergence of Parties in the Canadian House of Commons (1867–1908)" (Godbout and Høyland 2013). Copyrights Cambridge University Press. Reprinted with permission.

2 For Britain, see Eggers and Spirling (2016a); for eastern Europe, see Davidson-Schmich (2003) and Tavits (2011); and for the European Parliament, see Hix, Noury, and Roland (2006).

3 For a similar classification, see Godbout and Smaz (2016, 482–3).

4 Everyone over the age of twenty-one who was a British subject could vote. There were still restrictions for Indigenous peoples, certain religious groups, or citizens of Chinese or Japanese origins.

5 For instance, in 1891 the *Montreal Daily Witness* reported in great detail the outcome of two votes in the House of Commons on a proposed motion to support prohibition, including the names of each member on the division list. The reader was informed that a motion to adjourn this debate, introduced by the government whip, was soundly defeated. The article went on to explain that "Mister Savard of Chicoutimi, who is claimed as a Ministerialist, cast his first vote and put it against the Government side, while Mister Tarte, a former Conservative, did the same on both divisions" (*Montreal Daily Witness* 1891). Other examples are found in many nineteenth- and early twentieth-century newspapers, such as the Toronto

Globe, the Montreal *Gazette*, the *Ottawa Citizen*, the *Toronto Daily Mail*, the *Sarnia Observer*, and the *Irish Canadian*, which all had correspondents in Ottawa reporting on parliamentary activities. Finally, election pamphlets were also common, such as "Les principaux votes du dernier parlement: électeurs examinez la conduite de vos représentants et jugez-les," published in 1891, which discussed at length the results of several recorded divisions in Parliament.

6 Private members' business here implies time set aside for the "consideration of bills and motions presented and sponsored by members who are not Ministers or Parliamentary Secretaries" (O'Brien and Bosc 2009, 479).

7 Note that the data exclude bills that proposed name changes of constituencies. For the 1867–1909 period, the data were collected from Stewart (1977, 198–9). The rest were taken directly from the Library of Parliament Archives, online at http://www.lop.parl.gc.ca/parlinfo/compilations/HouseOfCommons/BillSummary.aspx, accessed 18 August 2016. The lines are local polynomial least squares regression (loess) fitted locally on the *x* axis to smooth the data.

8 For a similar approach, see McLean (2001, 47–50).

4. Legislative Records and Parliamentary Voting

1 The Journals are the official condensed reports of the House proceedings taken from the more extensive verbatim House of Commons (or Senate) Debates, which are sometimes referred to as the Hansards. Part of the text in this chapter is taken from the article "Unity in Diversity? The Development of Political Parties in the Parliament of Canada, 1867-2011" (Godbout and Høyland 2017). Copyright Cambridge University Press. Reprinted with permission.

2 This discussion of the voting procedure in the House of Commons is largely based on O'Brien and Bosc (2009, chap. 12).

3 Rule 84 in the 1868 version of the "Rules, orders and forms of proceeding of the House of Commons of Canada," adopted by the House in the first session of the first Parliament.

4 In several instances a member was listed as paired, but still voted yea or nay in a division. There is no way for us to determine if this was a clerical error in the recording of a vote or if a member really voted twice (see Dawson 1962 for a discussion on recorded divisions). A pairing error even brought down a government in 1926, when a member of the opposition was paired with a member of the government and voted by accident. There are other instances when members voted yea and nay in one division. I noted all of these in the coding scheme of the data. Overall, these coding anomalies represent less than 0.002 per cent of the total recorded individual votes in the House of Commons and 0.008 per cent of those in the Senate. Sometimes, following the absence of a member, his or her voting intention on a particular vote could be recorded in the Debates as well. A returning member would declare that he/she would have voted yea/nay

on a previously recorded division. These recordings are infrequent and are not reported in the data.

5 Note that, prior to 1991, these abstentions were not officially recorded in the Debates.

6 Elected Members of Parliament were assigned two specific identification numbers. The first is the HTML tag formerly used by the Parliament of Canada online database to identify uniquely each member who served in the House of Commons. Høyland and I supplemented this code by creating a separate numerical identification number to account for members who crossed the floor or became independent during a legislative session.

7 The thirty-first minority Parliament saw the lowest number of votes, with only eight recorded; the thirty-sixth Parliament saw the highest number of divisions, with 1,990 recorded votes.

8 Note that there were no recorded votes in the Senate during the twenty-fifth and thirty-first minority Parliaments.

9 Note that the distribution of the second dependent variable, party unity scores (not reported here), follows a similar pattern. In this case, the Rice index for both parties converges towards 100 during the first half of the twentieth century. In fact, more than 76 per cent (Liberals) and 68 per cent (Conservatives) of the total number of votes have a Rice index greater than 99 on the scale when we consider all of the recorded divisions between 1867 and 2011.

10 The data in the model end at the thirty-fifth Parliament because the Progressive Conservative Party only elected two MPs in 1993.

5. How Members Vote

1 This is the Neyman-Rubin model of causal inference (Rubin 1974, 690). See also Gelman and Hill (2006, chap. 9) for a discussion of causal inference in regression models.

2 In the online appendix to this chapter, I replicated the same analyses using fractional logit regression models, which account for variations in the standard unit interval of 0 to 1. These robustness tests show that the substantive results do not differ significantly from the standard linear model approach I use below. This appendix, the voting data, and all of the supplementary material used in the book can be found in the Dataverse repository entry: https://dataverse.harvard.edu/dataset.xhtml?persistentId=doi:10.7910/DVN/CVLGQW.

3 Parts of the text in this section is taken from the article "The Emergence of Parties in the Canadian House of Commons (1867–1908)" (Godbout and Høyland 2013). Copyright Cambridge University Press. Reprinted with permission.

4 Normally we would want to measure loyalty towards either one of the two major parties. However, since party lines were not clearly identified in the first three Parliaments, the dependent variable indicates the proportion of time an individual MP voted with the majority of the cabinet. This is an index of government support,

and is the same as the loyalty scores described in chapter 4. However, instead of measuring loyalty by looking at support for the party, I look at whether or not members voted with the majority position of all members of the cabinet.

5 Note that Macdonald's government was forced to resign because of the Canadian Pacific Railway scandal at the end of the second Parliament. Hence, in the third election, the incumbent government was the Liberal Party.

6 All of the variables in the model are coded as dummy (coded 1 or 0). The baseline category for region is Ontario. Government is coded 1 if the MP was affiliated with the governing party in a given term, 0 otherwise. Ministry is coded 1 if an MP was in the cabinet during a Parliament, 0 otherwise. Colonial is coded 1 if the MP was previously elected in a colonial assembly, 0 otherwise.

7 I also conducted the analysis separately in each term. The results remained virtually unchanged, but I find that government supporters elected in later polling days had on average lower levels of party loyalty only in the first Parliament.

8 Government supporters are captured by the interactive term (days × government) in the model, whereas independent and opposition members are captured by the number of days variable.

9 This result is obtained by calculating the unique effect of government affiliation in the model (the partial regression coefficient) on loyalty towards the cabinet, holding all other values constant in the analysis.

10 Note, however, that the franchise still excluded certain minorities, Indigenous peoples and communities, and women (until 1918).

11 I used the Canadian censuses of 1871, 1881, 1891, 1901, 1911, 1921, and 1931, and the Prairie provinces census of 1916 to compile data on the total number of voters in each electoral district between 1867 and 1935.

12 Note that I excluded colonial experience from this analysis. I also added a region dummy for the western provinces after the third Parliament. The data from the fifteenth Parliament are excluded because of the small number of votes and the almost perfect voting records of most party members.

13 Since I analyse each Parliament separately, I consider party affiliation by controlling for members who are on the government side (either Liberals or Conservatives), depending on the term. The complete results and the code for these analyses are reported in the online appendix to this chapter.

14 This index is calculated by dividing 1 by the sum of the squared proportion of votes obtained by each candidate in the district (Laakso and Taagepera 1979). Therefore, a value greater than 1 implies that competition increased in that district. In plurality elections, an index of 2 also indicates that the threshold needed to win a seat will be lower than 50 per cent; any value above this point will raise competitiveness in the district (because fewer than an absolute majority of votes will be required to win).

15 Each model also controls for whether an MP is a member of the governing party (Liberal or Conservative, depending on the term), region, or whether he/she has a cabinet position.

16 Author's translation; the original reads: "Quand le gouvernement change, le bureau de poste change."
17 Note that I excluded from this average the loyalty scores of members during their time in cabinet or after they were first appointed to this position – if, for example, they returned as backbenchers in the House. This was done to ensure that the measure truly captures the influence of party loyalty before a promotion was granted.
18 Note also that I deleted all first-term members from the analysis, as they had no voting records to speak of.
19 This variable includes all ministers, ministers without portfolio, and parliamentary secretaries.
20 The complete model used for this analysis is provided in the online appendix to this chapter.
21 Thus, a member who served four terms after being elected for the first time in 1900 is coded as having served one term in the ninth Parliament (1901–4), two in the tenth (1905–8), three in the eleventh (1909–11), and four in the twelfth (1911–17).
22 In terms of cohorts, the same member described above would be associated with the ninth cohort throughout his legislative career. In other words, in the twelfth Parliament, our member would be in the ninth cohort, and the fourth term of his career.
23 The full results are presented in the online appendix to this chapter.
24 Part of the text in this section is taken from the article "Unity in Diversity? The Development of Political Parties in the Parliament of Canada, 1867–2011" (Godbout and Høyland 2017). Copyright Cambridge University Press. Reprinted with permission.
25 The turnout variable reports the proportion of times a member voted in a given term. Since abstentions are not systematically recorded in Hansard, it is impossible to verify if a member abstained voluntarily or involuntarily.
26 In the previous analysis, I estimated the size of the voting population by reporting the total population of the riding from the decennial censuses. For this cumulative analysis, I use the total number of voters in the riding for a given election (because the franchise is not constant over time, and because I do not have the population size of the riding after 1935). Whenever an election was won by acclamation, I substituted the total number of voters by the average number of voters for all ridings in the election.
27 All variables in the models are dichotomous (coded 1 or 0), unless otherwise indicated.
28 For the regional variables, the baseline category is Ontario.
29 The baseline categories are the first cohort and the first Parliament.
30 In the earlier analysis, we could distinguish between Conservative and Liberal members with the government variable, since each regression analysis was done separately by term.

31 The online appendix to this chapter reports the results of the same analysis for government-sponsored motions only – described as whipped divisions earlier in the chapter. The results of these regressions show no substantive difference from the findings presented below.

6. How Parties Unite

1 I also replicate the final cumulative analysis in the online appendix of this chapter using a fractional logit regression model. These additional tests show that the substantive results do not differ significantly from the standard linear model approach, which has the advantage of being much more straightforward to estimate and interpret.
2 In earlier terms, members had to have a valid reason to be absent, unless a leave of absence was granted by the House. According to Dawson (1962, 89), any unauthorized absence was usually severely reprimanded.
3 I thus removed the following three Parliaments from the analysis: the thirty-first (1979), the twenty-fifth (1962–3), and the twenty-third (1957–8).
4 The coding for this variable is as follows: a Conservative-(Liberal-)sponsored motion for the Conservative (Liberal) Party equals 1, 0 otherwise.
5 Note that because only two Progressive Conservatives were elected to the thirty-fifth Parliament, I dropped this term from the analysis.
6 Part of the text in this section is taken from the article "The Emergence of Parties in the Canadian House of Commons (1867–1908)" (Godbout and Høyland 2013). Copyright Cambridge University Press. Reprinted with permission.
7 Since debates in reply to the Speech from the Throne were often voiced through several different addresses before 1903, it is possible that this voting category contains several of these motions as well.
8 For a discussion, see O'Brien and Bosc (2009, 1123) and Loewen et al. (2014, 191).
9 The analysis uses a different coding scheme here to simplify matters. Any vote taken over a bill falls into either the government or private members' bill category, depending on the sponsor. The same logic applies for all types of motions.
10 This is obtained from the combination of the parliament (positive) and parliament squared (negative) coefficients. Note that this last analysis is also reproduced in the online appendix to this chapter, where the dependent variable is replaced by a weighted Rice index, which considers abstentions as a potential vote choice. The results are substantively identical to those presented here.

7. Louis Riel and the Catholic Sort

1 These numbers are from the Canadian census, available online at: http://www.statcan.gc.ca/pub/11-516-x/sectiona/4147436-eng.htm#4.
2 As stipulated by Article 93.3 of the British North America Act and Article 22 of the Manitoba Act.

3 The Judicial Committee of the Privy Council in London ultimately ruled that the federal government could issue a Remedial Order on the Manitoba Schools Question, thus overruling a previous decision of the Supreme Court of Canada.
4 The party was successively led by an English Catholic, John Thompson, followed by an English Protestant, Mackenzie Bowell, who was grand master of the British North America Orange Order.
5 Blais (2005) and Johnston (2017) both use Canadian Election Study data to analyse the individual determinants of vote choice. Johnston also uses Gallup survey data going back to the 1950s. In each analysis, the relationship between Catholic voters and the Liberal Party is confirmed outside Quebec (Blais and Johnston) and across Canada (Johnston). Both authors, however, find that the strength of this relationship has declined over time.
6 In 1925, almost all Methodists, Congregationalists, and some members of the Presbyterian Church formed an association to constitute the United Church of Canada.
7 Using similar riding-level data between 1878 and 1921, Johnston confirms that religion played an indeterminate role in explaining this relationship prior to 1900 outside Quebec (Johnston 2017, 110–11). My analysis confirms this result; however, the remainder of this chapter also confirms the importance of religion in initiating this change prior to 1900.
8 I used the Canadian censuses of 1871, 1881, 1891, 1901, 1911, 1921, and 1931, and the Prairie provinces census of 1916 to compile the percentage of Catholics and Methodists from 1867 to 1930 in each electoral district. Census districts were matched to electoral districts using the documentation provided with each census and the Federal Electoral District Maps for the 1921 census. Data for the 1949–65 elections were taken from Blake (2011). To obtain the proportion of Catholics in each riding, Blake uses data from the 1951 and 1961 censuses.
9 In Quebec, support for this party was strongest in rural ridings, where the proportion of Catholics was high.
10 The models include dummy variables for each term (the baseline is the first Parliament). The full results are available in the appendix to this chapter.
11 The Canadian Election Study surveys in 1965, 1974, and 1979 asked respondents to name the party identification of their parents. The statistics reported are from two-way tables comparing the party identification of Catholics and Protestants.
12 These surprising results are partially explained by the fact that seventeen seats were won by acclamation in the 1882 election in Quebec (fifteen by Conservatives), while only six were won by acclamation in 1887 (three by Conservatives). Still, if we add the Liberal and the Nationalist votes together, the Conservatives' vote share dropped to 49 per cent – that is, 65,602 Conservative votes / (65,602 Conservative votes + 61,075 Liberal votes + 8,306 National votes).
13 When the information was not available in the Parliamentary Companions, every possible effort was made to match MPs with their publicly released historical census records where the religious affiliation is reported. Because the census is

organized by household, the names of spouses, parents, siblings, and children were sometimes used to cross-reference religious affiliation. In some cases, biographical information, obituaries, or school records were also used to verify the religion of MPs. Overall, I was able to confirm the religion of 98 per cent of all Members of Parliament in my dataset between 1867 and 1925.

14 French-Canadian MPs were identified by their first and last names. Additional steps were taken to determine the origin of certain MPs (such as schooling or spouse's name) whose names were not obviously classifiable.

15 The data (points) for the distribution of Catholics and Protestants in each party caucus are not reported in the graphic, only the loess curves calculated from these data.

16 The next three paragraphs are taken in part from the article "The Emergence of Parties in the Canadian House of Commons (1867–1908)" (Godbout and Høyland 2013, 786–90). Copyright Cambridge University Press. Reprinted with permission. And from Godbout (2014, 174–7).

17 This is because the cabinet has to maintain the confidence of a majority of the legislature in a parliamentary system, and opposition parties are more likely to vote against the government regardless of whether or not they support the cabinet. Hence, legislators who always support (oppose) the governing party will be located at one of the extremes, while those who sometimes vote with the government will be located near the middle. The gap between the two groups should widen as party unity increases.

18 For a more detailed account of OC, see Poole (2005). The data were pre-processed to exclude lopsided votes (those in which all but five MPs voted similarly on a motion). Legislators who participated in fewer than twenty-five votes were also dropped from the analysis, since their estimates were associated with a large degree of uncertainty. To ensure identification, the locations of two legislators were fixed. The leader of the government or the party whip (for example, Macdonald or Mackenzie) was fixed as polarity on the first dimension, and the leader of the French-Canadian opposition (for example, Dorion or Laurier) was fixed as polarity on the second dimension. This analysis relies on OC because the algorithm is nonparametric and no explicit utility function is specified (beyond the assumption of single-peaked preferences). Indeed, whipping and party-line votes violate some of the more fundamental assumptions of the spatial theory of legislative voting, as shown by Spirling and McLean (2007).

19 I use Poole's OC package in R (Poole et al. 2018).

20 In spatial terms, the algorithm could move Protestants downwards in the third and fourth quadrants of two-dimensional space, but also move Catholics upwards in the second and first quadrants. On the other hand, party-line votes would divide party members into the second and third quadrants (Conservatives) against the first and fourth quadrants (Liberals), while religious divisions would oppose the first and second quadrants (Catholics) against the third and fourth (Protestants).

21 The text for the remainder of this section is taken in part from the article "The Emergence of Parties in the Canadian House of Commons (1867–1908)" (Godbout and Høyland 2013, 788–92). Copyright Cambridge University Press. Reprinted with permission.

22 I also report the aggregated proportion reduction in error, which indicates how much the OC algorithm compares to a benchmark model (in this case, the smallest number of yeas or nays for each vote). This measure is 1 if there is no classification error in the model, 0 if the number of the spatial model error equals the value of the smallest number of yeas or nays. For a discussion, see Poole and Rosenthal (2007, 36).

23 See Godbout and Høyland (2011, 372–3) for a more detailed explanation.

24 The higher the value of the APRE, the better the classification fit of the spatial model; hence a large difference between the first- and second-dimension fit implies that the introduction of an additional dimension significantly improves the voting predictions of MPs.

8. Western Discontent and Populism

1 The rule change for private members' bills made it unnecessary to go into the committee of the whole to consider each individual piece of legislation; all private bills could now be referred to this committee for debate in one single motion (Dawson 1962, 249).

2 This is rule 17A, which I discuss further below.

3 Prior to 1920, the government also frequently had to introduce hoist amendments to postpone for several months the reading of private members' bills introduced by members of the same party (O'Brien and Bosc 2009, 746–7).

4 I used 1968 as the cutoff because this is when the committees of supply and ways and means were abolished and replaced by opposition days. After this point, it was no longer possible for a backbencher to amend the motion for the speaker to leave the chair before entering into these two committees.

5 For the Liberal (Conservative) analysis, the original motion had to be from a Liberal (Conservative) party member (coded 1, 0 otherwise). The full results of this analysis are available in the online appendix to this chapter.

6 I counted Mackenzie King and Fielding in the thirteenth Parliament as leaders of the opposition, since both were candidates for the leadership of the Liberal Party.

7 A total of sixty-five supply amendments were introduced by backbenchers during this period, fourteen of which were sponsored by MPs from the Prairies.

8 Part of the text in this section is taken from the article "Unity in Diversity? The Development of Political Parties in the Parliament of Canada, 1867–2011" (Godbout and Høyland 2017). Copyright Cambridge University Press. Reprinted with permission.

9 French-Canadian MPs represent 26 per cent of all members. Most have been elected from Quebec, but 15 per cent have been elected from outside that province. Still, all French-Canadian nationalists are from Quebec.

10 The full results are available in the online appendix to this chapter.
11 Note that the lines in the figure were obtained by local regressions.

9. Partisanship in the Senate

1 It has been announced that the new appointment process will be implemented in two phases. In the transitional phase, five appointments were made in March 2016 with the goal of immediately reducing "partisanship in the Senate and improve the representation of the provinces with the most vacancies (i.e., Manitoba, Ontario and Quebec)" (Canada 2015). Note that, in January 2014, Justin Trudeau expelled all the Liberal senators from the Liberal National Parliamentary Caucus and recommended that they sit as independent senators.
2 The senator-in-waiting from Alberta offers an example of an appointment reform that has not been followed by all subsequent prime ministers. So far, only Stephen Harper and Brian Mulroney have appointed elected nominees.
3 Senator Peter Harder was appointed government representative to the Senate by Justin Trudeau in 2016. Since then, the government representatives in the forty-second Parliament have grown with the addition of two new senators, Diane Bellemare and Grant Mitchell.
4 This is the same measure I used in chapters 4 and 6. The Rice index is obtained by taking the absolute value of the difference between the proportion of yeas and nays for a given party during a vote. I then take the average of these scores for both parties across each term. Note that this index ranges from 0 (perfect split) to 1 (perfect unity).
5 Note that I counted only members who voted in at least five divisions before June 2017. The Trudeau senators are those appointed by his government. I counted as independent other members who joined the Non-Affiliated Independent Group or Non-Affiliated Reform Group, which later became known as the Independent Senator Group.
6 Note that both Harder and Bellemare have the same voting records in these divisions.
7 I borrowed the term "crypto-Liberal" from the discussion of Prairie populism in Laycock (1990, chap. 2).

10. Conclusion

1 Part of the text in this section is taken from the article "Unity in Diversity? The Development of Political Parties in the Parliament of Canada, 1867–2011" (Godbout and Høyland 2017). Copyright Cambridge University Press. Reprinted with permission.
2 The decision by the farmers' movement to support the Progressive Party and Crerar as leader was made by the Canadian Council of Agriculture in 1920 (Morton 1950, 95).

3 The *Grain Growers' Guide* was a newspaper published by the Grain Growers' Grain Company (later the United Grain Growers), an influential cooperative representing western farmers.

4 I looked at elections in Manitoba, Saskatchewan, and Alberta during this period. Either the Liberals, the United Farmers, or the Social Credit in Alberta (1935 only) controlled the provincial governments. Note also that there is one exception: the 1930 election in Manitoba, which returned a majority of Liberals (the 1925 election in this province also returned seven out of fifteen seats for the Progressive Party).

5 The Liberal incumbent was Albert Champagne, a business owner and mayor of Battleford.

6 These numbers were taken from all the recorded divisions of the first session of the forty-second Parliament between 8 December 2015 and 31 January 2018.

7 Following the scandal, Macdonald's first ministry resigned in the second Parliament before a vote of confidence could be taken.

Bibliography

Acharya, Avidit, Matthew Blackwell, and Maya Sen. 2016. "The Political Legacy of American Slavery." *Journal of Politics* 78 (3): 621–41. https://doi.org/10.1086/686631.

Aldrich, John H. 1995. *Why Parties? The Origin and Transformation of Political Parties in America*. Chicago: University of Chicago Press.

Aldrich, John H. 2011. *Why Parties? A Second Look*. Chicago: University of Chicago Press.

Aldrich, John H., and David W. Rohde. 2005. "Congressional Committees in a Partisan Era." In *Congress Reconsidered*, edited by Lawrence C. Dodd and Bruce I. Oppenheimer, 249–70. Washington, DC: CQ Press.

Amyot, Chantal, and John Willis. 2003. *Le courrier est arrivé: la poste rurale au Canada de 1880 à 1945*. Gatineau, QC: Musée canadien des civilisations.

Atkinson, Michael M., and Paul G. Thomas. 1993. "Studying the Canadian Parliament." *Legislative Studies Quarterly* 18 (3): 423–51. https://doi.org/10.2307/439834.

Aydelotte, William O. 1977. "Constituency Influence on the British House of Commons, 1841–1847." In *The History of Parliamentary Behavior*, edited by William O. Aydelotte, 225–46. Princeton, NJ: Princeton University Press.

Azoulay, Dan Andre. 1999. *Canadian Political Parties: Historical Readings*. Toronto: Irwin Publications.

Bakvis, Herman, and Laura G. Macpherson. 1995. "Quebec Block Voting and the Canadian Electoral System." *Canadian Journal of Political Science* 28 (4): 659–92. https://doi.org/10.1017/S000842390001934X.

Balthazar, Louis. 2013. *Nouveau bilan du nationalisme au Québec*. Montreal: VLB.

Beauchesne, Arthur. 1922. *Rules and Forms of the House of Commons of Canada*. Toronto: Canada Law Book. Available online at https://catalog.hathitrust.org/Record/008877843, accessed 2 January 2019.

Beck, J. Murray. 1968. *Pendulum of Power: Canada's Federal Elections*. Scarborough, ON: Prentice-Hall of Canada.

Beelen, Kaspar, et al. 2017. "Digitization of the Canadian Parliamentary Debates." *Canadian Journal of Political Science* 50 (3): 849–64. https://doi.org/10.1017/S0008423916001165.

Behiels, Michael D. 1982. "The Bloc Populaire Canadien and the Origins of French-Canadian Neo-Nationalism, 1942–8." *Canadian Historical Review* 63 (4): 487–512. https://doi.org/10.3138/CHR-063-04-03.

Bélanger, Réal. 1983. *L'impossible défi: Albert Sévigny et les conservateurs fédéraux (1902–1918)*. Quebec City: Presses de l'Université Laval.

Bernard, André. 1978. *What Does Quebec Want?* Toronto: James Lorimer.

Berrington, Hugh. 1968. "Partisanship and Dissidence in the Nineteenth-Century House of Commons." *Parliamentary Affairs* 21 (June): 338–74. https://doi.org/10.1093/parlij/21.1968jun.338.

Black, Edwin R. 1975. *Divided Loyalties: Canadian Concepts of Federalism*. Montreal; Kingston, ON: McGill-Queen's University Press.

Blais, André. 2005. "Accounting for the Electoral Success of the Liberal Party in Canada: Presidential Address to the Canadian Political Science Association, London, Ontario June 3, 2005." *Canadian Journal of Political Science* 38 (4): 821–40. https://doi.org/10.1017/S0008423905050304.

Blake, Donald E. 1979. "1896 and All That: Critical Elections in Canada." *Canadian Journal of Political Science* 12 (2): 259–79. https://doi.org/10.1017/S0008423900048113.

Blake, Donald E. 2011. "Canadian Census and Election Data, 1908–1968." Ann Arbor, MI: Inter-university Consortium for Political and Social Research, 11 August. Available online at https://doi.org/10.3886/ICPSR00039.v2ICPSR00039-V2.

Blidook, Kelly. 2012. *Constituency Influence in Parliament: Countering the Centre*. Vancouver: UBC Press.

Bloc Populaire. 1943. "Programme fédéral du Bloc." Available online at https://www.bibliotheque.assnat.qc.ca/DepotNumerique_v2/AffichageNotice.aspx?idn=64627.

Blondel, Jean. 1968. "Party Systems and Patterns of Government in Western Democracies." *Canadian Journal of Political Science* 1 (2): 180–203. https://doi.org/10.1017/S0008423900036507.

Boily, Robert. 1982. "Les partis politiques québécois: perspectives historiques." In *Les partis politiques et les élections*, edited by Vincent Lemieux, 27–68. Montreal: Boréal.

Boix, Charles. 2009. "The Emergence of Parties and Party Systems." In *The Oxford Handbook of Comparative Politics*, edited by Charles Boix and Susan C. Stokes, 499–521. Oxford: Oxford University Press.

Borden, Robert Laird. 1938. *His Memoirs*. London: Macmillan.

Bourinot, John G. 1884. *Parliamentary Procedure and Practice, with an Introductory Account of the Origin and Growth of Parliamentary Institutions in the Dominion of Canada*. Montreal: Dawson Brothers.

Bourinot, John G. 1916. *Parliamentary Procedure and Practice, 4th ed.* Toronto: Canada Law Book.

Brady, David W., Joseph Cooper, and Patricia A. Hurley. 1979. "The Decline of Party in the U.S. House of Representatives, 1887–1968." *Legislative Studies Quarterly* 4 (3): 381–407. https://doi.org/10.2307/439581.

Breton, Raymond. 2005. *Ethnic Relations in Canada: Institutional Dynamics*. Montreal; Kingston, ON: McGill-Queen's University Press.

Brodie, M. Janine, and Jane Jenson. 1988. *Crisis, Challenge and Change: Party and Class in Canada Revisited*. Ottawa: Carleton University Press.

Brown, Robert C. 1975. *Robert Laird Borden: 1914–1937*. Toronto: Macmillan of Canada.

Brown, Robert Craig, and Ramsay Cook. 1974. *Canada, 1896–1921: A Nation Transformed*. Toronto: McClelland & Stewart.

Burke, Edmund. [1770] 1892. *Thoughts on the Present Discontents, and Speeches*. London: Cassel & Company.

Cairns, Alan C. 1968. "The Electoral System and the Party System in Canada, 1921–1965." *Canadian Journal of Political Science* 1 (1): 55–80. https://doi.org/10.1017/S0008423900035228.

Campbell, Colin. 1978. *The Canadian Senate: A Lobby from Within*. Toronto: Macmillan of Canada.

Campion, Gilbert. 1955. "Parliamentary Procedure, Old and New." In *Parliament: A Survey*, edited by Lord Campion et al., 141–67. London: George Allen & Unwin.

Canada. 1985. House of Commons Special Committee on the Reform of the House of Commons. *Report of the Special Committee on Reform of the House of Commons* [McGrath Report]. Ottawa: Canadian Government Publishing Centre, Supply and Services Canada.

Canada. 2015. "Government announces immediate Senate reform." 3 December. Available online at https://www.canada.ca/en/democratic-institutions/news/2015/12/government-announces-immediate-senate-reform.html, accessed 29 December 2018.

Canada. 2019. Independent Advisory Board for Senate Appointments. "Mandate and Members." Available online at https://www.canada.ca/en/campaign/independent-advisory-board-for-senate-appointments/members.html.

Carey, John M. 2007. "Competing Principals, Political Institutions, and Party Unity in Legislative Voting." *American Journal of Political Science* 51 (1): 92–107. https://doi.org/10.1111/j.1540-5907.2007.00239.x.

Carey, John M. 2008. *Legislative Voting and Accountability*. Cambridge: Cambridge University Press.

Carson, Jamie L., and Joel Sievert. 2015. "Electoral Reform and Changes in Legislative Behavior: Adoption of the Secret Ballot in Congressional Elections." *Legislative Studies Quarterly* 40 (1): 83–110. https://doi.org/10.1111/lsq.12066.

Carty, R. Kenneth. 1988. "Three Canadian Party Systems: An Interpretation of the Development of National Politics." In *Party Democracy in Canada*, edited by George Perlin, 15–30. Scarborough, ON: Prentice-Hall.

Carty, R. Kenneth, and William Cross. 2010. "Political Parties and the Practice of Brokerage Politics." In *The Oxford Handbook of Canadian Politics*, edited by John C. Courtney and David E. Smith, 191–297. Oxford: Oxford University Press.

Carty, R. Kenneth, Lisa Young, and William P. Cross. 2000. *Rebuilding Canadian Party Politics*. Vancouver: UBC Press.

CBC News. 2005. "Churchill MP quits NDP after nomination loss." 18 October. Available online at http://www.cbc.ca/news/canada/manitoba/churchill-mp-quits-ndp-after-nomination-loss-1.527707.

CCF (Co-operative Commonwealth Federation). 1933. *The Regina Manifesto*. Available online at https://www.socialisthistory.ca/Docs/CCF/ReginaManifesto.htm, accessed 31 October 2019.

Chhibber, Pradeep K., and Ken Kollman. 2004. *The Formation of National Party Systems*. Princeton, NJ: Princeton University Press.

Clark, Warren. 2003. "Pockets of Belief: Religious Attendance Patterns in Canada." *Canadian Social Trends* 68: 1–5. Available online at https://www150.statcan.gc.ca/n1/pub/11-008-x/2002004/article/6493-eng.pdf.

Clokie, Hugh McDowall. 1944. *Canadian Government and Politics*. Toronto: Longmans, Green.

Cochrane, Christopher. 2015. *Left and Right: The Small World of Political Ideas*. Montreal; Kingston, ON: McGill-Queen's University Press.

Corry, J.A. 1946. *Democratic Government and Politics*. Toronto: University of Toronto Press.

Corry, J.A. 1954. "Adaptation of Parliamentary Processes to the Modern State." *Canadian Journal of Economics and Political Science* 20 (1): 1–9. https://doi.org/10.2307/138408.

Cox, Gary W. 1987. *The Efficient Secret: The Cabinet and the Development of Political Parties in Victorian England*. Cambridge: Cambridge University Press.

Cox, Gary W. 1997. *Making Votes Count: Strategic Coordination in the World's Electoral Systems*. Cambridge: Cambridge University Press.

Cox, Gary W., and Mathew D. McCubbins. 2004. "Theories of Legislative Organization." *APSA-CP Newsletter* 15 (1): 9–12.

Cox, Gary W., and Mathew D. McCubbins. 2005. *Setting the Agenda: Responsible Party Government in the US House of Representatives*. Cambridge: Cambridge University Press.

Cruikshank, Ken. 1986. "The People's Railway: The Intercolonial Railway and the Canadian Public Enterprise Experience." *Acadiensis* 16 (1): 78–100.

Davidson-Schmich, Louise K. 2003. "The Development of Party Discipline in New Parliaments: Eastern German State Legislatures 1990–2000." *Journal of Legislative Studies* 9 (4): 88–101. https://doi.org/10.1080/1357233042000306272.

Dawson, Robert M. 1936. "The Canadian Civil Service." *Canadian Journal of Economics and Political Science* 2 (3): 288–300. https://doi.org/10.2307/136662.

Dawson, Robert MacGregor. [1947] 1960. *The Government of Canada*. Toronto: University of Toronto Press.

Dawson, William F. 1962. *Procedure in the Canadian House of Commons*. Toronto: University of Toronto Press.

"Debates of the House of Commons." Various years. Available online at http://parl.canadiana.ca/?usrlang=en.

"Debates of the Legislative Assembly, 1865." Available online at http://eco.canadiana.ca/view/oocihm.9_00952_25/5?r=0&s=1.

Depauw, Sam, and Shane Martin. 2009. "Legislative Party Discipline and Cohesion in Comparative Perspective." In *Intra-Party Politics and Coalition Governments*, edited by Daniela Gannett and Kenneth Benoit, 103–20. London: Routledge.

Desposato, Scott W. 2005. "Correcting for Small Group Inflation of Roll-Call Cohesion Scores." *British Journal of Political Science* 35 (4): 731–44. https://doi.org/10.1017/S0007123405000372.

Le Devoir (Montreal). 1911. "M. Monk à Nicolet." 16 June.

Dewan, Torun, and Arthur Spirling. 2011. "Strategic Opposition and Government Cohesion in Westminster Democracies." *American Political Science Review* 105 (2): 337–58. https://doi.org/10.1017/S0003055411000050.

Dion, Douglas. 1997. *Turning the Legislative Thumbscrew: Minority Rights and Procedural Change in Legislative Politics*. Ann Arbor, MI: University of Michigan Press.

Docherty, David C. 1997. *Mr. Smith Goes to Ottawa: Life in the House of Commons*. Vancouver: UBC Press.

Docherty, David C. 2002. "The Canadian Senate: Chamber of Sober Reflection or Loony Cousin Best Not Talked About." *Journal of Legislative Studies* 8 (3): 27–48. https://doi.org/10.1080/714003922.

Docherty, David C. 2005. *Legislatures*. Vancouver: UBC Press.

Dumont, Fernand, Jean-Paul Montminy, and Jean Hamelin. 1978. *Idéologies au Canada français*. Quebec City: Presses de l'Université Laval.

Durham, Earl of. 1839. Report on the Affairs of British North America. Montreal: Printed at the Morning Courier Office. Available online at https://catalog.hathitrust.org/Record/100136431.

Duverger, Maurice. [1951] 1958. *Les partis politiques*. Paris: Armand Colin.

Duverger, Maurice. 1954. *Political Parties: Their Organization and Activity in the Modern State*. London: Methuen.

Easterbrook, William T., and Hugh C. J. Aitken. 1988. *Canadian Economic History*. Toronto: University of Toronto Press.

Eggers, Andrew C., and Arthur Spirling. 2016. "Party Cohesion in Westminster Systems: Inducements, Replacement and Discipline in the House of Commons, 1836–1910." *British Journal of Political Science* 46 (3): 567–89.

Eggers, Andrew C., and Arthur Spirling. 2018. "The Shadow Cabinet in Westminster Systems: Modeling Opposition Agenda Setting in the House of Commons, 1832–1915." *British Journal of Political Science* 48 (2): 343–67. https://doi.org/10.1017/S0007123414000362.

Eggleston, Stephen D. 1988. "Party Cohesion in the Early Post-Confederation Period." Master's thesis, University of British Columbia. Available online at https://open.library.ubc.ca/cIRcle/collections/ubctheses/831/items/1.0097707.

Elgie, Robert, and Steven Griggs. 2008. *French Politics: Debates and Controversies*. London: Routledge.

English, John. 1977. *The Decline of Politics: The Conservatives and the Party System, 1901–20*. Toronto: University of Toronto Press.

Engstrom, Erik J. 2012. "The Rise and Decline of Turnout in Congressional Elections: Electoral Institutions, Competition, and Strategic Mobilization." *American Journal of Political Science* 56 (2): 373–86. https://doi.org/10.1111/j.1540-5907.2011.00556.x.

Epstein, Leon D. 1964. "A Comparative Study of Canadian Parties." *American Political Science Review* 58 (1): 46–59. https://doi.org/10.2307/1952754.

Epstein, Leon D. 1967. *Political Parties in Western Democracies*. New York: Praeger.

Fay, Terence J. 2002. *A History of Canadian Catholics: Gallicanism, Romanism, and Canadianism*. Montreal; Kingston, ON: McGill-Queen's University Press.

Finocchiaro, Charles J., and David W. Rohde. 2008. "War for the Floor: Partisan Theory and Agenda Control in the U.S. House of Representatives." *Legislative Studies Quarterly* 33 (1): 35–61. https://doi.org/10.3162/036298008783743273.

Flanagan, Tom. 2001. "From Riel to Reform (and a Little Beyond): Politics in Western Canada." *American Review of Canadian Studies* 31 (4): 623–38. https://doi.org/10.1080/02722010109481075.

Forsey, Eugene. 1963. "Government Defeats in the Canadian House of Commons, 1867–73." *Canadian Journal of Economics and Political Science* 29 (3): 364–7. https://doi.org/10.2307/139221.

Forsey, Eugene. 1964. "The Problem of 'Minority' Government in Canada." *Canadian Journal of Economics and Political Science* 30 (1): 1–11. https://doi.org/10.2307/139166.

Francis, Lloyd. 1984. "Speaker's Ruling: The Ringing of Division Bells." *Canadian Parliamentary Review* 7 (2): 26–7.

Franks, C.E.S. 1987. *The Parliament of Canada*. Toronto: University of Toronto Press.

Franks, C.E.S. 1999. "Not Dead Yet, but Should It Be Restructured? The Canadian Senate." In *Senates: Bicameralism in the Contemporary World*, edited by Samuel C. Patterson and Anthony Mughan, 120–61. Columbus: Ohio State University Press.

Friesen, Gerald. 1984. *The Canadian Prairies: A History*. Toronto: University of Toronto Press.

Gaines, Brian J. 1999. "Duverger's Law and the Meaning of Canadian Exceptionalism." *Comparative Political Studies* 32 (7): 835–61. https://doi.org/10.1177/0010414099032007004.

Garner, John. 1969. *The Franchise and Politics in British North America 1755–1867*. Toronto: University of Toronto Press.

Gazette (Montreal). 1982. "Is Parliament relevant anymore?" 29 May.

Gehlbach, Scott. 2006. "A Formal Model of Exit and Voice." *Rationality and Society* 18 (4): 395–418. https://doi.org/10.1177/1043463106070280.

Gelman, Andrew, and Jennifer Hill. 2006. *Data Analysis Using Regression and Multilevel/Hierarchical Models*. Cambridge: Cambridge University Press.

George, Alexander L., and Andrew Bennett. 2005. *Case Studies and Theory Development in the Social Sciences*. Boston: MIT Press.

Gerring, John. 1998. *Party Ideologies in America, 1828–1996*. Cambridge: Cambridge University Press.

Gidengil, Elisabeth. 2012. "An Overview of the Social Dimension of Vote Choice." In *The Canadian Election Studies: Assessing Four Decades of Influence*, edited by Mebs Kanji, Antoine Bilodeau, and Thomas J. Scotto, 101–20. Vancouver: UBC Press.

Godbout, Jean-François. 2014. "Parliamentary Politics and Legislative Behaviour." In *Comparing Canada: Methods and Perspectives on Canadian Politics*, edited by Luc Turgeon, Martin Papillon, Jennifer Wallner, and Stephen White, 171–97. Vancouver: UBC Press.

Godbout, Jean-François, and Bjørn Høyland. 2011. "Legislative Voting in the Canadian Parliament." *Canadian Journal of Political Science* 44 (2): 367–88. https://doi.org/10.1017/S0008423911000175.

Godbout, Jean-François, and Bjørn Høyland. 2013. "The Emergence of Parties in the Canadian House of Commons (1867–1908)." *Canadian Journal of Political Science* 46 (4): 773–97. https://doi.org/10.1017/S0008423913000632.

Godbout, Jean-François, and Bjørn Høyland. 2017. "Unity in Diversity? The Development of Political Parties in the Parliament of Canada, 1867–2011." *British Journal of Political Science* 47 (3): 545–69. https://doi.org/10.1017/S0007123415000368.

Godbout, Jean-François, and Martial Foucault. 2013. "French Legislative Voting in the Fifth Republic." *French Politics* 11 (4): 307–31. https://doi.org/10.1057/fp.2013.17.

Godbout, Jean-François, and Monika Smaz. 2016. "Party Development in the Early Decades of the Australian Parliament: A New Perspective." *Australian Journal of Political Science* 51 (3): 478–95. https://doi.org/10.1080/10361146.2016.1182618.

Gordon, Alan. 1999. "Patronage, Etiquette, and the Science of Connection: Edmund Bristol and Political Management, 1911–21." *Canadian Historical Review* 80 (1): 1–31. https://doi.org/10.3138/CHR.80.1.1.

Guay, Monique. 2002. "Parliamentarian's Dilemma: Party Discipline, Representation of Voters and Personal Beliefs." *Canadian Parliamentary Review* 25 (1): 7.

Hamelin, Marcel. 1974. *Les premières années du parlementarisme québécois (1867–1878)*. Cahiers d'histoire de l'Université Laval 19. Quebec City: Presses de l'Université Laval.

Hayward, Jack. 2004. "Parliament and the French Government's Domination of the Legislative Process." *Journal of Legislative Studies* 10 (2–3): 79–97. https://doi.org/10.1080/1357233042000322238.

Heard, Andrew D. 1991. *Canadian Constitutional Conventions: The Marriage of Law and Politics*. Toronto: Oxford University Press.

Heath, Gordon L. 2012. "The Protestant Denominational Press and the Conscription Crisis in Canada, 1917–1918." *Historical Studies* 78 (2): 27–46.

Hersh, Eitan D., and Clayton Nall. 2016. "The Primacy of Race in the Geography of Income-Based Voting: New Evidence from Public Voting Records." *American Journal of Political Science* 60 (2): 289–303. https://doi.org/10.1111/ajps.12179.

Hicks, Bruce M., and André Blais. 2008. "Restructuring the Canadian Senate through Elections." *IRPP Choices* 14 (15): 1–22.

Hill Times. 2018. "Lobbyists get 'too much time' in Senate committees, says ISG deputy ahead of back-to-Parliament meeting." 24 January. Available online at https://www.hilltimes.com/2018/01/22/lobbyists-get-much-time-senate-says-isg-deputy-ahead-back-parliament-summit/131427.

Hirschman, Albert O. 1970. *Exit, Voice, and Loyalty: Responses to Decline in Firms, Organizations, and States*. Cambridge: Harvard University Press.

Hix, Simon, Abdul Noury, and Gérard Roland. 2005. "Power to the Parties: Cohesion and Competition in the European Parliament, 1979–2001." *British Journal of Political Science* 35 (2): 209–34. https://doi.org/10.1017/S0007123405000128.

Hix, Simon, Abdul Noury, and Gérard Roland. 2006. "Dimensions of Politics in the European Parliament." *American Journal of Political Science* 50 (2): 494–520. https://doi.org/10.1111/j.1540-5907.2006.00198.x.

Hougham, G. M. 1963. "The Background and Development of National Parties." In *Party Politics in Canada*, edited by Hugh G. Thorburn, 1–13. Scarborough, ON: Prentice-Hall.

Howe, Paul, and David Northup. 2000. "Strengthening Canadian Democracy: The Views of Canadians." *Policy Matters* (Institute for Research on Public Policy) 1 (5): 1–104. Available online at http://irpp.org/research-studies/strengthening-canadian-democracy-the-views-of-canadians/.

Huber, John D. 1992. "Restrictive Legislative Procedures in France and the United States." *American Political Science Review* 86 (3): 675–87. https://doi.org/10.2307/1964130.

Huber, John D. 1996. *Rationalizing Parliament: Legislative Institutions and Party Politics in France*. Cambridge: Cambridge University Press.

Hug, Simon. 2010. "Selection Effects in Roll Call Votes." *British Journal of Political Science* 40 (1): 225–35. https://doi.org/10.1017/S0007123409990160.

Irvine, William P. 1974. "Explaining the Religious Basis of the Canadian Partisan Identity: Success on the Third Try." *Canadian Journal of Political Science* 7 (3): 560–3. https://doi.org/10.1017/S0008423900040786.

Irvine, William P., and Hyam Gold. 1980. "Do Frozen Cleavages Ever Go Stale? The Bases of the Canadian and Australian Party Systems." *British Journal of Political Science* 10 (2): 187–218. https://doi.org/10.1017/S000712340000209X.

Jenkins, Jeffery A. 1999. "Examining the Bonding Effects of Party: A Comparative Analysis of Roll-Call Voting in the US and Confederate Houses." *American Journal of Political Science* 43 (4): 1144–65. https://doi.org/10.2307/2991821.

Johnson, J.K., ed. 1930. *Affectionately Yours: The Letters of Sir John A. Macdonald and His Family*. Toronto: Macmillan of Canada.

Johnston, Richard. 1985. "The Reproduction of the Religious Cleavage in Canadian Elections." *Canadian Journal of Political Science* 18 (1): 99–113. https://doi.org/10.1017/S000842390002922X.

Johnston, Richard. 2008. "Polarized Pluralism in the Canadian Party System: Presidential Address to the Canadian Political Science Association, June 5, 2008." *Canadian Journal of Political Science* 41 (4): 815–34. https://doi.org/10.1017/S0008423908081110.

Johnston, Richard. 2017. *The Canadian Party System: An Analytic History*. Vancouver: UBC Press.

Johnston, Richard, André Blais, Henry E. Brady, and Jean Crête. 1992. *Letting the People Decide: Dynamics of a Canadian Election*. Stanford: Stanford University Press.

Jones, Mark P., and Wonjae Hwang. 2005. "Party Government in Presidential Democracies: Extending Cartel Theory beyond the US Congress." *American Journal of Political Science* 49 (2): 267–82. https://doi.org/10.1111/j.0092-5853.2005.00122.x.

Joyal, Serge. 2003. *Protecting Canadian Democracy: The Senate You Never Knew*. Montreal; Kingston, ON: McGill-Queen's University Press.

Kam, Christopher. 2006. "Demotion and Dissent in the Canadian Liberal Party." *British Journal of Political Science* 36 (3): 561–74. https://doi.org/10.1017/S0007123406000299.

Kam, Christopher. 2009. *Party Discipline and Parliamentary Politics*. Cambridge: Cambridge University Press.

Kam, Christopher. 2014. "Party Discipline." In *The Oxford Handbook of Legislative Politics*, edited by Kaare Strøm and Shane Martin, 399–417. Oxford: Oxford University Press.

Katznelson, Ira. 2011. "Historical Approaches to the Study of Congress: Toward a Congressional Vantage on American Political Development." In *The Oxford Handbook of the American Congress*, edited by George C. Edwards III, Frances E. Lee, and Eric Schickler, 116–38. Oxford: Oxford University Press.

Kerby, Matthew, and Kelly Blidook. 2011. "It's Not You, It's Me: Determinants of Voluntary Legislative Turnover in Canada." *Legislative Studies Quarterly* 36 (4): 621–43. https://doi.org/10.1111/j.1939-9162.2011.00029.x.

Key, Valdimer O. 1955. "A Theory of Critical Elections." *Journal of Politics* 17 (1): 3–18. https://doi.org/10.2307/2126401.

Koop, Royce, and Amanda Bittner. 2013. "Parties and Elections after 2011: The Fifth Canadian Party System?" In *Parties, Elections, and the Future of Canadian Politics*, edited by Royce Koop and Amanda Bittner, 308–31. Vancouver: UBC Press.

Kornberg, Allan. 1964. "The Rules of the Game in the Canadian House of Commons." *Journal of Politics* 26 (2): 358–80. https://doi.org/10.2307/2127601.

Kornberg, Allan. 1966. "Perception and Constituency Influence on Legislative Behavior." *Western Political Quarterly* 19 (2): 285–92. https://doi.org/10.2307/445192.

Kornberg, Allan. 1967. *Canadian Legislative Behavior: A Study of the 25th Parliament*. New York: Holt, Rinehart, and Winston.

Kornberg, Allan, and William Mishler. 1976. *Influence in Parliament: Canada*. Durham, NC: Duke University Press.

Krehbiel, Keith. 2000. "Party Discipline and Measures of Partisanship." *American Journal of Political Science* 44 (2): 212–27. https://doi.org/10.2307/2669306.

Kunz, Frank A. 1965. *The Modern Senate of Canada 1925–1963*. Toronto: University of Toronto Press.

Laakso, Markku, and Rein Taagepera. 1979. "'Effective' Number of Parties: A Measure with Application to West Europe." *Comparative Political Studies* 12 (1): 3–27. https://doi.org/10.1177/001041407901200101.

Laurier, Wilfrid. 1908. Letter to R. Pepper: Election Bill and Closure – House of Commons. 21 May. Available online at http://collectionscanada.gc.ca/pam_archives/index.php?fuseaction=genitem.displayItem&lang=eng&rec_nbr=479401, accessed 2 January 2019.

Laycock, David. 1990. *Populism and Democratic Thought in the Canadian Prairies, 1910–1945*. Toronto: University of Toronto Press.

Laycock, David H. 2002. *The New Right and Democracy in Canada: Understanding Reform and the Canadian Alliance*. Don Mills, ON: Oxford University Press.

Lee, Frances E. 2009. *Beyond Ideology: Politics, Principles, and Partisanship in the US Senate*. Chicago: University of Chicago Press.

Lee, Frances E. 2016. *Insecure Majorities: Congress and the Perpetual Campaign*. Chicago: University of Chicago Press.

Lemco, Jonathan. 1988. "The Fusion of Powers, Party Discipline, and the Canadian Parliament: A Critical Assessment." *Presidential Studies Quarterly* 18 (2): 283–302.

Lemieux, Vincent. 2008. *Le Parti libéral du Québec: alliances, rivalités et neutralités*. Quebec City: Presses de l'Université Laval.

Liberal-Conservative Party. 1913. "What 'The Globe' Said." In *Liberals First Advocated Closure: Their Statements Then and Now*. Ottawa: Canadian Institute for Historical Microreproductions.

Liberal Farmers Association of the Battleford Constituency. 1911. "Statement to the Electors." Available online at http://peel.library.ualberta.ca/bibliography/3620/3.html.

Lijphart, Arend. 1977. *Democracy in Plural Societies: A Comparative Exploration*. New Haven, CT: Yale University Press.

Linteau, Paul-André, René Durocher, and Jean-Claude Robert. 1989. *Histoire du Québec contemporain: de la Confédération à la crise (1867–1929)*. Montreal: Boréal.

Lipset, Seymour Martin. 1954. "Democracy in Alberta." *Canadian Forum* (November–December): 175–98.

Lipset, Seymour, and Stein Rokkan. 1967. *Party Systems and Voter Alignments: Cross-National Perspectives*. New York: Free Press.

Loewen, Peter John, Royce Koop, Jaime Settle, and James H. Fowler. 2014. "A Natural Experiment in Proposal Power and Electoral Success." *American Journal of Political Science* 58 (1): 189–96. https://doi.org/10.1111/ajps.12042.

Lowell, Abbott L. 1908. *The Government of England*. London: Macmillan.

Lower, Arthur R.M. 1961. *Colony to Nation: A History of Canada*. Toronto: Longmans Canada.

Lynch-Staunton, John. 2000. "Role of the Senate in the Legislative Process." *Canadian Parliamentary Review* 23 (2): 10.

MacGuigan, Mark. 1978. "Parliamentary Reform: Internal Impediments to Enlarging the Role of Backbencher." *Legislative Studies Quarterly* 3 (4): 671–82. https://doi.org/10.2307/439620.

MacKay, Robert A. 1926. *The Unreformed Senate of Canada*. New York: Oxford University Press.

MacKay, Robert A. 1963. *The Unreformed Senate of Canada*. Montreal; Kingston, ON: McGill-Queen's University Press.

MacLean, Raymond. 1976. "The Highland Catholic Tradition in Canada." In *The Scottish Tradition in Canada*, edited by W. Stanford Reid, 93–117. Toronto: McClelland & Stewart.

Macpherson, Crawford B. 1953. *Democracy in Alberta: The Theory and Practice of a Quasi-Party System*. Toronto: Toronto University Press.

Madison, James. [1787] 2003. *"Federalist No. 10."* New York: Bantam Dell.

Malloy, Jonathan. 2002. "The "Responsible Government Approach" and Its Effect on Canadian Legislative Studies." *Parliamentary Perspectives* 5. Ottawa: Canadian Study of Parliamentary Group.

Malloy, Jonathan. 2003. "High Discipline, Low Cohesion? The Uncertain Patterns of Canadian Parliamentary Party Groups." *Journal of Legislative Studies* 9 (4): 116–29. https://doi.org/10.1080/1357233042000306290.

Mannion, John. 1974. *Irish Settlements in Eastern Canada: A Study of Cultural Transfer and Adaptation*. Toronto: University of Toronto Press.

March, Roman R. 1974. *The Myth of Parliament*. Scarborough, ON: Prentice-Hall.

Marland, Alex. 2016. *Brand Command: Canadian Politics and Democracy in the Age of Message Control*. Vancouver: UBC Press.

Marleau, Robert, and Camille Montpetit. 2000. *House of Commons Procedure and Practice*. Ottawa: House of Commons.

Massicotte, Louis. 2009. *Le parlement du Québec de 1867 à aujourd'hui*. Quebec City: Presses de l'Université Laval.

McCarthy, D'Alton. 1889. *D'Alton McCarthy's Great Speech Delivered in Ottawa, December 12th, 1889*. Toronto: Toronto Equal Rights' Association. Available online at http://archive.org/details/daltonmccarthysg00mcca, accessed 29 December 2018.

McKelvey, Richard D. 1976. "Intransitivities in Multidimensional Voting Models and Some Implications for Agenda Control." *Journal of Economic Theory* 12 (3): 472–82. https://doi.org/10.1016/0022-0531(76)90040-5.

McLauchlin, Kenneth. 1986. "'Riding the Protestant Horse': The Manitoba School Question and Canadian Politics, 1890–1896." Canadian Catholic Historical Association, *Historical Studies* 53: 39–52.

McLean, Iain. 2001. *Rational Choice and British Politics: An Analysis of Rhetoric and Manipulation from Peel to Blair*. Oxford: Oxford University Press.

Meisel, John. 1962. *The Canadian General Election of 1957*. Toronto: University of Toronto Press.

Meisel, John. 1964. *Papers on the 1962 Election: Fifteen Papers on the Canadian General Election of 1962*. Toronto: University of Toronto Press.

Mill, John Stuart. [1861] 2004. *Considerations on Representative Government*. Whitefish, MT: Kessinger Publishing.

Miller, James R. 1974. "'This Saving Remnant': Macdonald and the Catholic Vote in the 1891 Election." *CCHA Study Sessions* 41: 33–52.

Miller, James R. 1985. "Anti-Catholic Thought in Victorian Canada." *Canadian Historical Review* 66 (4): 474–94. https://doi.org/10.3138/CHR-066-04-03.

Monet, Jacques. 1966. "French Canada and the Annexation Crisis, 1848–1850." *Canadian Historical Review* 47 (3): 249–64. https://doi.org/10.3138/CHR-047-03-03.

Montreal Daily Witness. 1891. "Prohibition debate and two divisions." 22 May. Available online at https://news.google.com/newspapers?nid=125&dat=18910522&id=3yQEAAAAIBAJ&sjid=YiwDAAAAIBAJ&pg=1924,5762509&hl=en.

Morgenstern, Scott. 2004. *Patterns of Legislative Politics: Roll Call Voting in the Latin America and the United States*. Cambridge: Cambridge University Press.

Morton, William L. 1950. *The Progressive Party in Canada*. Toronto: University of Toronto Press.

Müller, Wolfgang C., and Kaare Strøm. 1999. *Policy, Office, or Votes? How Political Parties in Western Europe Make Hard Decisions*. Cambridge: Cambridge University Press.

National Post. 2015a. "The post-patronage era: Trudeau's Senate appointments could lead to dynamism – or chaos." 13 November. Available online at http://nationalpost.com/news/politics/the-post-patronage-era-trudeaus-senate-appointments-could-lead-to-dynamism-or-chaos.

National Post. 2015b. "'We would like a more independent, less partisan Senate': LeBlanc becomes Trudeau's emissary to Senate." 6 November. Available online at https://nationalpost.com/news/politics/we-would-like-a-more-independent-less-partisan-senate-leblanc-becomes-trudeaus-emmisary-to-senate.

Le Nationaliste. 1907. "Armand Lavergne." 10 February.

Neatby, Hilda. 1973. *Laurier and a Liberal Quebec*. Toronto: McClelland and Stewart.

Nunn, Nathan. 2009. "The Importance of History for Economic Development." *Annual Review of Economics* 1 (1): 65–92. https://doi.org/10.1146/annurev.economics.050708.143336.

O'Brien, Audrey, and Marc Bosc, eds. 2009. *House of Commons Procedure and Practice*, 2nd ed. Ottawa: House of Commons. Available online at http://www.ourcommons.ca/procedure-book-livre/Document.aspx

?sbdid=7C730F1D-E10B-4DFC-863A-83E7E1A6940E&sbpidx=1 &Language=E&Mode=1.

O'Brien, Gary. 1981. "The Senate Order Paper." *Canadian Parliamentary Review* 4 (4): 26–8.

O'Neil, Juliet. 2007. "Tory expelled for opposing budget bill." *Ottawa Citizen*, 6 June.

Ostrogorski, Moisei. 1902. *Democracy and the Organization of Political Parties: By M. Ostrogorski, Translated from the French by Frederick Clarke, with a Preface by the Right Hon. James Bryce*. London: Macmillan.

Özbudun, Ergun. 1970. *Party Cohesion in Western Democracies: A Causal Analysis*. Thousand Oaks, CA: SAGE.

Patten, Steve. 2017. "The Evolution of the Canadian Party System: From Brokerage to Marketing-Oriented Politics." In *Canadian Parties in Transition*, 4th ed., edited by Alain-G. Gagnon and A. Brian Tanguay, 3–27. Toronto: University of Toronto Press.

Pelletier, Yves Y.J. 2000. "Time Allocation in the House of Commons: Silencing Parliamentary Democracy or Effective Time Management?" *Canadian Parliamentary Review* 23 (4): 20–8.

Perin, Roberto. 1998. *L'église des immigrants: les allophones au sein du catholicisme canadien, 1880–1920*. Ottawa: Société historique du Canada.

Pierson, Paul. 2004. *Politics in Time: Institutions, History, and Social Analysis*. Princeton, NJ: Princeton University Press.

Pinard, Maurice. 1971. *The Rise of a Third Party: A Study in Crisis Politics*. Englewood-Cliffs, NJ: Prentice-Hall.

Poole, Keith T. 2005. *Spatial Models of Parliamentary Voting*. Cambridge: Cambridge University Press.

Poole, Keith T., and Howard Rosenthal. 1997. *Congress: A Political-Economic History of Roll Call Voting*. Oxford: Oxford University Press.

Poole, Keith T., and Howard L. Rosenthal. 2007. *Ideology and Congress*. New Brunswick, NJ: Transaction Publishers.

Poole, Keith T., Jeffrey B. Lewis, James Lo, and Royce Carroll. 2018. "Package 'OC.'" Available online at https://cran.r-project.org/web/packages/oc/oc.pdf.

Pope, Joseph. 1921. *Correspondence of Sir John Macdonald*. Garden City, NY: Page.

Porter, John Arthur. 1965. *The Vertical Mosaic: An Analysis of Social Class and Power in Canada*. Toronto: University of Toronto Press.

Power, Charles G. 1968. "Quebec Nationalism in My Time." *Queen's Quarterly* 75 (1): 1–20.

Rae, Nicol C. 2007. "Be Careful What You Wish for: The Rise of Responsible Parties in American National Politics." *Annual Review of Political Science* 10: 169–91. https://doi.org/10.1146/annurev.polisci.10.071105.100750.

Rask, Bjorn E. 2014. "Institutional Foundations of Legislative Agenda-Setting." In *The Oxford Handbook of Legislative Politics*, edited by Kaare Strøm and Shane Martin, 455–80. Oxford: Oxford University Press.

Reid, Escott M. [1932] 1963. "The Rise of National Parties in Canada." In *Party Politics in Canada*, edited by Hugh G. Thorburn, 14–21. Scarborough, ON: Prentice-Hall.
Reid, Escott. 1936. "The Saskatchewan Liberal Machine before 1929." *Canadian Journal of Economics and Political Science* 2 (1): 27–40. https://doi.org/10.2307/136645.
Rennie, Bradford James. 2000. *The Rise of Agrarian Democracy: The United Farmers and Farm Women of Alberta, 1909–1921*. Toronto: University of Toronto Press.
Rice, Stuart A. 1925. "The Behavior of Legislative Groups: A Method of Measurement." *Political Science Quarterly* 40 (1): 60–72. https://doi.org/10.2307/2142407.
Riker, William H. 1982. "The Two-Party System and Duverger's Law: An Essay on the History of Political Science." *American Political Science Review* 76 (4): 753–66. https://doi.org/10.1017/S0003055400189580.
Rohde, David W. 1991. *Parties and Leaders in the Postreform House*. Chicago: University of Chicago Press.
Rohde, David W. 2013. "Reflections on the Practice of Theorizing: Conditional Party Government in the Twenty-First Century." *Journal of Politics* 75 (4): 849–64. https://doi.org/10.1017/S0022381613000911.
Rousseau, Jean-Jacques. [1762] 1992. *Du contrat social*. Paris: Flammarion.
Rubin, Donald B. 1974. "Estimating Causal Effects of Treatments in Randomized and Nonrandomized Studies." *Journal of Educational Psychology* 66 (5): 688–701. https://doi.org/10.1037/h0037350.
Rush, Michael, and Philip Giddings. 2011. *Parliamentary Socialisation: Learning the Ropes or Determining Behaviour*. Basingstoke, UK: Palgrave Macmillan.
Saalfeld, Thomas, and Kaare W. Strøm. 2014. *Political Parties and Legislators*. Oxford: Oxford University Press.
Salkind, Neil J. 2007. *Encyclopedia of Measurement and Statistics*. Thousand Oaks, CA: SAGE.
Samara Centre for Democracy. n.d. "MP Exit Interviews." Available online at http://www.samaracanada.com/research/political-leadership/mp-exit-interviews.
Sanguinetti, Sonja P. 1969. "Common Misperceptions of the Events Relating to the Rise of the Protest Movements on the Prairies." Master's thesis, University of British Columbia.
Sartori, Giovanni. 1976. *Parties and Party Systems: A Framework for Analysis*. New York: Cambridge University Press.
Savoie, Donald J. 1999. *Governing from the Centre: The Concentration of Power in Canadian Politics*. Toronto: University of Toronto Press.
Scarrow, Susan. 2006. "The Nineteenth-Century Origins of Modern Political Parties: The Unwanted Emergence of Party-Based Politics." In *Handbook of Party Politics*, edited by Ricahrd S. Katz and William J. Crotty, 16–47. Thousand Oaks, CA: SAGE.
Schumpeter, Joseph. [1942] 1975. "Creative Destruction." In *Capitalism, Socialism and Democracy*. New York: Harper & Row.
Sekhon, Jasjeet. 2008. "The Neyman-Rubin Model of Causal Inference and Estimation via Matching Methods." In *The Oxford Handbook of Political Methodology*, edited

by Henry E. Collier and Janet M. Box-Steffensmeier, 271–99. Oxford: Oxford University Press.

Semple, Neil. 1996. *Lord's Dominion: The History of Canadian Methodism*. Montreal; Kingston, ON: McGill-Queen's University Press.

Sharman, Campbell. 2015. "Upper Houses." In *Constitutional Conventions in Westminster Systems: Controversies, Changes and Challenges*, edited by Brian Galligan and Scott Brenton, 157–72. Cambridge: Cambridge University Press.

Shepsle, Kenneth A., and Barry R. Weingast. 1981. "Structure-Induced Equilibrium and Legislative Choice." *Public Choice* 37 (3): 503–19. https://doi.org/10.1007/BF00133748.

Siegfried, André. [1906] 1966. *The Race Question in Canada*. Montreal; Kingston, ON: McGill-Queen's University Press.

Silver, Arthur I. 1997. *The French-Canadian Idea of Confederation, 1864–1900*. Toronto: University of Toronto Press.

Silver, Arthur I. 1999. "The Union of the Canadas." In *As I Recall/Si je me souviens bien: Historical Perspectives*, edited by John Meisel, Guy Rocher, and Arthur Silver, 45–54. Montreal: Institute for Research on Public Policy.

Simpson, Jeffrey. 1988. *Spoils of Power: The Politics of Patronage*. Toronto: HarperCollins Canada.

Sinclair, Barbara. 2016. *Unorthodox Lawmaking: New Legislative Processes in the US Congress*. Washington, DC: CQ Press.

Sircar, Indraneel, and Bjørn Høyland. 2010. "Get the Party Started: Development of Political Party Legislative Dynamics in the Irish Free State Seanad (1922–36)." *Party Politics* 16 (1): 89–110. https://doi.org/10.1177/1354068809341056.

Skogstad, Grace. 2003. "Who Governs? Who Should Govern? Political Authority and Legitimacy in Canada in the Twenty-First Century." *Canadian Journal of Political Science* 36 (5): 955–73. https://doi.org/10.1017/S0008423903778925.

Smiley, Donald V., and Ronald L. Watts. 1985. *Intrastate Federalism in Canada*. Toronto: University of Toronto Press.

Smith, David E. 1981. *The Regional Decline of a National Party: Liberals on the Prairies*. Toronto: University of Toronto Press.

Smith, David E. 1985. "Party Government, Representation and National Integrations in Canada." In *Party Government and Regional Representation in Canada*, edited by Peter Aucoin, 1–68. Toronto: University of Toronto Press.

Smith, David E. 2003. *The Canadian Senate in Bicameral Perspective*. Toronto: University of Toronto Press.

Smith, David E. 2007. *The People's House of Commons: Theories of Democracy in Contention*. Toronto: University of Toronto Press.

Smith, Denis. 1963. "Prairie Revolt, Federalism, and the Party System." In *Party Politics in Canada*, edited by Hugh G. Thorburn, 126–37. Scarborough, ON: Prentice-Hall.

Spirling, Arthur. 2014. "British Political Development: A Research Agenda." *Legislative Studies Quarterly* 39 (4): 435–7. https://doi.org/10.1111/lsq.12053.

Spirling, Arthur, and Iain McLean. 2007. "UK OC OK? Interpreting Optimal Classification Scores for the UK House of Commons." *Political Analysis* 15 (1): 85–96. https://doi.org/10.1093/pan/mpl009.

Squire, Peverill. 2012. *The Evolution of American Legislatures: Colonies, Territories, and States, 1619–2009*. Ann Arbor, MI: University of Michigan Press.

Stevenson, Garth. 1997. *Ex Uno Plures: Federal-Provincial Relations in Canada, 1867–1896*. Montreal; Kingston, ON: McGill-Queen's University Press.

Stewart, Gordon T. 1986. *The Origins of Canadian Politics: A Comparative Approach*. Vancouver: UBC Press.

Stewart, Ian. 1980. "Of Customs and Coalitions: The Formation of Canadian Federal Parliamentary Alliances." *Canadian Journal of Political Science* 13 (3): 451–79. https://doi.org/10.1017/S0008423900033539.

Stewart, John B. 1977. *The Canadian House of Commons: Procedure and Reform*. Montreal; Kingston, ON: McGill-Queen's University Press.

Strahl, Chuck. 2001. "Toward a More Responsive Parliament." *Canadian Parliamentary Review* 24 (1): 2.

Supreme Court of Canada. 2014. *Reference Re Senate Reform. CSC 32*. Available online at https://scc-csc.lexum.com/scc-csc/scc-csc/en/item/13614/index.do?r=AAAAAQANc2VuYXRlIHJlZm9ybQE.

Tavits, Margit. 2011. "Power within Parties: The Strength of the Local Party and MP Independence in Postcommunist Europe." *American Journal of Political Science* 55 (4): 923–36. https://doi.org/10.1111/j.1540-5907.2011.00520.x.

Thomas, Paul G. 1996. "Parties in Parliament: The Role of Party Caucuses." In *Canadian Parties in Transition*, 2nd ed., edited by Brian Tanguay and Alain-G. Gagnon, 252–81. Toronto: Nelson Canada.

Thomas, Paul G. 2003. "Comparing the Lawmaking Rules of the Senate and the House of Commons." In *Protecting Canadian Democracy: The Senate You Never Knew*, edited by Serge Joyal, 189–228. Montreal; Kingston, ON: McGill-Queen's University Press.

Toronto Star. 2016. "Justin Trudeau names seven new senators." 18 March. Available online at https://www.thestar.com/news/canada/2016/03/18/justin-trudeau-names-seven-new-senators.html.

Toronto Star. 2017. "Unpredictable Senate causing trouble for Trudeau's agenda, documents show." 23 April. Available online at https://www.thestar.com/news/canada/2017/04/23/unpredictable-senate-causing-trouble-for-trudeaus-agenda-documents-show.html.

Trudeau, Justin. 2016. "Prime Minister announces intention to recommend the appointment of seven new senators." 18 March. Available online at http://pm.gc.ca/eng/news/2016/03/18/prime-minister-announces-intention-recommend-appointment-seven-new-senators.

Trudeau, Pierre Elliott. 1958. "Some Obstacles to Democracy in Quebec." *Canadian Journal of Economics and Political Science* 24 (3): 297–311. https://doi.org/10.2307/138618.

Tsebelis, George. 2002. *Veto Players: How Political Institutions Work*. Princeton, NJ: Princeton University Press.

Underhill, Frank H. 1935. "The Development of National Political Parties in Canada." *Canadian Historical Review* 16 (4): 367–87. https://doi.org/10.3138/CHR-16-04-01.

Venne, Pierrette. 2003. "Parliament and Democracy in the 21st Century: The Role of MPs." *Canadian Parliamentary Review* 26 (1): 2.

Wade, Mason. 1955. *The French Canadians, 1760–1945*. London: Macmillan.

Walchuk, Brad. 2012. "A Whole New Ballgame: The Rise of Canada's Fifth Party System." *American Review of Canadian Studies* 42 (3): 418–34. https://doi.org/10.1080/02722011.2012.705867.

Ward, Norman. 1966. *A Party Politician: The Memoirs of Chubby Power*. Toronto: Macmillan of Canada.

Watt, James T. 1967. "Anti-Catholic Nativism in Canada: The Protestant Protective Association." *Canadian Historical Review* 48 (1): 45–58. https://doi.org/10.3138/CHR-048-01-03.

Wearing, Joseph. 1998. "Guns, Gays, and Gadflies: Party Dissent in the House of Commons under Mulroney and Chrétien." Paper presented at the Annual Meeting of the Canadian Political Science Association, Ottawa, June.

Western, Bruce, and Meredith Kleykamp. 2004. "A Bayesian Change Point Model for Historical Time Series Analysis." *Political Analysis* 12 (4): 354–74. https://doi.org/10.1093/pan/mph023.

Westmacott, Martin. 1983. "Whips and Party Cohesion." *Canadian Parliamentary Review* 6 (3): 14–19.

White, Graham. 1991. "Westminster in the Arctic: The Adaptation of British Parliamentarism in the Legislative Assembly of the Northwest Territories." *Canadian Journal of Political Science* 24 (3): 499–523.

White, Graham. 2005. *Cabinets and First Ministers*. Vancouver: UBC Press.

Williams, John R. 1956. *The Conservative Party of Canada: 1920–1949*. Durham, NC: Duke University Press.

Wiseman, Nelson. 1973. "The CCF and the Manitoba 'Non-partisan' Government of 1940." *Canadian Historical Review* 54 (2): 175–93. https://doi.org/10.3138/CHR-054-02-03.

Young, Walter D. 1969. *The Anatomy of a Party: The National CCF, 1932–1961*. Toronto: University of Toronto Press.

Index

www.ingramcontent.com/pod-product-compliance
Lightning Source LLC
LaVergne TN
LVHW040159080826
844660LV00001B/43

9781487507039